P9-APD-820

1993

# The Professional Charcuterie Series

## (Volume 2)

# The Professional Charcuterie Series

Volume 2

Pâtés, Terrines and Ballotines
made with Poultry, Veal, Pork and Liver
Andouilles and Andouillettes – Foie gras

**Marcel Cottenceau**
**Jean-François Deport and Jean-Pierre Odeau**
under the direction of
**Pierre Michalet**

*Translated by Anne Sterling*

A copublication of
**CICEM** (Compagnie Internationale
de Consultation *Education* et *Media*)
**Paris**

and

**Van Nostrand Reinhold**
**New York**

# The Authors

## Marcel COTTENCEAU

Born in 1924 in the town of Cheroy, southeast of Paris, Marcel Cottenceau followed in the professional footsteps of his father and grandfather, both charcutiers.

He is one of the leading members of the charcuterie profession, who the trade magazine " Charcuterie et Gastronomie " aptly dubbed " the one-man band " of charcuterie.

His early training was in this family's business, established in 1893. In 1947, Marcel Cottenceau set up shop in Montrouge where over the last 30 years his endeavors have met with remarkable success, especially in his expanding catering activities. Mr. Cottenceau has won several awards--" Oscar de la Charcuterie ", " Concours d'Arpajon " (in both charcuterie and cuisine), "Grand Prix de la Charcuterie Française ", and in 1961 he was awarded the prestigious title of " Meilleur Ouvrier de France ".

Teaching has always formed an integral part of Marcel Cottenceau's professional activities. Specifically, he is in charge of the technical seminars offered by the professional development branch of the Paris Charcutiers' Union.

Mr. Cottenceau has been instrumental in the development of CEPROC, of which he is Vice-President of the Administrative Council. Since 1978 he holds the official position of Technical Advisor to the " Confederation Nationale des Charcutiers-Traiteurs Français ". He is also deeply involved with union activities. During the last 20 years he has been first Administrator then Vice-President of the Paris Charcutiers' Union.

In 1990, he was awarded the " Insignes d'Officier de l'Ordre National de Mérite ".

Marcel Cottenceau is the author of numerous important publications including the " Encyclopedie de la Charcuterie ", which he co-authored, and his 1987 work " Marcel Cottenceau's 80 Terrines ".

His professional background makes Mr. Cottenceau an ideal contributor to Editions St. Honoré's series on traditional charcuterie. His work on the series gives him another valuable opportunity to contribute to the improvement and development of his professional colleagues as well as providing a means to share with professionals outside of France the traditional techniques which have given French charcuterie its excellent reputation.

*" * President of the Confédération Nationale des Charcutiers-Traiteurs " et Traiteurs de France*

*The major goal of the French Confederation of Charcutiers-Caterers is to train and inform the men and women of the industry.*

*Therefore as president of this confederation, it is a great honor for me to introduce this extensive series on charcuterie written by three of the top " Meilleurs Ouvriers de France " in our business:*

- *The Technical Director of CEPROC, Marcel COTTENCEAU, is the former owner of a well-known family charcuterie and in recent years has dedicated himself to teaching the art to aspiring charcutiers.*
- *Two instructors of CEPROC and charcuterie owners as well, Jean-François DEPORT and Jean-Pierre ODEAU are talented young charcutiers with a creative spirit and dedication to the classic techniques and traditions.*

*These three qualified professionals have collaborated on this detailed book of recipes and techniques, clearly explained and accompanied by photographs that illustrate each step.*

*It is only natural that the recipes for this book were prepared at CEPROC (" École Supérieure de la Charcuterie "), the foremost instructional facility for the charcuterie industry in Europe. The future of charcuterie is indeed bright with talented chefs working in a technically advanced environment. I wish them great success.*

Claude VIGNON*

# Experience and Talent

## Jean-François DEPORT

Jean-François Deport, born in 1949, is a key figure in the profession, especially in his role as President of the Association de Meilleurs Ouvriers de France Charcutiers-Traiteurs.

His early training consisted of receiving his C.A.P. at age 17, followed by apprenticeships in various establishments in the region south of Paris.

In 1968, his job in Sens helped accelerate his professional advancement, leading to the opening of his own business in Arpajon in 1971, which very quickly earned an excellent reputation in the region. In 1988 he transferred his business to Châlons-sur-Marne, where his large and diverse enterprise continues to thrive.

He was awarded the prestigious title of Meilleur Ouvrier de France in 1979 and he remains instrumental in encouraging other professionals to seek and earn this award. As President of the Association des Meilleurs Ouvriers de France de la Charcuterie, Jean-Francois Deport leads training sessions at the CEPROC and participates in the development and programming of professional training seminars and apprenticeships.

Jean-François Deport is married and has two children.

## Jean-Pierre ODEAU

Jean-Pierre Odeau was born in 1954 into a family of charcutiers in the Sarthe, a region of France known for its fine charcuterie. He is considered by some as the child prodigy of the profession. He received his C.A.P. in Le Mans and began his professional career in La Chartre-sur-le-Loir. He went next to Paris where he earned his " Diplôme de Compagnon " in 1974, returning to Le Mans to hone his skills by working with Roland Russe for six months. His culinary training was polished by a spell at one of the top restaurants of the time, Le Gue des Grues. During his military service, he was responsible for the officers mess at the base in Le Mans.

After the military, he alternated between working in his family's business and working in the Normandy resort town of Deauville during several seasons. In 1976 he received a higher level of certification, the Brevet de Maitrise No. 2, and returned to Paris.

The year 1979 was a significant one for Jean-Pierre Odeau, because that year, at the age of 25, he won the Concours d'Arpajon and was awarded the title Meilleur Ouvrier de France – the youngest person ever to receive the honor.

In 1981 he set up shop in Houilles, then transferred in 1984 to St. Germain-en-Laye, where he continues to develop his growing business. Jean-Pierre Odeau frequently participates in the CEPROC's training programs. He is married and has three children.

# Introduction to Volume 2

**Volume 1 of this series covers the basic preparations and recipes of traditional French charcuterie. Volume 2 builds on this information and elaborates on more complex products.**

**This volume, like the first, is an indispensable tool for professional charcuteries-caterers as well as enthusiastic amateurs.**

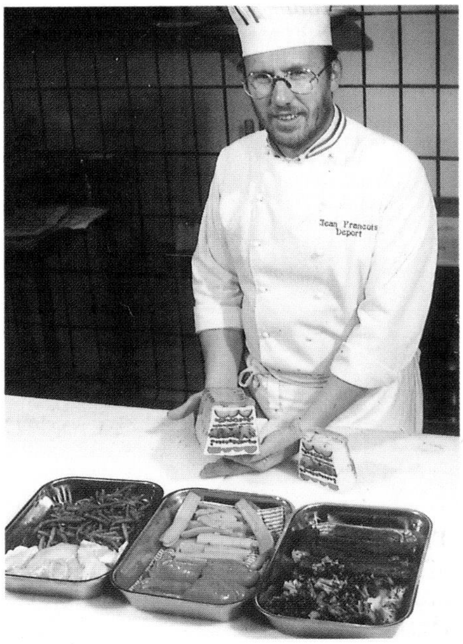

### Chapter 1 – *Review of Techniques*

To further explain several very important techniques, this volume begins with information to clarify the recipes presented in volume 2.

### Chapter 2 – *Roast Pork, Brined Pork Products and Pig's Feet*

All cuts of pork can be cured in brine for presentation in the shop. They can be cooked and ready to eat hot or cold or uncooked for the custumer to prepare at home.

### Chapter 3 – *"Andouilles" and "Andouillettes"*

Each province of France offers its own versions of these wonderful products. The best known sausages in this category are described.

### Chapter 4 – *Pâtés and Terrines made with Liver*

This is an important line of products for the French charcutier who has always used the pork liver to make delicious preparations especially pâtés and terrines.

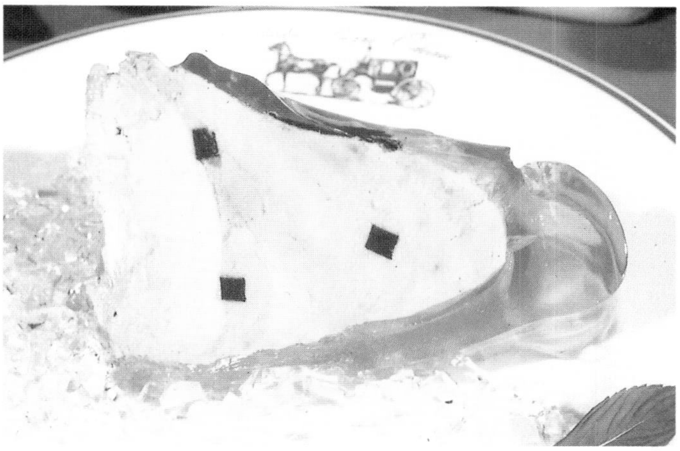

## Chapter 5 – *Foies Gras*

The most luxurious ingredient of all is the fattened liver of force fed ducks and geese; " foie gras ". The variety of products that can be made from foie gras is impressive. Here is a chance for the professional charcutier to add some new variations to his reperatoire for holiday business and throughout the year. The authors explain the important grading process in France and include information on regulations concerning foie gras and truffles.

## Chapter. 6 – *Terrines, Galantines and Roulades made with Veal and Pork*

Veal and pork, both delicate in flavor and light in color are popular choices of French charcutiers for making terrines and galantines. Their subtle taste makes veal and pork perfect partners witn ideal for the elaborate forcemeats used in elegant galantines and terrines.Roulades are easily formed from a boned breast of veal.

## Chapter 7 – *Pâtés and Terrines made with Poultry*

This is a superb selection of original recipes featuring a variety of poultry, rabbit and game. The authors have chosen preparations that succeed on all levels: harmonious marriages of ingredients for delicious flavor, homogeneous forcemeat mixtures for neat slicing and decorative touches for an attractive presentation.

# Table of Contents



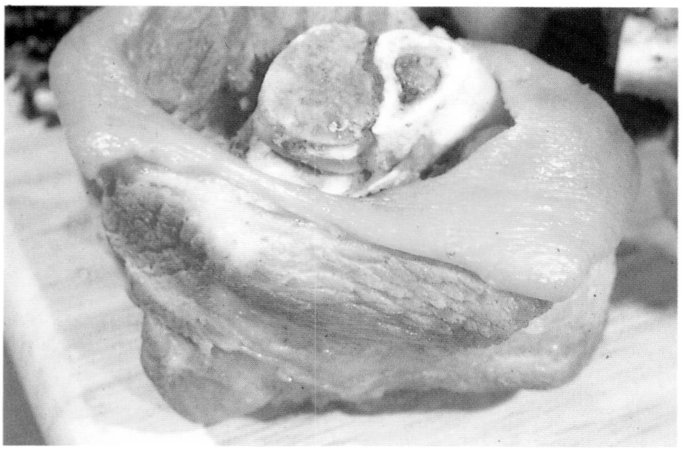

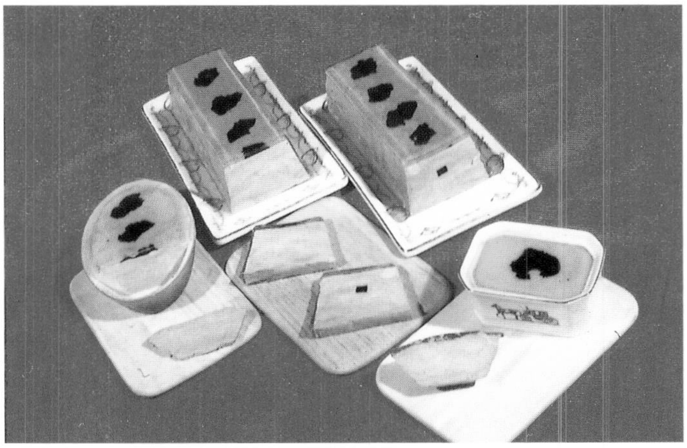

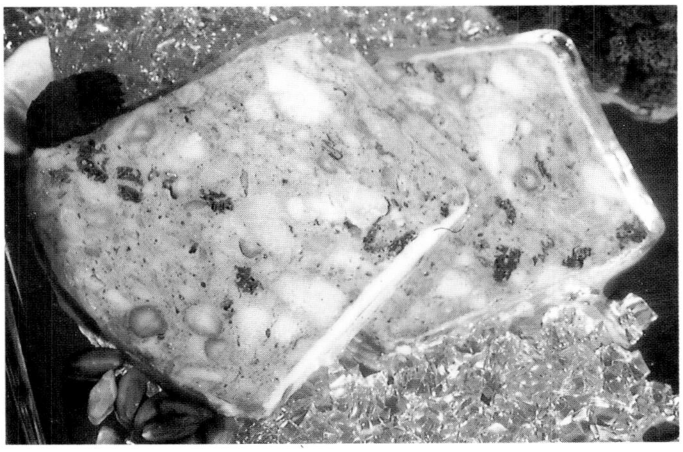

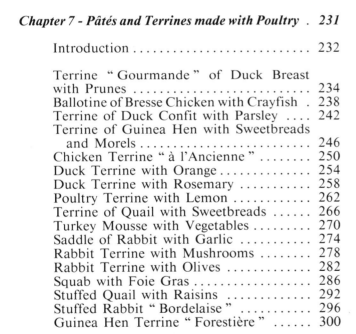

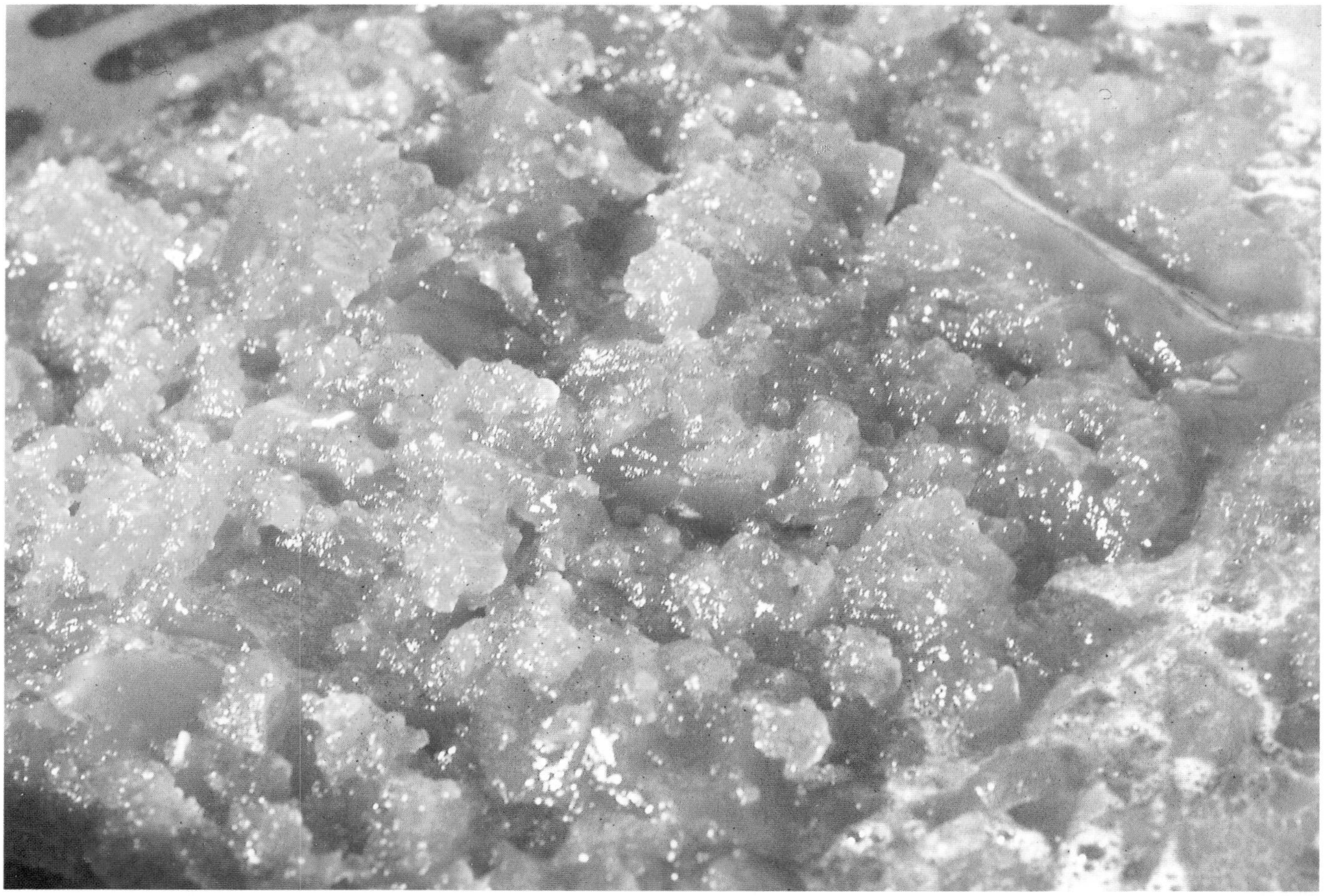

# *Chapter 1*
# *Review of Techniques*

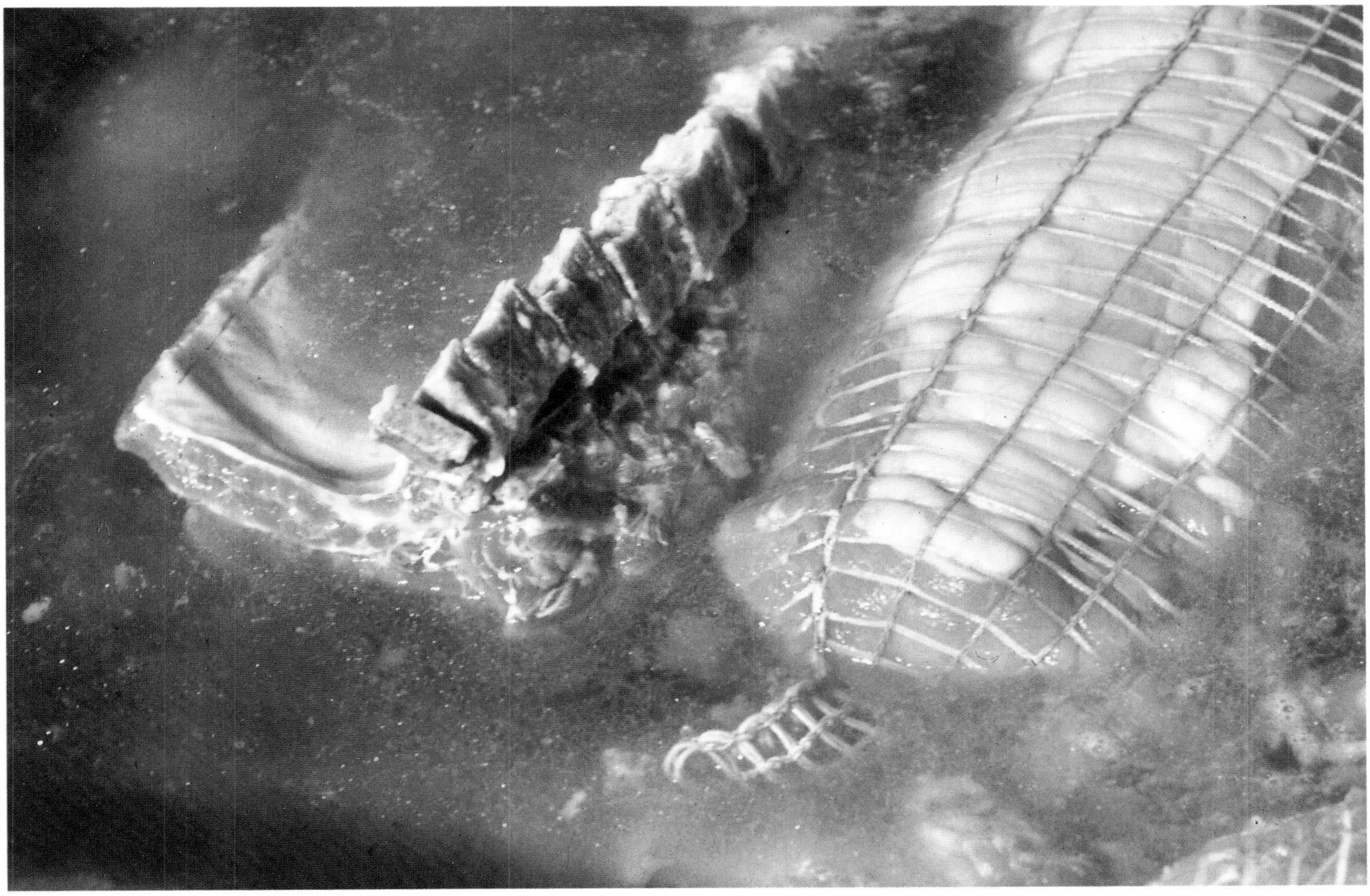

# *Additional Technical Information*

*In volume 1 of " Professional French Charcuterie " we described the basic operations performed by the charcutier and the equipment needed to perform those tasks efficiently. Several categories of basic products were also covered. Volume 2 explains additional categories of basic preparations; primarily the brined cuts of pork and pâtés and terrines. Technical information pertaining to these products has been added here to clarify the recipes that follow.*

- *Variety Meats and Uses*
- *" Hachages " (grinding methods)*
- *" Gratins " (chicken liver mixture for terrines) and Techniques for Enhancing Flavor*
- *Stocks, Aspics, Clarifications and Reductions*
- *Cooking Techniques for Pork*

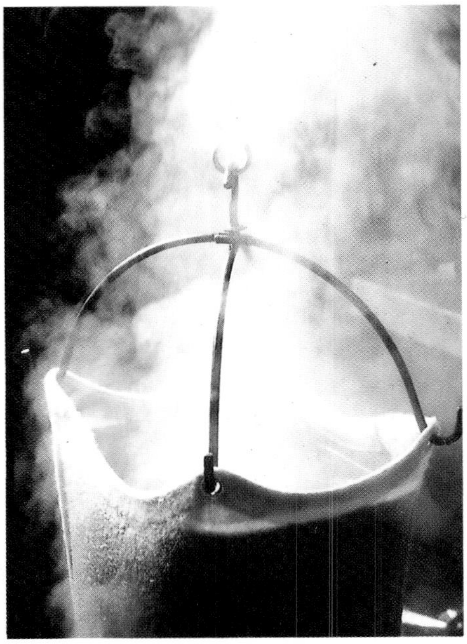

# Variety Meats and Uses

### Introduction

The saying that " the whole pig can be cooked except the squeal " is certainly true in French traditional charcuterie.

The only part that is removed from the pig are the nails from the feet. All other parts find their way into a culinary preparation.

The fact that pigs can be easily raised on a wide assortment of table scraps has made them an ideal animal for small farms. As a result traditional recipes flourish using pork. With the exception of the followers of the muslim and jewish religions, pork has been a major source of meat for people thoughout the world and throughout history.

### Categories

Here we group the variety meats (also known as " offal ") in anatomical groups and follow the carcass from the head to the tail. We describe the principle preparations, in charcuterie and in cooked dishes, which is a varied and rich selection.

### The Head

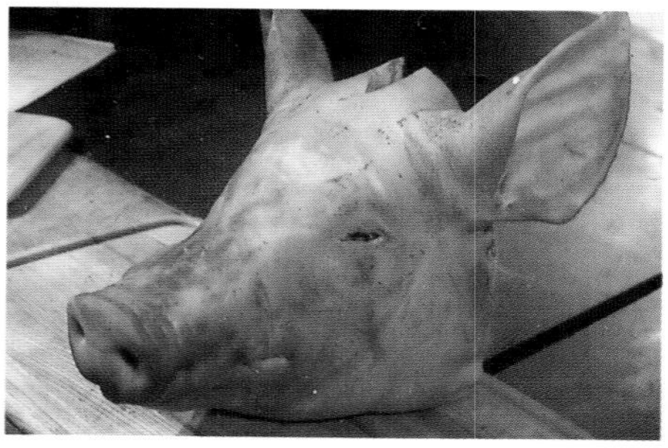

The head (" tête ") represents about 6% of the carcass and generally weighs 4-6 kilos (9-13 lbs). The head is separated from the carcass at the slaughterhouse with a cut between the first and second vertabrae. The cheek is cut out and remains attached to the carcass and becomes the jowl and is therefore sold as meat and not offal.

The tongue (with pharnyx attached) is removed using a thin-bladed knife.

The head is then scraped and washed thoroughly then rinsed in cold running water. The head is then split in two and the brain is removed in one piece.

In industrial-scale slaughtering houses machines are used with a specially designed curved blade which cuts open the head without damaging the brain.

*Uses*

*The tongue (" langue ")* weighs about 500 g (1 lb). To remove the skin, the tongue is blanched in 70 °C (160 F) water to loosen the skin and facilitate peeling.

The peeled tongue is thoroughly rinsed then injected with brine then immersed in brine for 12-24 hours.

Tongue is sold cured and un-cooked in French charcuteries. It is an important ingredient in a variety of headcheese-type products (" hure ", " museau " or " tête roulée "). Its firm texture and pink color make it a good choice for adding a decorative touch to products.

*The brain (" cervelle ")* of the pig is not as refined as the brains of calves and lambs, but certainly better than cow's brain. It is usually poached then sautéed in butter and served hot.

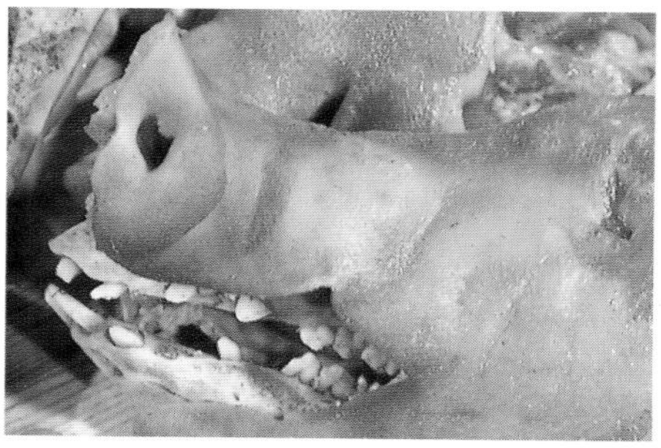

The fine texture also is delicious when added to forcemeat mixtures, ground or in large pieces.

*The whole head* (after the tongue and brain are removed) is injected with brine and sometines immersed in brine for 12-24 hours.

The head is sold cured and uncooked but is primarily made into headcheese and related products.

All of these preparations are made from the meat and skin of the head after it has been thoroughly cooked.

In some regions, the cheek is left on the head. It is removed before the brining process and made into cooked dishes that reflect the traditions of the region.

The ears (" oreilles ") are the only parts that are sold cooked on their own in the charcuterie (presented cold, glazed with aspic).

For fancy presentations featuring the entire head, boned and stuffed, the head must be sectioned with the jowl and neck attached. Since this is not the usual method, it is done on special request.

### The Heart and Lungs

The heart and lungs and esophagus are removed together from the carcass after the sternum has been cut.

#### *The Heart*

The heart (" cœur ") is detached form the lungs and drained of all remaining blood and rinsed with cold running water.

Not as refined as calf's heart it can be prepared in the same way: cut in slices and pan-fried. But it is primarily used in pâtés that feature variety meats and country pâtés used along with liver.

#### *The Lungs*

Lungs (" poumons " or " mou ") are also called " lights ". For many years the lungs were the least expensive meat and eaten mostly by the poor in stews. They made a delicious dish at a low price.

The demand has greatly dropped and it is now more profitable to sell the lungs directly to companies producing canned animal food and is rarely sold fresh.

#### *The Esophagus*

This part is attached to the heart and lungs.

The cylindrical muscle (after the outer skin is removed) can be used much like the heart in pâtés that feature variety meats. More often it is sent directly to animal food companies.

## The Digestive Tract

Of all the animals raised by man for consumption, the pig is the only one with a digestive tract used in its entirety. Some products are made entirely of intestines (andouilles) or are a blend of intestines and ground meat. The intestines serve primarily as natural sausage casings for a variety of products.

When the intestines are removed the outer covering is carefully pulled off. This thin skin is the peritone also known as caul fat (" crépine " or " epiploon ").
It is preserved in salt and after rinsing is used to wrap certain preparations such as flat sausages, molded pig's feet or used to cover the top of terrines.

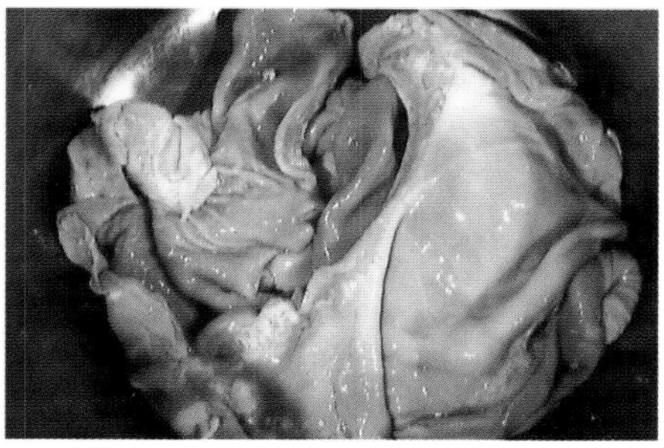

The actual intestines can be divided in sections, each with a different use:

***The stomach (" panse ")*** weighs about

500 g (1 lb). It is split open to clean it thoroughly then blanched to facilitate removal of the mucous membrane. It is used in the making of certain " andouillettes ".

***The " menu " (small intestine)*** is about 15-20 cm (6-8 in) in length with a diameter which graduates from 2.5-5 cm (1-2 in). It is rarely used to make andouilles because it is used as sausage casings for a variety of products which includes white sausage (" boudin blanc ") and Toulouse sausage.
It is scraped clean, leaving a thin skin which is cut in lengths according to diameter and packed in salt.

***The large intestine*** includes several parts:
***The " sac " or caecum*** is the first portion which is in the form of a pocket and measures about 30 cm (12 in).
***The " chaudin "*** is the long portion (up to 3 meters (about 3 yards)) of the intestine that follows the large intestine. This is used primarily in the making of andouilles and andouillettes.
***The " robe "*** follows the " chaudin " and got its name from its use as a casing or covering for andouillettes and other sausages. It measures about 1 meter (about 1 yard) with a diameter of about 4-6 cm (1 1/2-2 1/4 in).
***The " fuseau " (rectum)*** is the last portion which ends at the anus. It is conical and is used as a casing for several traditional sausages (" rosette " and " fuseau ").

***The " vessie " (bladder)*** of the pig is trimmed of all exterior fat and emptied. It is then soaked in water with salt or baking soda. The cleaned bladder is then blown up like a balloon to dry.
It is used in fancy resturants as a cooking bag for baked chicken (" poularde au vessie) ". In days gone by the bladder was made into a tobacco pouch.

## Liver, Kidneys and Spleen

These meats can also be grouped with the heart and lungs.

### *The Liver*

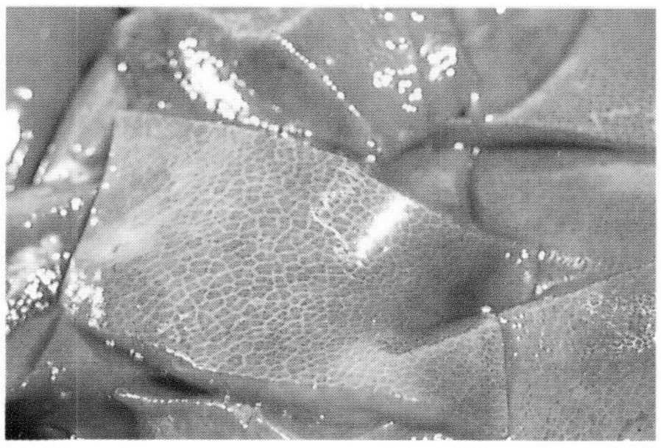

When the innards are removed, the liver (" foie ") is attached to the heart and lungs.
The first operation is to clean the liver and it must be done very carefully. The duct leading to the bile sack is cut without letting any of the bile into the liver. The bile, a green substance which often leaves stains on the liver is extremely bitter. If the sack is pierced the bile could coat the liver and ruin it.
The pork liver is used in many cooked dishes and is prepared like calf's liver (which is more flavorful).
The pork liver is used primarily for charcuterie products as illustrated throughout this series.

### *The Kidneys*

The kidneys (" rognons ") filter blood and secrete urine.
They are used in cooked dishes after the urine sacks are removed.
They are used in pâtés that feature variety meats and are prepared like the heart.

### *The Spleen*

The spleen (" rate ") used to be sold by the charcutier for animal food but is now sent with the lungs directly from the slaughterhouse to companies that make canned pet food.

## The Feet

The feet (" pieds ") are cut off at the slaughterhouse and are sold separately. In some cases the rear feet re-

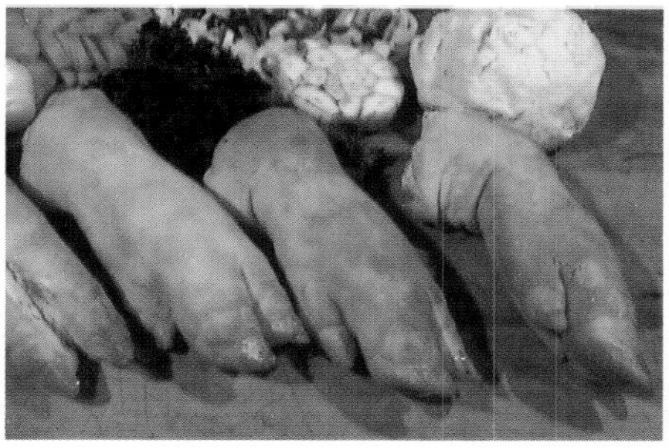

main attached to the ham and the front feet remain attached to the shoulder.
The feet are scraped and shaved, then washed and rinsed. They are split before being prepared into a variety of delicious dishes: molded pig's feet, breaded pig's feet, or the famous " pieds à la St-Menehould ".

### *The Tail*

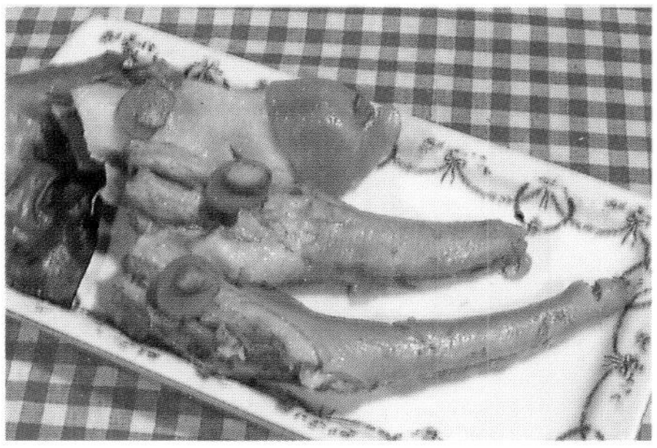

The tail (" queue ") can be prepared like the feet.
A popular dish a few decades ago was pork tail stuffed with foie gras which was much appreciated by connoisseurs.
Unfortunately, the tail is often removed from young piglets to guard against cannibalism among the animals. The portion that is left on the adult pig is usually not used in cooking.

# Grinding Techniques " Hachages "

In volume 1 we described " hachage " as the operation of mechanically grinding or chopping lean meat and fat into the desired " grain " or texture for a particular product.

The equipment available for the grinding process was also described. The choice of machines is vast and the chef should select the size and type that best suit his style and product line.

To review, a well equipped charcuterie kitchen will have the following:

***Grinder (" broyeur-hachoir ")*** with

large worm screw which guides the meat to the turning blade and fixed disk (also called plate or die) . The size of the holes in the disk vary from 2-10 mm (1/12-3/8 in).

***Mixer (" mélangeur ")*** with variable

speeds and three attachments: hook, paddle and whisk.

***Horizontal chopper (" cutter hoizon-***

***tal ")*** also known as buffalo chopper, is available with a fixed bowl or one that rotates. It is equipped with 3-6 blades that chop at variable speeds.

***Food processor (" cutter vertical ")*** also known as a robot coupe, these machines have a small capacity with a knife attachment that turns on a central arm.

A moderate-sized enterprise may choose to have just one " cutter ". A large capacity food processor can do the work of the horizontal chopper in the hands of a skilled worker.

The chef-owner must match the size and type of equipment to the volume of business and type of products that are most in demand. If a large and expensive machine is used only 15 minutes a day it will probably not be paying for itself in the long run. Smaller machines can often do the same work.

The goal of the grinding process is to cut up the meat into specific sized pieces to create forcemeats and stuffings with a variety of textures.

The mixtures are usually a blend of lean and fat in different ratios depending on the product.

The size of the cut or " grain " is achieved with disks (for grinder) with holes of various sizes. Obtaining the desired grain in the chopper is a more delicate operation as it is a function of how long the machine turns and how many blades. For a smooth, finely textured mixture the chopper is best because the machine turns until the meat is puréed.

Recipes sometimes refer simply to the size of the grain. The size of the grain can be grouped in three categories:

- Large grain: 8-10 mm (about 1/3-3/8 in)
- Medium grain: 4-6 mm (about 1/8-1/4 in)
- Small grain: less than 4 mm (1/8 in)

An important factor when grinding forcemeats is the nature of the two elements--lean and fat. It is usually desirable to grind the fat more finely so that it is not apparent in the slice (the consumer enjoys the texture of a pâté with fat in the mixture but does not always want to see it in the slice).

The fat however could melt a little due to friction if forced through too small a disk. The fat should be passed through a large or medium disk first then passed a second time through a small disk. With mousses and other fine-textured mixtures this is not a problem.

Another technique when processing in the chopper is to cut the meats into even sized cubes. Not only will the meat marinate more evenly, but when the blades turn, there will not be any piece of meat that needs more chopping than another.

It is also important that the blades be well-sharpened at all times so that the meat is chopped and not crushed which could heat the mixture.

Another machine, not mentioned in volume 1, that saves time in a large-scale charcuterie is a " lardonneuse ".

A " lardon " is a cube or short strip of meat. Slab bacon is often cut into " lardons " to use as a garnish on salads and cooked dishes. The " lardonneuse " cuts meats such as slab bacon and fatback into very neat cubes and strips. It can also be used to cut up the cooked meat from the pig's head to make headcheese. The cubes of fat used in " mortadella " and other preparations is cut neatly and quickly with this machine.

# " Gratins " and Guidelines for Enhancing Flavor

The top priority in cooking is to make products that taste delicious. Elaborate decorations are wasted on a dish that does not satisfy the palate.

Chefs face many obstacles as they strive to bring out maximum flavor in food.

A modern dilemna is industrial breeding. Pigs and poultry are raised in crowded conditions that do not allow the flesh to develop the flavor and texture of meat raised on farms in years past. We are not criticizing the system, the advantages of modern breeding are evident--higher quantities at lower prices. However it is important to realize that the flavor has diminshed and measures must be taken to compensate.

Secondly, the cooks of today must face the fact that consumers have been greatly influenced by reports of the medical community that high consumption of fat is harmful to health. This message is carried to the public by the press, especially the women's magazines.

French charcuterie, which traditionally contains substantial amounts of animal fats, has had to be adapted to meet the new demands. Charcutiers are researching methods for lowering the fat content while maintaining taste and texture.

Fat however is an excellent conductor of flavor and aromas (fats are used in making perfumes). Fats also make products moist and unctuous.

Synthetic flavorings are available. However the artisan charcutier can use his skill and knowledge to develop techniques to enhance flavor without artificial flavors.

The first step is to always choose the freshest and highest quality ingredients which will naturally have more flavor.

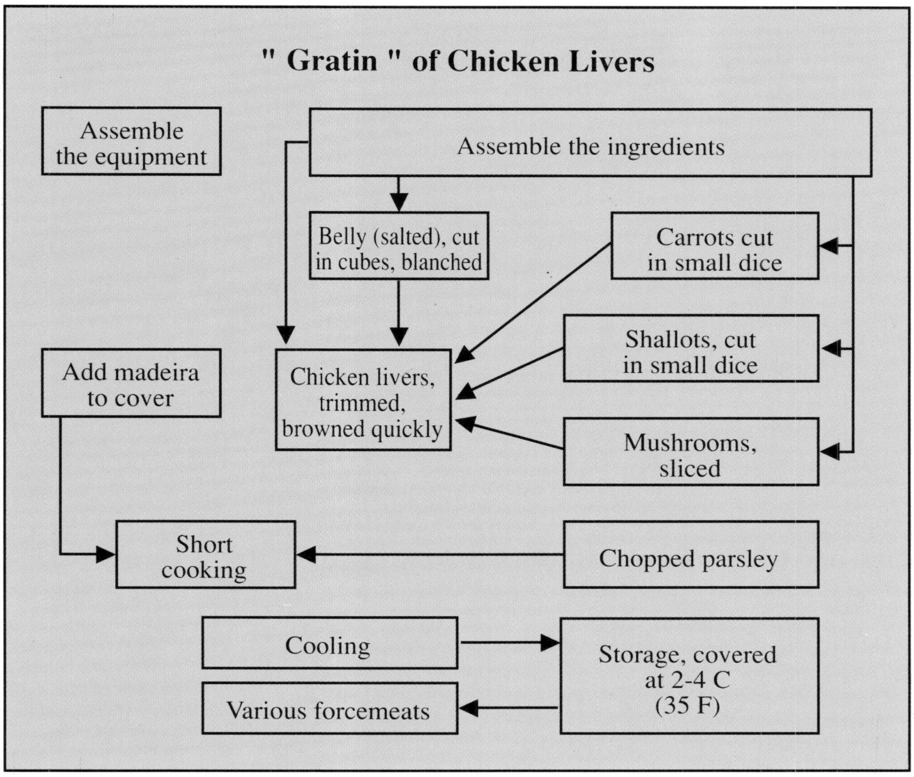


In addition there are two simple techniques used by the charcutier to intensify the natural flavors in his products:

***Reductions and meat glazes*** made from stocks are described in this chapter.

***" Gratins "*** are seasoned mixtures of chicken livers (or liver of particular animal featured in dish) and aromatic vegetables with madeira. The livers are lightly browned to add flavor but remain uncooked so they add a velvety texture to the forcemeat when it is cooked. The gratin is usually marinated then ground along with the other forcemeat ingredients.

A recipe is given on pages 259-260.

Reductions and gratins add primarily to taste. To compensate for the moisture that is lost when fat is eliminated from a recipe, cream can be substituted (animal fat is 80-90% fat, cream is 20-30%). Note that UHT cream (sterilized at " ultra high temperatures ") is used.

Lastly, attention to detail throughout processing, in conjuction with natural flavor enhancers, will ensure that products are seasoned to perfection, blended to the right consistency and cooked under the proper conditions.

# Stock, Aspic, and Reductions

### Introduction

Many charcuterie products are cooked in liquid. The type of liquid varies depending on the taste, texture and type of outer covering of the product.

The most basic liquid used is *water;* sometimes with salt added or food color for adding a tint to the casing of certain sausages (sausages from Strasbourg for example).

Water, of course, is the main ingredient of flavored cooking liquids, the simplest being " bouillon ". Not really a " court bouillon " or a stock, bouillon is the water flavored by cooking meats, notably those that are cured in brine.

The charcutier begins by adding aromatic vegetables to the stock pot or jacketed kettle in which the brined meats will cook. Water is added to cover and as the meats cook, they absorb flavors from the vegetables and meat juices escape into the liquid. Impurites are skimmed throughout cooking and the resulting liquid is a " bouillon ".

Between uses the flavorful liquid is boiled, skimmed and strained. It is then used to cook more brined meats. Aromatic vegetables are always added to the pot and water is blended with the bouillon to keep it from getting too strong and salty and to perpetuate the supply.

There are reknowned kitchens in Lyon that poach the famous chickens from Bresse in bouillon that is continually " topped up ".

The bouillon serves another important function: the cooked meats are covered with bouillon (boiled, skimmed and strained) for airtight storage.

In all cases, the bouillon must be cooled as quickly as possible as it is a very favorable environment for bacteria expecially when the temperature is between 20-45 °C (68-112 F).

## Pork Stock (" Jus ")

Stock is a fundamental ingredient in many charcuterie preparations. Either " as is " or reduced, stock adds flavor to a wide range of products.

The recipe for the stock used in charcuterie is similar to the aspic (" gelée ") recipe that follows. The main difference is the addition of browned bones in the stock recipe. Note that this gelatinous stock differs from the classic stock or " fond " that is used in restaurant kitchens. The charcutier's stock is known as " jus " or " juice ".

The term " jus " may come from the deglazing procedure. The bones and aromatic vegetables (onions and carrots) are first browned in a little fat (a process known as " rissoler " in French; often " rissolage " is done in the oven for even browning). The " juices " that adhere to the pan are then deglazed before more liquid is added to cover.

To add natural gelatin to the " jus ", pork skin (" couenne ") is added. It should be very fresh. If stock is made only a few times a week, the skin from the daily trimming of carcasses should be stored in salt then rinsed before using. The skin is always blanched and rinsed before being added to the stock.

### Ingredients

10 L (about 11 qts) water
2.5 kg (5.5 lbs) bones
6 kg (13 lbs) pork skin

*Aromatic vegetables:*
400 g (14 oz) onions
300 g (10 oz) carrots
3 branches celery
2 bouquet garnis
4 cloves
0.5 L (2 cups) dry white wine
Lard or goose fat

Coarse salt is added; 5 g (1/6 oz) per liter (qt), which draws out the flavor of the ingredients without making the stock salty. This " jus " is used to make full-flavored stocks and reductions so it should not be salty.

### Procedure

Saw the bones into pieces and remove the marrow.

Wash the vegetables, peel and cut in thick slices.

Place the bones in a greased roasting pan (lard or goose fat) and brown in a hot oven. Add the carrots and onions and brown, stirring often to brown evenly without burning.

Pour off the fat and deglaze with dry white wine.

Transfer the bones and vegetables to a large stockpot or jacketed kettle, add the remaining seasonings (celery, clove, bouquet garni) and cover the bones generously with water.

Bring to a boil, skimming all fat and impurities that rise to the surface.

Lower to a simmer and cook the stock for 6 hours. The stock can be started at the end of the work day and left to cook slowly all night.

When the stock is cooked, strain through a large colander to remove the bones and vegetables. Return the liquid to the heat and bring slowly to a boil, skimming all fat and impurities that rise to the surface. Strain through a fine mesh conical sieve and cool quickly.

It is preferable to store the stock in several small containers so that only the amount needed is removed from the refrigerator.

Stored at cold temperatures (2-4 °C (35 F)), the stock will stay fresh for 8-10 days.

### Uses

This " jus " is used " as is " to poach galantines, ballotines, foies gras and pigs' feet. It is also the binding ingredient in head cheese and similar products (the " bouillon " that the head is cooked in is not gelatinous enough to set up firmly).

For products made with a specific meat (such as quail, duck, rabbit...), this pork stock is added to the browned bones of that animal or bird to make a full-flavored stock. This stock with the characteristic taste of the quail or rabbit etc. can be poured over the cooked terrine for added moistness and can be reduced and added to the forcemeat to reinforce the flavor of the meat.

The stock can also be clarified to make a clear glaze.

## Pork Aspic (" Gelée ")

The aspic is made like the stock but *without bones or browning in fat.*

The proportion of skin (6-7 kg (13-14 lbs) per 10 L (11 qts) of water) is the same to obtain a liquid that will remain firm at 16-18 °C (62-64 F). The skin should be fresh and is prepared in the same way.

The liquid must be skimmed often and strained following the same guidelines as for stock.

Without bones and browning in fat, the " gelée " is much clearer than stock. (Technically this is not a true aspic but rather a " gel ".) Unclarified it is used as a cooking liquid (for andouillettes for example). It is clarified for glazing the top of finished products.

## Clarifying Stock (" Jus ") and Aspic (" Gelée ")

Even if the aspic is strained carefully it will not be crystal clear unless it is clarified. Stunning presentations depend on aspic that is perfectly transparent.

The clarifying process therefore removes the remaining fat and impurites.

This is accomplished with the addition of substances high in protein; eggs whites, blood or ground beef (lean, tough cut).

When the proteins coagulate at 63-66 °C (150 F) they absorb the fat and impurities. The liquid is then strained through a conical cloth filter (" alambic ").

No matter which method is used, a small amount of vinegar (1.5 % (150 ml (generous 1/2 cup) for 10 L (11 qts) is added to the stock or aspic to add flavor and help the coagulation process. The clarified aspic with vinegar keeps better as well.

Before the liquid is clarified, a small portion is chilled to verify the setting power. Powdered of leaf gelatin is added to achieve the desired firmness (the gelatin dissolves in cold stock and melts during the clarification process).

## Clarifying " Gelées " and " Jus " *(continued)*

**Procedure**

### *Blood Method*

10 L (11 qts) aspic or stock
1.25 L (1.25 qt) blood
150 ml (generous 1/2 cup) vinegar

Verify the gelatin content of the aspic or stock. Place the liquid in a stockpot, season with salt if necessary and add vinegar.

Bring to a boil and skim all fat and impurities that rise to the surface.

Whisk the blood into the boiling liquid, lower the heat to 95 °C (200 F) and cook gently 15-20 minutes.

Turn the heat off and let the liquid sit undisturbed for 15 minutes.

Ladle the liquid through a conical cloth strainer. For best results strain the first three liters (qts) twice.

Cool as quickly as possible.

### *Egg White Method*

10 L (11 qts) aspic or stock
450-500 g (1 lb) egg whites
150 ml (generous 1/2 cup) vinegar

This method is different; the egg whites are whisked into cold stock.

Whisk the liquid continuously as it is heated to 85 °C (185 F), stop stirring and simmer 15 minutes.

Turn the heat off and let the liquid sit undisturbed for 15-20 minutes.

Ladle the liquid through a conical cloth strainer. Strain the first three liters (qts) twice.

Cool the liquid as quickly as possible.

*The photographs illustrate the " blood method "*

Our preference is for the " egg white method ". The aspic or stock will pick up some flavor from the blood, especially if it is not perfectly fresh whereas the egg whites are neutral in taste.

However, the blood does add a lovely amber color (the egg whites do not change the color).

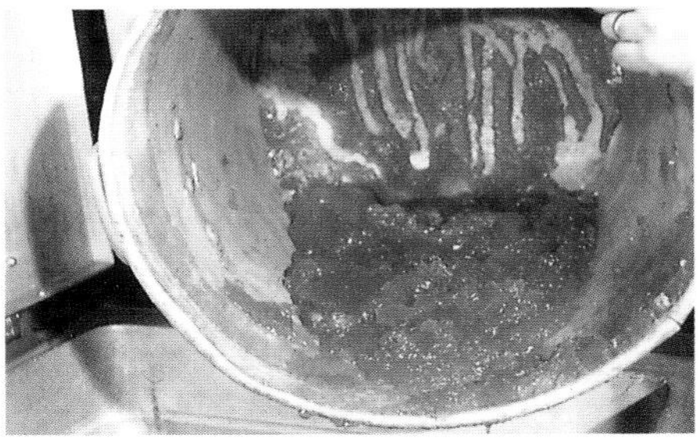

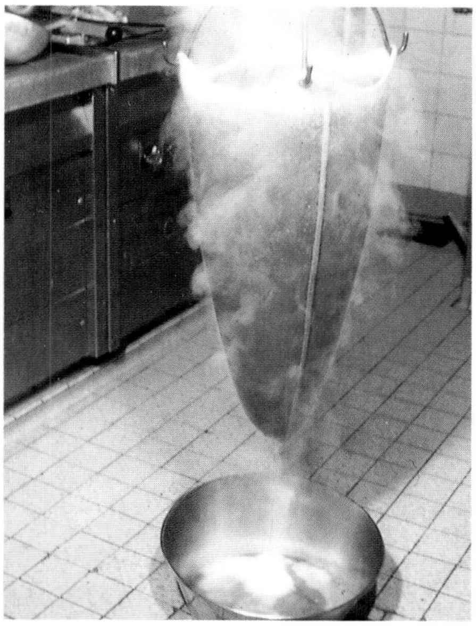

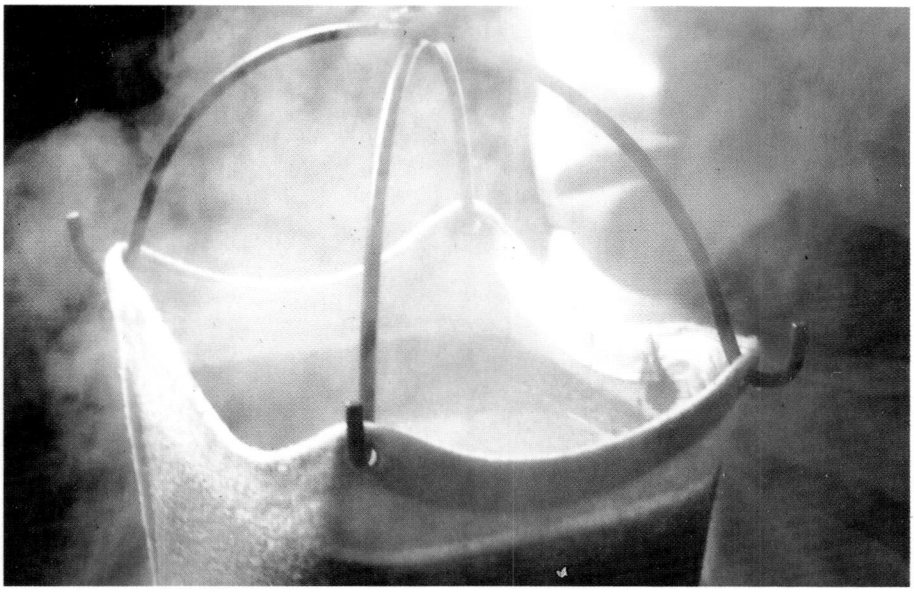

## Reductions and Glazes

The full-flavored stocks described in the first section (made by adding pork stock (" jus ") to the browned bones (quail, duck etc.)) can be made into reductions and glazes.

Before these stocks are reduced, they must be boiled and skimmed of all fat and impurites. They are then simmered to slowly evaporate the liquid and concentrate the flavor. Note that the salt does not evaporate; the original stock should not be salty.

A *reduction* is obtained by simmering the stock until it is thick and concentrated but still liquid.

A *glaze* is obtained by reducing further until the stock is syrupy and will coat a spoon. A meat glaze is also called an " essence ".

The intense flavor is ideal for reinforcing the characteristic taste in a ground meat mixture without changing the texture. The glaze should always marry with the other flavors in the preparation.

The long cooking and the lack of moisture in the final result, means that reductions and glazes will keep relatively well. In a closed glass container, stored in the refrigerator (2-4 °C (35 F)), the reductions will keep fresh for several weeks.

The process requires no special skill or equipment. The liquid should be skimmed and stirred so that it does not stick to the bottom of the pot. As the volume decreases, transfer the liquid to a smaller pot. (Dissolve any stock that adheres to the pot with water and add to stock that is being made.)

# Cooking Techniques

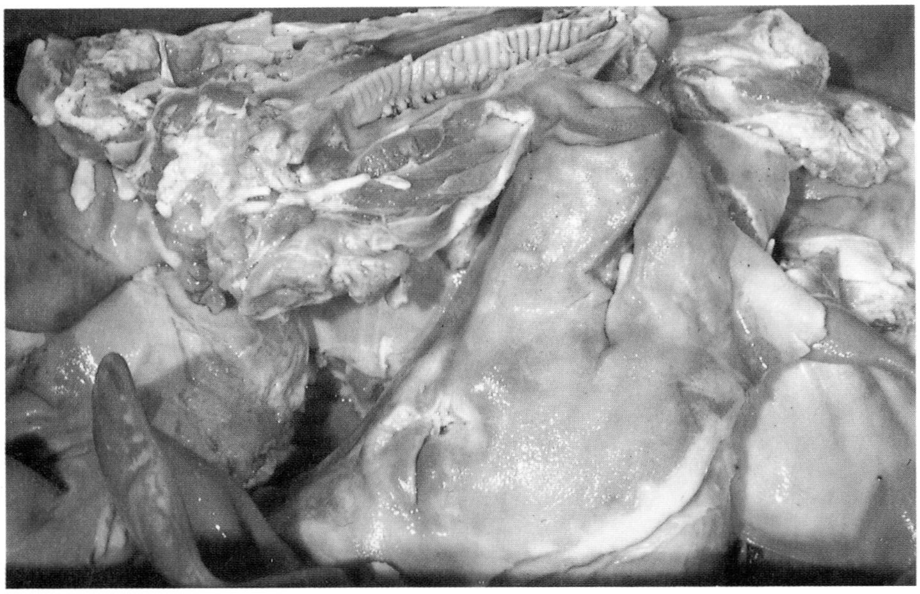

## The Effects of Cooking

The term "charcutier", as we explained in Volume 1, comes from two French words – "chair" meaning flesh or meat and "cuit" meaning cooked. The original charcutiers were "chair-cuitier" or those who prepared cooked meat.

The modern charcutier follows in this tradition and has supplemented his selection with other items and is often trained as a caterer as well.

When man discovered fire, he found that heated food, and meat in particular, had a better taste, was more easily digested and could be stored for longer periods.

What are the physical changes that take place in meat during the cooking process?

### The Effect of Cooking on the Basic Components of Meat

***Water***

Water makes up about 70% of muscle. Water evaporates when heated, most notably from the surface of the meat. This evaporation can be blocked by searing the surface of the meat with direct contact with the cooking recipient heated to a high temperature. The outer "crust" that forms when the meat is seared reduces the weight (in the form of moisture) that would have been lost through evaporation therefore making the finished product more moist and succulent.

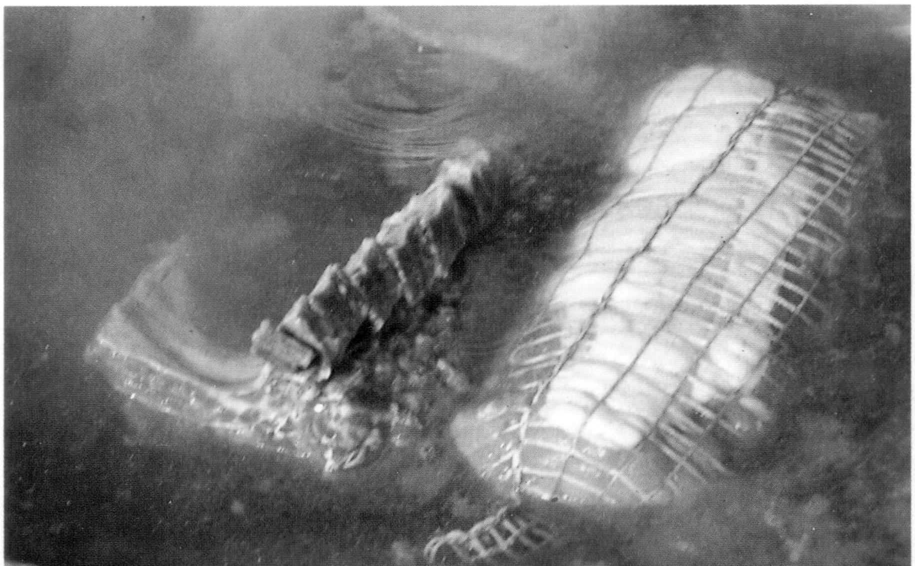

Meat that is cooked in liquid loses some of its water content but through osmosis absorbs moisture from the cooking liquid.

### *Fat*

Animal fats melt at relatively low temperatures. When meats are seared, fats melt on the surface, forming a thin protective film which then flows down and collects in the baking dish. This fat should be spooned up and used to baste the meat throughout cooking to maintain the protective film of fat.

Fat is adversely affected by temperatures exceeding 200 °C (400 F). This breaks down the fat resulting in a sour and bitter flavor and in some cases can render the fat toxic.

### *Protein*

Proteins begin to coagulate at 55 °C (131 F). The muscle fibers begin to shrink and force the juices from the meat. The coagulation process is irreversible and definitive.

The collagen melts at high temperatures then solidifies when the meat is chilled. This gelatinous substance facilitates the slicing of cold meats.

### Effect on Microorganisms

The destruction of microorganisms in foods that could eventually cause the meat to spoil is an important role of cooking at high temperatures.

The microorganisms present in all foods must be treated so that the bacteria are destroyed. However while some bacteria are destroyed at 55 °C (131 F) others are not easily destroyed even by boiling.

Guidelines have been set to establish safe parameters for the production of food products.

For a product to be considered safe the internal temperature must reach 70 °C (159 F). The products of the artisan charcutier sold within a few days of fabrication should follow this general rule.

Complete pasteurization requires higher temperatures. Products that are sterilized in jars and cans for prolonged storage are heated to 121 °C (250 F).

Sterilization does not happen with high temperatures alone. The length of cooking plays a dual role with the temperature level. Therefore different combinations of time and temperature are used to suit various products.

For more scientific information French charcutiers consult the " Encyclopédie de la Charcuterie " a technical, highly regarded reference work. The authors of this series had the honor of collaborating on this book.

Therefore the artisinal charcutier strives for the perfect balance between safety and taste. For each product there is a point of optimal quality – the heat has been sufficient to destroy bacteria and the full flavor and texture of the product has been maintained.

Another important consideration is the weight lost during cooking. Here again a balance is met so that the product produces as many portions as possible within the taste and safety guidelines.

These precise cooking techniques require competence and a feel for the product. (There is a saying that one can learn to make sauces but one is born a roaster of meats.) Technical developments in the form of thermostats and probe thermometers are essential tools for the charcutier which help him judge the temperature accurately.

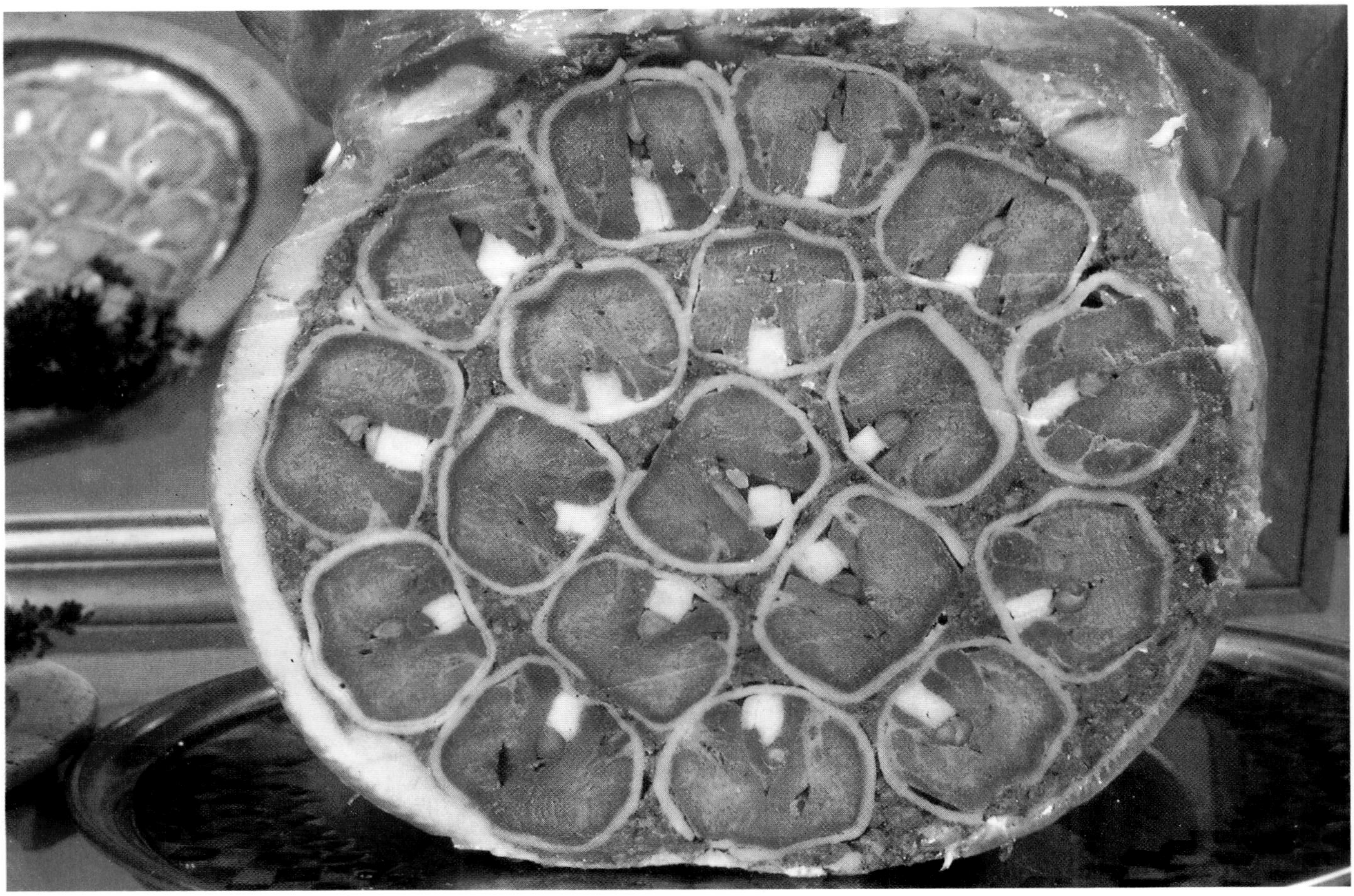

# Chapter 2
# Roast Pork, Brined Pork Products and Pig's Feet

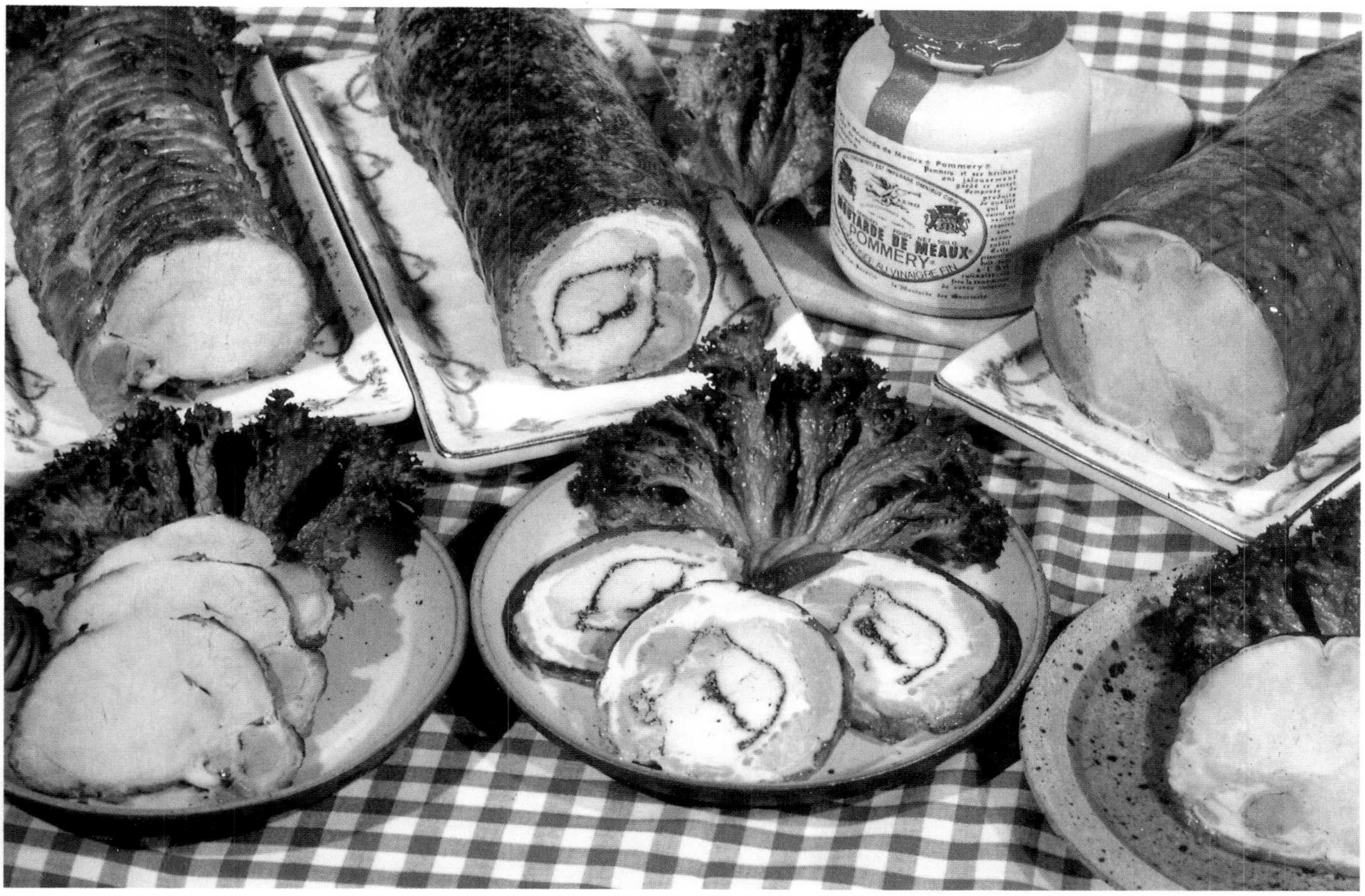


## Delicious Traditional Preparations

*This chapter demonstrates the saying "In the pig, you can cook everything but the squeal!".*

*These recipes complete the selection of basic traditional preparations in Volume 1 which includes hams, sausages, white and blood sausages, rillettes and confits.*

*These classic products are best when prepared by a skilled artisan charcutier.*

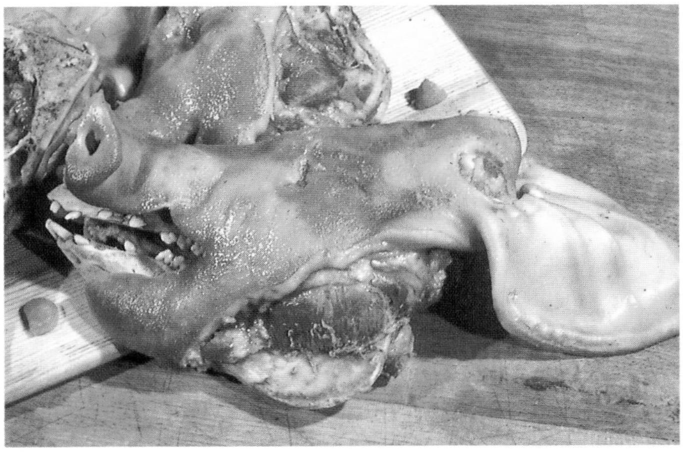

# Presentation

### *Categories covered in volume 1*

*The following products are described in volume 1:*

- *Hams (8 varieties)*
- *Sausages (14 varieties)*
- *Specialty Cooked Sausages (7 varieties)*
- *Blood Sausages (6 varieties)*
- *White Sausages (12 varieties)*
- *Rillettes and Rillons (9 varieties)*
- *Confits (5 varieties)*
- *Smoked Pork Products*

#### *Cuts of Pork*

The preparation of hams is described in volume 1. In this volume, products that use the cooked ham such as ham with parsley (" jambon persillé ") are explained. In addition to this classic version, another recipe is given using the blade end (" palette ").

From the vast selection of roast pork products, three representative recipes are described.

Pork products cured with brine, from the " jambonneau " (ham shank) to the Boston shoulder (" échine ") and spareribs (" travers ") are traditional in French charcuteries and form the base for many basic dishes.

#### *Pig's Head*

This portion of the pig is used by the French charcutier in many original and traditional products.

The most classic preparation is head cheese (" fromage de tête ") and " hure ". The hure which refers to the entire head, is presented in an elaborate presentation and a simpler one assembled in a mold.

Tongues as well as pig's ears are presented here in delicious, original dishes.

#### *Extremities*

Pig's feet is a favorite dish in France and can be made plain or fancy. The elaborate products described in this volume include two popular specialities; " pieds à la Saint-Menehould " and molded pig's feet which are offered by many top quality charcutiers in France.

The arm steak and ham hock (" jarret " and " jarrotin ": which sometimes come attached to the front feet are delicious additions to choucroute.

The tail of the pork has long been a favorite of connoisseurs and adds a characteristic touch to many dishes.

**Cured Pork Roast (page 27)**

**Roast Pork " Ménagère " (page 28)**

**Roast Pork with Crushed Pepper (page 30)**

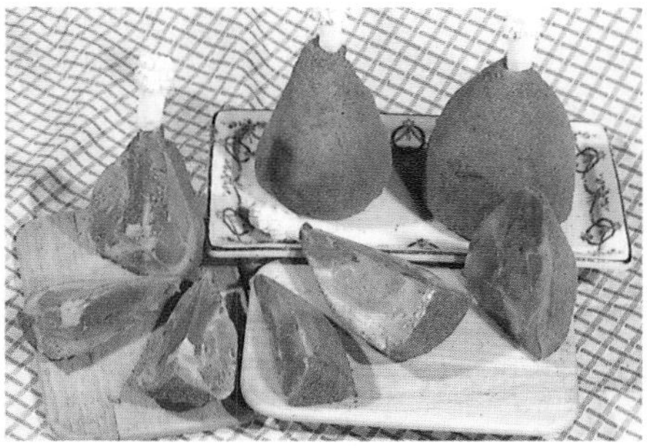

Cooked Ham Shanks
(page 32)

Brined Pork Products
(page 36)

Arm Steaks and Ham
Hocks (page 40)

Pork Cuts for Choucroute
(page 43)

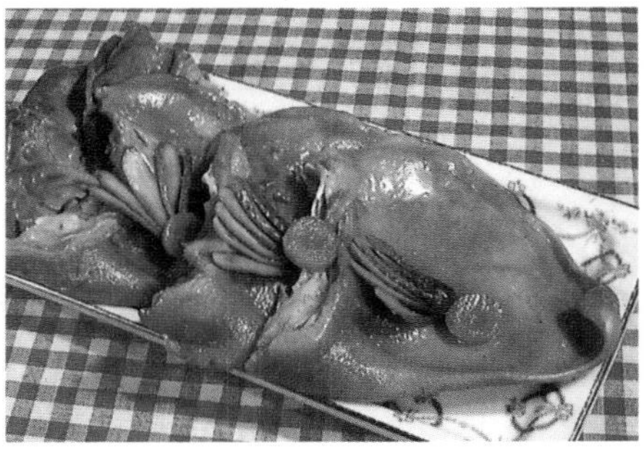

Ears
(page 44)

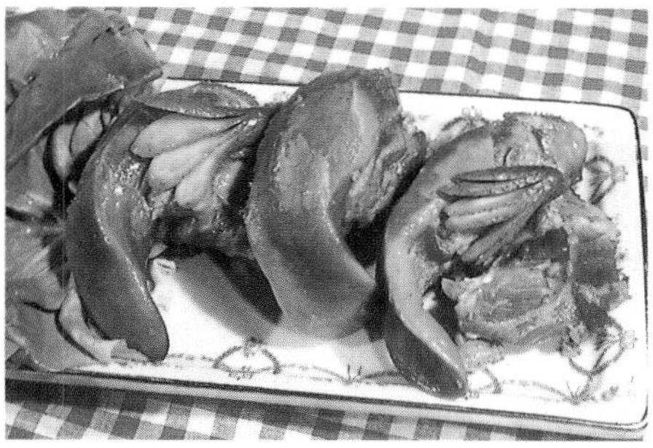

Tongues
(page 45)

Tails
(page 45)

Head Cheese
(page 46)

" Museau "
(page 49)

Molded Ham with Parsley
(page 50)

" Hure à la Parisienne "
(page 56)

Molded " Hure "
(page 62)

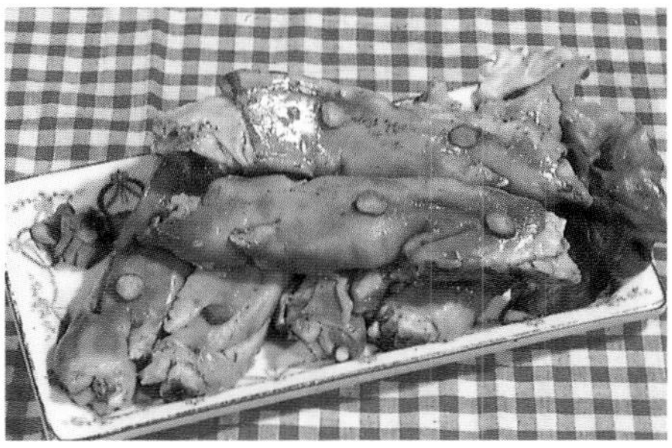

Pig's Feet Cooked in Aspic
(page 64)

Pig's Feet St-Menehould
(page 66)

Molded Pig's Feet
(page 70)

# General Advice for Roast Pork

All cuts from the loin of pork as well as the ham (whole or sliced) can be successfully roasted. Boston shoulder (" échine ") and blade end (" palette ") are good choices. The best cuts of all are the rib roast (" carré de côtes ") and filet. (*Note:* U.S. and French cuts differ slightly.)

Pork cuts for roasting in France are sold in two forms:

- Fresh, most often purchased by home cooks to be roasted with prunes or plain and served with vegetables...
- Cured in a light brine (" demi-sel "). Some customers will select a fresh cut of pork and request that it be brined to order. The final preparation and cooking is done in the customer's kitchen.

*What are the differences between these two products?*

***Color:*** The fresh, uncured meat is a grayish color after cooking. This is the case with all meats that are cooked " well done " (veal, pork, poultry...). When beef and duck breast are served " pink ", it is because the temperature at the center of the cut did not reach 50 °C (131 F) and therefore the proteins did not coagulate.

The cured meat will retain its rosy color when cooked.

***Taste:*** The injection of brine into the meat seasons it from within and also adds moisture which makes it more succulent. In addition, cured meat is usually cooked in bouillon or other flavored liquid. At home, the cured roast would be cooked in a covered pot in the oven where it is continually basted in its own juices.

The osmosis that takes place when the roast cooks in bouillon (as with hams, and other cuts) assures a meat that is moist as well as flavorful.

Fresh pork roast is often stuffed with fruits (prunes, olives, kiwis) which adds flavor and moisture, The chef can choose from many possible garnishes without changing the cooking method.

The brined pork roast is a standard product in French charcuteries. It is a favorite item in the summer when it is consumed cold.

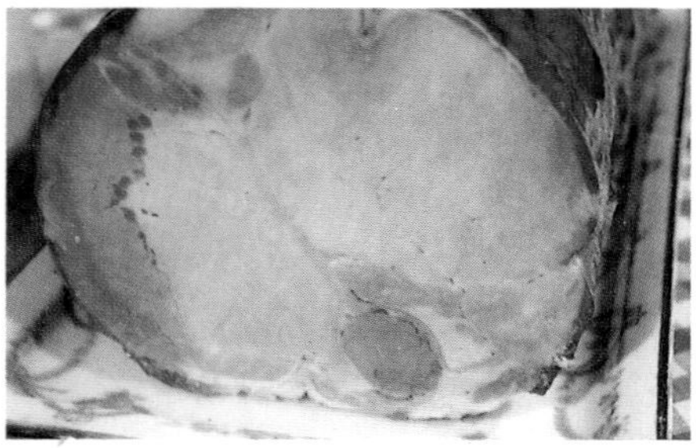

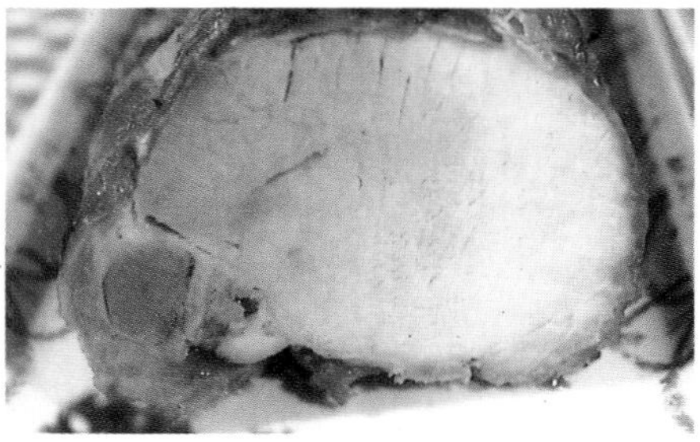

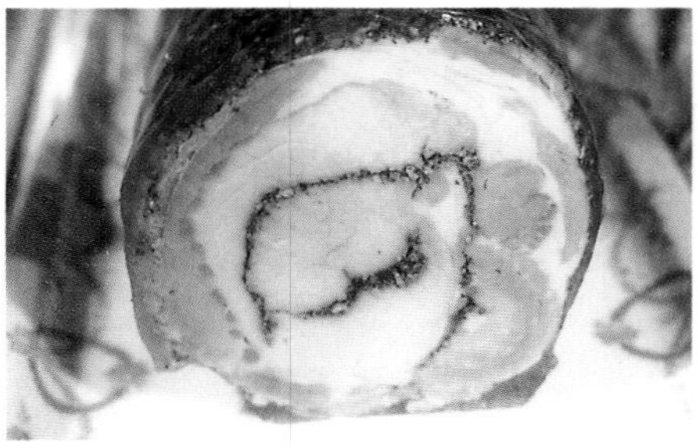

# Brined Pork Roast

**Procedure**

This roast is usually prepared from the whole loin with the point removed.

The loin is boned and trimmed then injected with brine (density and amount is same as for hams) then immersed in brine for 12 hours.

The meat is then rinsed thoroughly under cold running water before the draining and maturing process.

The roast is then placed into an elastic net to hold its shape. It can also be tied in the classic way with kitchen string.

**Cooking**

The drained roast is patted dry with paper towels before cooking. Lard or oil is heated in a large sauté pan then the roast is browned on all sides in the hot fat. The seared meat is then placed in a pot of bouillon. Professional charcuteries will use large kettles that can hold several cuts of meat at once. Brined meat is added throughout the day and removed when the correct internal temperature is achieved.

This roast is cooked until the center registers 75 °C (167 F) on a thermometer. It is then transferred to a deep recipient. Some of the cooking liquid is brought to a boil, skimmed then strained over the meat to cover. It is then cooled as quickly as possible and stored in this liquid in the refrigerator.

It is chilled for at least 24 hours before slicing. For presentation in the shop, wipe the surface and glaze with aspic (chilled and slightly thickened) by either dipping the roast in the aspic or using a pastry brush.

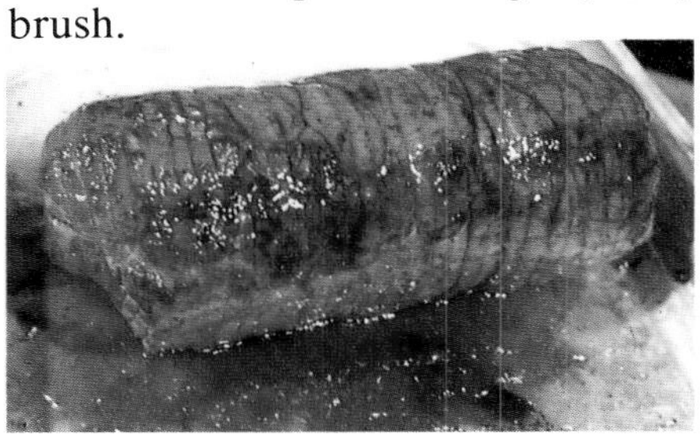

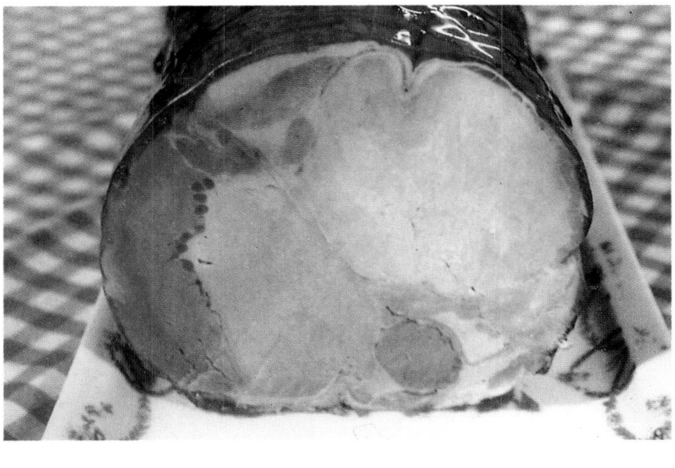

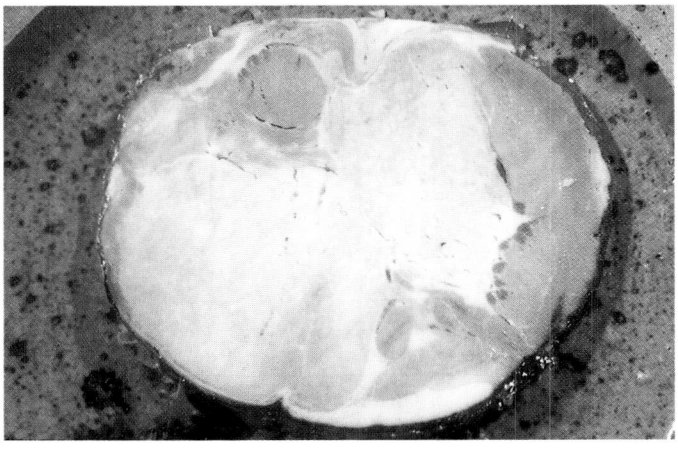

# Homestyle Roast of Pork (“ Ménagère ”)

This is the classic homestyle pork roast. With more women back in the work force and no longer full-time housewives (“ ménagères ”), the French charcutier-caterer often offers this simple dish for busy families to eat at home.

This is an easy preparation which requires a basic knowledge of roasting techniques which is traditionally passed from mother to daughter in the French household.

**Equipment**

Knife, kitchen string, roasting pan or cocotte.

**Ingredients**

Pork roast, aromatic vegetables (onions, carrots, celery, garlic), bouquet garni.

**Procedure**

All the cuts from the pork loin can be roasted in this way. The rib roast however is the best choice as it is more moist than the filet and not as fatty as the Boston shoulder. The blade end has similar qualities and would also be a good choice.

The rib roast is first boned and trimmed following the classic method. The boned side is then seasoned with salt and pepper, several peeled garlic cloves are arranged on the meat then it is rolled and tied securely with kitchen string.

The aromatic vegetables are peeled, rinsed and sliced then spread evenly in the roasting pan and the meat is placed on top of the vegetables. Several small nuggets of lard are placed on top of the roast so that the fat melts over the meat, producing a protective film.

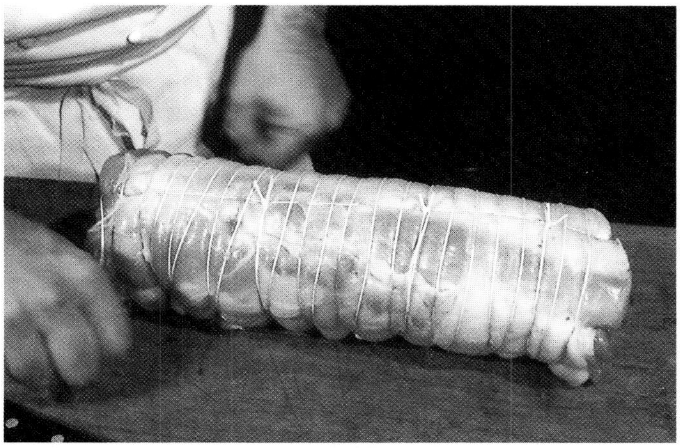

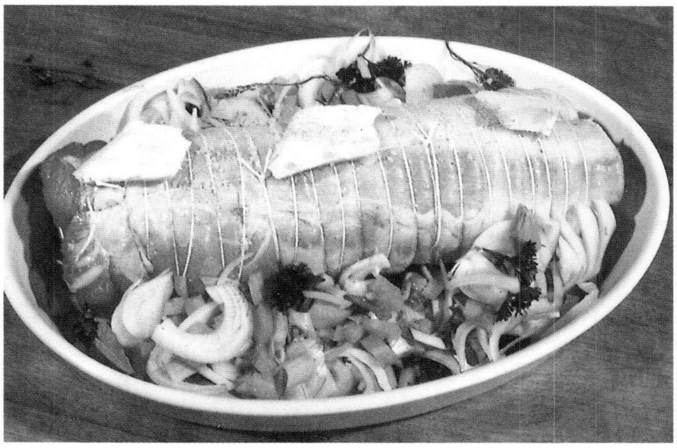

**Cooking**

Place the roast in a preheated 180 °C (350 F) oven. Turn the meat so that it browns on all sides.

When the meat is browned, turn down the heat to 140-150 °C (300 F). Cooking time will vary according to the size of the roast--about 1 1/2 hours for a medium sized roast. About halfway through the cooking time, the pan is removed from the oven and the fat from the pan is poured off.

The pan is then deglazed. The chef can choose from many liquids; white wine and water, chicken or veal stock, consommé, or bouillon from " pot-au-feu ". The pan is then returned to the oven and the meat is basted often during the remainder of the cooking so that the meat is moist.

**Presentation**

In French charcuteries, pork roast is sometimes sold warm and ready to consume as a main course. In this case, the pan juices are packaged for the customer to take home and serve with the roast.

The roast is also sold cold and sliced to order. In this case, the meat should be cooled immediately and quickly and kept refrigerated (2-4 °C (35 F)). The slices of cold pork are served with tart pickles (" cornichons ") and a variety of mustards.

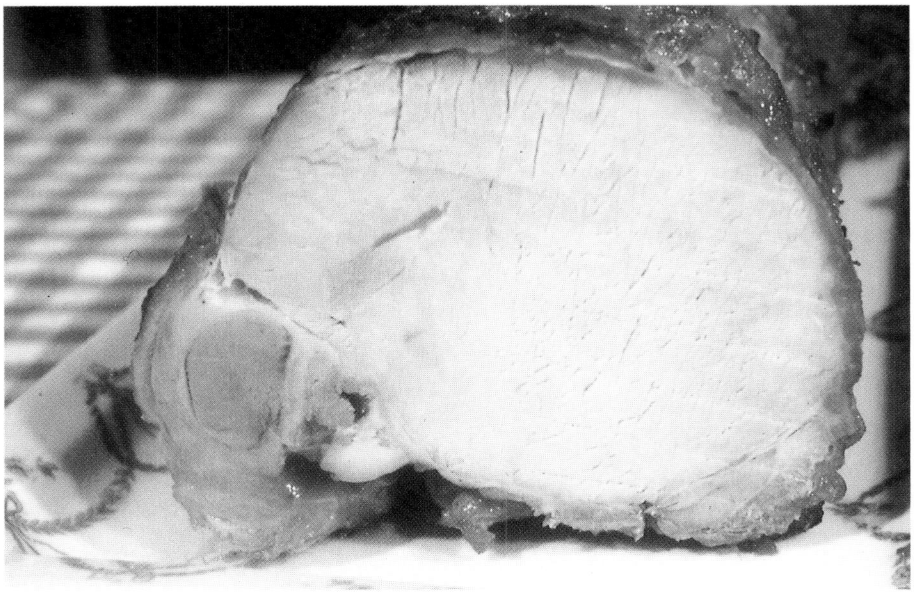

# Pork Roast with Crushed Pepper

This preparation is made with a cut of pork which is seasoned with coarsely crushed pepper (" mignonette "). This spicy addition makes it a favorite dish to serve in the summer. The cuisines of the tropical countries are proof that hot foods actually make the consumer feel cooler.

**Equipment**

Knife, kitchen string or net, brining pump, saucepan, marmite.

**Procedure**

The rib roast is also the best choice for this recipe. It is completely boned and trimmed.

At this stage the chef decides whether to cure the meat or use it fresh.

• For the curing procedure, refer to the explanation for curing, draining and maturing explained in this volume.

• If the pork is to be roasted " fresh ", proceed by first butterflying the meat by making a neat slice through the thick portion and opening it flat.

Cover the entire surface with coarsely crushed pepper. We recommend making your own " mignonette ". Pre-ground products quickly lose their flavor and aroma. It is best to crush the pepper with a bottle, rolling pin or the bottom of a pot just before it is used. In this way, the pepper is the most flavorful.

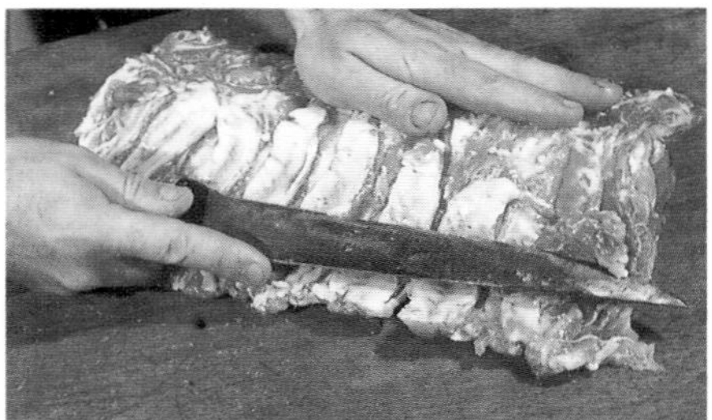

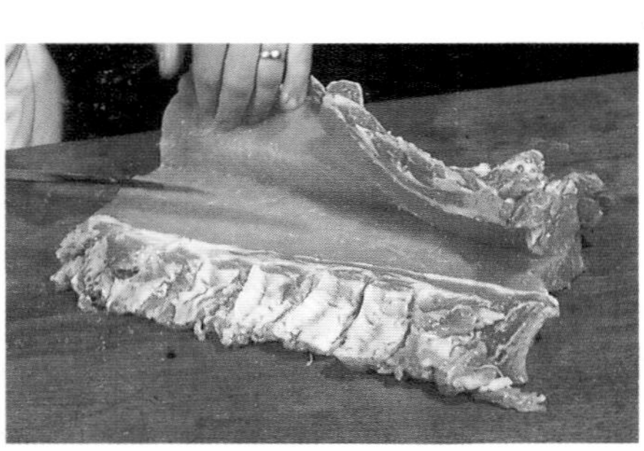

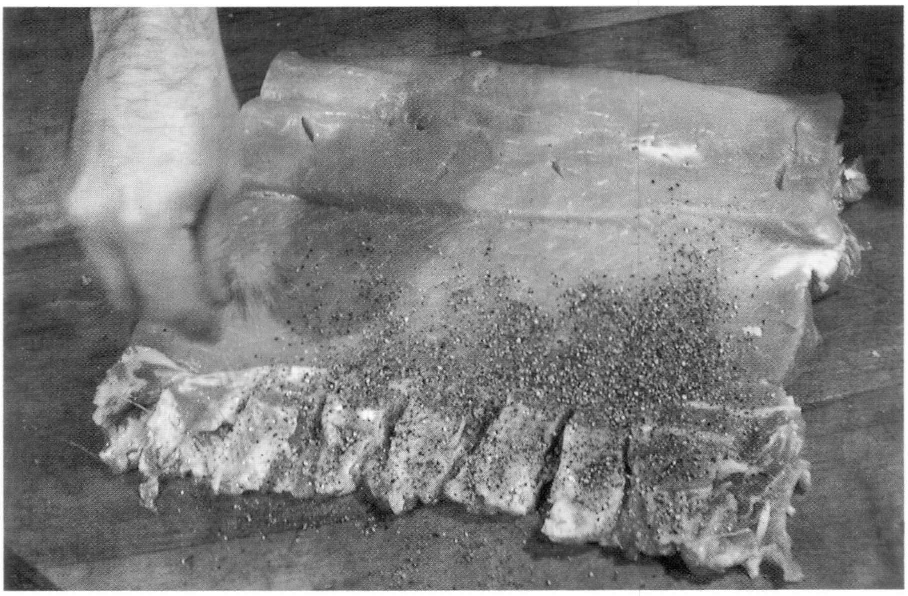

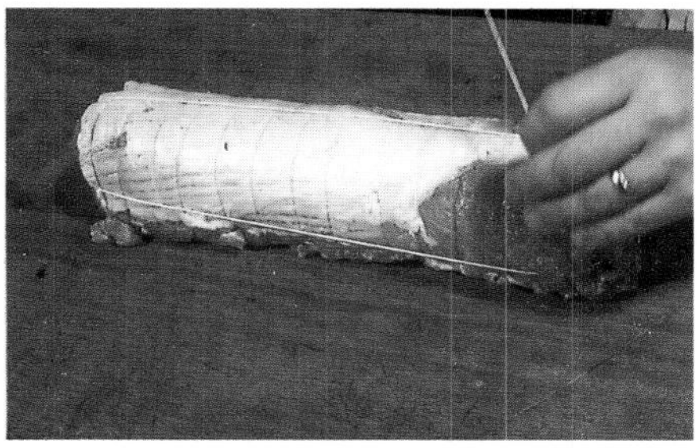

Roll the meat to reform the roast and tie it securely but not too tight. This is an important guideline for all roasted meats--if the string is pulled too tight, flavorful juices will be forced out of the muscle.

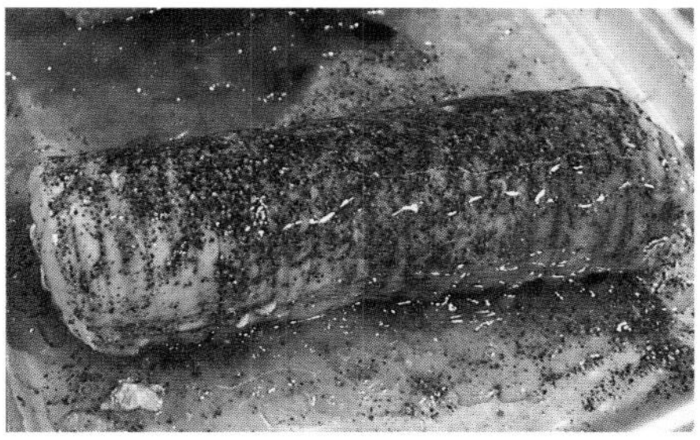

**Cooking**

This roast is cooked in a flavorful bouillon in the classic manner until the internal temperature reaches 75 °C (167 F).

The roast is then placed in a deep recipient and covered with the bouillon (boiled and skimmed and strained) and cooled quickly.

**Presentation**

As with classic brined pork roast, pork roast with crushed pepper is glazed with aspic for presentation in the charcuterie.

***Important Advice***

This product can be very successfully cooked using the modern vacuum pack method.

The procedure is the same as previously described up to the browning stage.

The browned roast is then cooled quickly to 2-4 °C (35 F) before being placed in the vacuum pouch.

The meat in the pouch can be cooked in plain water as the plastic allows for no osmosis.

There are several advantages with this method. All the juices are held inside the pouch so that the meat is very moist. The weight loss during cooking is greatly reduced so that the yield is higher.

The cooked meat should be quickly cooled in the pouch either in a special cooling chamber or in a basin of ice water.

The meat can be left in the cooking pouch until it is sold. To prolong storage the meat in the cooking pouch can be placed in a special vacuum pouch developed for better conservation.

# Cooked Ham Shank (" Jambonneau ")

**Introduction**

The shank or " jambonneau " is the tip of the ham that is attached to the end of the tibia and fibula (in the case of the hind legs).

These are not to be confused with the hocks from the front legs that are attached to the radius and ulna.

On the wholesale market, the shank is usually sold with the ham and is removed with a straight cut at a right angle to the shank bone at the stifle joint.

The " jambonneau " is a very tender and succulent cut if cooked.

**Equipment**

Knife, razor, brining pump, stock pot or jacketed kettle, " jambonneau " mold, handtowel or special cooking pouch.

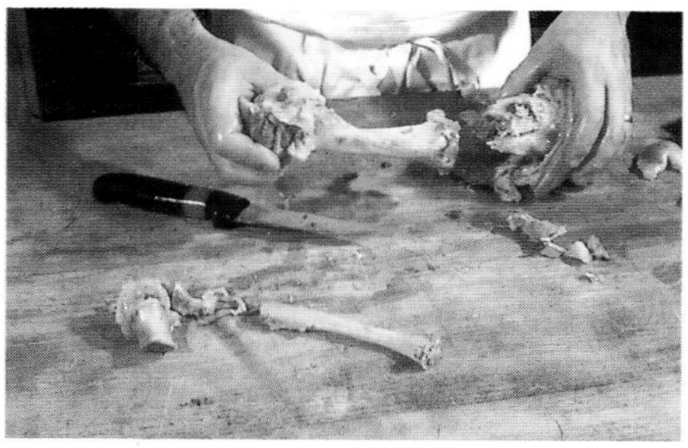

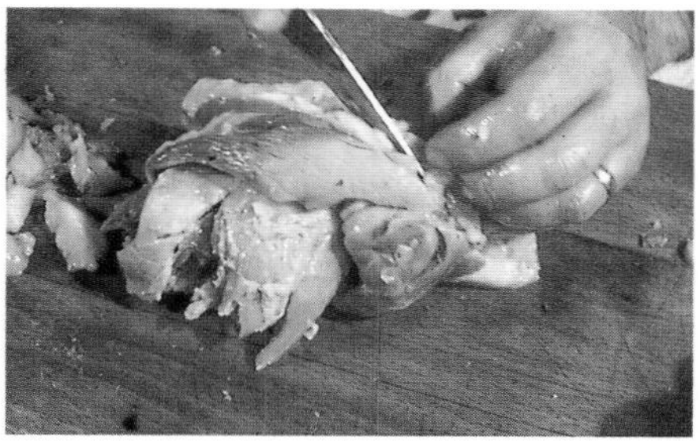

**Procedure**

The " Parisien " method for cutting up the pork carcass (illustrated in Volume I) provides the best hams. The best shanks (cut from hams destined to be " jambons supérieur ") are cut fresh from the ham when it is boned.

The shank must be carefully shaved and rinsed to remove hairs. It is then injected with standard ham brine then immersed in brine for 12-24 hours.

As with all brined products, the shank is thoroughly rinsed in cold running water to remove excess brine then drained and left to rest and " mature ". This process can take up to several days.

The modern method of " mixing " hams with brine in a tumbler (" malaxeur ") can also be used for ham shanks.

Following the guidelines in volume I for hams, the shanks are placed in the tumbler with 12-15 % of their weight in brine. The tumbler is then operated in " massaging " and rest cycles to allow the muscles to rest to ensure an even and thorough absorption of the brine.

**Cooking**

The cooking is also similar to the procedure for hams.

A flavorful bouillon with aromatic vegetables is brought to a boil and skimmed of all fat and impurities.

The shanks are added and the temperature is regulated to 85 °C (185 F). The ham shanks cook until they are tender and pull away from the bone.

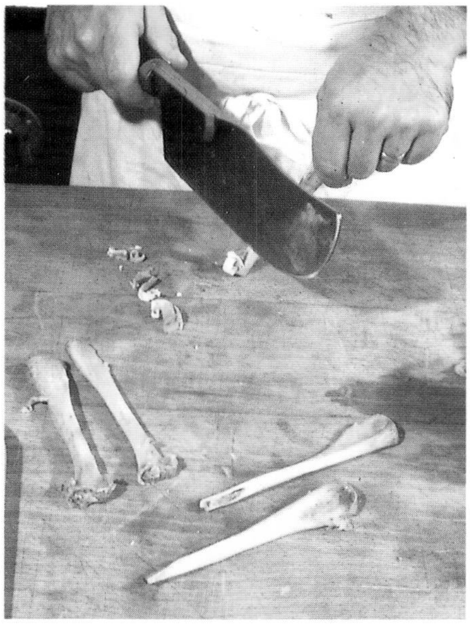

If the charcutier is equipped with a reliable jacketed kettle that can be set at 72 °C (160 F), the cooking can take place overnight.

The lengthy cooking at low temperatures produces a higher yield and a moist product. This is also a technique used with hams.

**Molding**

The ham shanks are boned by hand while they are still warm.

The tibia is set aside and replaced in the center when the "jambonneaux" are reformed and placed in the molds. The bone is often cut at an angle and decorated with a paper frill or "papillotte" for presentation in the shop.

The shanks are also trimmed of excess fat. The skin should remain intact but as much fat as possible should be cut away from under and around the skin.

When the jambonneaux are shaped in French charcuteries, the

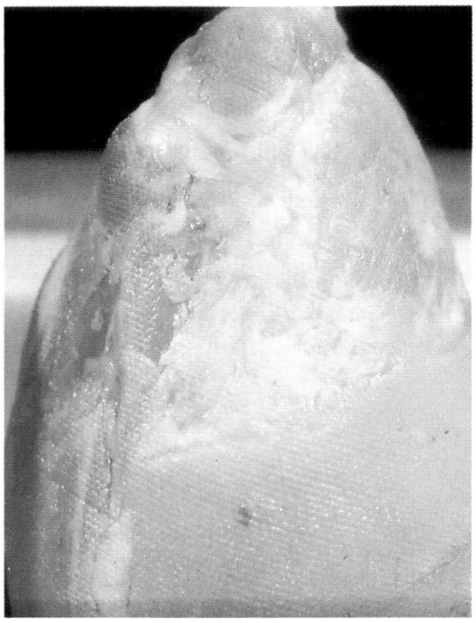

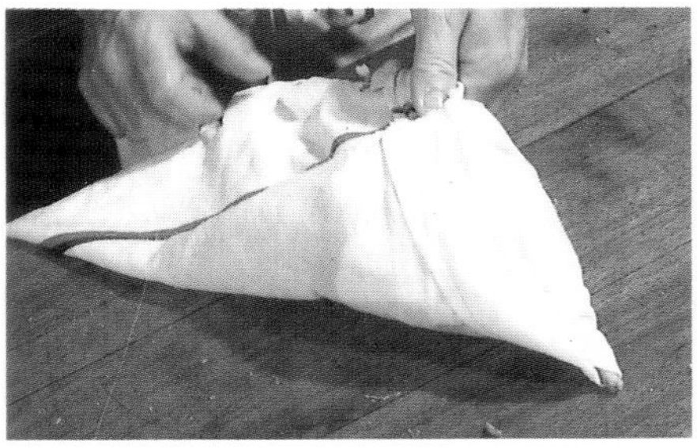

mold is sometimes filled out with pieces of lean blade end or shoulder to ensure a tightly packed conical shape. This meat replaces the bone and fat that was removed and is a legal procedure in making jambonneaux.

The molding procedure can be done in two days:

***Molding in a "Jambonneau Mold"***

The skin is placed against the sides of the mold then the trimmed meat is fitted in to completely fill the mold. The bone is placed in the center with the end protruding through the hole that is designed for this purpose.

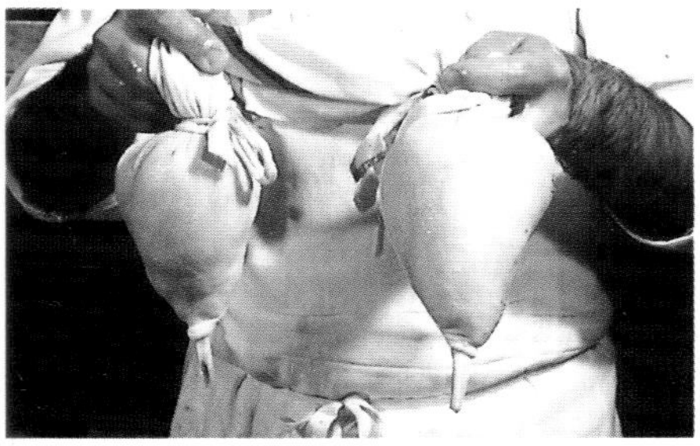

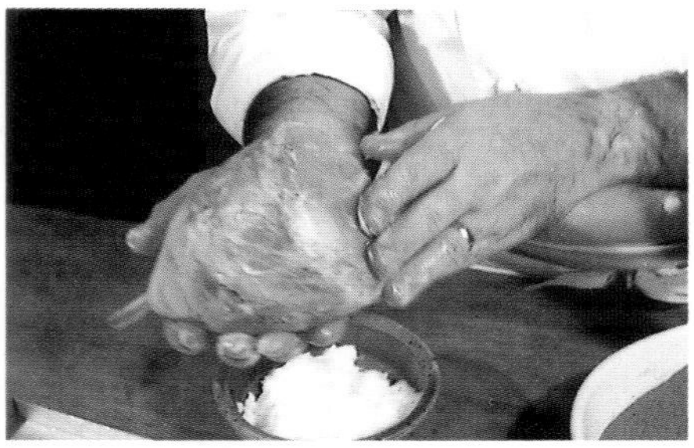

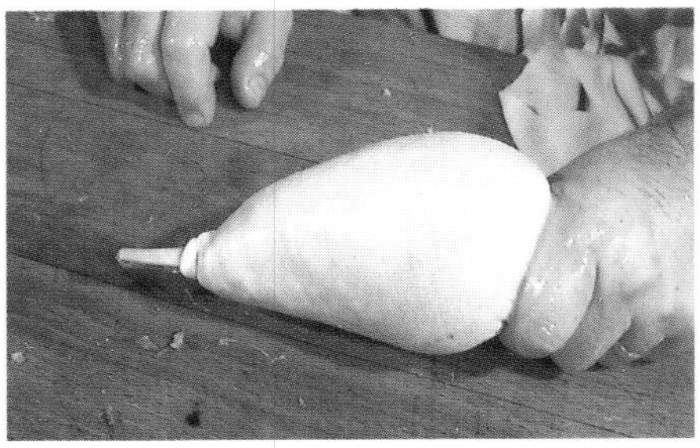

The top is placed on the mold and the contents are pressed lightly to compact them without forcing out juices which would result in a dry product.

It is recommended to place the molds in boiling bouillon for 15 minutes. They are then cooled as quickly as possible in fresh bouillon that has been boiled and skimmed.

They can be stored for 8-10 days in the refrigerator.

***Molding in a Handtowel***

The ham shank is first reformed in the mold with the bone just like the preceding method. It is then carefully transferred to a clean

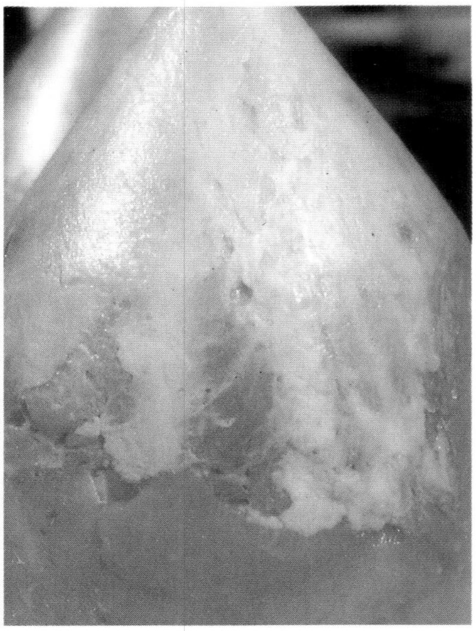

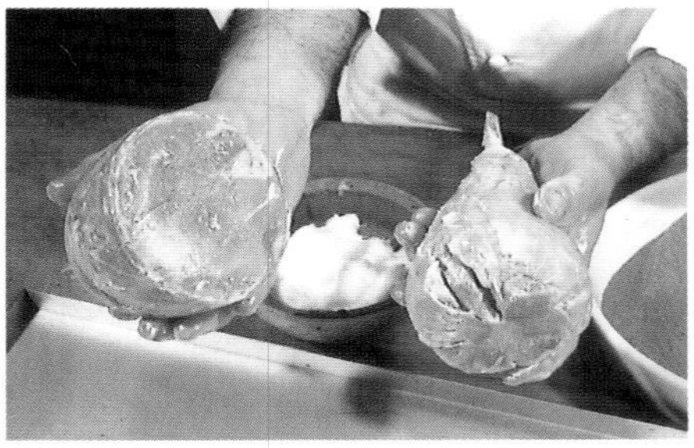

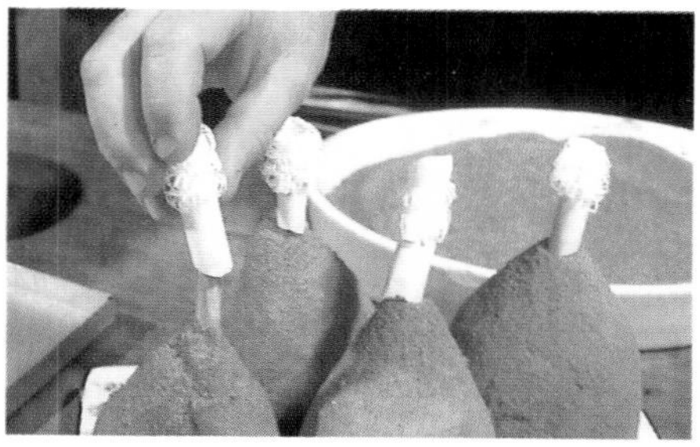

handtowel which is spread out on the work surface. It is then wrapped to maintain the conical shape and securely tied at the base.

This is the method that we recommend. The meat is not pressed as tightly therefore resulting in a moister product. Also more flavor is absorbed from the cooking liquid. The shaping procedure requires some dexterity but is not difficult.

*Variation on the Handtowel Method*

In France, jambonneau is such a popular item that special pouches are available in the form of the ham shank with a hole for the bone. This requires less expertise and has all the advantages of the handtowel method.

For the handtowel and pouch method the procedure is similar to the mold method. The reformed ham shank is first cooked in bouillon for 15 minutes then covered with fresh bouillon and cooled quickly. As with all delicate charcuterie products, care must be taken to handle the cooked item with clean utensils following the guidelines of good hygiene.

For easier storage, the cooled jambonneau can be removed from the bouillon, wiped dry and placed in a vacuum pouch. In this case it is better to reform the ham shank without the bone as it might pierce the plastic vacuum pouch.

**Presentation**

The classic presentation of the French jambonneau is the same no matter which method was used to form it.

The cooled ham shank is removed from the mold or handtowel, wiped off then coated with light breadcrumbs.

The ham shanks are arranged neatly on a platter with the bones standing straight up. The bones can be decorated with a paper frill or " papillote " for an elegant touch.

In France the jambonneau is usually served cold in thin slices. Since it is featured in menus that call for cold meats it is most in demand in the summer months when they are in short supply. In winter when the demand falls off, the charcutier must often use the ham shank in other preparations.

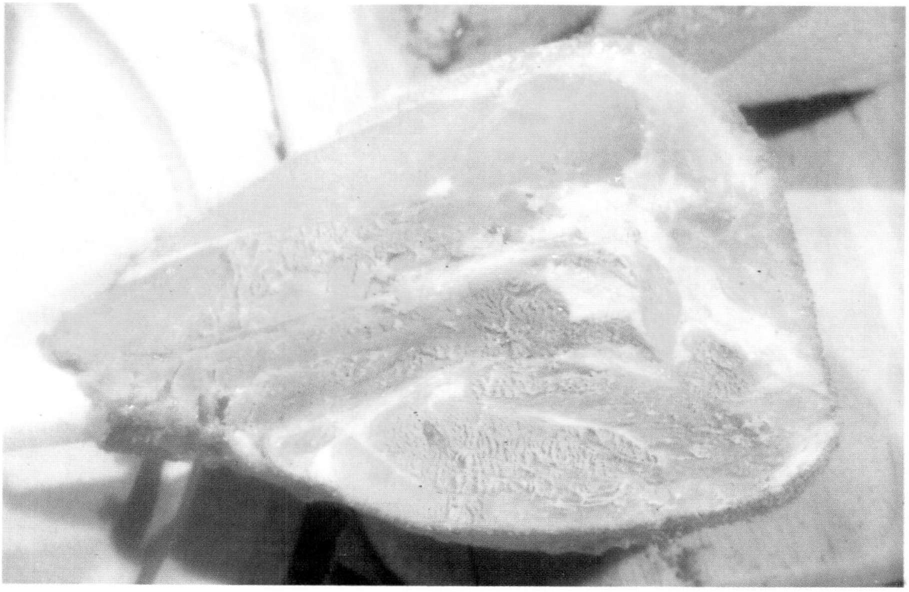

# Boston Shoulder, Spareribs and Picnic Shoulder

**Introduction**

These cuts are cured in brine and sold uncooked alongside other cured products (" demi-sel ").

Curing the meats is not done primarily to store them for lengthy periods. The main objective of brining is to maintain the bright pink color of the meat and to season it evenly throughout the muscle. In addition meat that has been injected and/or soaked in brine does keep longer than fresh meat.

Salt has been used to preserve meats since ancient times. Even at the turn of this century on farms in the French countryside salt was used to preserve meats (before refrigeration became widely available). The various cuts were layered with coarse salt in earthenware pots and

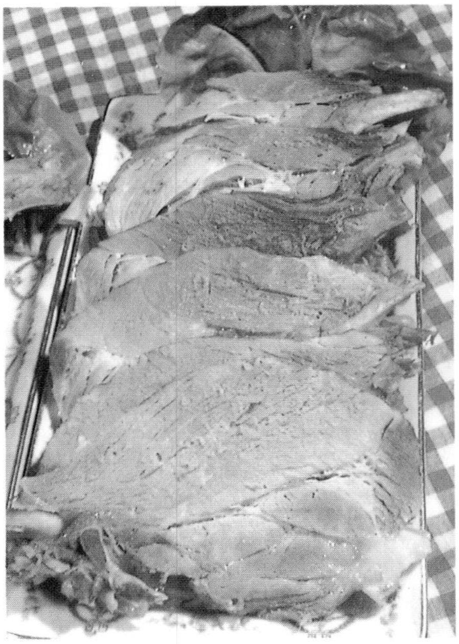

# The Boston Shoulder (" Echine ")

kept in a cool dry place for cooking throughout the winter months.

Today however the consumption of large quantities of salt has become a prime health concern. Modern refrigeration and the availability of freezers for home use have practically eliminated the farm tradition of preserving meats in salt.

The taste of meats treated with brine echos the slow-salted meats of yesteryear so the tradition lives on in the modern charcuterie. The brine is just salty enough to season and maintain the pink color. Proper conservation is assured by maintaining cold temperatures throughout processing.

Pork prepared this way is an excellent accompaniment to winter vegetable dishes such as cooked cabbage and choucroute, lentils, and white beans.

*Note: The French cuts shown here do not correspond exactly to American or English cuts of pork. The Boston shoulder or shoulder butt comes from the top shoulder like the French " échine " and the U.S. spareribs includes portions of the French " travers " and " plat de côtes ". The " plat de côtes also extends into the U.S. picnic shoulder (" hachage ").*

## The Boston Shoulder

The corresponding cut in France (échine) is the end cut of the loin which includes part of the shoulder. The échine includes the cervical vertabrae and the first five ribs (when cut " à la Parisienne ").

This cut is marbled with fat which makes it a tender, moist cut of pork.

To cure, inject 12-15% brine with the pump then immerse the shoulder in brine for 12 hours.

It is also important to follow each brining with a thorough draining (12 hours for this cut) during which time the flavor develops. This resting and maturing period allows the brine to be completely absorbed and will not exude during cooking.

Like other brined cuts, the shoulder is soaked in a basin with cold running water to remove excess brine before it is cooked.

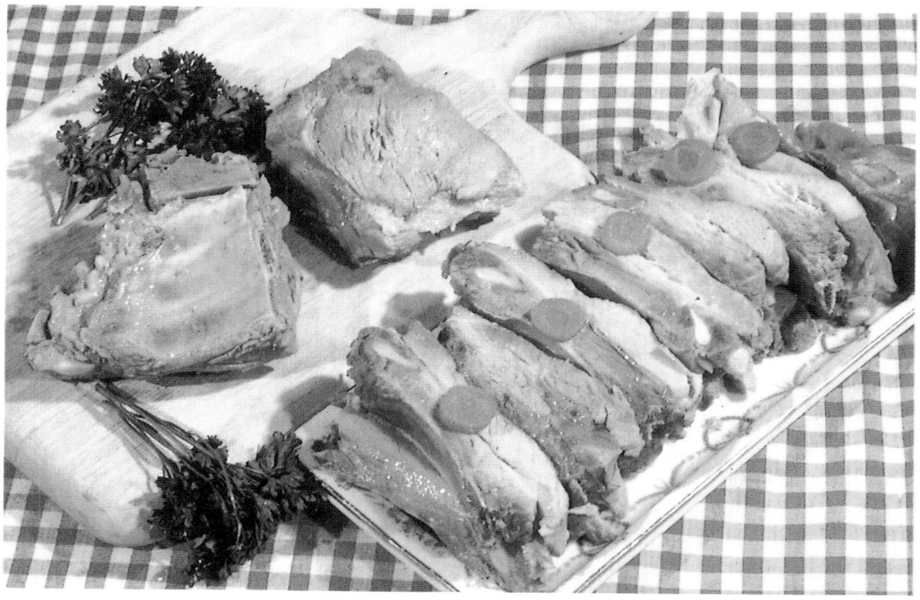

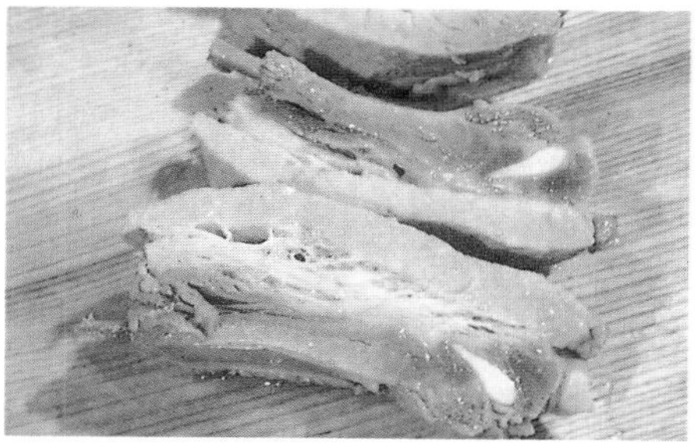

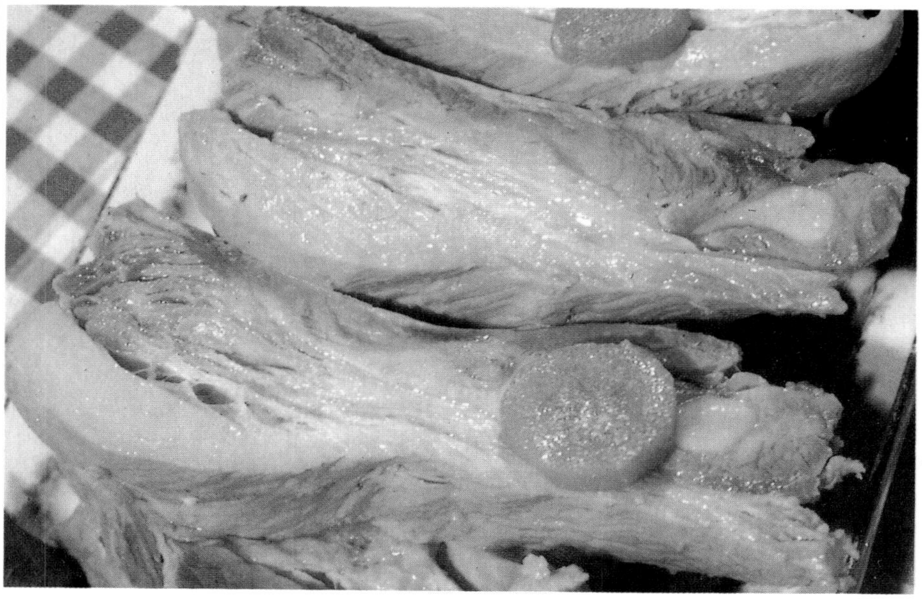

# The Spareribs (" Travers ")

**Equipment**

Knives, brining pump, brining tank, platters.

Every part of the pig from the head to the tail can be cured in brine.

The loin which includes the filet, rib roast and blade end, the sow-belly, ham and shank--all destined for different final products--can be brined.

In this section we study the uses of the Boston shoulder, spareribs, and picnic shoulder after brining.

**Presentation**

The spareribs compare most closely to the French " travers " which is pictured here. Only the " Parisienne " cut produces this cut of pork.

This is a band that is cut lengthwise from the loin on the rib side. A good-sized " travers " is 4-5 cm (1 1/2-2 in) thick.

The boneless end (near the ham) is usually removed and used in ground meat products.

The " travers " is placed directly in the brine for 12 hours, then is left to drain and mature for 12 hours.

The ribs must then be soaked in a basin of cold running water for 1-2 hours.

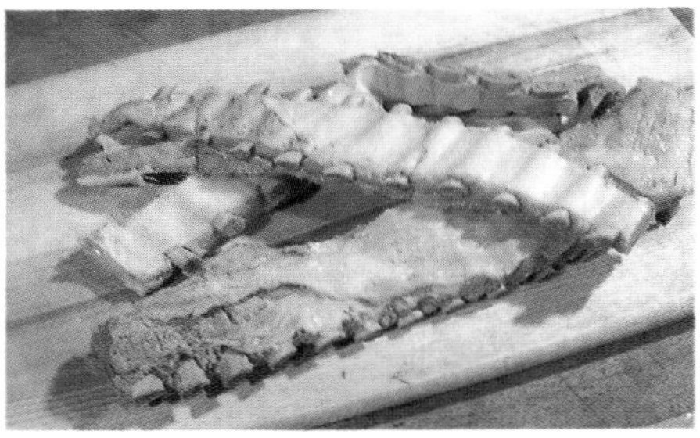

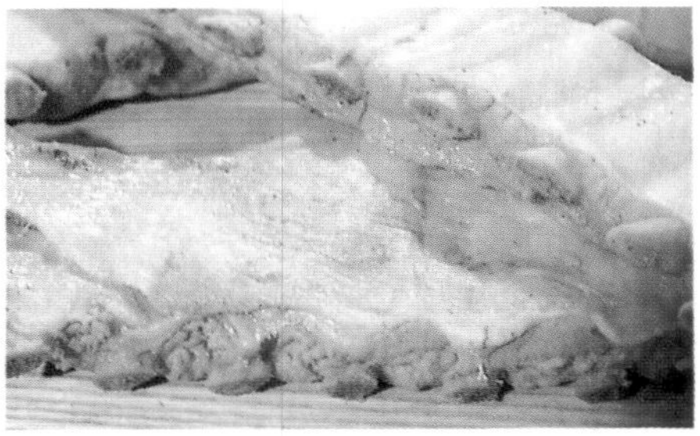

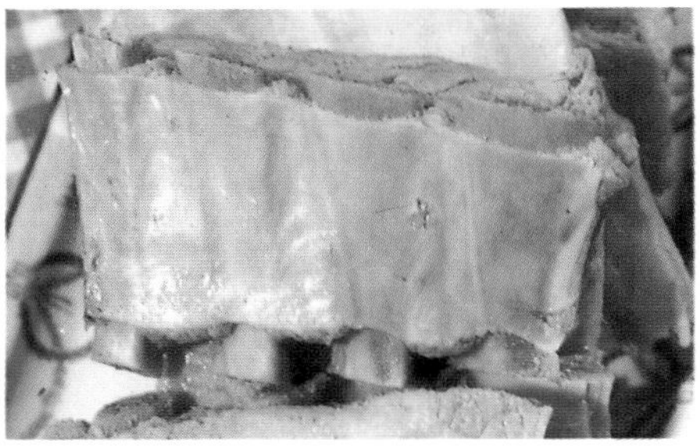

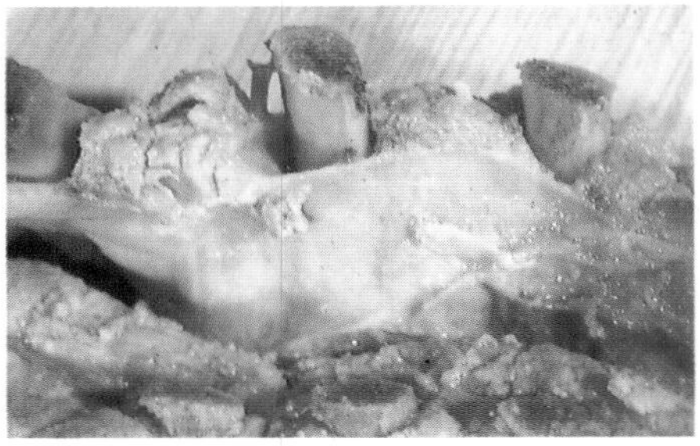

# The Picnic Shoulder (" Plat de côtes ")

**Presentation**

The picnic shoulder actually corresponds most closely to the cut called the " hachage ".

The piece of pork called the " plat de côtes " is the portion of the " hachage " sectioned from the rib side and contains part of the sternum and the ends of about 4-5 ribs. In the " Parisienne " cut, the " plat de côtes " is cut about 2.5-3 cm (1 in) thick to include some of the meat from the " hachage ".

It is cured in brine exactly like the " travers ".

**Cooking**

These brined pork products are generally cooked in bouillon, chilled and stored in fresh bouillon until ready to present in the shop of the charcuterie.

They are removed from the bouillon with a clean utensil, wiped dry and arranged on platters.

They are most often consumed as " cold cuts " along with a green salad or cold vegetables or on their own with a zesty mustard from Meaux or Dijon.

It is also possible to reheat these products in bouillon or along with beans (white beans or lentils).

Often the charcutier will provide the customer with some bouillon to reheat these meats.

Although the French do not usually indulge in an " American style breakfast ", these cured preparations are often featured for a hearty brunch before a day of fishing or hunting.

Sliced, cured, cooked pork makes a delicious snack anytime.

# Arm Steaks and Ham Hocks

**Introduction**

Cured arm steaks and ham hocks belong to the family of brined pork products (" demi-sel ") which are cooked in bouillon. All of the preparations in this group are cured with brine by injection and/or immersion in brine to season the entire muscle of the meat and maintain the pink color.

Arm steaks and ham hocks are often served with choucroute. They are also delicious with lentils or white beans, vegetable stew (" potée ") and fresh cooked cabbage.

**Equipment**

Brining pump, knives, saw, jacketed kettle or large stock pot

**Procedure**

The arm steak is the shank or " jambonneau " from the front leg of the pig.

It is the part of the picnic shoulder (" hachage ") that extends into the leg of the animal and is cut just before the foot.

The ham hock is the forward section of the arm steak. To cut the hock, it is easier to cut it before the arm steak is sectioned from the picnic shoulder.

It is removed about 3.5-4 cm (1 1/2 in) from the foot end of the ham hock.

The remaining portion of the arm steak is then used in the fabrication

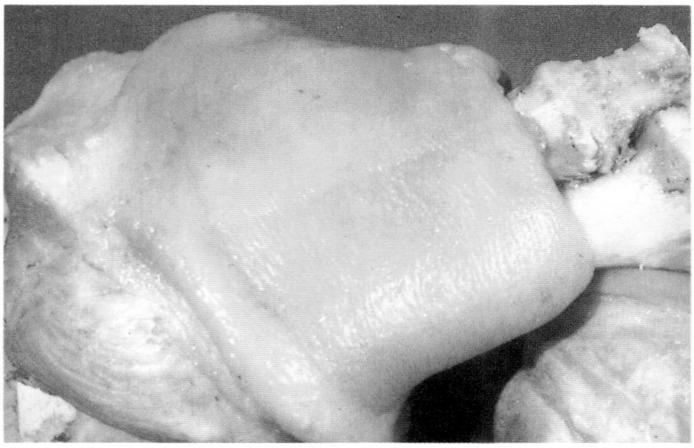

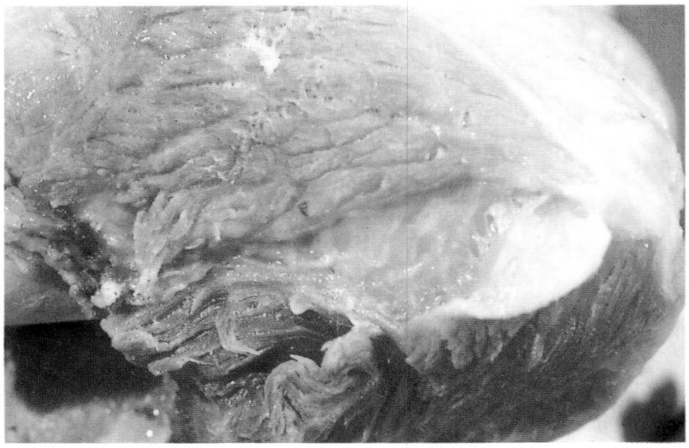

of ground meat products such as sausages and forcemeat.

*Note:* The names of the U.S. cuts given here are the closest equivalent to the French cuts pictured in this section -- " jarret " and " jarrotins ".

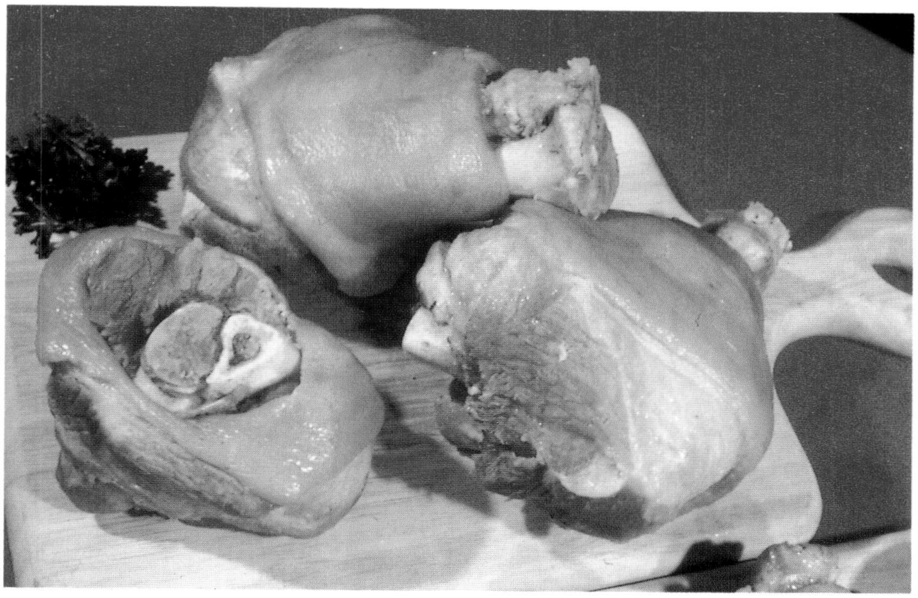

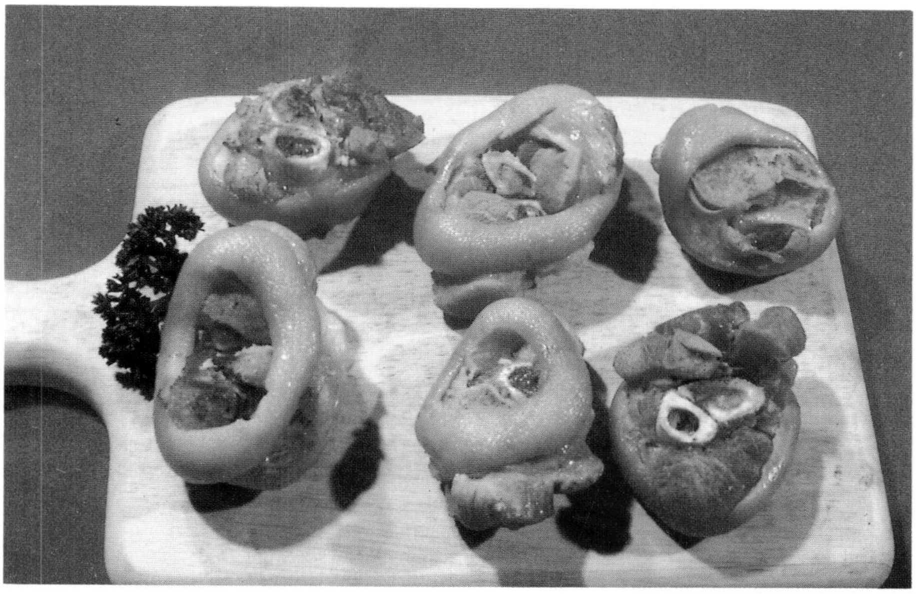

### Procedure

The ham hock and arm steak are cleaned and cured in the same way as the other brined pork products.

First they are shaved to remove all hair and bristles. This is a very important step for all products that are cooked and sold with the skin (" couenne ") attached.

The skin is the source of a great concentration of bacteria. Scientific analysis has shown that the frequent handling of the carcass from the slaughterhouse to the preparation kitchen of the charcutier puts the carcass in contact with a multitude of bacteria.

### Brining

The trimmed ham hocks and arm steaks are then cured in brine (same as for hams).

The arm steak, which is a larger cut, is first injected with about 15% brine. The soaking period for both cuts is about 1 hour.

The meat is then drained for the same amount of time (1 hour) during which time the flavor " matures ".

### Cooking

Before cooking, soak the ham hocks and arm steaks in cold running water for 2-3 hours.

They are then cooked in bouillon.

Check the saltiness of the bouillon in advance; if it is too salty to the taste, add water to cut the strength.

The bouillon is flavored with an addition of aromatic vegetables as with all these products.

Bring the bouillon to a boil and skim all fat and impurities that rise to the surface. Regulate the temperature to 90 °C (195 F).

The meat is then lowered into the bouillon and cooked until the meat begins to detach from the bones. The smaller ham hock will be cooked before the larger arm steaks. The meat should not be overcooked; the cuts are sold with the bones attached.

### Presentation

Charcuteries often time the cooking of these products so that they can be sold warm directly from the cooking liquid.

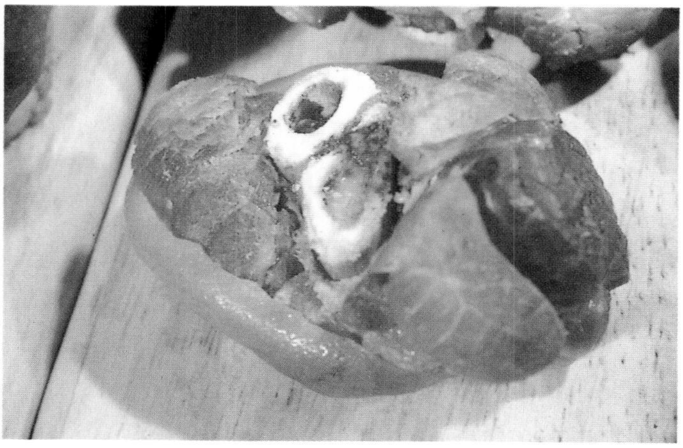

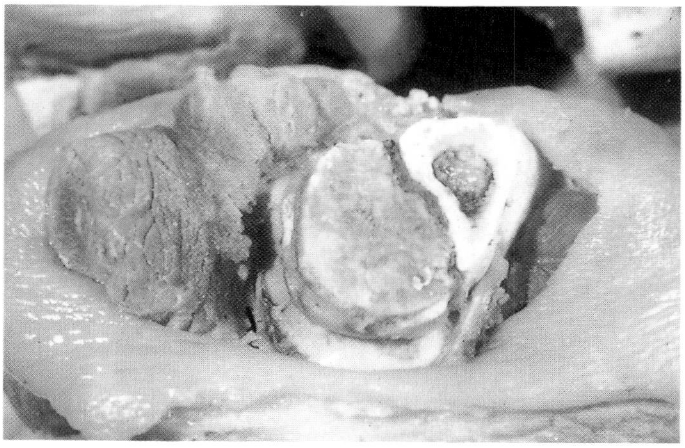

They can be reheated with choucroute or beans either at home or in the shop.

The cooked ham hocks and arm steaks can be covered with fresh bouillon (boiled, skimmed and strained) and stored for several days in the refrigerator.

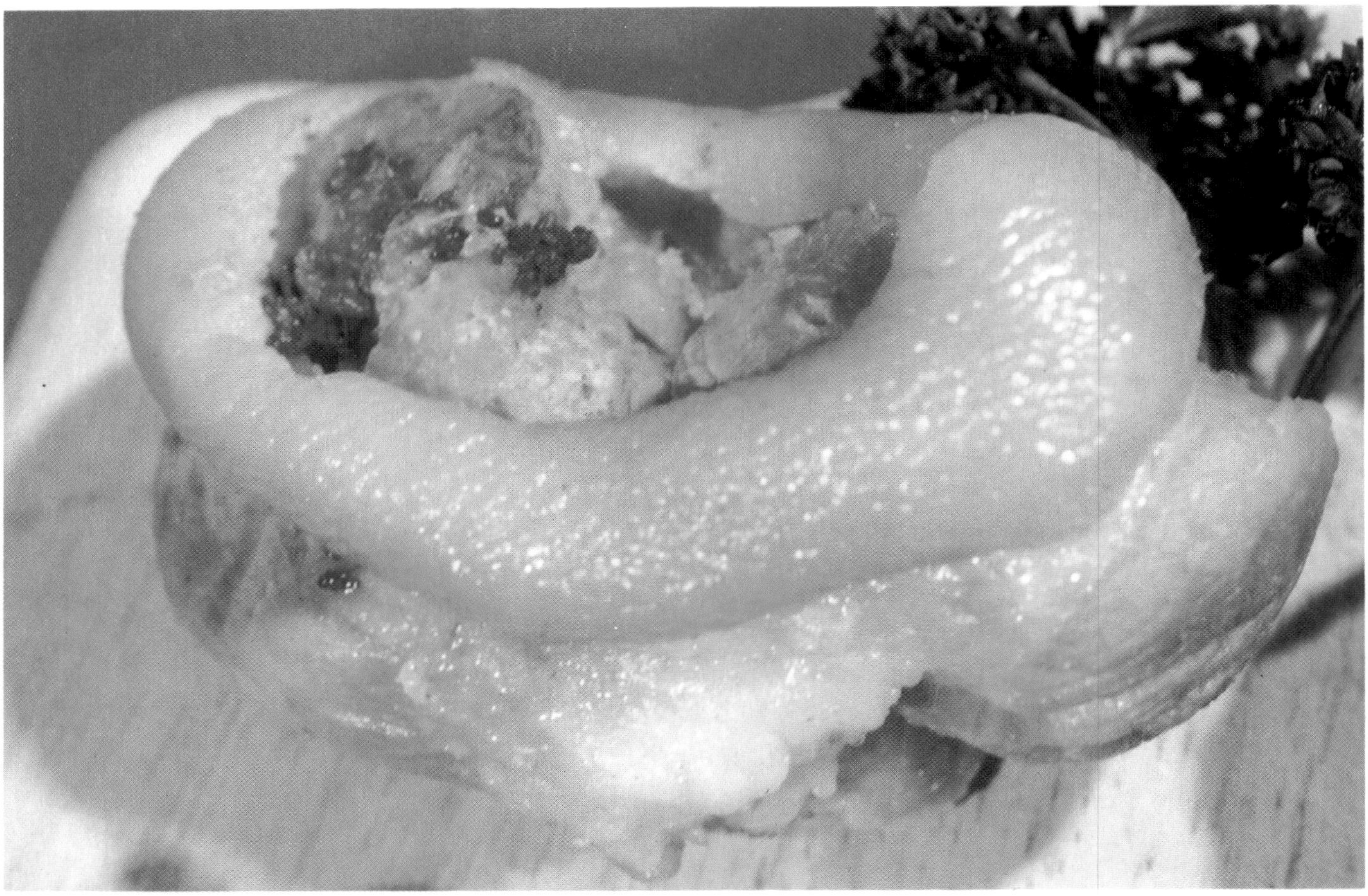

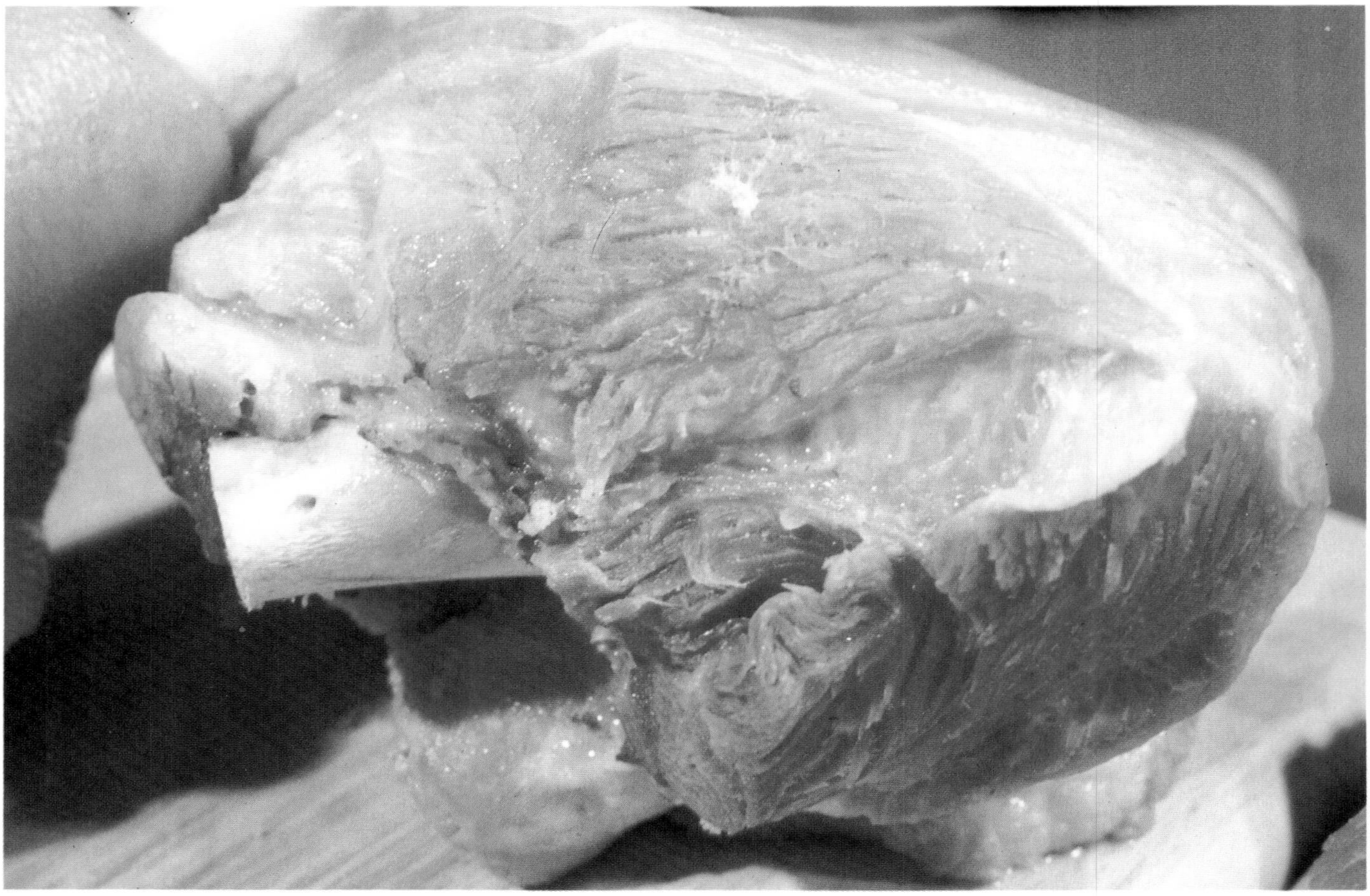

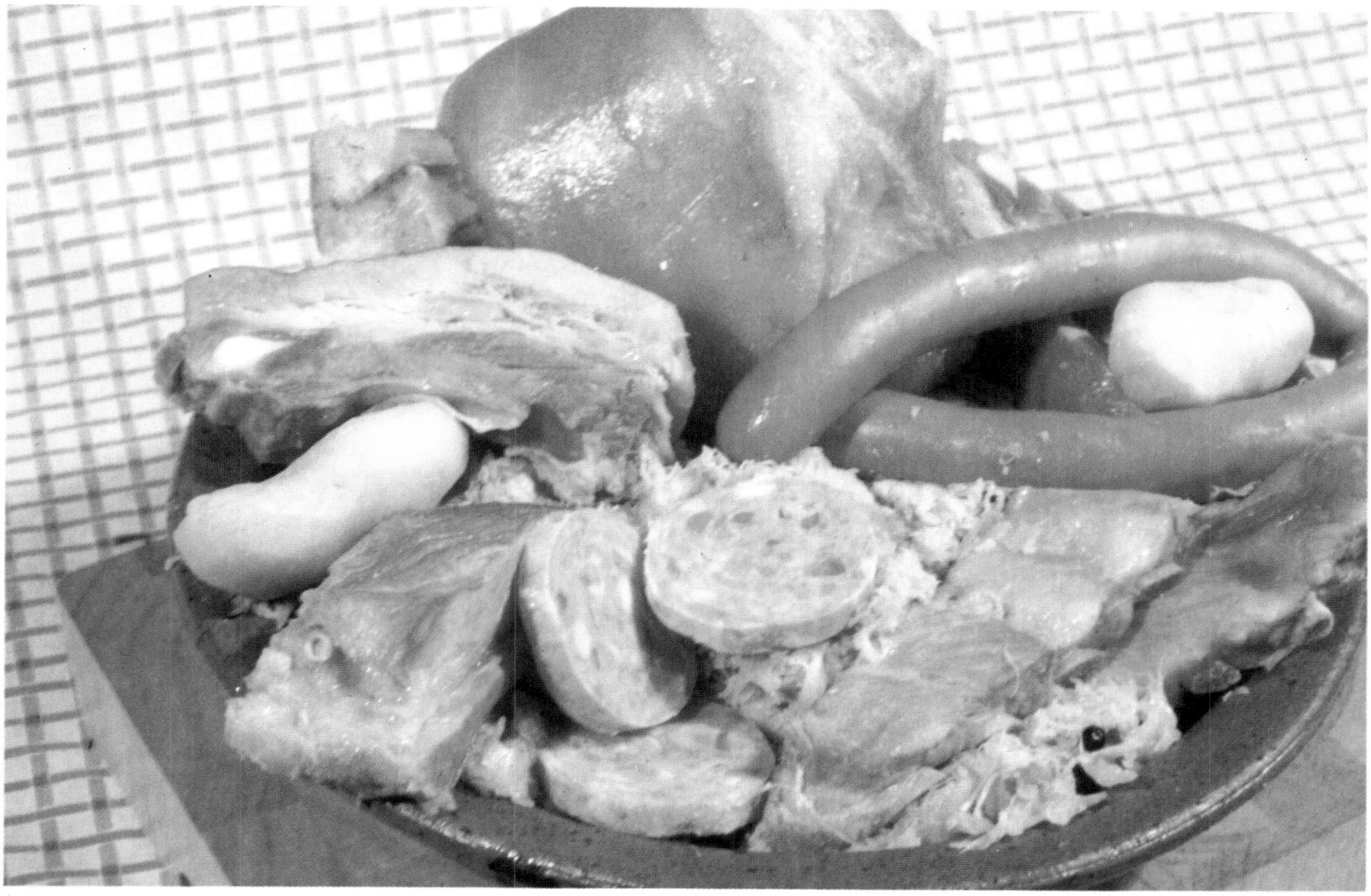

# Ears, Tongue and Tail of Pork

The tail is usually sold attached to one half of the pig and the ears and tongue are obtained when the pig's head is purchased. These parts of the pig are often overlooked but can be made into delicious dishes.

## The Ears

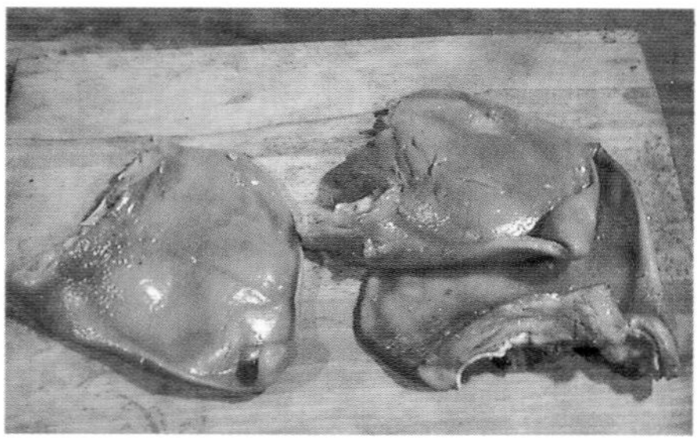

After the head is cooked the ears are removed close to the head and excess fat is removed. They are covered with bouillon that has been brought to a boil, skimmed and strained. The ears must be cooled quickly, then they can be stored in the refrigerator for up to 8 days. When ready to serve, remove the ears from the bouillon with a clean fork.

*Presentation*

The ears are removed from the bouillon and wiped off. They are then dipped in aspic that has been chilled to thicken slightly so that it adheres to the ears in a smooth layer. In the shop of the charcuterie, the ears are sold whole decorated with pieces of tart pickle ("cornichon"), tomato or lemon cut in attractive shapes. Pigs' ears are usually eaten cold with mustard. They can also be reheated on a bed of cooked beans (lentils for example).

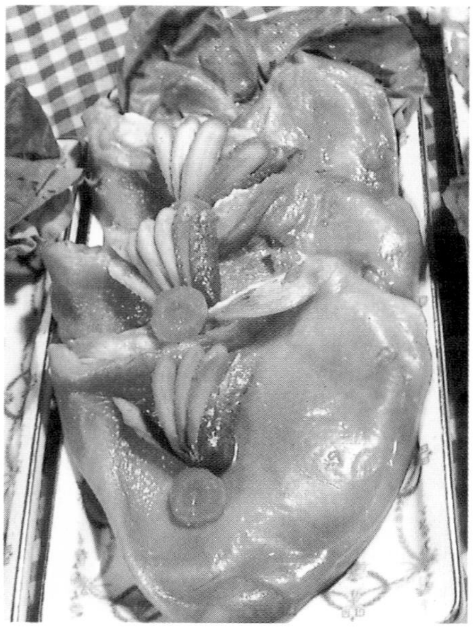

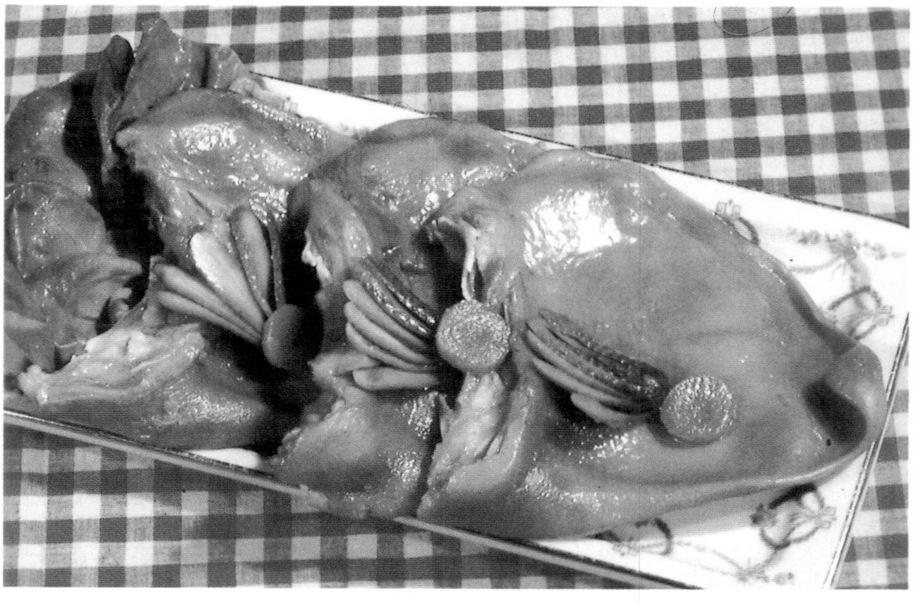

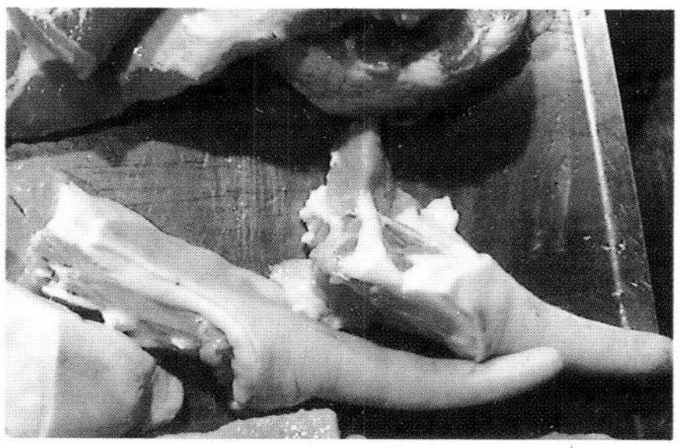

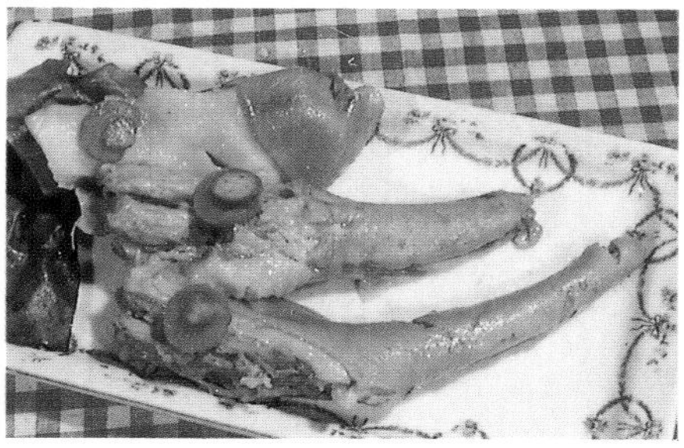

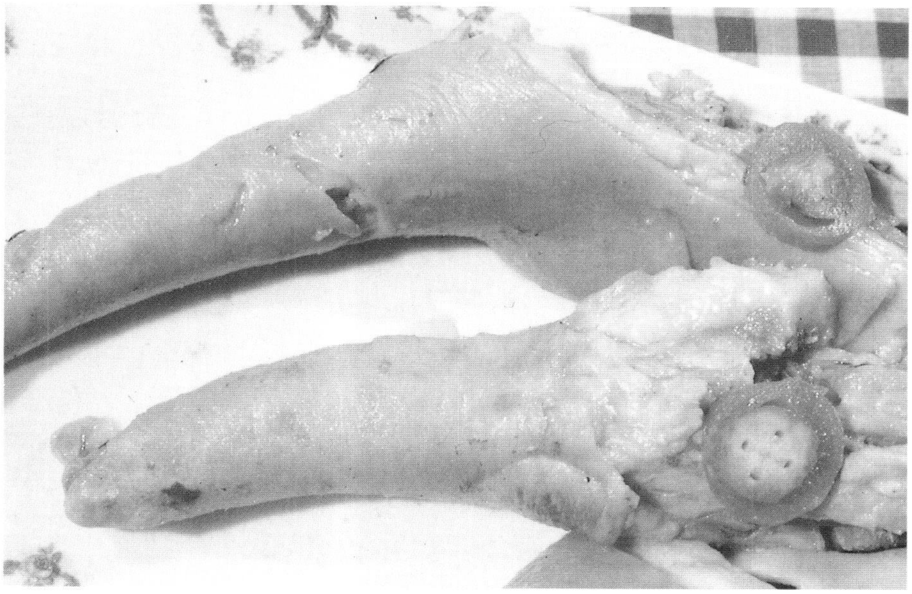

***The Tail***

The loin of the pig is marketed in two halves and the tail is left attached to one side. It is separated from the carcass by cutting between the bones close to the body.

*Preparation*

The tail must be shaved to eliminate all remaining hair and bristles then scrubbed and rinsed to clean it thoroughly.

Like the head, the tail is immersed in brine for 12 hours.

The cured tail is then rinsed under cold running water to remove excess brine and drained.

The tip of the tail is cut off.

*Cooking*

The tail can be cooked along with the head and other brined cuts that are cooked in bouillon.

It is also common to cook tails along with the feet using consommé as the cooking liquid.

The tail is cooked when the meat detaches easily from the bones.

*Presentation*

The tail can be coated with aspic like the ears and tongue (to be served cold) or covered with breadcrumbs (to be served grilled).

Charcuteries in France also sell cured uncooked tails (" demi-sel ") which can be cooked with vegetables for added flavor and served as an accompaniment.

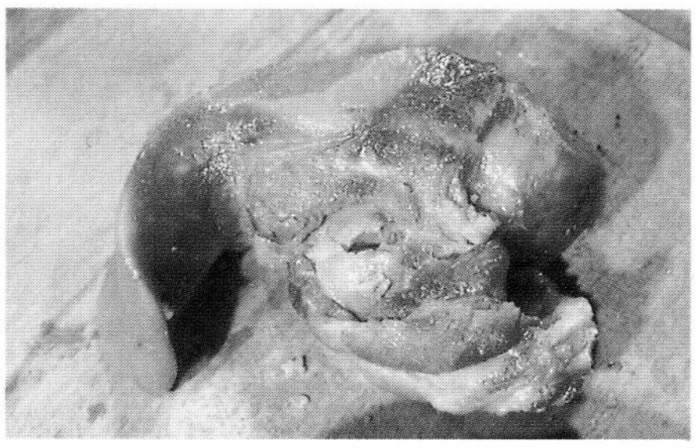

***The Tongue***

Tongue is injected with brine then immersed in brine for 12 hours. After thorough rinsing, it is cooked in bouillon until tender.

After the tongue is cooked it is trimmed to eliminate any remaining cartilage and small bones (from the larynx).

As with the other preparation in this section, the tongue is stored in bouillon and removed from the bouillon with a clean utensil.

As a general rule, all products that are stored in bouillon should not be handled at this stage.

Bouillon is a haven for bacteria and even hands that have just been cleaned may cause contamination to the bouillon or the product being removed if the hands are used. Following the basic rules of hygiene is important for everyone in the charcuterie.

*Presentation*

Tongue is presented whole after being dipped in thickened aspic to coat it evenly.

Tongue can be decorated in the same way as the ears. It is also served cold with mustard but can also be heated gently and served warm.

Note that the tongue is completely lean making it an excellent choice for low fat diets.

# Head Cheese (" Fromage de Tête ")

**Introduction**

Head cheese is a classic preparation in French charcuteries. It is a molded mixture of the boned meats of the head cooked with the skin in full-flavored clarified gelatinous pork stock.

Sometimes the tongue is used and in some cases the ham hock from the front leg is added as well.

The quality of the stock which binds this product is crucial to the success of the head cheese.

**Equipment**

Paring knife, sauté pan, large stainless steel bowl, terrine mold.

**Ingredients**

1 pig's head, cooked
2 tongues
100 g (3 1/2 oz) cooked carrots
100 g (3 1/2 oz) tart pickles (cornichons)
50 g (1 3/4 oz) chopped parsley
Clarified pork stock

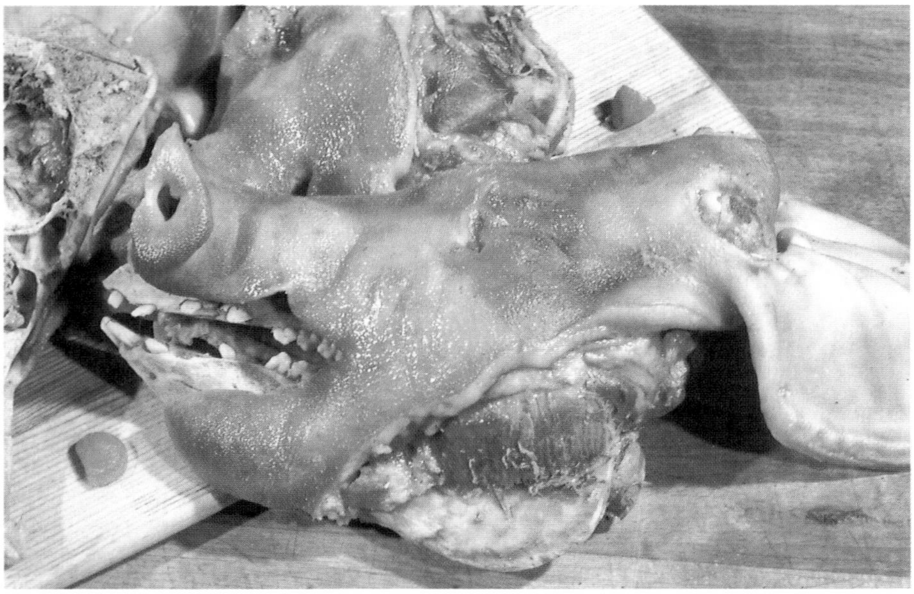

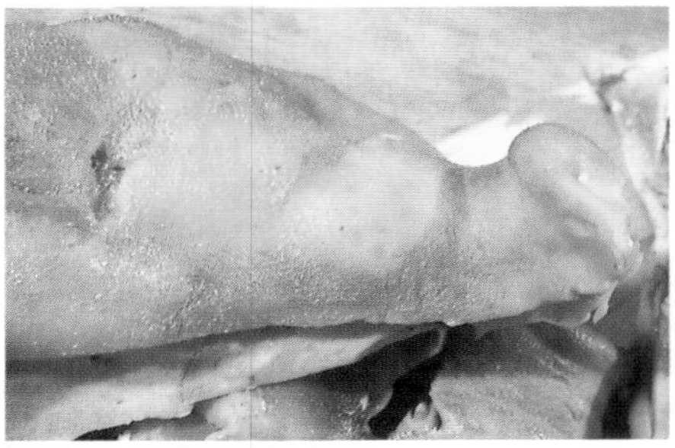

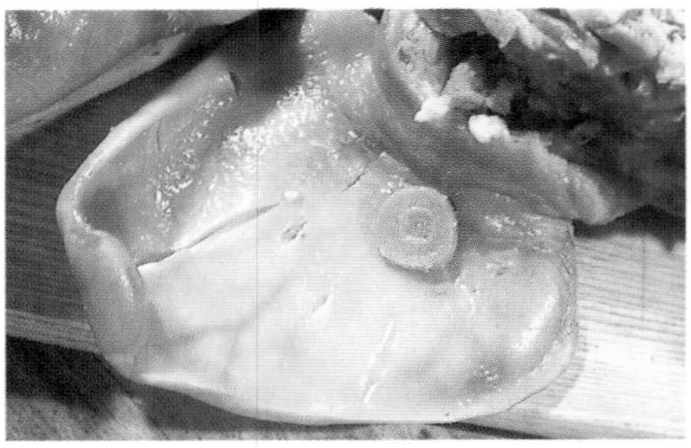

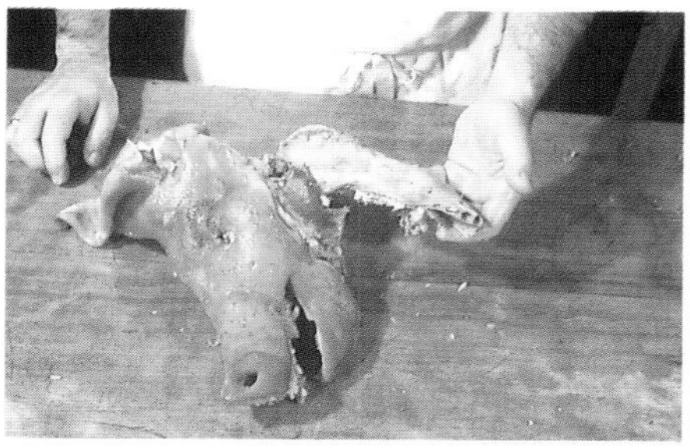

**Procedure**

***The Head***

The head is first scraped, cleaned and rinsed. The tongue and the larynx are cut out. It is then split open and the brain is removed. The opening from the larynx is cut open to away any remaining food matter.

The head is then injected with brine in the meaty portions of the cheek then the whole head is immersed in brine.

The skin and meat of the head harbor bacteria. Therefore the brine is used only once or twice.

It is also possible to salt the head by rubbing with dry salt. It rests on the bed of salt for at least 12 hours in the refrigerator (2-4 $^0$C (35 F)).

***The Tongues***

The tongues are blanched to facilitate the peeling process. Once trimmed, they are injected with brine then immersed along with the head.

The cured tongues are scraped then rinsed in a basin with cold running water.

**Cooking**

The head and tongues are cooked in bouillon with aromatic vegetable cooking liquid is first brought slowly to a boil, skimming all impurities that rise to the surface.

The bouillon is regulated to about 90 $^0$C (195 F). The head is cooked when the jawbone detaches easily. This usually requires about 2 1/2 hours of cooking.

The head is boned while it is still warm. The eye is eliminated. The types of meat--lean, fat, snout, ears and tongue are arranged in separate stainless steel recipients to be chilled before being cut into neat pieces.

**Assembling the Head Cheese**

The meats will be easier to cut into neat dice if they are throughly chilled.

In small scale charcuteries the meats are cut up by hand. In large enterprises an automatic cutter is used called a " lardonneuse " which cuts the meats into just the right size dice (" lardon ").

The lean is cut into even dice (1 cm (3/8 in)). The fat is cut as small possible. The tongues are left whole.

Assemble a blend of about 75 % lean (including the tongue) and 25 % fat. The ears are in addition and are cut into large dice or strips.

The cornichons and the carrots are cut in thin slices. (Note that the carrots can be cooked in the bouillon along with the meats.) The parsley is washed, trimmed and chopped.

Cool a little of the pork aspic to be sure that it is sturdy enough to sliced. Toss the meats together to blend evenly then add enough aspic cover.

Stir to disperse the stock evenly and season to taste. Ladle the mixture into the molds.

Even if the pork stock was brought to a boil before adding to the meats, it is recommended to bring the mixture to a boil in the terrines for about 15-20 minutes. (This is a safety measure because the preparation requires a lot of handling which can cause contamination.)

Prepared in this way, the head cheese can be stored in the refrigerate for 8-10 days.

**Presentation**

Unmold the head cheese. Wash the mold then coat it with a thin layer of aspic. Chill then add a little more

aspic to coat all sides and insert the head cheese. Once the outer protective layer of aspic has set, it is unmolded onto a serving platter.

Head cheese is cut into thick slices.

This is a warm weather dish that is very popular in France. Many charcutiers embellish the classic head cheese with personal accents such as an addition of white wine, aged vinegar or mustard.

# Pressed Head of Pork

**Introduction**

This preparation is known by many names--" museau (snout) de porc ", " tête roulée " (" rolled " head), as well as " tête pressée " (pressed head). It is made with the whole head like head cheese but without an addition of pork stock. The natural collagen in the meat and skin of the head hold together.

**Ingredients**

This product is made exclusively with the meat from the head without addition of stock or diced vegetables. The cooking of the head is identical to that of head cheese.

**Procedure**

Line the mold with a thin sheet of barding fat. Remove the bones from the cooked pig's head while it is still warm. Trim and remove any pockets of fat that are too large.

While the pieces of meat are still warm, fill the mold.

**Presentation**

The pressed head is most often served sliced and arranged on a plate with vinaigrette and chopped onions, shallots and parsley.

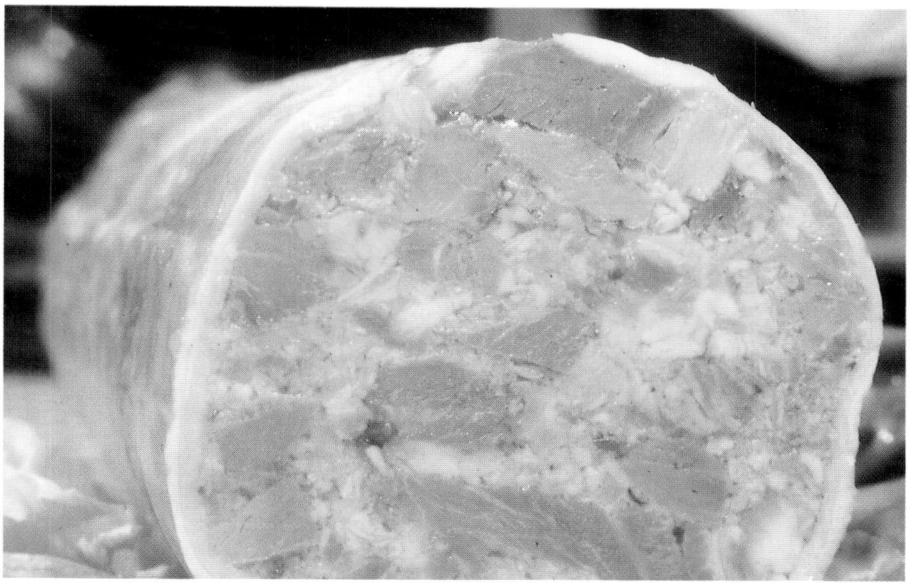

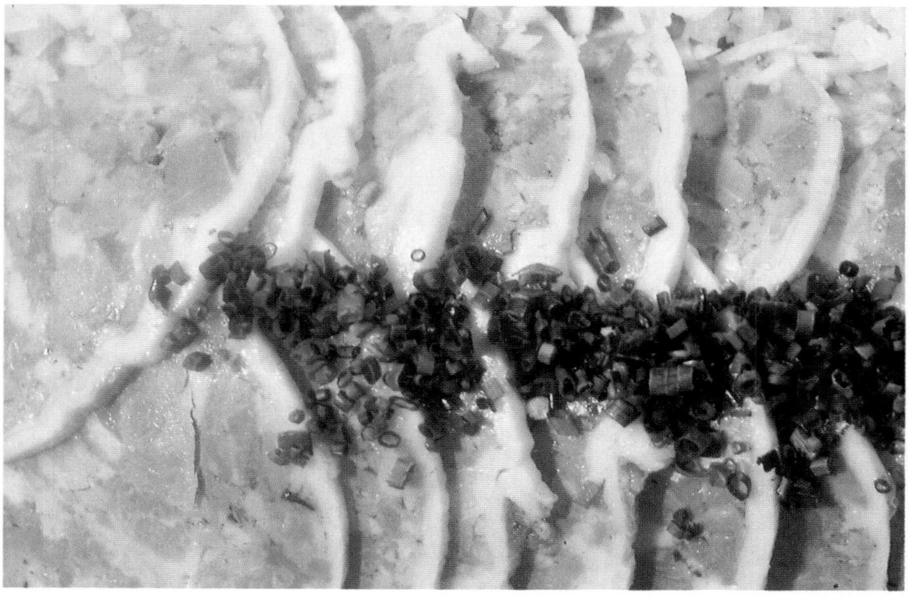

# Cured Ham Molded with Aspic and Parsley (" Jambon Persillé ")

**Introduction**

In this section we present two presentations of this dish which are made with different cuts of pork.

The regions of Burgundy and the Morvan are well known for their " jambons persillés " and the variations here are inspired by the products of those regions.

These preparations differ from the Burgundy version because a meaty filling (" farce " or forcemeat) made with pigs' and calves' feet has been added.

The French Charcuterie Code defines the classic " jambon persillé " as the following:

*" Prepared with pieces cut from the shoulder and ham with aspic flavored with white wine and a large amount of chopped parsley. The net weight of meat cannot be less than 60%. "*

Note that there are only two products in France that can be called " Jambon " (ham) without containing 100% meat from the ham section--" Jambon Persillé " and " Jambon de Reims ".

Following the traditional technique we propose two variations:

- A rectangular mold filled with aspic and pieces of pork from the shoulder (blade end).
- A round mold using meat from the ham.

**Equipment**

Knives, brining pump, horizontal chopper, jacketed kettle or large stock pot, molds

**Ingredients**

Recipe A: 8 kg (17.5 lbs) cured blade end
Recipe B: 8 kg (17.5 lbs) cured ham

*Filling*

600 g (1 lb 5 oz) cooked pig' feet
600 g (1 lb 5 oz) cooked calves' feet
500 g (1 lb) flat parsley
100 g (3 1/2 oz) onions
50 g (1 3/4 oz) shallots
150 g (1/3 lb) tart pickles (" cornichons ")

*Seasonings*

18 g (about 1/2 oz) saltpeter (check manufacturer's instructions)
2 g (1/16 oz) ground pepper
0.5 g (1/64 oz) ground nutmeg
White wine vinegar
Dry white wine 2L (about 2 qts)
2 liters of " jus " (pork stock) (aspic plus cooking liquid)
Powdered gelatin

**Procedure**

***The Meat***

The blade end and the ham are prepared following the same guidelines; boned, trimmed of fat and nerves then injected with 15% brine (same type used for hams).

The meats are then immersed in brine for 12 hours followed by a draining period during which time the flavors develop and the color of the meat deepens a little.

Before cooking the meat is soaked in a basin of cold running water for 6 hours.

***The Filling***

This filling is the " cement " that holds the pieces of meat in place.

The cooked feet provide natural gelatin. They are cooked the traditional way and boned while still warm.

Chop the shallots and onions into small dice.

Wash the parsly thoroughly, first in a basin of cold water with a little bleach then rinsed in fresh water. The parsley is then drained and squeezed dry. It is important that the parsley is washed very carefully because it is being used fresh and all uncooked vegetables present the possibility of bacterial contamination. The bleach in the first washing will keep this problem under control.

## Cured Ham Molded with Aspic and Parsley *(continued)*

Pluck the leaves from the parsley for this dish and reserve the stems to make bouquet garnis for other preparations.

Note that the recipe calls for flat parsley which is more flavorful than curly parsley.

In the horizontal chopper, place the warm meat from the feet, the parsley, shallots and onions.

Add the seasonings and process at moderate speed adding the same quantity (in this case 2 L (about 2 qts) of aspic blended with chilled bouillon from cooking the hams.

This mixture should be bright green and very gelatinous.

Test the setting power by chilling a small portion. Add powdered gelatin accordingly to obtain a gel that sets very firmly (30-50 g (1-1 3/4 oz) per liter (qt) of liquid).

To add the powdered gelatin, dissolve in some cold liquid then heat to 80-90 °C (195 F) to melt it.

Once the gelatin mixture is added to the forcemeat it will set up quickly, therefore the meats must be cooked and cut and the molds prepared in advance.

**Cooking the Meats**

The blade end and ham are cooked in the same type of bouillon used for other brined pork products.

Add the aromatic vegetables (carrots, onions, celery, bouquet garni) to the cold bouillon.

Bring to a boil and skim all fat and impurities that rise to the surface.

Lower to a simmer, add the meat and cook the blade end until the meat begins to detach from the bones.

Remove the meats and drain.
Measure the bouillon needed for making the forcemeat, bring to a boil, skim and strain.
Bone the cooked meats while still

warm and remove the skin. Place in a single layer in a hotel pan and refrigerate to chill thoroughly.

**Assembly**

***Round Mold with Ham***

Cut the chilled ham into neat cubes (about 3 cm (1 in)).

The parsley filling should be slightly thickened but still liquid at this point. Chop the corresponding amount of cornichons and stir into the filling.
Check that the mold is perfectly clean (glass molds are usually used).
Alternate layers of meat and filling until the molds are filled.

## Cured Ham Molded with Aspic and Parsley *(continued)*

***Rectangular Mold with Blade End***

Cut the blade end into slices about 2 cm (3/4 in) thick. Slice the corresponding amount of cornichons, set aside.

Alternate layers of sliced blade end, the parsley filling and the cornichons to fill the mold.

The slices of blade end and cornichons should form neat layers in the finished slice.

In both cases the filled molds are covered and chilled as quickly as possible.

**Storage**

These preparations are not heated through after assembly.

They are therefore very perishable and the storage time is limited.

## Terrine prepared with Blade End in Aspic with Parsley

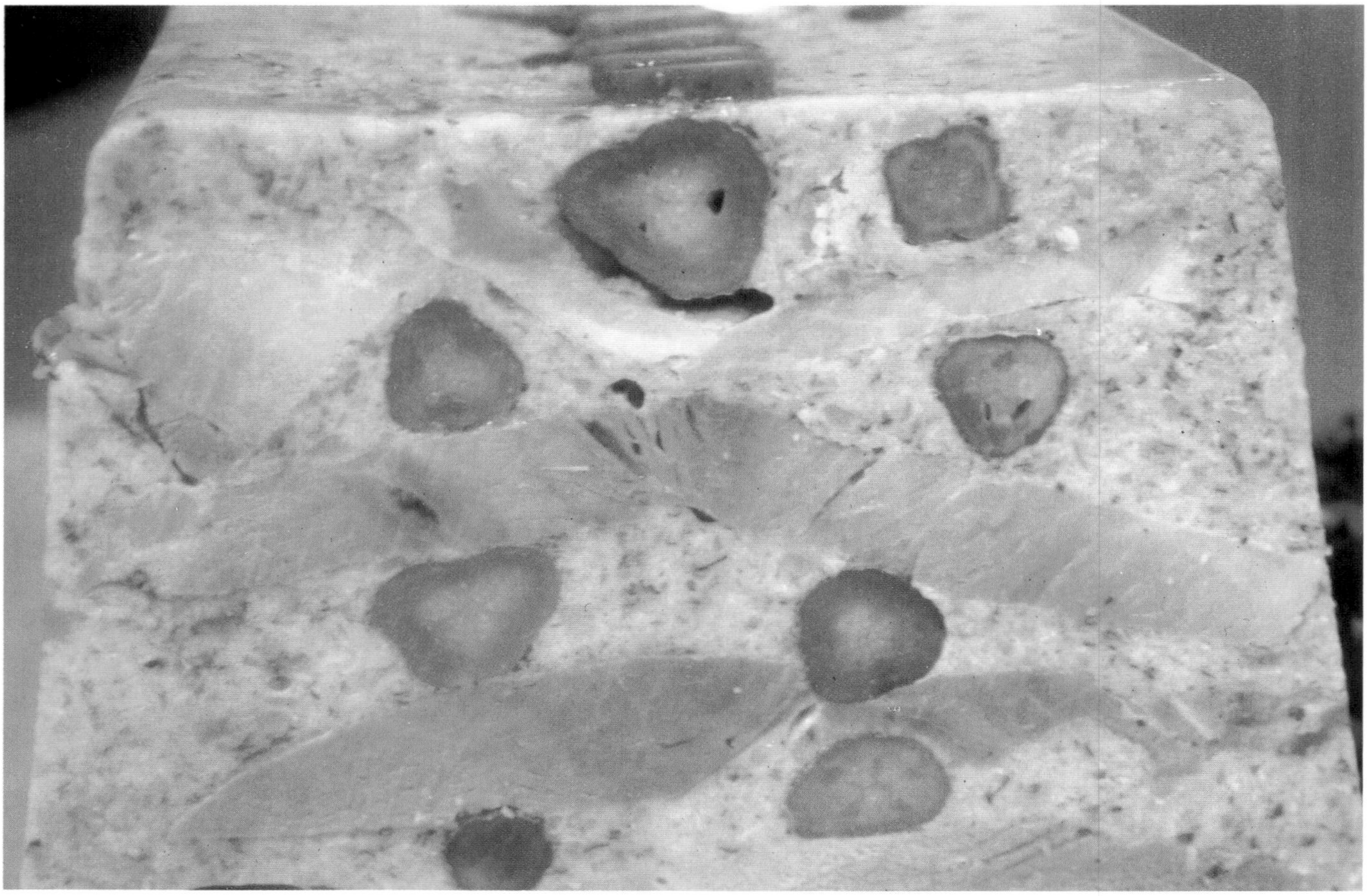

This is why certain precautions must be taken during the preparation of all of the ingredients: thorough washing of the parsley, and refrigeration of the meats before assembly.

The fabrication of the filling presents the most danger.

The temperature of the mixture must be kept as low as possible without letting the gelatin set up before assembly.

The jambon persillé must be sold within 3-4 days after it is made. It is stored in the refrigerator or refrigerated display case of the shop.

## Terrine prepared with Ham in Aspic with Parsley

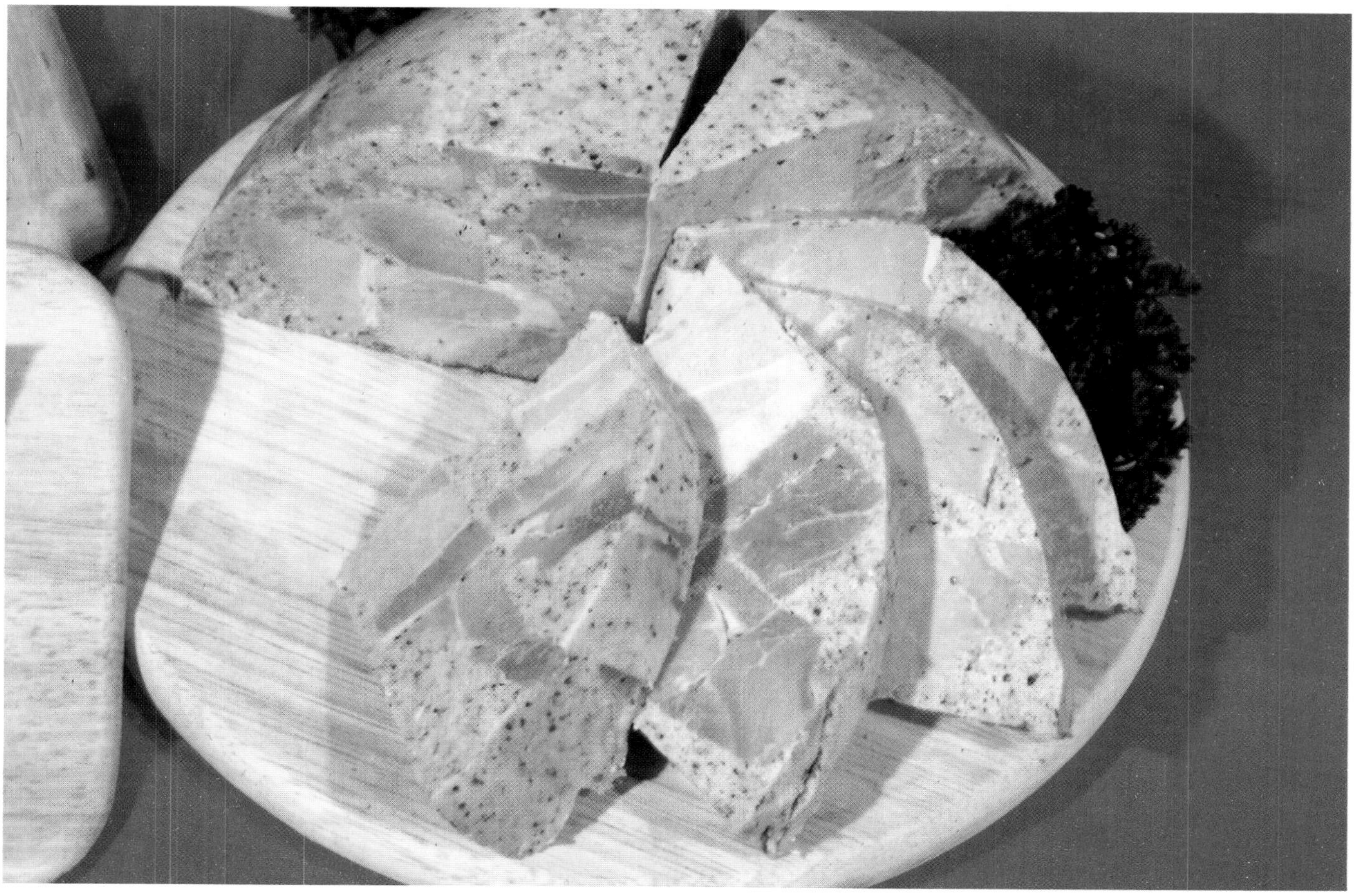

# " Hure " of Pork (" à la Parisienne ")

## Introduction

" Hure " is the head of a wild boar. Preparations that are shaped like the head of a pig are often given this name. Hure has also become a general term used for molded aspics made with pork or other ingredients.

The presentation here is spectacular. It is more appropriate as a showpiece for the shop window or centerpiece for a grand buffet in the hope of attracting customers for the classic hure which is simply formed in a rectangular mold.

## Equipment

Knives, bowls, stockpot, wooden spoon, food processor, hotel pan, handtowel, brining pump, galantine band, kitchen string, plastic bucket (8-10 L (8-10 qts)).

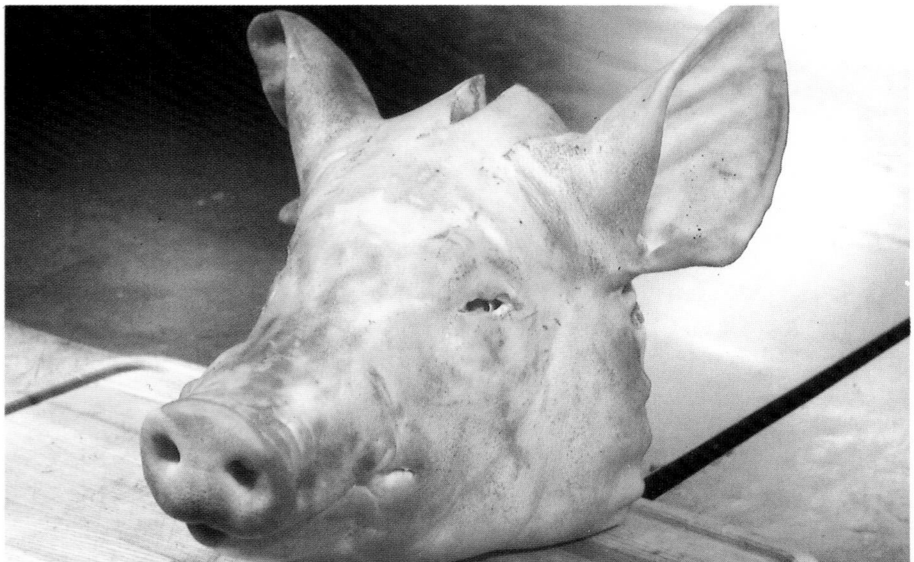

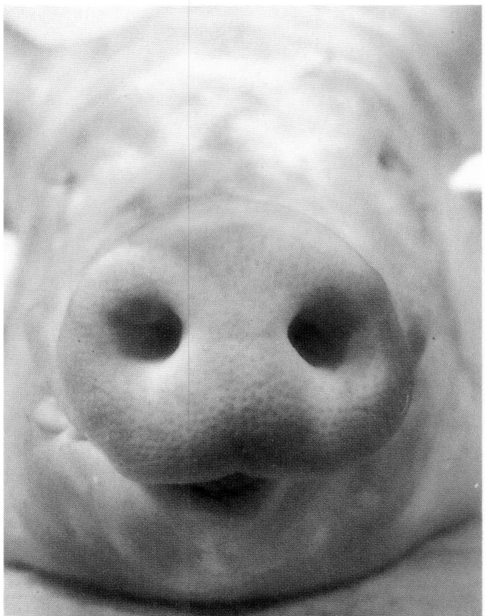

**Ingredients**

1 pig's head
(see " preparation ")
24 tongues (pork)
Pistachios (peeled)
Fatback cut in strips
Cooked pork skin
Barding fat

*Seasonings*

500 ml (2 cups) red wine
Powdered gelatin
Pepper
Nutmeg
Saltpeter
200 g (7 oz) shallots
100 g (3 1/2 oz) flat parsley

**Preparing the Ingredients**

***The Pig's Head***

If possible, procure a pig's head with the neck attached to facilite stuffing. They are usually marketed cut at the base of the head. To have it specially butchered it will have to be ordered directly from the slaughterhouse.

Since this may be difficult, it is possible to fashion a neck from out pieces of skin to complete the presentation.

The head is boned as far as the snout. The top portion is left unboned so that the head keeps its form. Remove large pieces of fat so that just thin even layer remains about the thickness of a sheet of barding fat.

It is important to select a head that is free of bruises as the appearance of the outside is crucial to the presentation. Il must be shaved to eliminate all remaining hair and bristles.

The boned and cleaned head is then immersed in brine for 12 hours.

The cured head is then soaked in cold running water to remove excess brine and drained for 12 hours in the refrigerator until completely dry.

During all manipulation of the head (especially boning) it is important to not pierce skin.

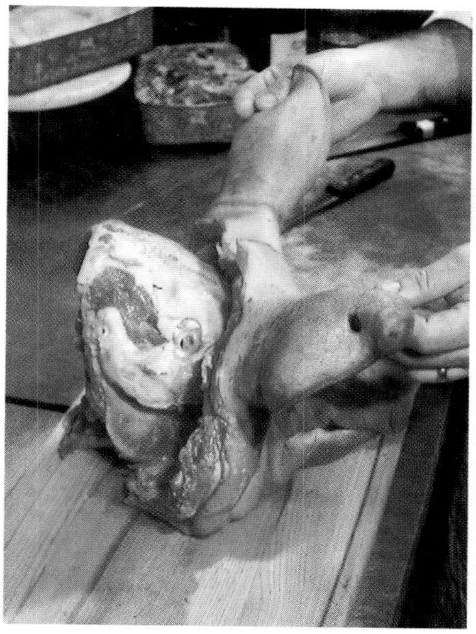

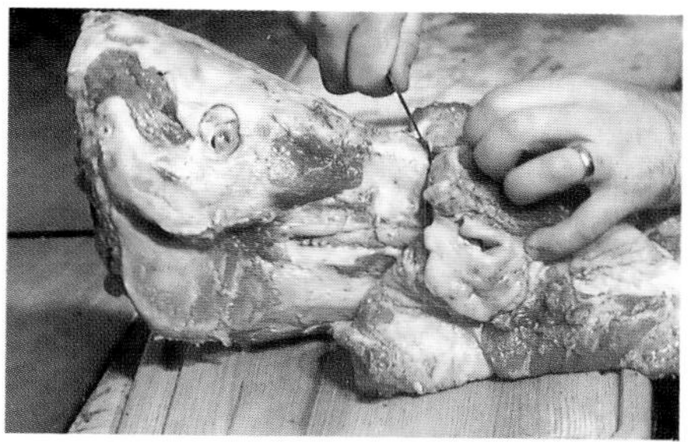

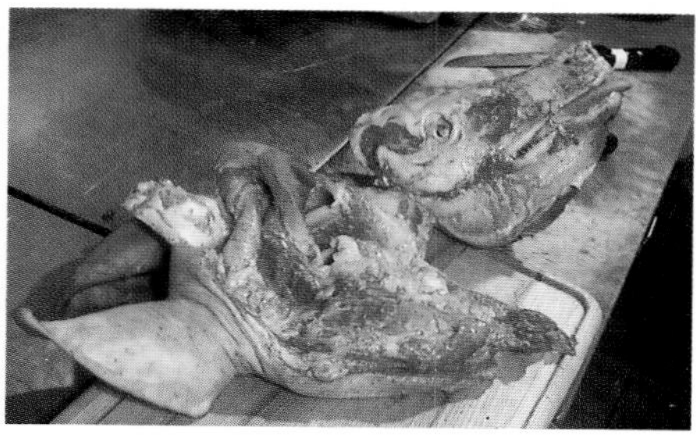

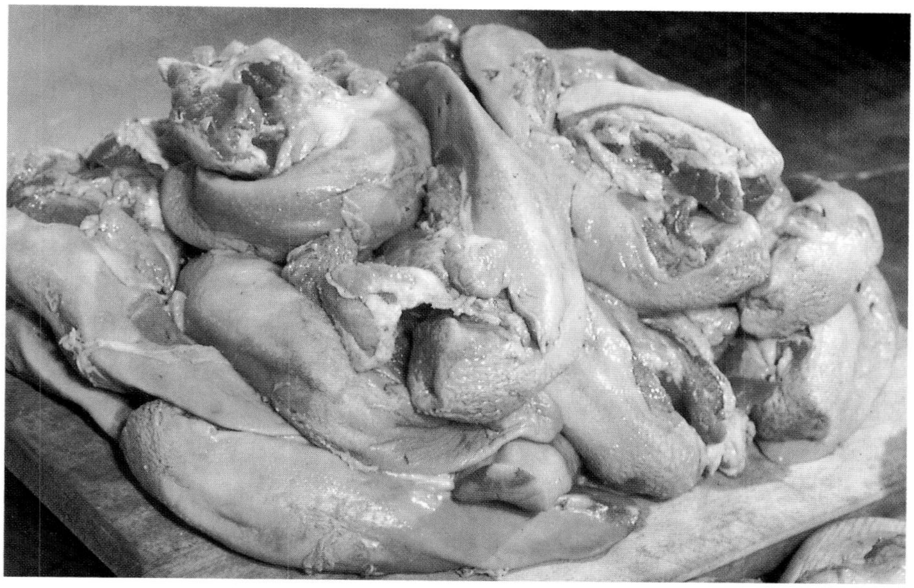

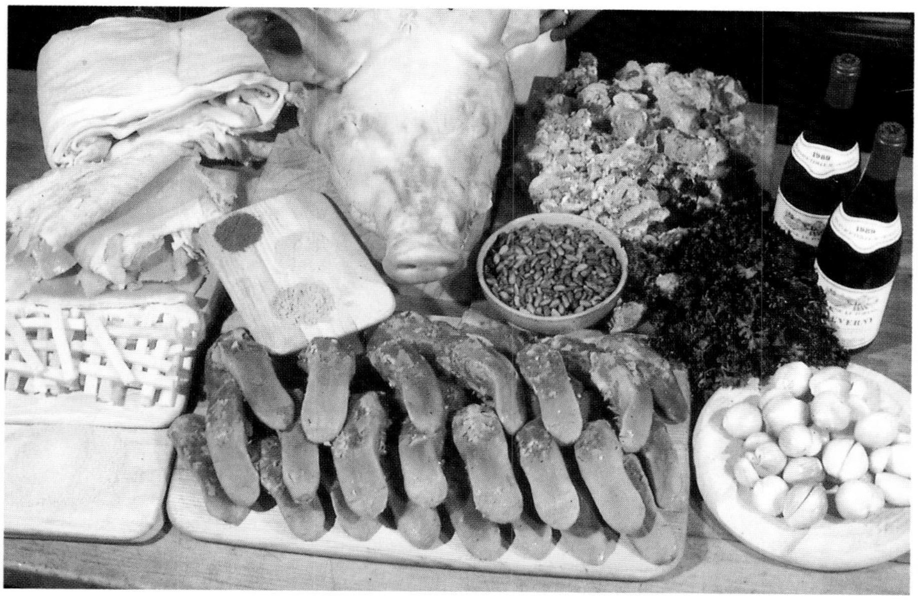

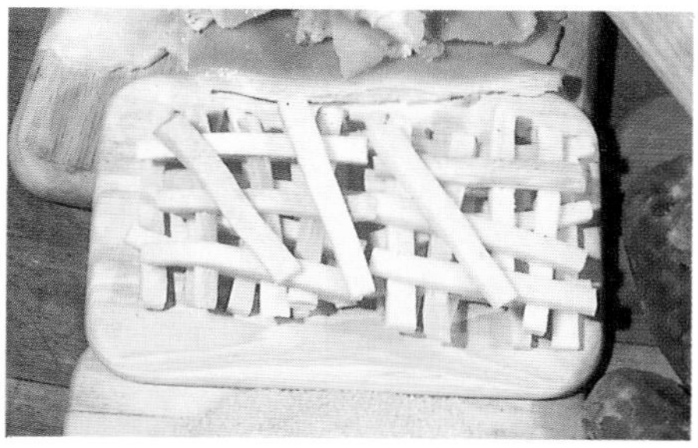

# Preparing the Tongues

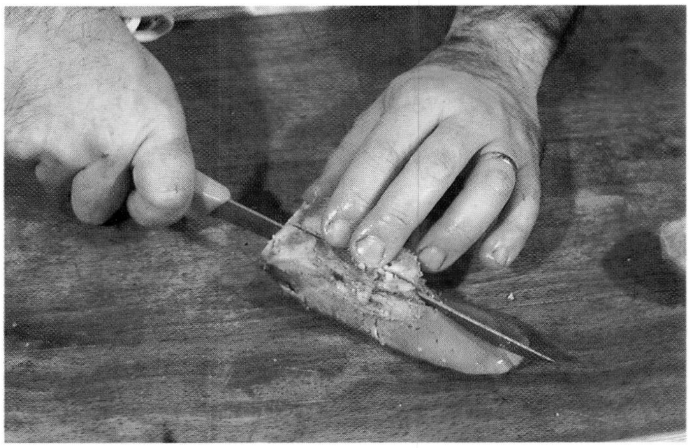

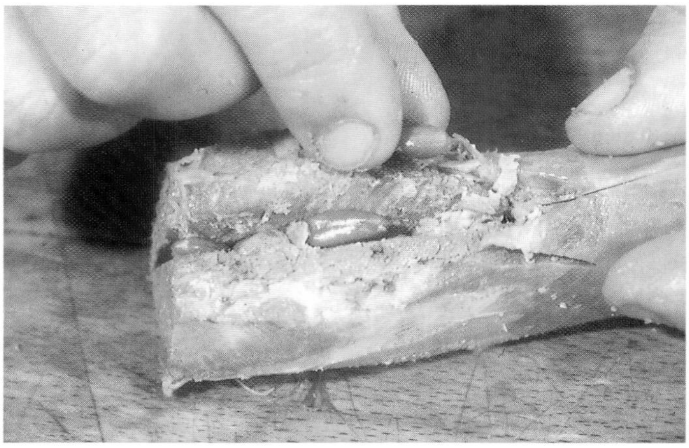

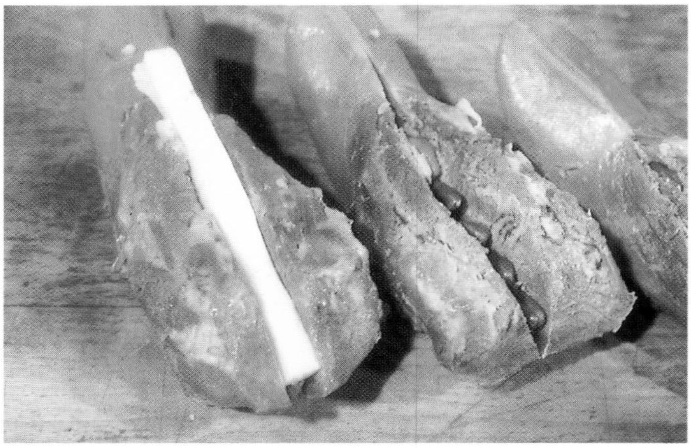

*Preparation*

Remove the larynx from each tongue.

Blanch the tongues in boiling water to facilitate the removal of the white skin that covers them. This skin should be completely removed.

The trimmed tongues are cooled in cold running water then injected with brine (same brine as for hams).

They are then immersed in brine for 12 hours then rinsed in cold running water.

*Cooking*

The tongues are cooked in the classic way in bouillon with an addition of sliced onions, carrots, celery and bouquet garni.

When they are tender, they are trimmed to make evenly shaped tongues.

While they are still warm place a board or baking sheet on top and place a weight on top to compress the tongues and keep them from curling. It is also possible to pack them into a rectangular ham press with a small baking sheet between each layer.

If placed in the mold, heat them through again to set the shape by immersing in simmering bouillon for 15 minutes.

Cool as quickly as possible and chill for 12 hours at 2-4 °C (35 F) with a weight on top so that they keep their uniform shape.

*Garnishing*

Remove the tongue from the mold or weight. Clean all traces of bouillon from the surface and dry.

Cut a slit about 3/4 of the way into each tongue.

Arrange a row of peeled pistachios in the bottom of each slit. On top of the pistachios arrange a row of cooked strips of fat (from the jowl--cut about 5 mm (1/4 in) across).

Wrap each tongue in a thin sheet of barding fat, arrange them on a plate and refrigerate (2-4 °C (35 F)).

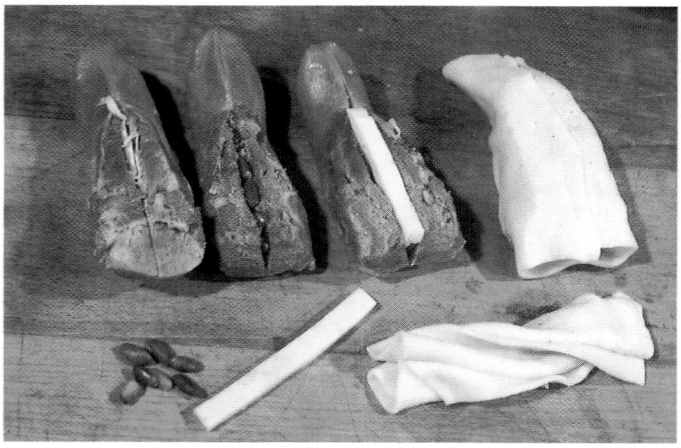

# Preparing the Forcemeat

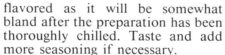

The forcemeat must be solid enough after cooking to hold the tongue in place so that the " hure " slices very neatly.

Therefore the preparation of this forcemeat is crucial to the success of the " hure ".

*Preparation*

Chop the shallots and parsley separately in the food processor.

Chop the tongue trimmings in the food processor until the pieces are about 1 mm (1/12 in).

Chop the cooked skin in the food processor. This skin can come from the production of aspic (see chapter on Stocks and Aspic). It is trimmed on all hair and cooked during the preparation of the aspic. Il should be warm when chopped and added to the mixture--the liaison of the ingredients in the forcemeat is better achieved.

Reduce the red wine by half.

Cook the chopped shallots in lard until soft but not browned. Add the chopped trimmings of tongue, the chopped skin, the reduced red wine and the chopped parsley.

Cook this mixture over low heat, stirring constantly.

Season with pepper, nutmeg and saltpeter (check label for amount).

This forcemeat should be strongly

flavored as it will be somewhat bland after the preparation has been thoroughly chilled. Taste and add more seasoning if necessary.

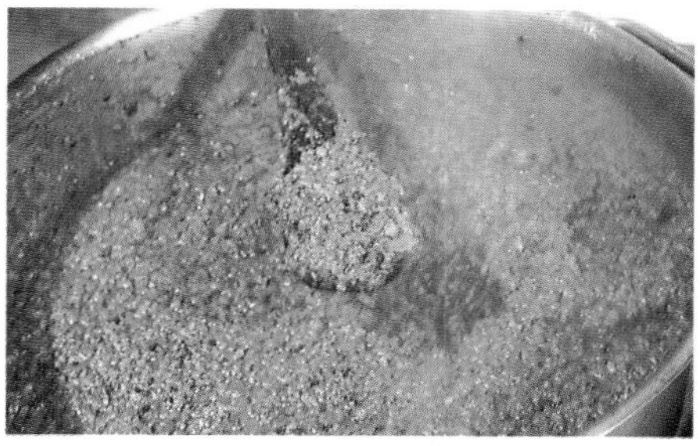

The tongues have simply been seasoned in the brine so the forcemeat is supplying most of the flavor in the filling.

# Hure of Pork *(continued)*

When the mixture is well cooked add 250 g (1/2 lb) of powdered gelatin to reinforce the binding properties of the forcemeat.
This mixture will solidify around the tongues and provide a firm text that will slice easily.

**Assembly**

***The Tongues***

The assembly of the hure is difficult because the appearance of each slice depends on accurately placing the tongues in an even pattern instead the head.
Spread each tongue with forcemeat.
Spread a 2 cm (3/4 in) layer of forcemeat in a bowl. Arrange four tongue standing on this layer, held together by forcemeat. Tie a string around this pyramid to hold the shape.
When the pyramid has set up, remove the string and arrange another row around the first layer enlarging the circumference of the pyramid. Tie string (not too tight) to secure.
Level the top and spread with forcemeat.
Repeat the operation to form a second tier. The final result should be a uniform cone with all the cracks between the tongues filled with forcemeat so that the outer layer is smooth.

***Final Assembly***

Cut a circle of skin the width of the plastic bucket (that will serve as a container during assembly). This skin will later cover the back of the during cooking.
Place the head in the bucket, snout side down. Remove all the strings from around the tongues and position the pyramid next to the bucket. Then turn the head in the bucket over the pyramid of tongues which should fit neatly inside.
Turn the bucket over and press lightly on the tongues to secure their position in the head.
Using a trussing needle and string, attach the circle of skin to the of the pig's head to cover completely.
Remove from the bucket and add a few more " stitches " if necessary to hold the covering securely in place.

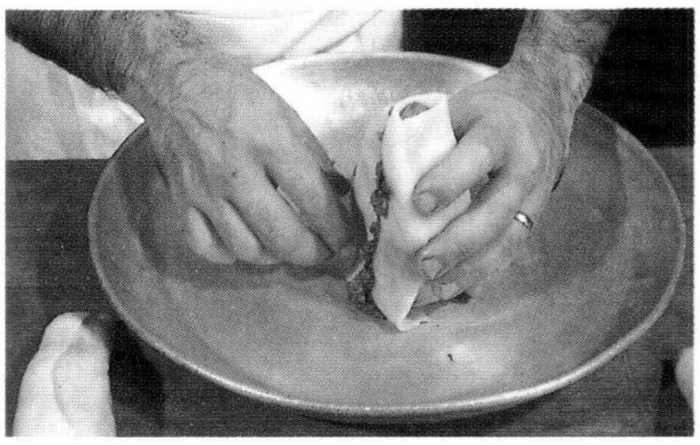

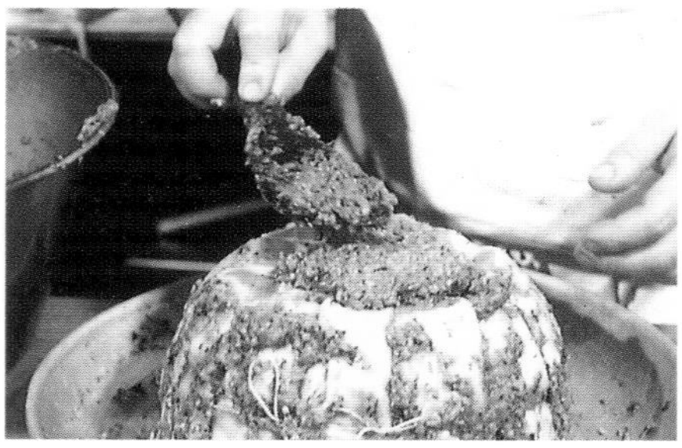

Wrap the head in cheesecloth with the ears sticking out. Preserve the conical shape of the head as the head is wrapped snugly.

Secure the cheesecloth in place with a linen strip (used for pigs' feet) and to further compress the head into the right shape.

**Cooking**

Bring a large pot of bouillon to a boil, skim all fat and impurities that rise to the surface and regulate the temperature to 90 °C (195 F).

Lower the head carefully into the bouillon and cook long enough to cook the skin on the outside--the filling ingredients are already completely cooked.

However, to be sure that bacteria have been destroyed it is recommend to cook until the internal temperature reaches 65-67 °C (150-155 F).

Transfer the cooked hure to a large recipient. Bring the bouillon to boil, skim and pour over the head. Cool as quickly as possible then refrigerate. The hure is so large that it must be chilled for at least 24 hours (up to 48 hours) before serving.

**Presentation**

Carefully remove the cloth band and the cheesecloth. Rinse under hot running water to remove bouillon that is attached to the head then rinse thoroughly under cold running water. Wipe the surface and place in the refrigerator to dry completely.

Decorate the surface with cut-out pieces of vegetables, fruits or truffles. Stir aspic over ice to thicken slightly then brush a thin coat over the decorations.

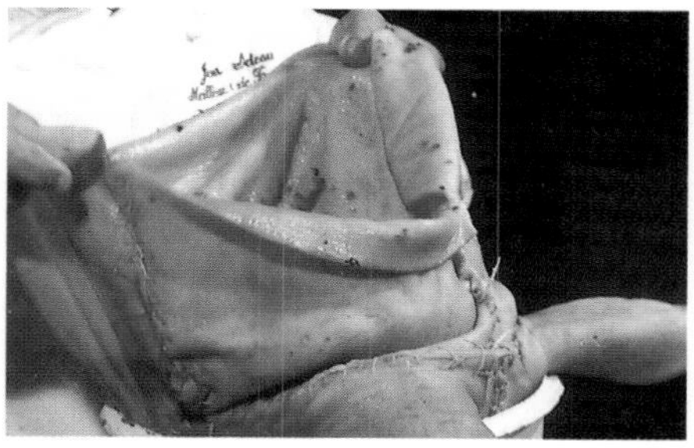

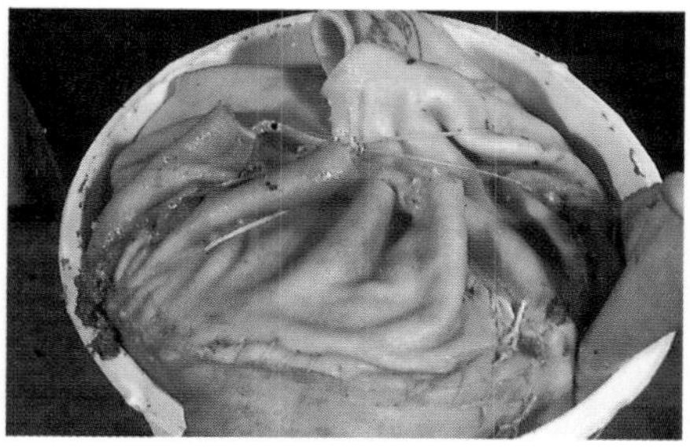

Cut out rounds from hard cooked egg white and make eyes for the hure.

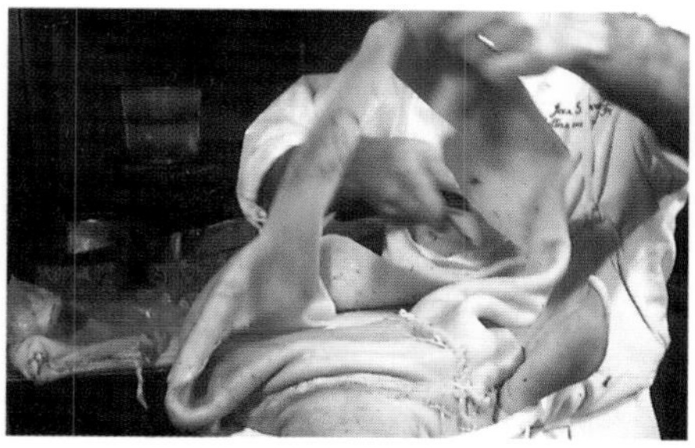

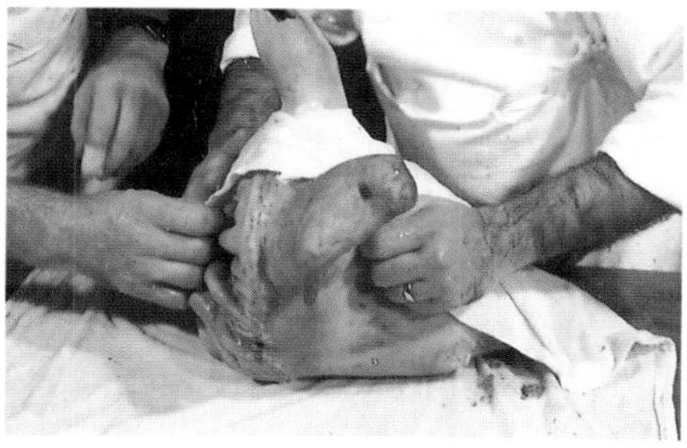

Place on a platter and brush on another coat of aspic.

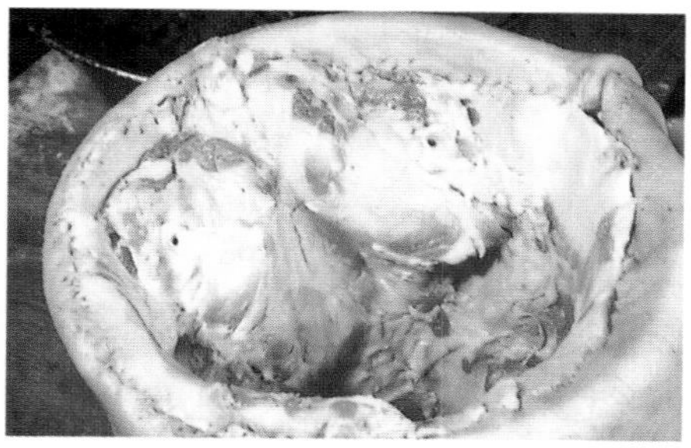

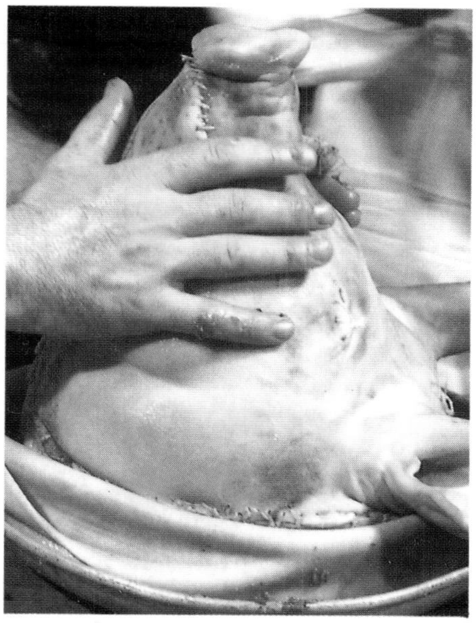

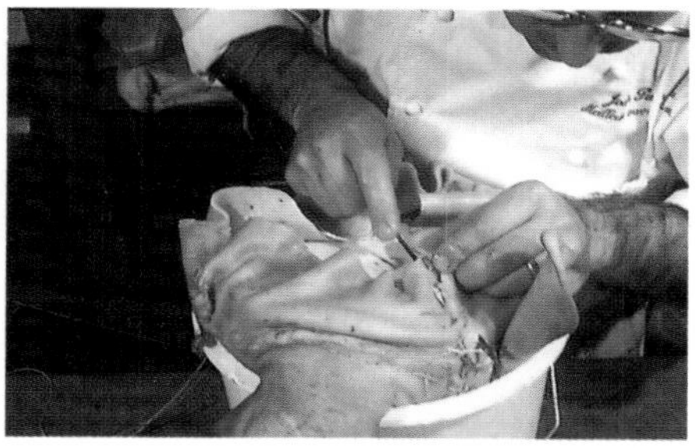

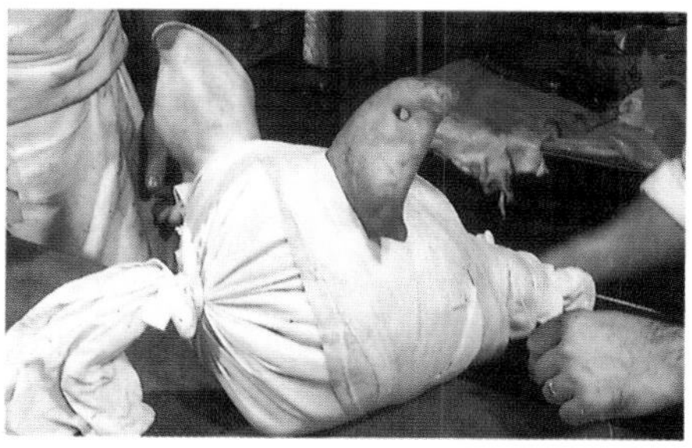

# " Hure " Made in a Mold

As we explained earlier the assembly of the hure inside the boned head of the pig is a long procedure that requires skill and practice. This presentation is reserved for special occasions and is used more as a showpiece than as a dish to be served. However the elaborate hure can be sold by weight. The charcutier will not make enough profit to compensation him for his time, but the clients have the opportunity to see the artistic talents of the chef.

" Hure à la Parisienne " is usually made in a special truncated mold so that it can be assembled and sliced easily.

The preparation of the ingredients is identical to the first recipe.

**Assembly**

Spread a large sheet of barding fat with forcemeat and line the mold.

Spread forcemeat on the tongues as in the other recipe and layer them the mold with the thin ends overlapping the thicker ends so that each layer is even.

Fill the mold to the top and cover with a piece of barding fat. Place a small baking sheet on top and secure it with string.

Bring the bouillon (used to cook the tongues) to a boil and skin. Lower the mold into the bouillon and cook at a simmer (85-90 °C (190-195 F) until the internal temperature reaches 65 °C (150 F) to assure that the ingredients are free of bacteria.

Place a weight (1 kilo (about 2 lbs)) on top of the cooked hure to compress it slightly.

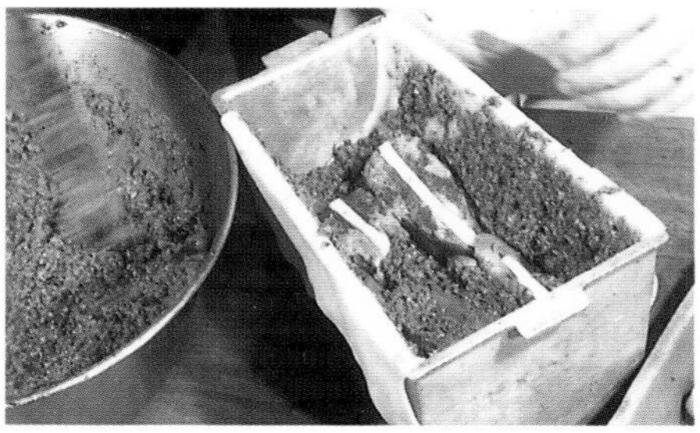

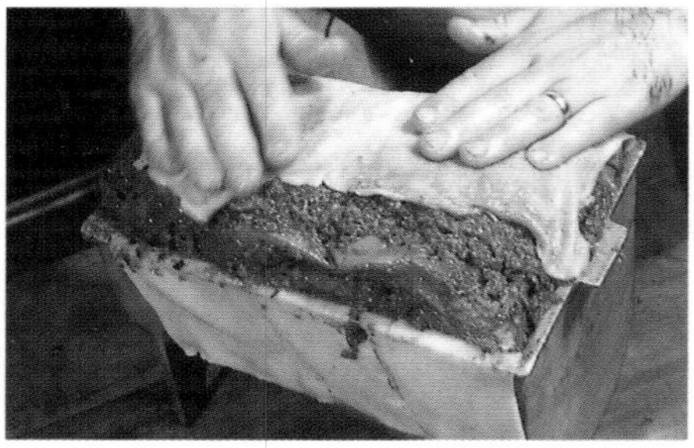

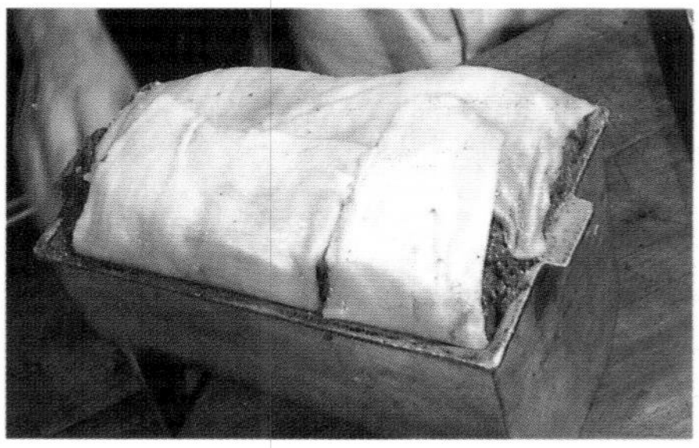

**Presentation**

Unmold the hure, clean the mold and coat with amber-colored aspic. Place it back into the mold to coat it evenly with aspic.

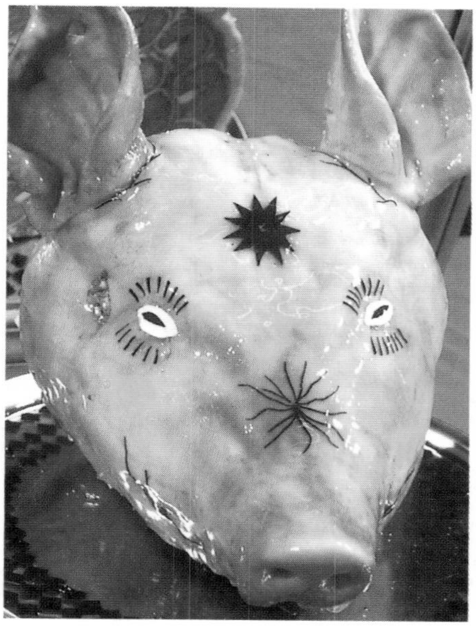

Unmold the hure onto a platter and slice by hand (or by machine if not glazed).

The hure can be consumed on its own or accompanied by tart pickles (" cornichons "), mustard, and/or olives. Purists enjoy this dish served simply with bread.

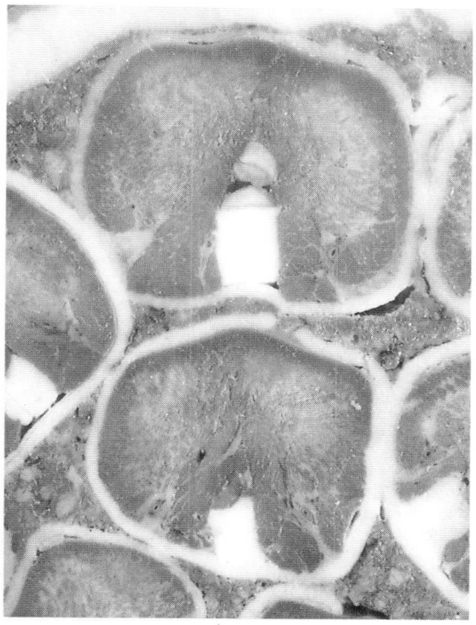

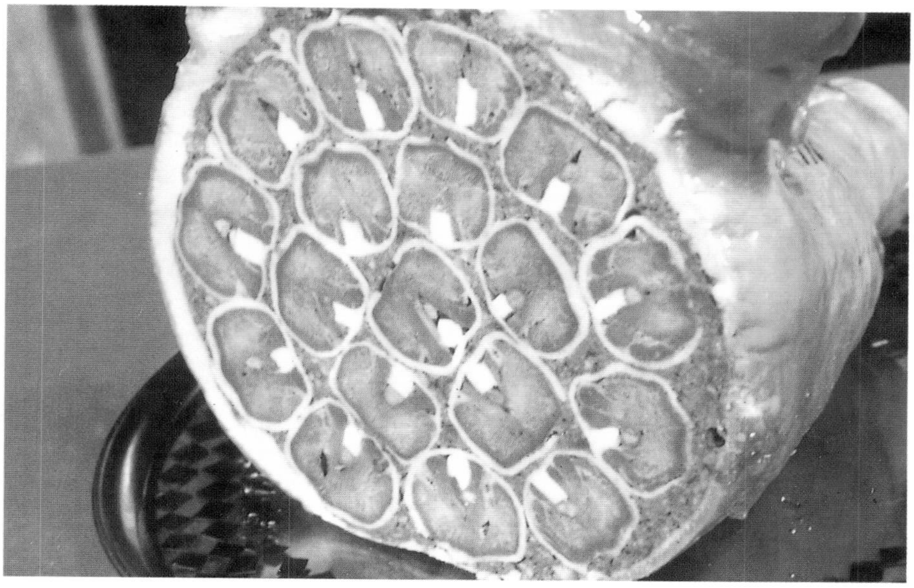

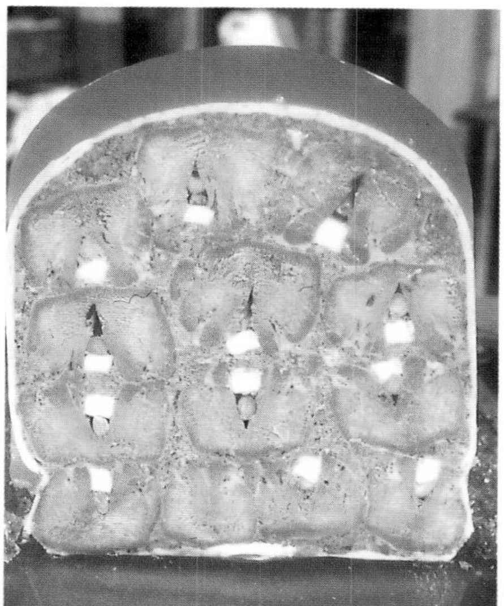

# Pigs' Feet Cooked in Aspic

## Introduction

The saying " all parts of the pig can be cooked except the squeal " is proved true with this recipe.

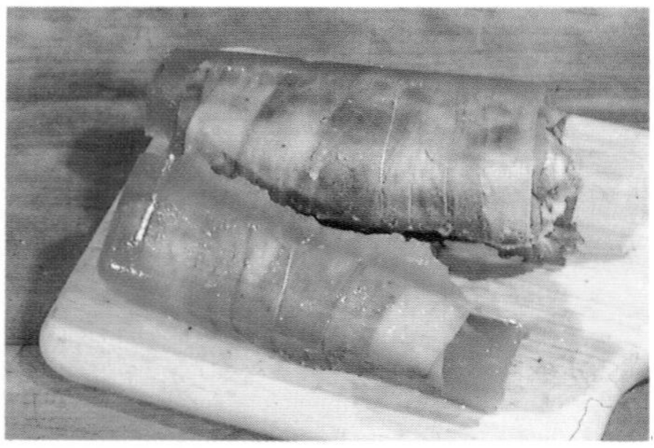

Pigs' feet which are composed of 60% bones and 40% skin with tendons and small muscles attached can be transformed into a succulent product much appreciated by gourmets.

## Equipment

Knives, cleaver, razor, baking sheet, linen band, stainless steel hooks, meat saw, deep hotel pan for storage

## Ingredients

Pigs' feet (from front and back)
Aspic

## Procedure

Modern day charcutiers rarely purchase the entire pork carcass. They choose only the individual cuts (loin, hams, picnic shoulder...) that are used in their standard selection. Therefore the feet, also known as trotters, are removed at the wholesale butcher and sold separately. The front feet are the best for dishes such as this because they are slightly more meaty than the hind feet.

First the nails are pulled out using the meat hook.

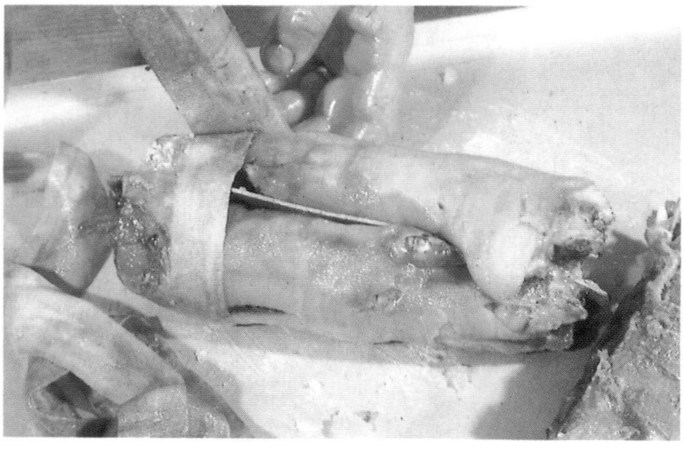

Next each foot is carefully shaved to remove all remaining hair and bristles which tend to be quite tough on the feet. It is also necessary to clean well between the toes where the skin often has become detached. Scrub the feet with a vegetable brush and wash well in cold water then rinse under cold running water.

Split the large bone exposed at the cut end with a cleaver or saw (hand-held or mechanical).

Tie up the feet; individually or two together (pointing in opposite directions) and attach them to a small metal sheet. In France, where this item is offered in practically every charcuterie, special linen bands are available called " cordon de pieds " (band for feet) to secure the feet. Handtowels or other robust cloth cut in long strips can be used. Wrap these bands tightly around the feet so that they sit flat on the metal sheet.

Special cooking vessels are also used with lids that can be clamped down to compress the feet as they cook. The feet are arranged in neat layers, separated by the small sheets and a rack is placed between each layer.

**Cooking**

The feet are cooked pork aspic.

Add a good quantity of aromatic vegetables to the cooking liquid and check that it is salted enough. Add more salt if necessary.

Bring the liquid to a simmer and skim all fat and impurities that rise to the surface.

Regulate the temperature to 90 °C (195 F), add the feet and cook until tender, generally 8-10 hours. (The cooking is usually done overnight.)

To check the cooking, press a finger into one of the feet--the skin of the foot should feel very soft and give under the pressure. Transfer the feet to a deep hotel pan. Bring the cooking liquid to a boil, skim and strain over the feet to cover.

**Storage**

Chill the cooked feet as quickly as possible then refrigerate (2-4 °C (35 F)). The feet can be served after 24 hours in the refrigerator covered with aspic.

**Presentation**

***Pigs' Feet in Aspic***

Lift the feet out of the aspic and remove the bands of cloth.

Remove the aspic that adheres to the feet with your fingers. Glaze the feet with aspic by dipping them in a container of aspic or using a pastry brush to apply a thin coat.

Decorate with cut-out pieces of vegetables (carrots, pickles...) and brush on another coat of aspic.

Pigs' feet in aspic are served cold with vinaigrette.

***Breaded Feet***

Remove the bands and excess aspic as in the previous presentation. The feet are then spread (by hand) with a very thin layer of lard. They can be split in half or left whole. They are then rolled in light breadcrumbs and arranged on platters.

Breaded pigs' feet are reheated in the oven and served with mustard.

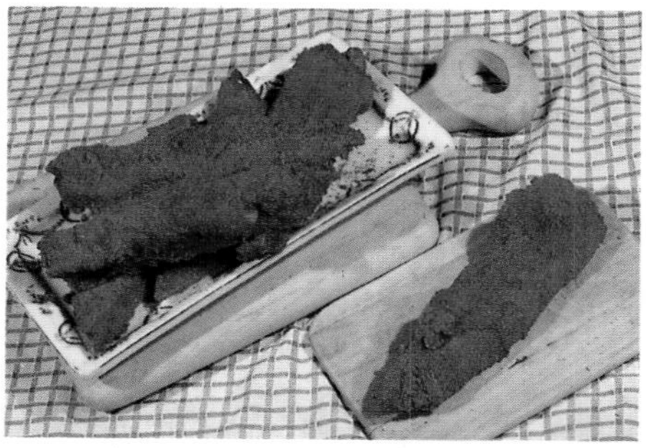

# Pig's Feet " Saint Menehould "

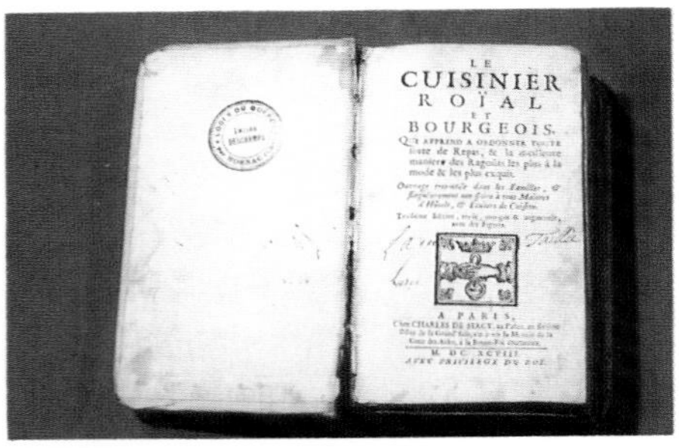


### Introduction

The cooking of the eastern region of Lorraine has contributed many well-known preparations that are part of culinary history.

• According to history, puff pastry was " invented " by the great artist Claude Gelée known as " Le Lorrain ".

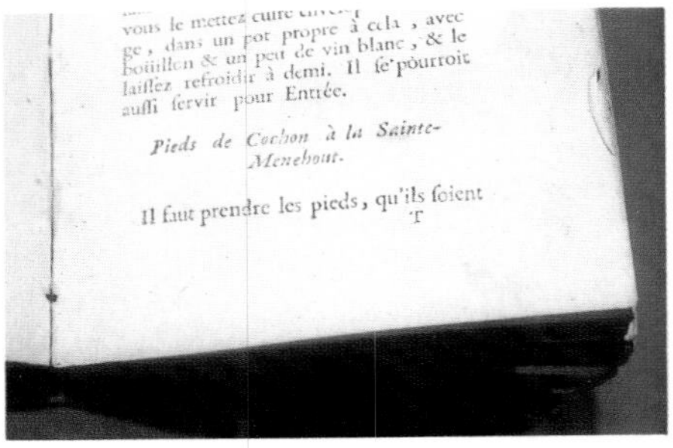

vous le mettez cuire ... ge, dans un pot propre à cela, avec boüillon & un peu de vin blanc, & le laissez refroidir à demi. Il se pourroit aussi servir pour Entrée.

*Pieds de Cochon à la Sainte-Menehout.*

Il faut prendre les pieds, qu'ils soient

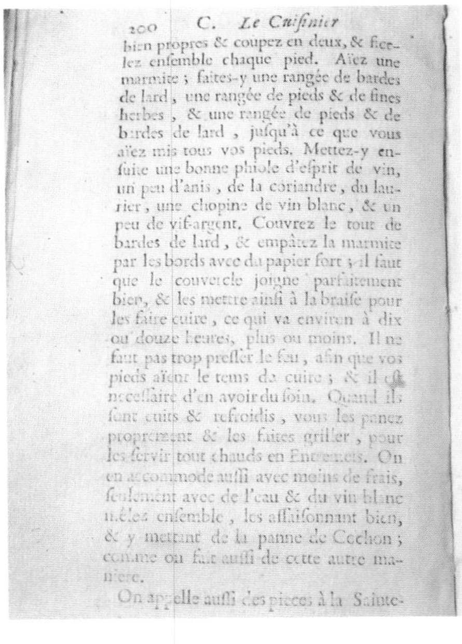

200 C. *Le Cuisinier*

bien propres & coupez en deux, & ficelez ensemble chaque pied. Aïez une marmite; faites-y une rangée de bardes de lard, une rangée de pieds & de fines herbes, & une rangée de pieds & de bardes de lard, jusqu'à ce que vous aïez mis tous vos pieds. Mettez-y ensuite une bonne phiole d'esprit de vin, un peu d'anis, de la coriandre, du laurier, une chopine de vin blanc, & un peu de vif-argent. Couvrez le tout de bardes de lard, & empâtez la marmite par les bords avec du papier fort; il faut que le couvercle joigne parfaitement bien, & les mettre ainsi à la braise pour les faire cuire, ce qui va environ à dix ou douze heures, plus ou moins. Il ne faut pas trop presser le feu, afin que vos pieds aïent le tems de cuire; & il est necessaire d'en avoir du soin. Quand ils sont cuits & refroidis, vous les panez proprement & les faites griller, pour les servir tout chauds en Entremets. On en accommode aussi avec moins de frais, seulement avec de l'eau & du vin blanc mêlez ensemble, les assaisonnant bien, & y mettant de la panne de Cochon; comme on fait aussi de cette autre maniere.

On appelle aussi des pieces à la Sainte-

• The famous dish " Les Pieds à la " Sainte-Menehould " is the product of a long and rich tradition of the chefs of this small town in the Lorraine.

These celebrated pigs' feet have been written about by many great authors.

The best known tale claims that King Louis XVI, while fleeing the Revolution in Paris, could not resist stopping to sample this dish en route. According to one report, he was recognized while eating his pigs' feet, arrested, and returned to Paris and an untimely end.

Was history changed by a dish of pigs' feet? No one will ever know, for the story has never been authenticated, and Louis XVI, although a heavy eater and a connaisseur, no doubt was occuppied at that moment more by politics than by gastronomy (according to the Dictionnary of Cooking by Alexander Dumas).

In any case this specialty is certainly worth a detour and many tourists from the surrounding countries to the east and north, as well as Frenchmen from other provinces, find their way to Saint Menehould where all the restaurants offer the renowned pigs' feet and the charcutiers-caterers sell them to reheat at home.

The reputation that this dish enjoys, in France and abroad, inspired us to research an authentic recipe. The " Traité de Cuisine Royale et Bourgeoise " written in the 17th century provided the guidelines for this recipe.

**Equipment**

Knives, cleaver or meat saw, large iron pot with cover, gratin dish

**Ingredients**

For this exceptionnal dish, use only the meatier front feet.

*For 8 front feet:*

Aromatic vegetables (onions, carrots, celery, bouquet garni)
Full-bodied red wine
Pork aspic
Lard
2 garlic cloves
Flour
Barding fat

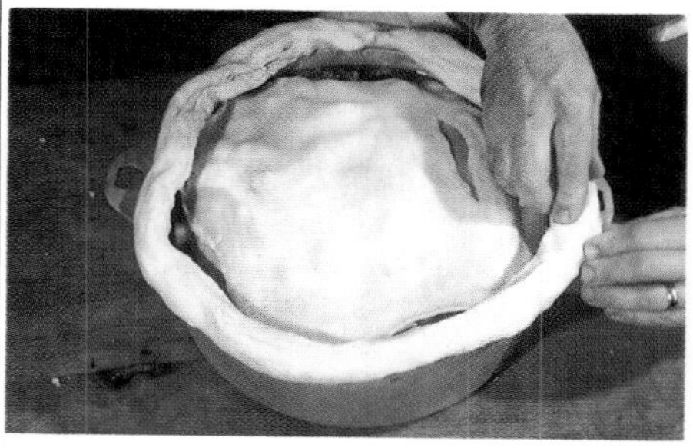

**Procedure**

Follow the instructions for preparing the feet described in the section on pigs' feet cooked in aspic.

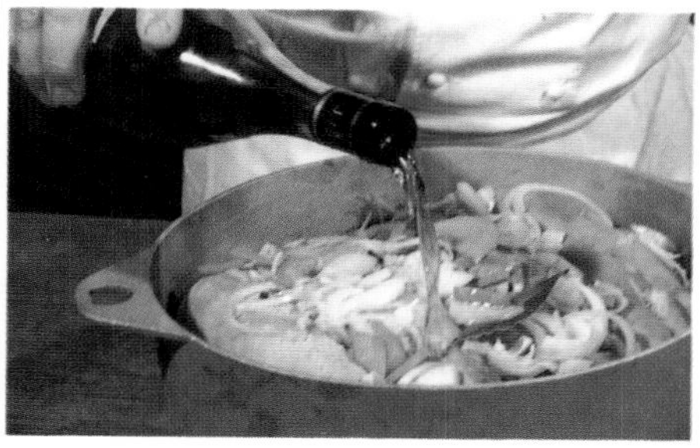

Removing the hair, cleaning and wrapping is done in the same manner.

Prepare the aromatic vegetables. Peel and slice the carrots and onions, cut up the celery and make the bouquet garni and stick a whole onion with several cloves.

Rub garlic on the bottom and sides of the pot.

Line the bottom of the pot with a sheet of barding fat.

Cover the bottom with half of the aromatic vegetables and the garlic cloves.

Place the feet in two layers in the pot.

Place the remaining vegetables on top.

Add 1/2 bottle of red wine and enough full-flavored pork aspic to completely cover the feet.

Place a second sheet of barding fat over the top.

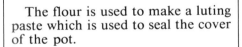

The flour is used to make a luting paste which is used to seal the cover of the pot.

Mix the flour with cold water to make a sticky dough which is applied around the edge of the pot, then place the cover into the luting paste to seal.

**Cooking**

Place the feet in a hot oven to bring the liquid to a simmer then lower the heat to 95-100 °C (200 F).

Since it is impossible to check the temperature of the cooking liquid, verify the temperature of the oven during the long cooking.

Cook the feet for about 10 hours. The combination of long cooking and low temperature is important for the success of the dish.

After 10 hours, remove the luting paste then the cover and skim the fat from the surface of the cooking liquid.

Remove the feet very carefully; they should be ***very well cooked,*** the bones are practically soft enough to eat.

**Presentation**

Remove the bands and arrange the feet in a gratin dish.

Pour a little of the strained cooking liquid (with some of the vegetables) over the feet and cover with a thin layer of light breadcrumbs.

Reheat in a hot oven before serving.

In the charcuterie, the feet can be prepared with the breadcrumbs and placed in disposible aluminum containers, ready for the customer to reheat in his own kitchen.

# Molded Pigs' Feet

**Introduction**

It is hard to believe that this delicious dish is no longer being made in many charcuteries. (This dish is called " pieds farcis " in France.)

Not only are molded pigs' feet delicious but they are relatively easy to prepare.

It is hard to say if it is the taste of the customers or the style of the charcutiers that is changing.

Molded pigs' feet are still popular for feasts celebrating the new year but do not deserve to be forgotten the rest of the year.

**Equipment**

Grinder, large stockpot or kettle, knives, plastic scraper, metal spoon, rectangular mold.

**Ingredients**

1 kg (about 2 lbs) cooked pigs' feet
300 g (10 oz) cooked pigs' tails
1 kg (about 2 lbs) pigs' snouts
700 g (1 lb 7 oz) cooked arm steaks (or hocks)
250 ml (1 cup) red wine
750 ml (3 cups) reduced pork stock
250 g (1/2 lb) shallots
500 g (1 lb) white mushrooms
Caul fat
Pork forcemeat (fine)

*Seasonings*

Saltpeter
Freshly ground pepper
Ground nutmeg
200 g (7 oz) chopped parsley
Truffles for presentation

The preparation of molded pigs' feet is done in three stages: the first step is the cooking of the pigs' feet, snouts and tails which must be done 24 hours in advance and cooled thoroughly.

**Preparing the Ingredients**

***The Pork Extremities***

The feet, snouts and tails (called collectively the " bouts de pieds " in French) are cooked in the classic manner described in this volume. The amount indicated in this recipe is for the weight of the meat off the bone. The " bouts de pieds " adds up to 4 kg (8.8 lbs) with the addition of the arm steak.

***The Forcemeat***

" Farce " (forcemeat) in France refers to a classic blend of ground fat and lean (usually belly and jowl) which is an ingredient in mixtures or used to bind (as in the making of a " rosace "). " Farce " is also a general term for all ground meat fillings (which sometimes include the simple fat and lean " farce " like in this recipe).

The " gratin " of chicken livers is described on page 15.

The finely ground forcemeat described here is a product sold in French charcuteries during the holidays because it is a favorite stuffing for the geese and turkeys served for Christmas dinner.

*Ingredients*
5 kg (11 lbs) " forcemeat " (belly, jowl, picnic shoulder)
500 g (1 lb) " gratin " of chicken livers (recipe pp. 259-260)
Reduced chicken stock
10 eggs
500 ml (2 cups) heavy cream

*Seasonings (per kilo (2.2 lbs))*

18 g (generous 1/2 oz) curing salt (sodium nitrite with fine salt)
2 g (1/16 oz) white pepper
0.5 g (1/64 oz) ground nutmeg
Cognac

Marinate the meats and the cooled gratin with the seasonings for 12 hours in the refrigerator.

Refrigerate the bowl of the chopper to maintain a cold temperature (14 °C (58 F)) throughout processing.

Chop the marinated meats then add the reduced stock, eggs. When smooth add the cream and process until homogeneous.

Set aside in the refrigerator. (The fine forcemeat can be used for many preparations.)

***The Aromatic Vegetables***

Wash and peel the mushrooms then cut in large dice.

Remove the stems from the parsley, wash thoroughly, chop finely.

Peel and chop the shallots.

### *Preparing the Cooked "Bouts de Pieds"*

Grind the cooked meats from the feet, snouts, tails and armsteaks through a disk with holes measuring 6 mm (1/4 in) and place in a large casserole.

Cook the chopped shallots in goose fat until soft but not browned, add 1/2 bottle of good red wine, reduce by a third and set aside.

Sauté the mushrooms in hot goose fat (or oil and butter) until browned, transfer to a strainer to cool and add the cooking liquid to the reduced wine. Add the parsley, mushrooms and red wine/shallots to the chopped meats and cover with full-flavored gelatinous pork stock. (Chill a little stock to verify that it sets up firmly.)

Add the seasonings (saltpeter, pepper, nutmeg, spices) (*Note:* the saltpeter here is blended with red food color, check manufacturer's suggestion for amounts.)

No further seasonings is added at this stage because the extremities were cured in brine and therefore salted. Cook the mixture over low heat for about 10 minutes.

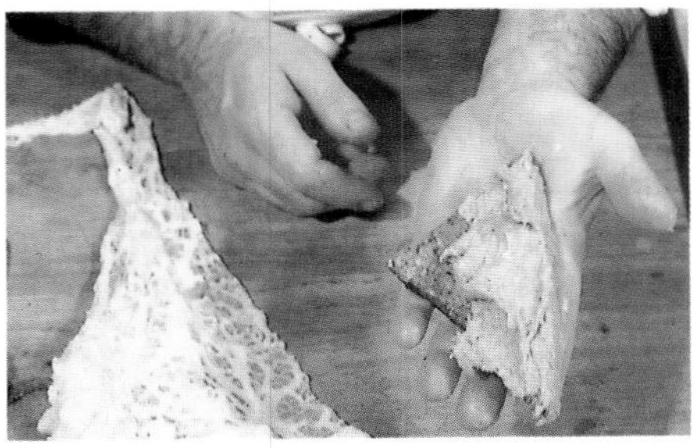

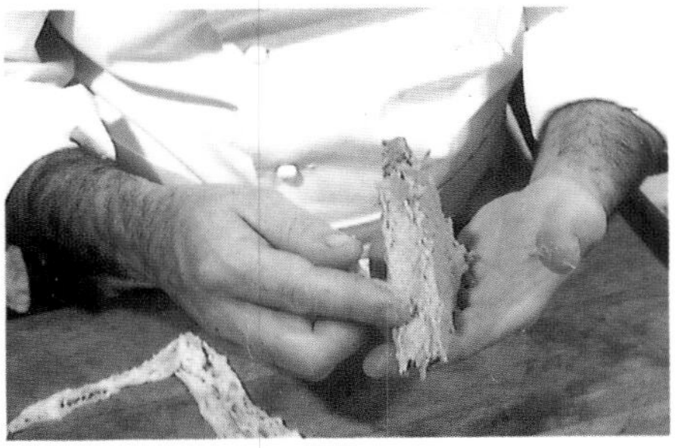
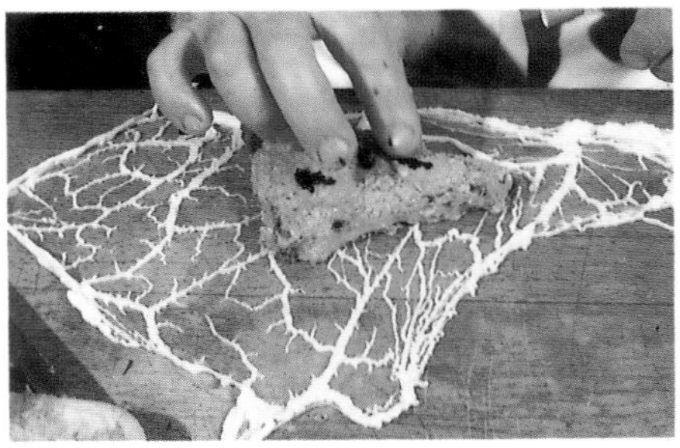
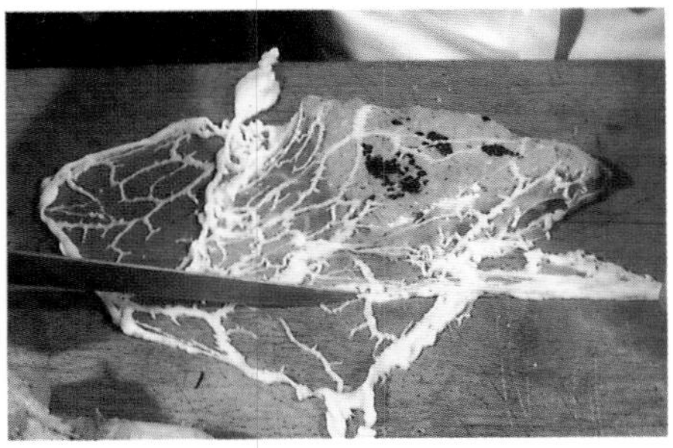

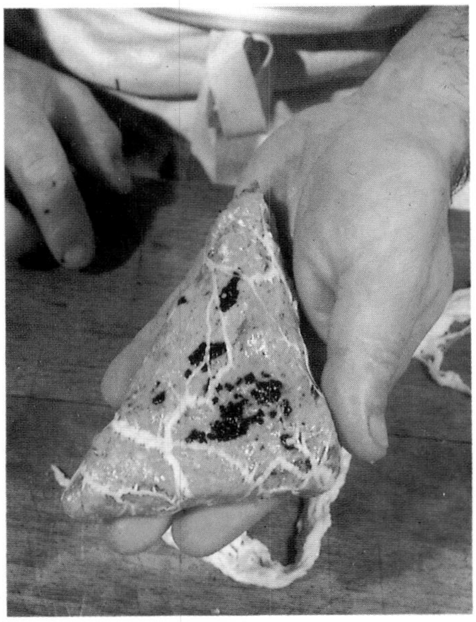

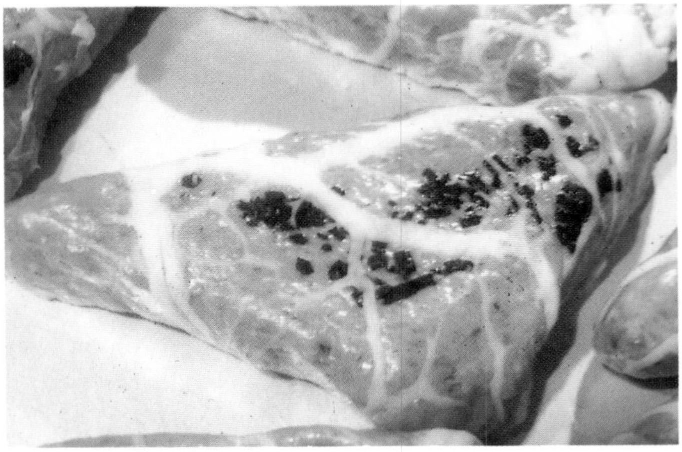

**Assembly**

Ladle the mixture into rectangular molds to a height of 8-10 cm (3-4 in).

Cool as quickly as possible (in an ice bath or cooling chamber).

Refrigerate for 12 hours to set the gelatin completely.

**Making the " Pieds Farcis "**

Unmold the chilled " bout de pieds ".

Cut slices about 1 cm (3/8 in) (by hand or by machine; using a machine gives neater, more even slices).

Cut each rectangle in half on the diagonal to form two triangles.

Spread the sheets of caul fat on the work surface and cut into pieces large enough to wrap around the triangles. (The caul fat is washed, rinsed and squeezed dry.)

Using a spatula or plastic scraper, cover the triangles of chopped extremities with an even layer of forcemeat.

Cover one side with chopped parsley. Chopped truffles can be used which would add a wonderful flavor however the food cost increases substantially.

Wrap the caul fat around each triangle to cover. Refer to recipe for flat sausages (volume 1) for further instruction on using caul fat.

Press on the wrapped triangles to make the shapes even and neat.

**Storage**

The blend of forcemeat and cooked feet is particularly perishable.

This product should be eaten within 48-72 hours of being made.

**Presentation**

The molded pigs' feet are sold uncooked. Arrange them in a neat pattern on a platter.

To prepare, the triangles are grilled or pan-fried. Only the caul fat and the forcemeat need to be cooked through; the molded extremities in the center are already cooked.

The result is a charcuterie product that is moist and delicious which deserves to be better known.

# Chapter 3

# " Andouilles " and " Andouillettes " (Chitterlings Sausages)

## Products from the French Countryside

*Each province of France offers its own version of these rustic products. Only in France is there such a diverse selection of " andouilles ".*

*As you travel throughout France, you discover many small towns tucked in the countryside; each one boasts its own " andouille ", the fruit of a long tradition.*

*" Andouilles " and " andouillettes " are usually made of pork intestines but can also be made from the intestines of other animals such as calf and sheep and even horse. Ground pork is sometimes added.*

*Even though sausages are made with chitterlings in the U.S., there is not the diversity or refinement found in this family of French products.*

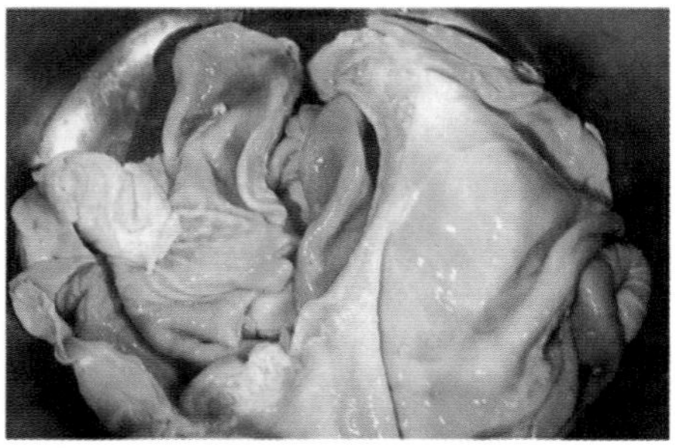

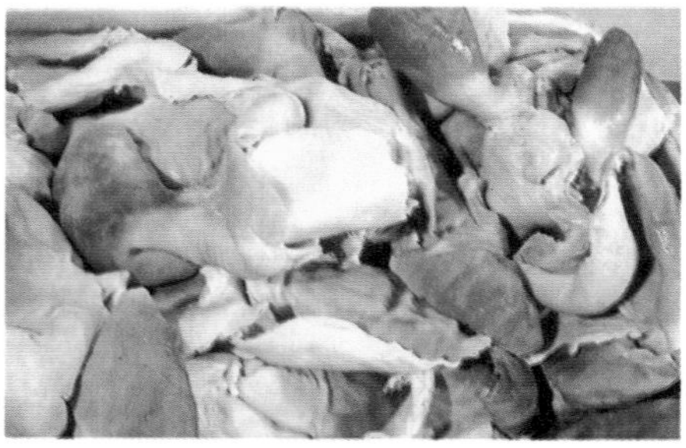

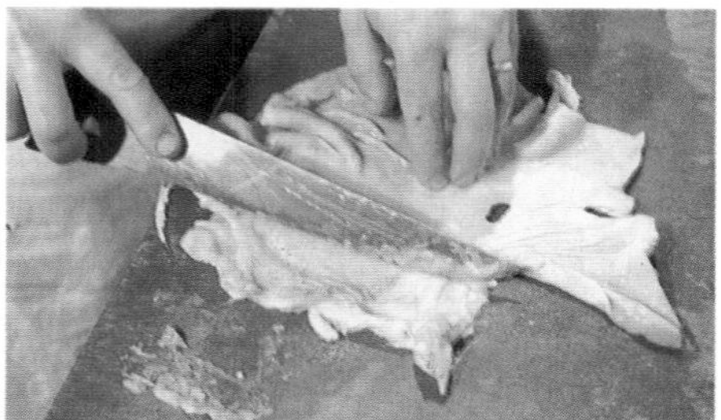

# General Information

The origin of these products is not exactly clear. We know that intestines were used in cooking as early as the Middle Ages, often mixed with other meats such as rabbit, pheasant or partridge.

The commom ingredient for all of the products in this category is pork intestine.

Local ingredients come into play and the creativity of the chef adds new dimension to this favorite traditional sausage.

The perfect andouille depends on following precise procedures during each step of production:

***Cleaning*** is done at the slaughterhouse. Traditionally this was done by hand but is now efficiently accomplished with machines.

Immediately following the slaughter of the animal, the intestines are removed, emptied and washed.

The slaughtering of animals in France is done exclusively in government approved facilities (some farmers will slaughter their own pigs but they are not offered for public consumption). Routine inspection by the health department assures top hygienic conditions.

This is all important because the intestine of all mammals (humans included) is a factory that produces the bacteria necessary for proper digestion. At work in the live animal, the bacteria serve an important function but must be destroyed once the animal is slaughtered.

The second important rule is to ***process the intestine as quickly as possible.*** The " chaudin " or large intestines should be made into sausages as soon as they are delivered to the charcutier.

Respecting these two guidelines, the intestines can be made into a variety of wonderful products.

**" Andouille "**

" Andouille " is a large sausage, stuffed into casings from the wide portion of the intestine (or beef casings). It is served cold in slices or heated.

The most famous variations are the ones from Normandy and Brittany. The towns of Guémené and Vire vie for the top honors.

Delicious andouilles, each a little different, are also made in Jargeau, Revin, the Lorraine and Auvergne regions. These artisinal sausages are often labeled simply " country andouilles ".

**" Andouillette "**

" Andouillette " is a smaller version of the andouille, usually an individual portion that is served hot.

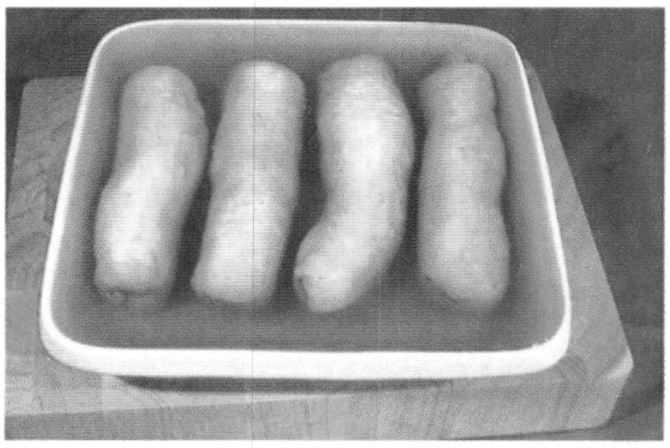

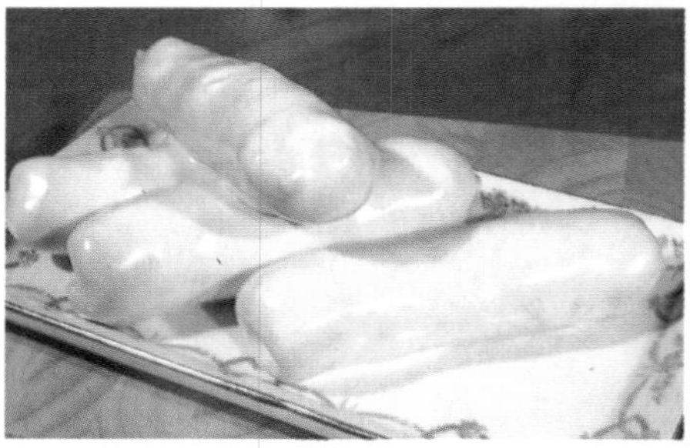

**Country-style " Andouille "**
**(p. 78)**

**Country-style " Andouillette "**
**(p. 82)**

**" Andouille " from Vire (p. 86)**

**" Andouillette " from Troyes (p. 90)**

(pictured below) **" Andouille " from Guéméné** (recipe not given)

The most famous andouillette is from Troyes. Other good varieties are made in Cambrai, Jargeau, Lyon, Rouen and in the provinces of Provence and Perigord.

In this series we describe four sausages from this vast category. The selection includes the most traditional and well-known.

All of these products keep very well and the andouille is smoked which prolongs storage.

The storage time can be prolonged by placing the sausages in a vacuum pouch which also protects them during transport.

The andouille is presented " as is ", sliced to order for the customer. Andouillettes are often glazed with aspic or a coating of lard to keep them fresh. Some varieties are covered with dried herbs.

# Country-style Andouille

## Introduction

The filling of this andouille is a classic blend of chopped pork intestine with pork jowl and seasonings.

The light smoking gives it a characteristic taste that is very popular.

This particular sausage can be eaten cold or warm. Cold, it is sliced thinly and eaten as an hors d'œuvre. It also can be heated on a bed of lentils or in a vegetable stew or simply poached in water with a bouquet garni.

## Equipment

Knives, food processor, hotel pan, bowls, large stock pot or jacketed kettle, smoker, string, skimmer, plastic scraper

## Ingredients

*For 10 kg (22 lbs) of sausages*

6 kg (13 lbs) large pork intestine (" chaudin ")
2.25 kg (about 5 lbs) pork stomach (" panse ")
1.75 kg (3.85 lbs) pork jowl, trimmed

*Seasonings (per kg (2.2 lbs))*

35 g (generous 1 oz) salt
2 g (1/16 oz) pepper
1 g (1/32 oz) four spice powder
1 g (1/32 oz) nutmeg
50 ml (1/4 cup) wine vinegar

*For the cooking:*

Bouquet garni
Onion skins

## Procedure

The preparation of the intestines is the same for all andouilles.

The first step is to clean them.

To thoroughly clean the intestines they are gently scraped to remove the mucous membrane and fat. Wash thoroughly in cold water.

Before the cleaning process the intestine is first cut into sections of different sizes:

- " Panse " (stomach)
- " Menu " (small intestine which is generally used for sausage casings)
- " Chaudin " (first section of large intestine)
- " Baudruche " (largest section of the large intestine)
- " Robe " (section following the " baudruche " used as casing for andouilles)
- " Fuseau " (rectum)

The " robe " is cleaned separately and set aside to be used for the casing. Care must be taken to not pierce the casing.

The remaining sections of the intestines are all cleaned in the same manner. They are first cut open with a knife and scraped to remove most of the gastric juices that adhere to the mucous lining. Then they are degorged for 2-3 hours in cold water with a little salt and vinegar.

When the soaking is completed they are blanched in boiling water for a few minutes. The blanching process stiffens the intestines slightly and greatly reduces or destroys harmful bacteria.

The blanched intestines are then rinsed under cold running water then scraped with a knife to eliminate all remaining fat and mucous.

The stomach, which is thicker and tougher is cooked after the cleaning process. It is poached for one hour in lightly salted water with aromatic vegetables (onion stuck with cloves, carrots, bouquet garni).

After cooking, the stomach is rinsed under cold running water.

The pork jowl is trimmed in the classic manner, removing skin, the large glands and blood spots. It is cut into pieces and chilled.

## Making the Mixture

Process the chilled pork jowl until coarsely chopped.

The stomach is chopped slightly more coarsely than the jowl.

Mix the jowl and stomach together with a few turns of the chopper.

By hand, cut the intestines into big pieces. Add to the other meats and add seasonings and vinegar.

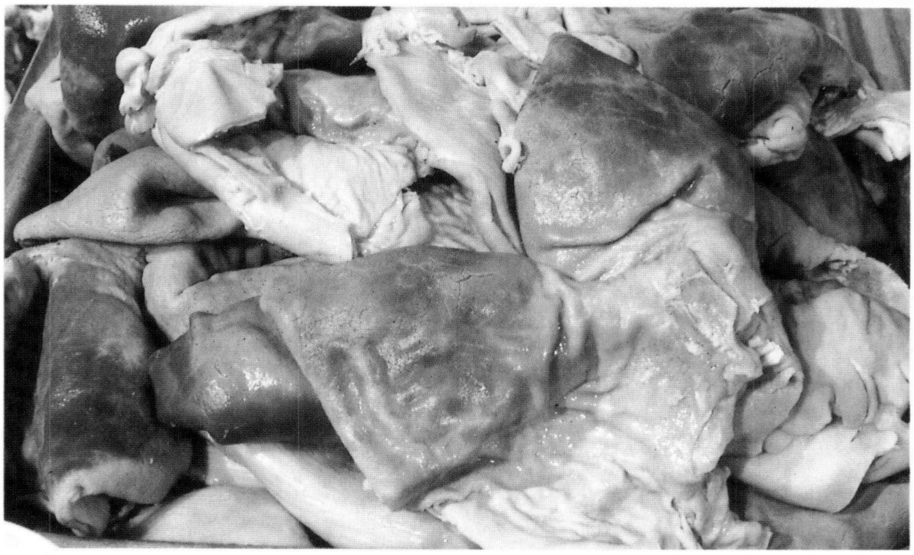
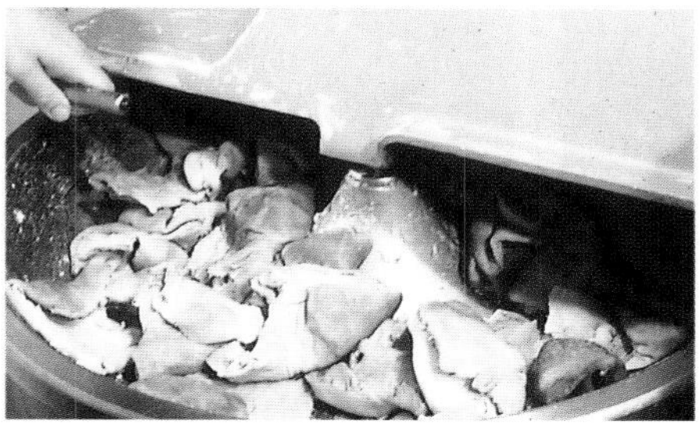

Process briefly to chop the meats to a grain of about 8-10 mm (3/8 in).

Transfer the chopped meats to a non-reactive recipient, cover and marinate in the refrigerator for 10 hours.

### Filling the Casings

Stir the marinated meats to blend and transfer to the stuffing machine.

Check the casings which have been previously soaked and scraped. The walls of the casings may have been worn thin during cleaning and might burst during cooking.

Stuff the mixture into the casings using the classic method described in volume 1.

Tie the sausages about 20-22 mm (8-9 in) long.

Cut into individual links or into pairs.

Hang to dry at room temperature for 6 hours.

### Smoking

The sausages are " cold-smoked " which means that the temperature is under 30 °C (86 F) and the humidity is about 75%.

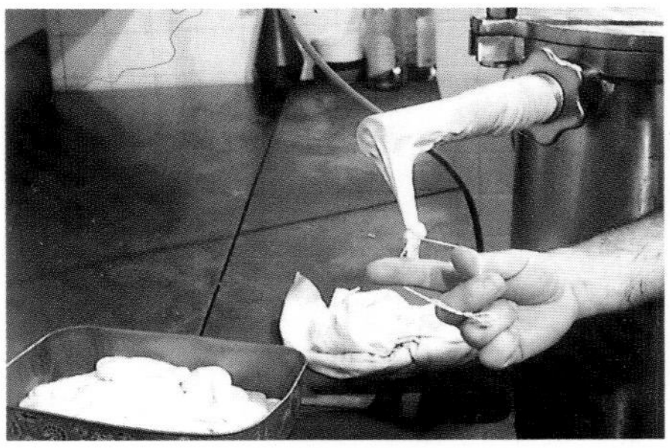

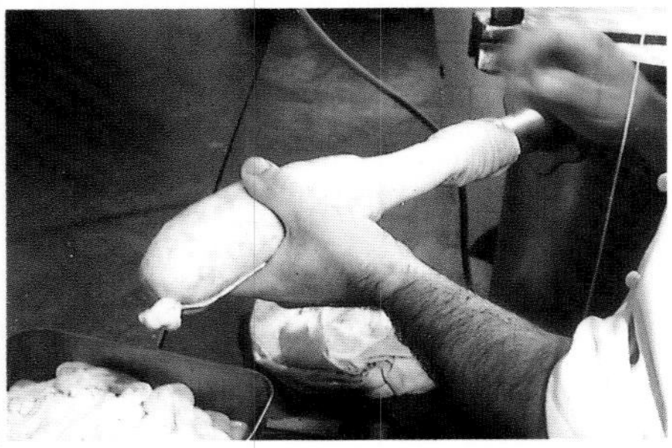

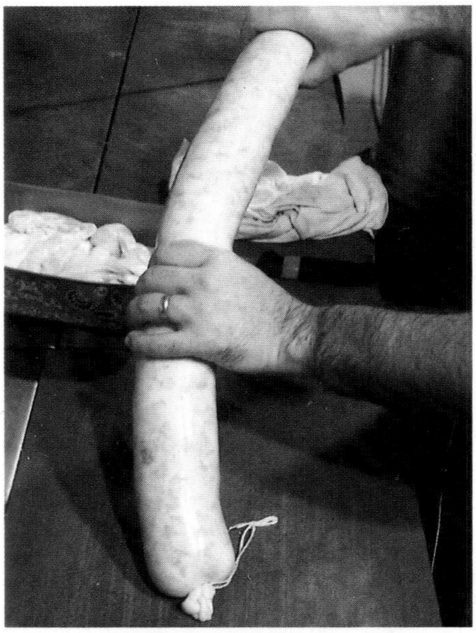

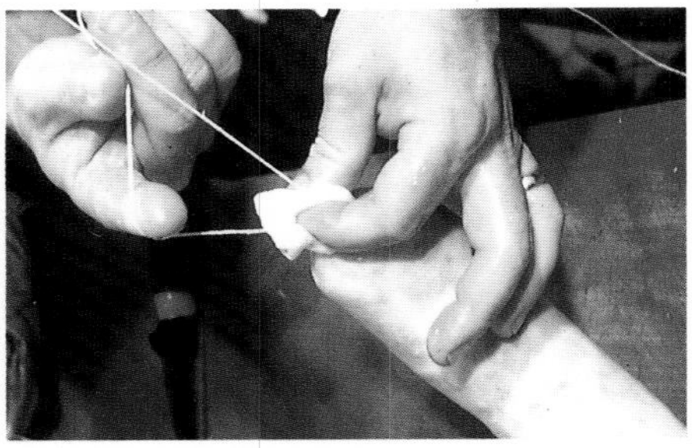

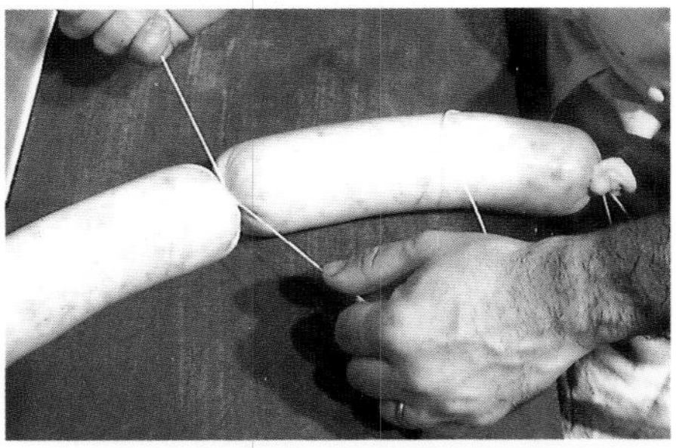

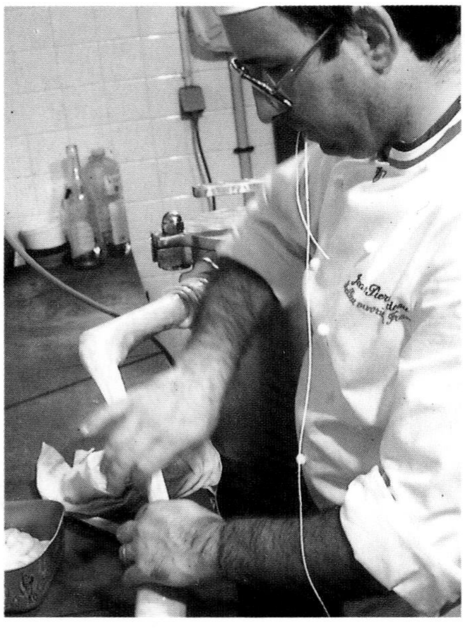

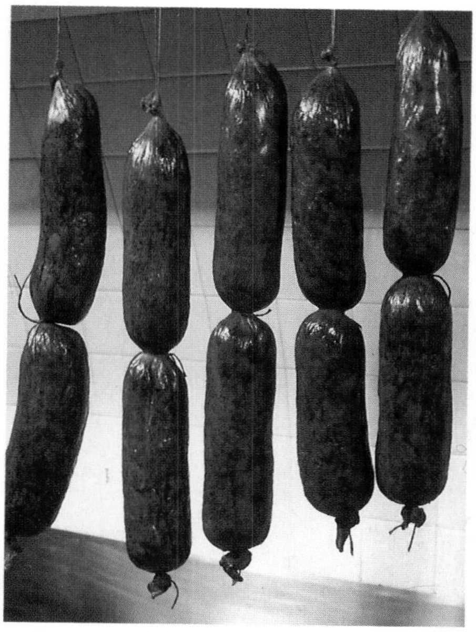

The smoking can be done overnight. The smoked sausages are smooth, completely dry and brick red in color.

### Cooking

The smoked sausages are poached in water with a bouquet garni and onion peels.

The onion peels flavor the water and also release a natural golden color which adds a nice tone to the andouilles.

The temperature of the liquid should never exceed 85 °C (185 F) so that the sausages do not burst.

The cooking time will depend on how large the sausages are. Generally they cook for 5-6 hours until the internal temperature is 85 °C (185 F).

The cooked sausages are carefully transferred to an ice bath.

When they are completely cooled the andouilles are hung to dry.

### Storage

As with all products that have been

smoked, andouilles will keep very well. In the refrigerator, the andouilles will keep for three weeks and even longer if they are placed in a vacuum pouch after being completely cooled and dried.

### Presentation

The andouilles are simply arranged neatly on platters. They can be sold sliced to be eaten cold with mustard or whole to be reheated with a dish of dried beans.

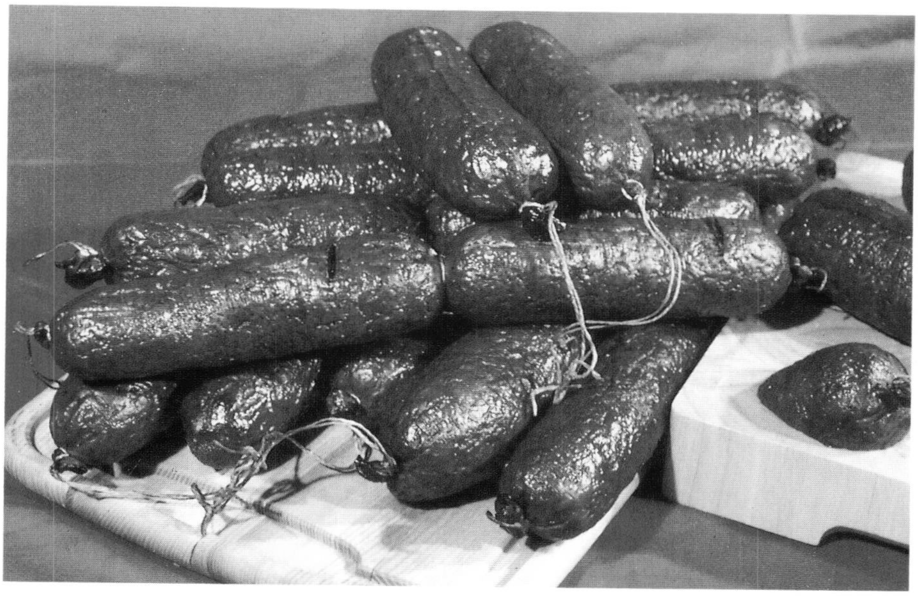

# Country-style " Andouillette "

**Introduction**

The essential difference between andouilles and andouillettes is the size. Andouillette is smaller than andouille; a single serving that is always served hot. It is usually grilled but can also be heated in the oven.

The seasonings differ as well and unlike the country-style andouille, this sausage is not smoked.

**Equipment**

Knives, horizontal chopper, stainless steel bowls and hotel pans, sausage stuffer, stock pot or jacketed kettle, casserole, skimmer, plastic scraper

**Ingredients**

*For 10 kg (22 lbs) of mixture*

6 kg (13 lbs) large intestine
2 kg (4.4 lbs) stomach (" panse ")
2 kg (4.4 lbs) pork jowl, trimmed
1 kg (2.2 lbs) onions, peeled
200 g (7 oz) strong mustard
250 ml (1 cup) wine vinegar
Parsley, chopped - Aromatic vegetables

*Seasonings (per kilo (2.2 lbs))*

35 g (generous 1 oz) fine salt
3 g (1/8 oz) pepper
1 g (1/32 oz) nutmeg
2.5 g (1/10) four spice powder

***The Seasonings***

Note that curing salt (sodium nitrite with fine salt) is not used for these products. Traditionally these products are not pink inside but are the natural pale grey color.

A rosy color would not be out of place if the chef chose to add sodium nitrite as a measure of security to retard bacterial growth.

Charcuterie products such as this that are made in advance and stored, transported and displayed in the shop undergo changes of temperature and are exposed to bacteria along the way. Sodium nitrite or ascorbic acid can guard against spoilage. The salt used here is " sel gris " a greyish salt with a pronounced flavor.

Also note that in France starch ingredients are not permitted in products made with intestines. However if the andouillettes are sold with a sauce for reheating at home, the sauce can be made with flour or other starch.

**Preparing the Ingredients**

The ingredients are the same as the country-style andouille but the proportions are different. Therefore the techniques for cleaning and blanching are exactly the same.

**Procedure**

The meats are chopped separately. The chilled pieces of pork jowl are chopped finely to a grain of about 4 mm (1/6 in).

The stomach, also chilled, is chopped a little more coarsely than the jowl (about 6 mm (1/4 in)). The " chaudin " is cut into large pieces. When making small quantities, this procedure can be done by hand.

The onion is chopped finely.

The chopped ingredients are transferred to a mixer where they are blended at slow speed until the mixture is homogeneous. This can be done by hand in a large bowl.

Stir the mustard into the vinegar to make it easier to incorporate into the mixture. Add the mustard/vinegar and the seasonings. Lastly add chopped parsley (quantity can vary according to taste).

Blend in these ingredients and transfer the mixture to a stainless steel hotel pan, cover and marinate in the refrigerator for 12 hours.

**Filling the Casings**

Transfer the marinated mixture to the sausage stuffer.

Cut the casings (" robe ") into sections about 20 cm (8 in) in length (which allows about 3 cm (about 1 in)) at both ends for closing.

Fill each casing then fold in the ends with the handle of a stainless steel spoon. The andouillette is now ready to be cooked (it is not smoked like the andouille).

Note that the marinating process can take place after the sausages are stuffed. Cover and refrigerate for 12 hours.

**Cooking**

Once the marinating is completed (before or after filling the casings) and the sausages are shaped with the ends secured, they are cooked immediately without being smoked.

The cooking liquid is pork aspic (see chapter 1) with an addition of aromatic vegetables (onions, carrots, celery and bouquet garni).

The liquid is maintained at a constant temperature of 85 °C (185 F) for about 3 hours. When the andouillettes are cooked they are very soft to the touch. The cooked andouillettes are gently transferred to a casserole. Using a wire cooking basket is practical because all the sausages can be re-

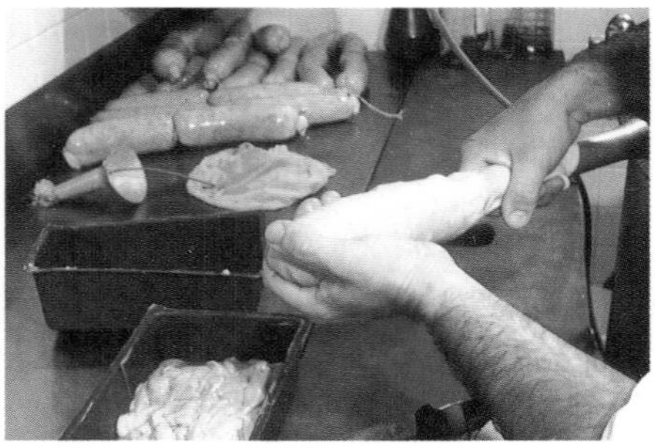

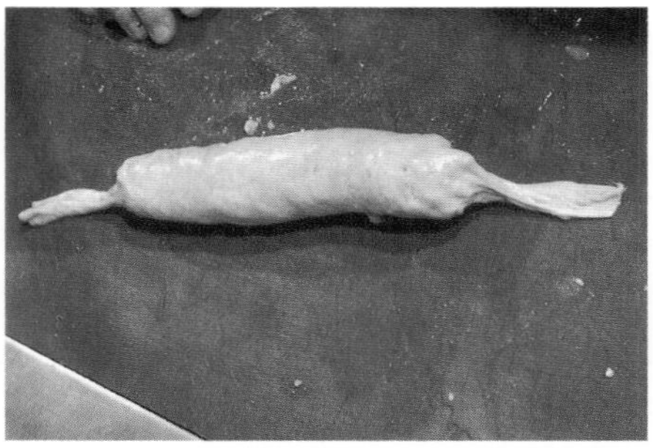

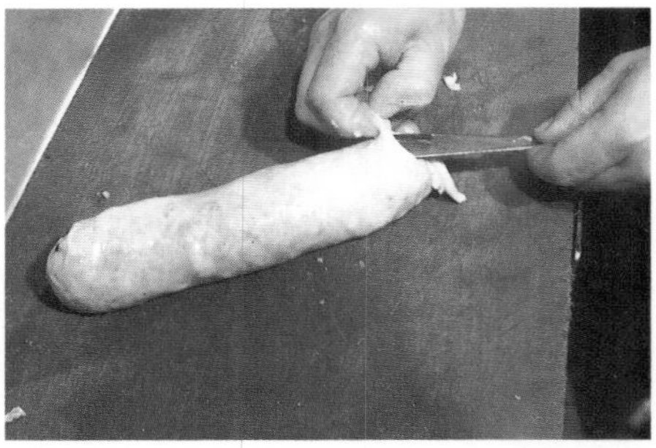

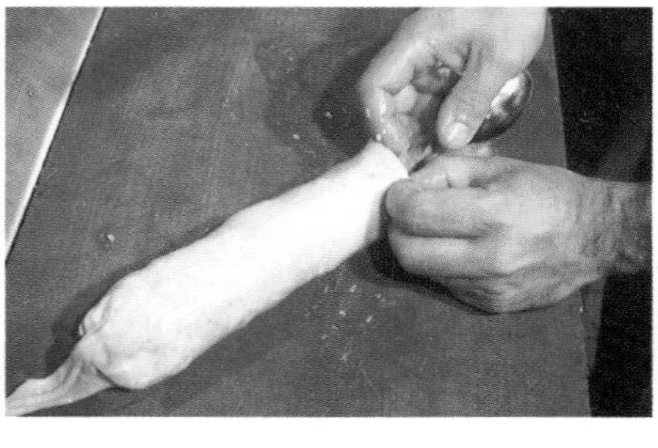

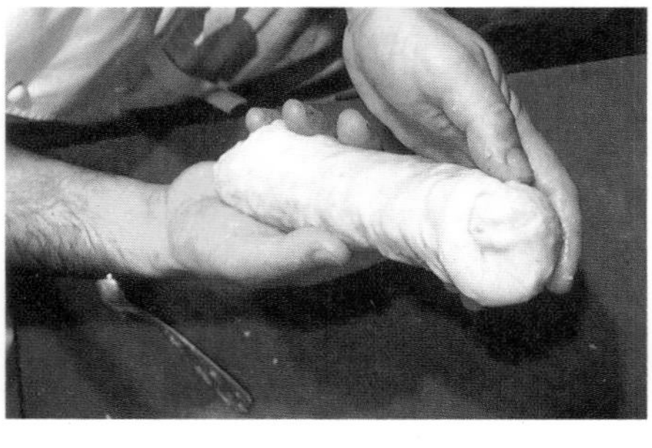

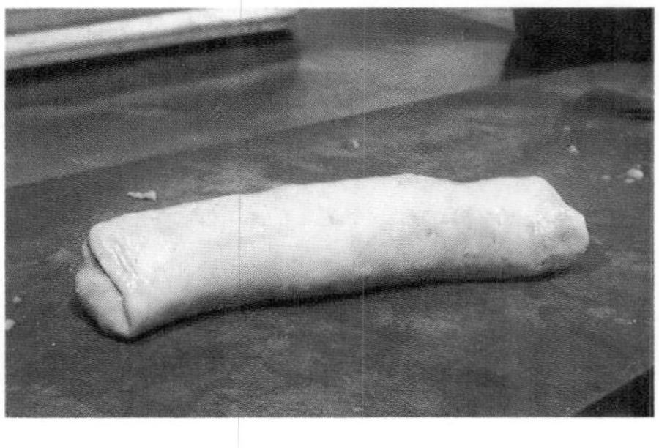

moved from the cooking liquid together.

Arrange the andouillettes neatly in the casserole with a stainless steel sheet between each layer. Bring the cooking liquid to a boil, skim and strain. Cover the sausages with the cooking liquid and cool as quickly as possible. (Special ventilated cooling chambers are available to do this.)

**Storage**

Covered with the cooking liquid, the andouillettes will keep up to two weeks in the refrigerator.

As the andouillettes are needed for display in the shop, lift them out carefully with a skimmer or tongs. Do not use your hands to remove the sausages as this could cause bacterial contamination. Keep the sausages covered but remove excess aspic as the sauages are removed.

**Presentation**

To present the andouillettes in the shop first rinse off the aspic that adheres to them with boiling water. Dry them and arrange neatly on platters.

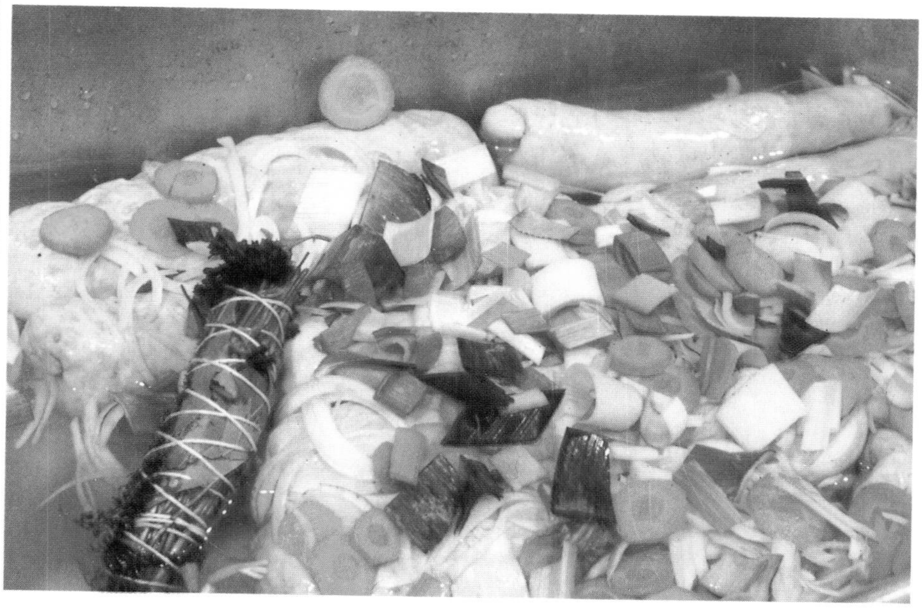

The sausages can also be coated with a thin layer of lard and rolled in dried herbs or breadcrumbs.

A nice idea is to display the andouillettes plain and coated to give the customer a choice.

This andouillette is grilled or heated in the oven and consumed hot. In France it is always served with mustard. They can be served with a variety of vegetables; purées, potatoes in any form, dried beans...

# " Andouille " from Vire

**Introduction**

This wonderful product from the city of Vire in Normandy is well known throughout France and beyond.

In Vire there is an official decree that protects the product and this sausage is also officially described in the " Code de la Charcuterie ".

The authentic product is made from the original recipe and fabricated within the city limits of Vire. The label reads " Véritable Andouille de Vire " or " Andouille de Vire Tradition ".

Charcutiers all over France make products that are inspired by the original recipe and are called simply " Andouille de Vire ". This is the version that we describe here.

**Equipment**

Knives, smoker, stock pot or kettle, stainless steel bowls and hotel pan

**Ingredients**

*For 10 kg (22 lbs) of mixture*

5 kg (11 lbs) " chaudin " (large intestine)

3 kg (6.6 lbs) " panse " (stomach)

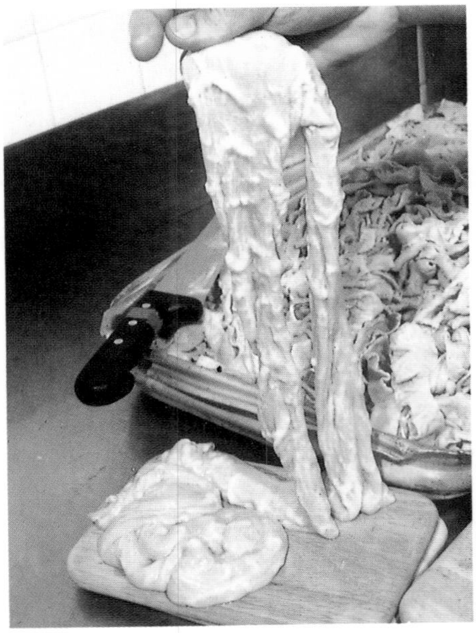

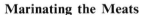

2 kg (4.4 lbs) pork jowl, trimmed
Large beef casing (" baudruche ")
Aromatic vegetables
Wine vinegar (aged)
*Seasonings (per kg (2.2 lbs) of mixture)*
35 g (generous 1 oz) fine salt
4 g (scant 1/6 oz) pepper
2 g (1/16 oz) four spice powder
1 g (1/32 oz) nutmeg

**Preparing the Ingredients**

The preparation of the ingredients is exactly the same as the previous recipes. The chitterlings are cleaned and blanched. The stomach is cooked for one hour and all elements are scraped to remove fat and mucous.

The procedure is completly different from the country-style sausages already described. All of the elements are fashioned into long " ropes ".

To cut the pork jowl into long strips, begin by slicing about 6-7 mm (1/4 in) thick (like barding fat). Cut each slice into strips (6 mm (1/4 in) across) but do not cut through the end, alternating as shown to obtain a continuous strip from each slice.

The cooked stomach is cut in the same way. Finally the intestines (blanched and cooled) are split lengthwise to make strips about 1 cm (3/8 in) across.

**Marinating the Meats**

Season each element separately with the corresponding amounts of spices. Toss each one with your hands to coat the ingredient evenly with the seasonings without tearing the strips.

**Shaping the Andouilles**

This can only be done by hand.

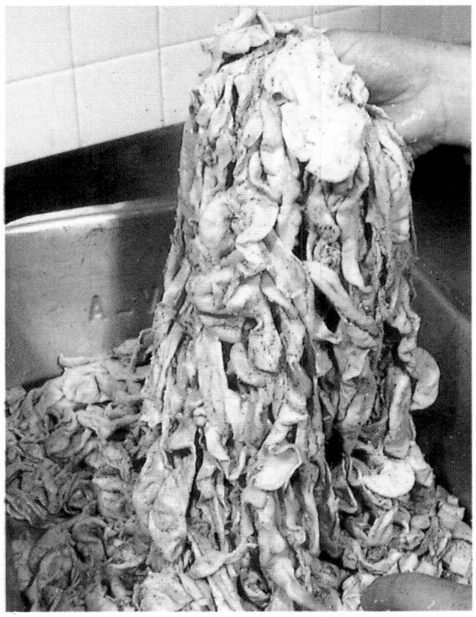

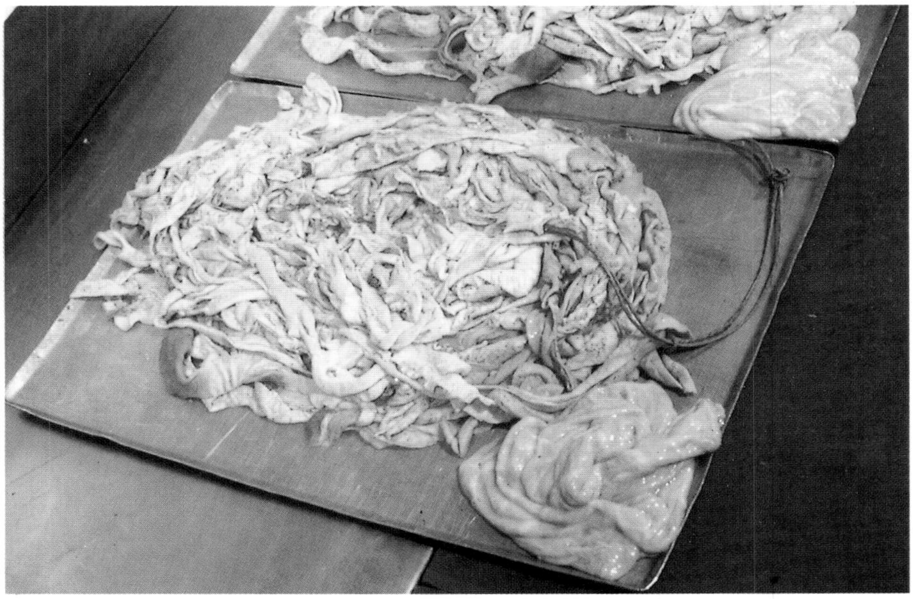

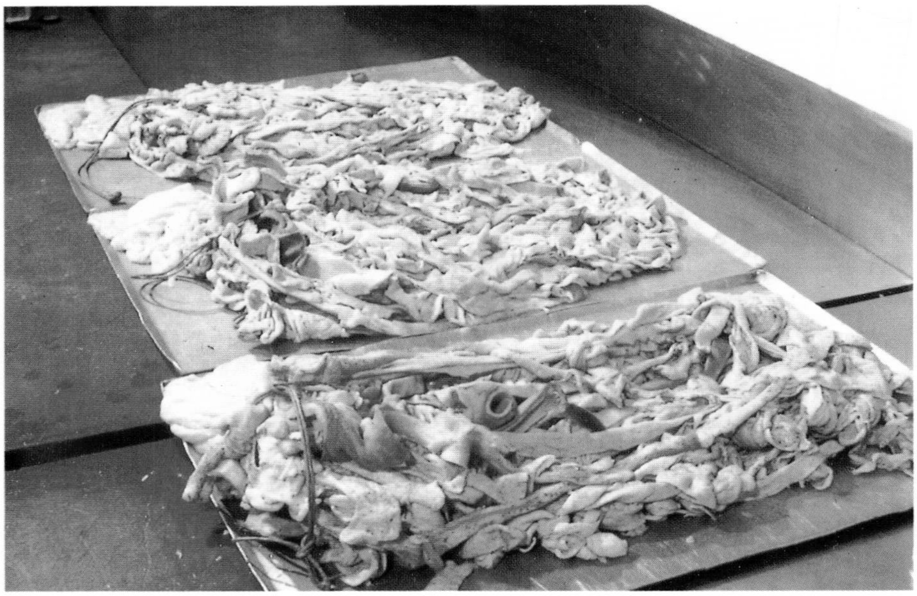

To form each sausage, take some of each element, respecting the following proportions: 50% intestine, 30% stomach, 20% pork jowl.

Each sausage should contain enough of each ingredient to form a coiled hank with a diameter of about 10-12 cm (4-5 in).

Tie one end of the hank with string to facilitate the stuffing process.

The casing is a " baudruche " or large beef casing (beef bung) which must be soaked in water with a little vinegar to rinse it and make it elastic and supple. The coiled meats are pulled into the casings. The string is used to later hang the sausages during the drying process (étuvage) which lasts 6-8 hours.

**Smoking**

The andouilles are " cold smoked " at 30-35 °C (85-95 F). Smoke over sawdust (non resin) overnight. The smoked sausage will be a lovely deep golden brown and the skin will be very dry but still supple. Tie the ends tightly and tie a string around the sausage, crossing the string to compress the meats. The casing should be slightly stretched by the string.

**Cooking**

The andouilles are cooked in water with aromatic vegetables (with a

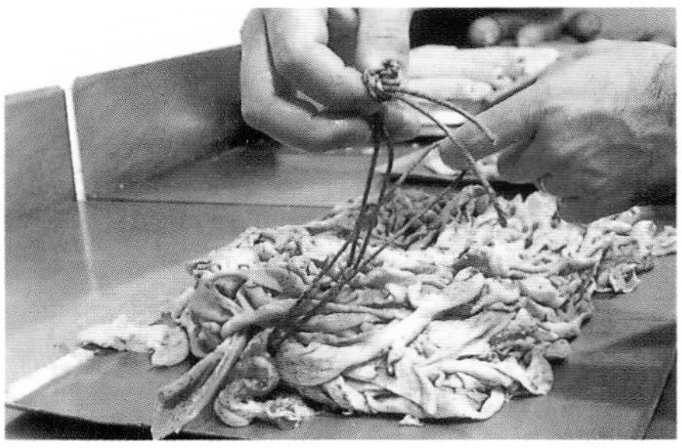

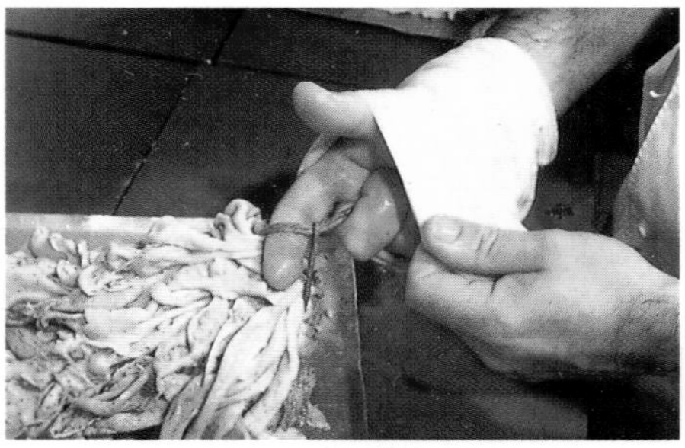

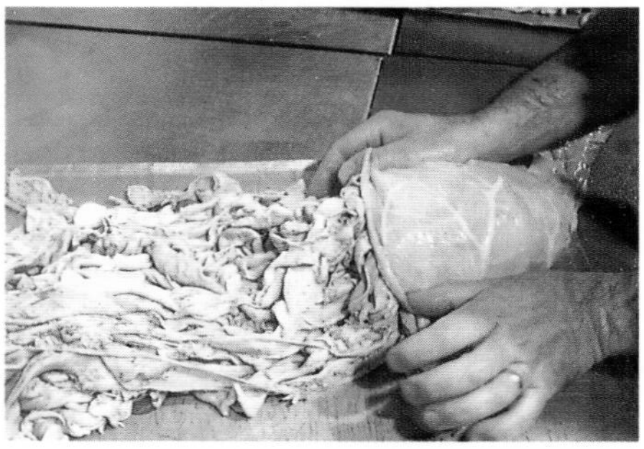

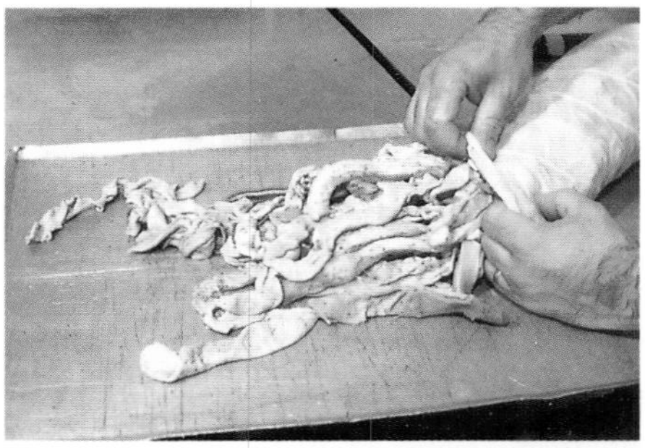

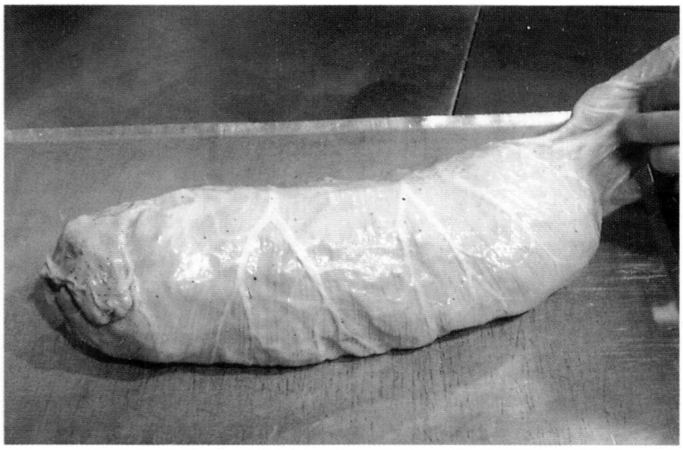

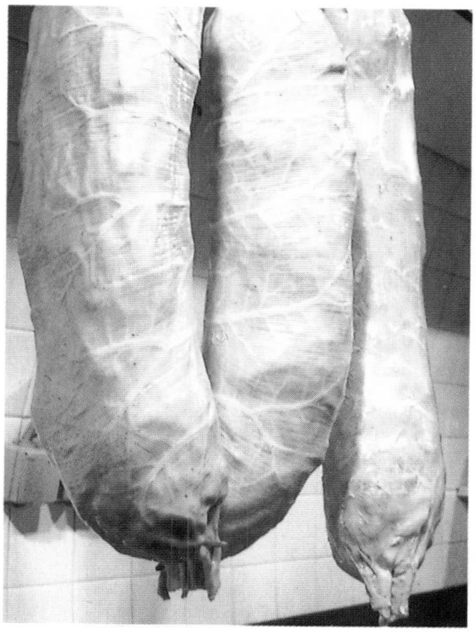

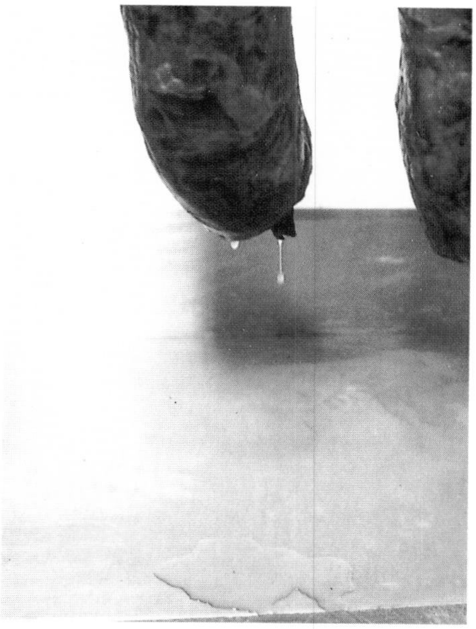
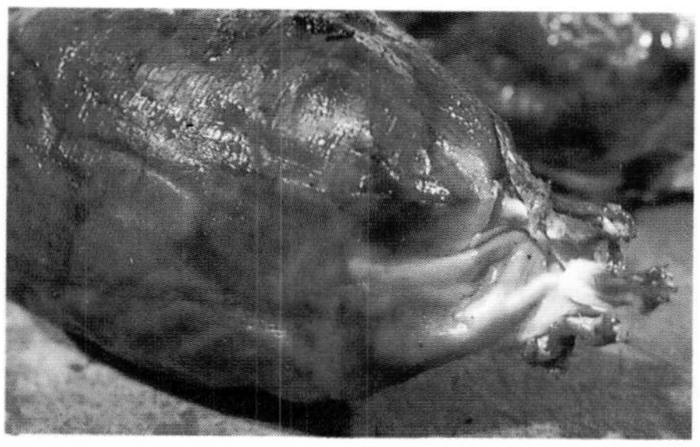
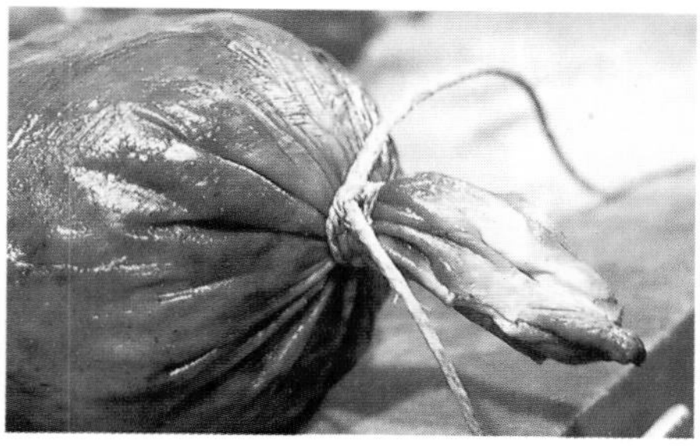
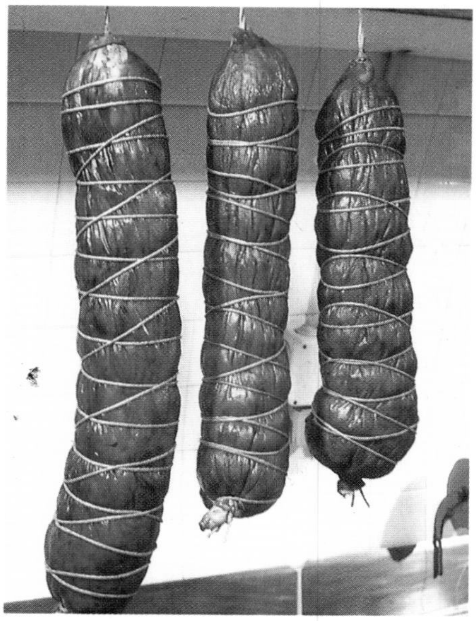

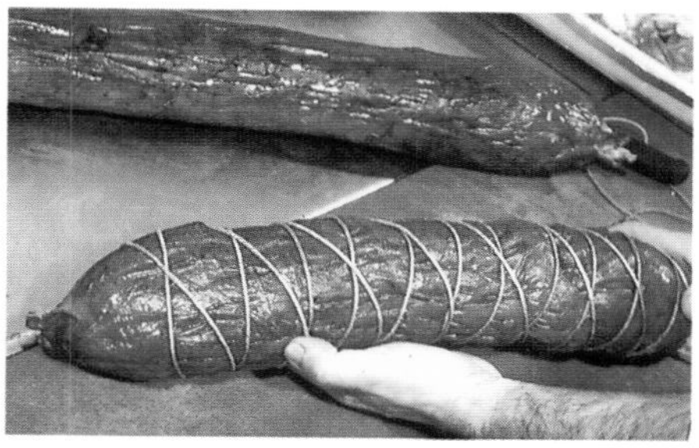

good quantity of onion peelings (which provide color and flavor).

Bring the temperature of the liquid to 85 °C (185 F) and maintain the heat for about 6 hours. The cooking time depends on the size of the andouilles.

**Storage and Presentation**

Due to the long smoking and thorough cooking the andouille from Vire will keep for several weeks. To prolong storage, the sausage, cooled in the refrigerator for 48 hours, can be placed in a vacuum pouch.

The andouille from Vire is eaten cold, sliced thin. The characteristic marbled appearance of the cross section is attractive.

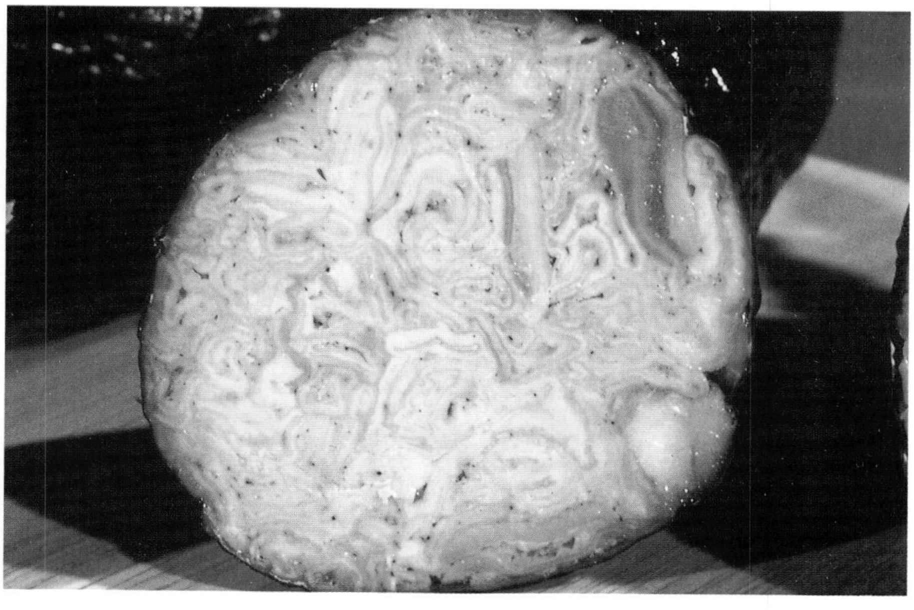

# " Andouillette " from Troyes

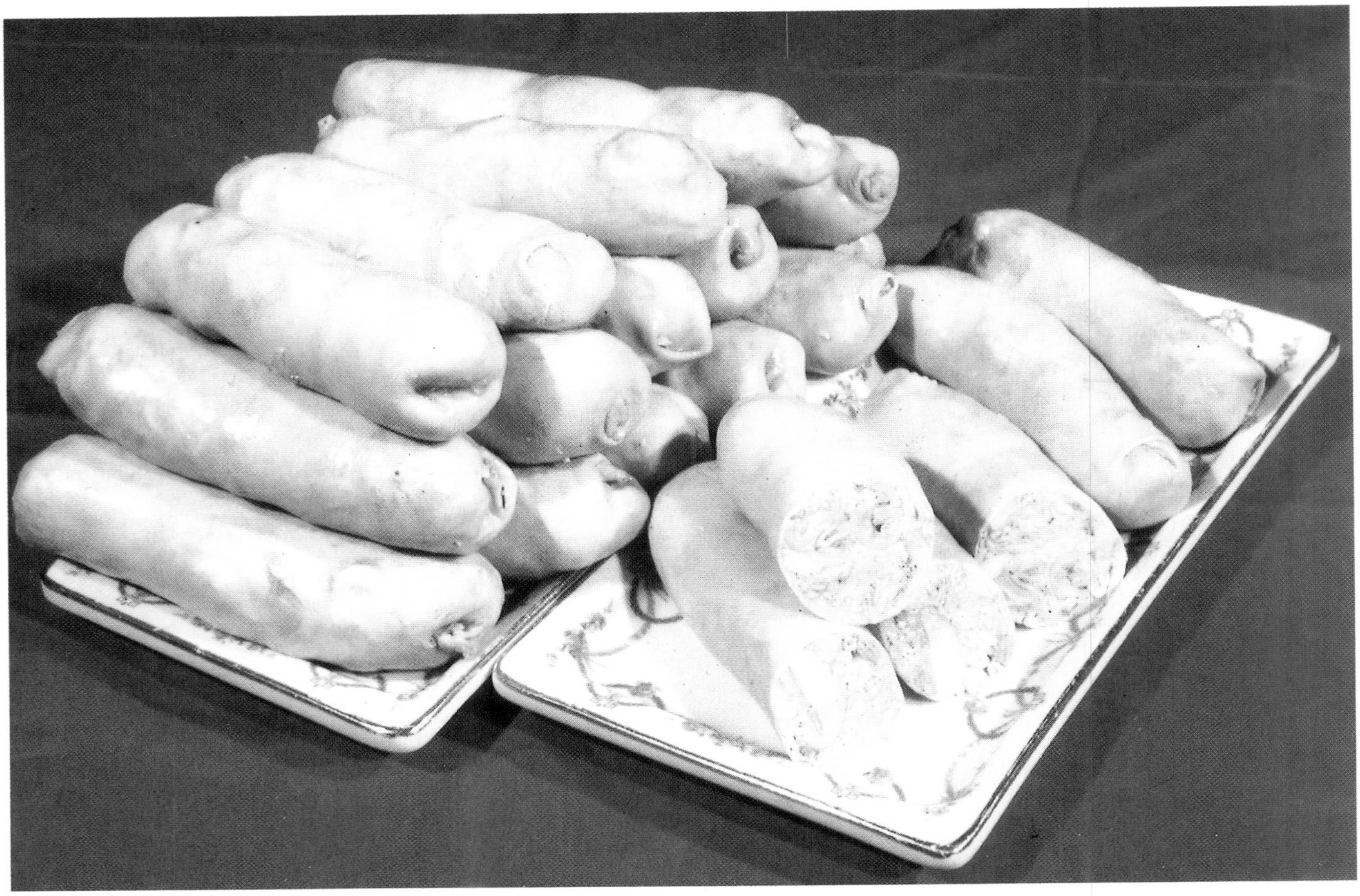

**Introduction**

The andouillette from Troyes, a city in eastern France, is one of the most popular of all French products made with chitterlings.

This andouillette is an individual portion like the country-style andouillette previously described. The procedure however is similar to the andouille from Vire.

The intestine, stomach and pork jowl are coiled into hanks and stuffed in casings made from the " robe " (a portion of the large intestine).

To achieve just the right texture, the meats are prepared by hand which justifies the high price.

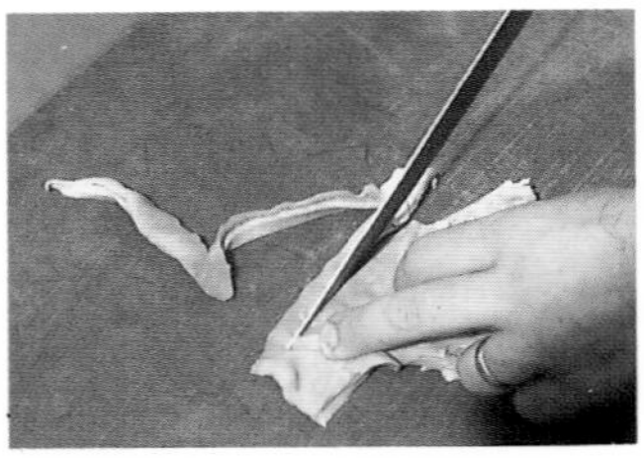

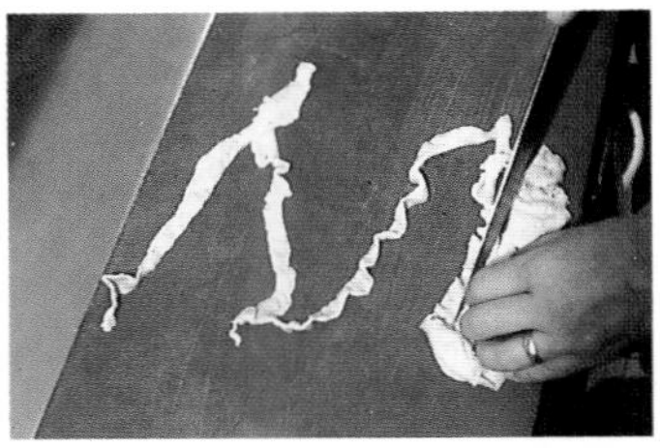

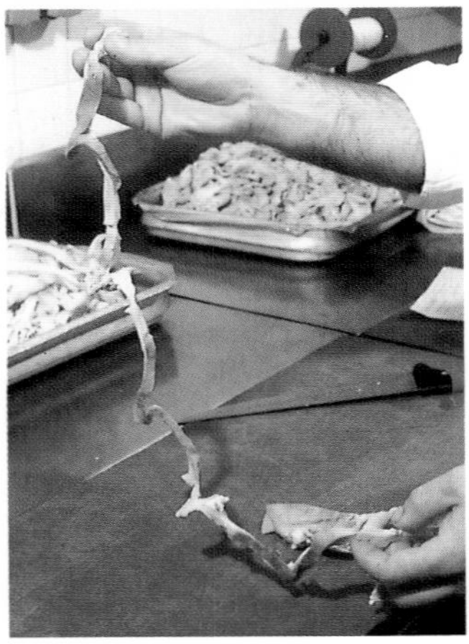

**Equipment**

Knives, stainless steel bowls and hotel pan, casserole, skimmer, plastic scraper

**Ingredients**

*For 10 kg (22 lbs) of mixture*

6 kg (13 lbs) large intestine (" chaudin ")
3.5 kg (7.7 lbs) stomach (" panse ")
500 g (1 lb) pork jowl, trimmed

*Note* that the French Charcuterie Code limits the amount of pork jowl to 5% and the " chaudin " cannot be less than 50%.

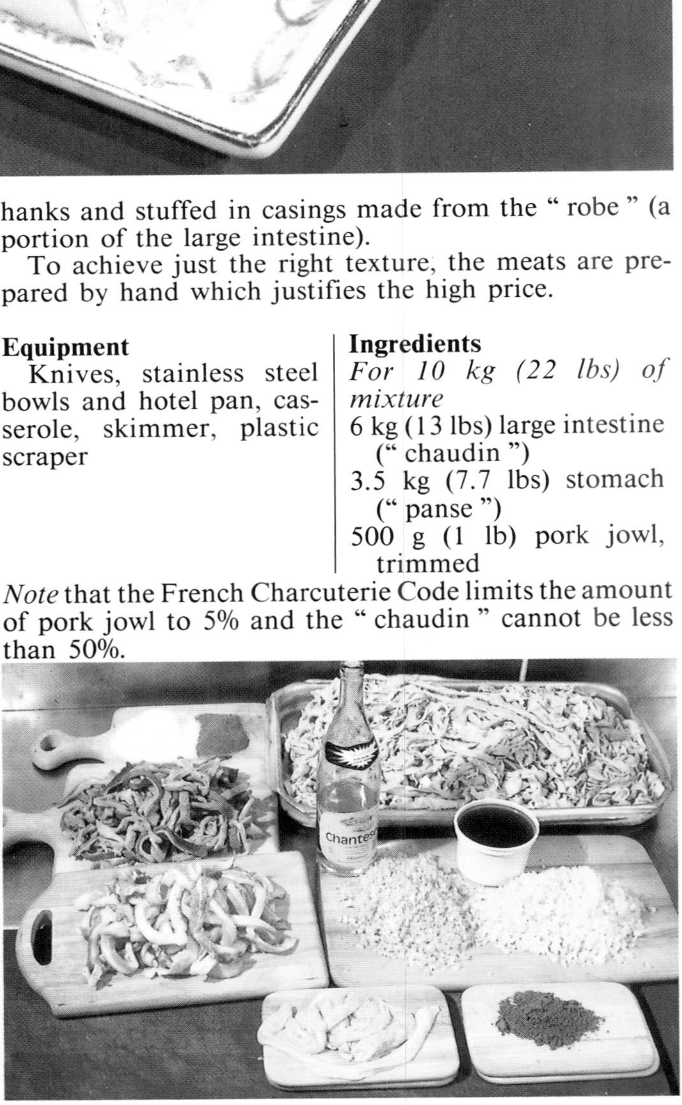

*Seasonings (per kilo (2.2 lbs))*
35 g (generous 1 oz) fine salt
4 g (scant 1/6 oz) pepper
2 g (1/16 oz) four spice powder
50 g (1 3/4 oz) onions, chopped
50 g (1 3/4 oz) shallots, chopped
500 ml (2 cups) white wine vinegar
500 ml (2 cups) dry white wine
30 g (1 oz) strong mustard

**Preparing the Ingredients**

The preparation of all the meats is exactly the same as described in the recipe for country-style andouilles. The elements are cleaned, blanched and scraped. The stomach is also cooked for one hour.

The onion is chopped slightly more coarsely than the shallots. Note that the " chopping " is actually slicing and cutting into neat dice. The chopped onions and shallots are tossed together.

Mix the spices together to blend.

Stir the mustard into the wine and vinegar to make it easier to spread evenly on the meats.

**Procedure**

The " chaudin ", stomach and pork jowl is cut into long " ropes " like for the andouille from Vire.

Each hank is coiled by hand. As each sausage is assembled, verify that the proportion of each element meets the estimated percentage of 60% for the intestine, 35% for the stomach and 5% for the pork jowl.

Cut the end of each hank and arrange them on the work surface in neat rows with no space between with the cut ends away from you.

Sprinkle evenly with the spices, vinegar/mustard and onions/shallots.

All the andouillettes should be evenly coated with all of the seasonings.

Prepare the casings as described in the recipe for country-style andouillette.

Cut them in lengths about 5 cm (2 in) longer than the hanks.

**Filling the Casings**

This operation should be done quickly and demands practice and dexterity.

Tie a string through the uncut end of each hank.

Twist each hank to give it a cylindrical form.

Turn the casing inside out and hold it open with the forefinger and thumb.

Take the end of the string and pull the hank into the casing, turning it rightside out as the intestines fill the casing. Carefully pull out the string without disturbing the filling.

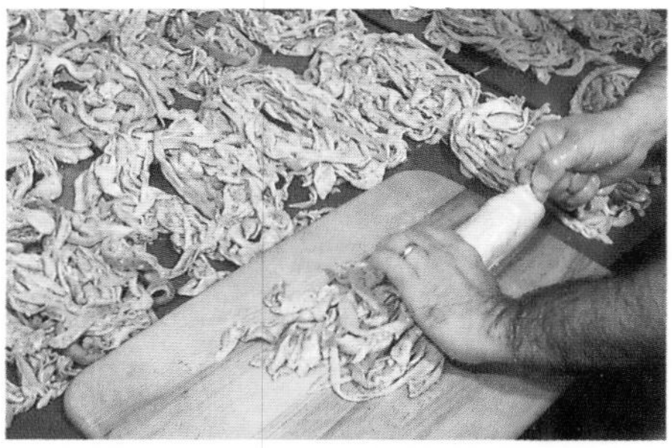

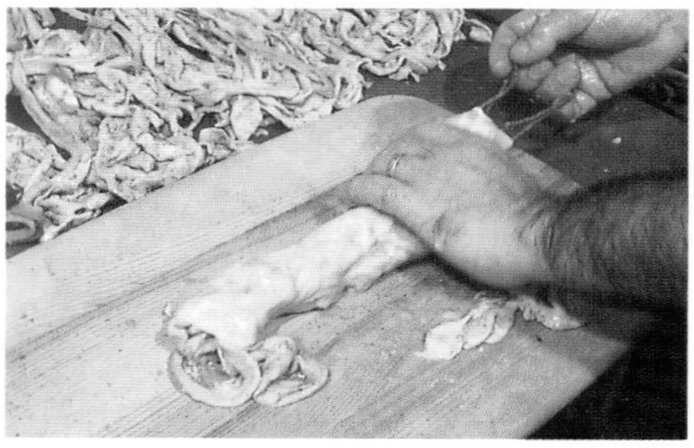

Tuck the ends of the casing in with your fingertips or the handle of a spoon.

Arrange the andouillettes side by side in a casserole.

Use a plastic scraper to scoop up the spices and liquid on the work surface and sprinkle over the sausages.

Cover the recipient and marinate in the refrigerator for 24 hours.

The hanks can also be marinated before they are stuffed into the casing.

Place the tied hanks into the casserole and coat evenly with the seasonings.

Place a sheet of plastic wrap between each layer to trap the marinade which tends to settle to the bottom (an inconvenience of this method.)

After 24 hours, the marinated hanks are stuffed into the casings following the same method.

**Cooking**

The andouillettes are cooked in the same casserole that they were marinated in.

Cover the sausages with unsalted water.

The best method is to cook them in a steamer (vents closed).

They are cooked very slowly at 80-82 °C (175-180 F) for 10-12 hours.

Cooking in a casserole with a small amount of water results in a moister product and higher yield than cooking in a kettle of salted water with aromatic vegetables.

Transfer the cooked sausages to a clean casserole and bring the cooking liquid to a boil, skim and strain over the sausages. Cool as quickly as possible, using a well-ventilated " cooling chamber " if available.

Skimming the fat form the cooking liquid is very important. All fats are very efficient insulators.

A layer of fat on the surface would trap heat inside and prevent the liquid from cooling.

Bacteria multiplies most quickly between 15-40 °C (60-105 F). All cooked preparations that are sold cold must pass through the " danger zone " as quickly as possible.

**Storage**

Covered with the liquid, the andouillettes will keep in the refrigerator for 10-12 days.

It is important to use a skimmer or tongs to gently remove them from the liquid; do not use your hands.

Rinse the andouillettes and dry to present them for sale.

**Presentation**

These andouillettes are usually arranged on platters and displayed " as is ".

However if the charcutier would like to offer some variety there are several possibilities.

• Rub a little lard on the outside and roll the andouillettes in breadcrumbs or dried herbs.

• Brush on a coat of aspic which has been chilled to thicken it slightly. This will keep the sausages from drying out.

• The andouillette can also be sold in vacuum pouches. This method facilitates transport and handling.

Andouillettes from Troyes are served hot; grilled, pan-fried, heated in the oven or even cut into pieces and made into brochettes.

They go well with many vegetables; mashed potatoes, lentils, peas, dried beans. Mustard from Dijon is a classic accompaniment.

# Chapter 4

# Pâtés and Terrines made with Liver

## A long-term culinary tradition

*This chapter presents one of the most important products of the French charcutier-caterer.*

*The common denominator in all these preparations is liver, the largest organ of the digestive system.*

*It is a complex chemical factory, serving as a filter to separate, organize, direct and store the nutrients that nourish the body.*

*Liver based pâtés and terrines are traditional and new; they have been made since ancient times and the modern charcutier offers classic products as well as creations featuring a variety of ingredients.*

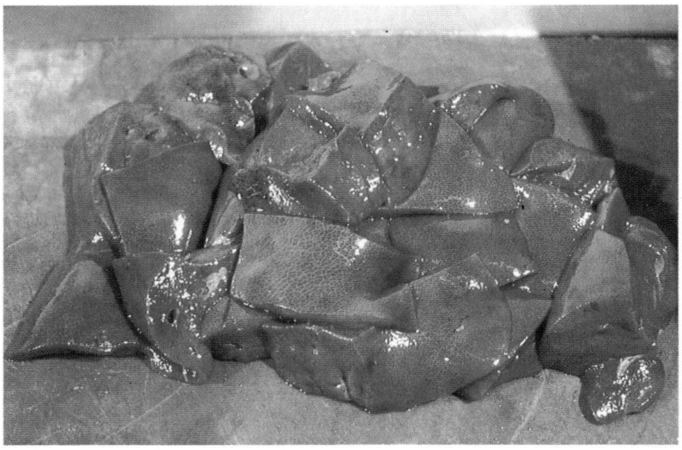

# Introduction

The art of pâté making can be traced back to the Greeks and Romans. In France until the Middle Ages only cooks could prepare and sell meat. In the 15th century a group emerged called the " chair-cuitiers " (cookers of meat) which received royal consent to prepare meat for sale to the general public.

The proud descendents of these meat cooks of the Middle Ages are the charcutiers-caterers of today who have become an important part of French gastronomy.

**Pâté or Terrine?**

Alas, what is the difference between a pâté and a terrine?

Pâté actually means " wrapped in pastry " (" pâte " means pastry or dough) so to be true to its name a pâté should always be contained within a crust of some kind and the term " pâté en croûte " is redundant.

The terrine takes its name from the earthenware (" terre cuit " or terra cotta) mold that it is cooked in.

Therefore in principle distinguishing between the two is easy:

- A pâté is a preparation cooked in a crust.
- A terrine is a preparation cooked directly in a mold.

The two terms are often used interchangeably and are thought to be the same thing.

Even the French Charcuterie Code does not make a clear distinction between pâté and terrine.

According to the " Code ", pâté is considered to be the term that includes all the ground meat products, divided into categories:

- Pâtés for slicing
- " Crèmes ", mousses and spreadable pâtés
- Galantines
- Pâtés " en croûte " (in pastry) and " friands "

Terrine is defined as " the best recipient in which to cook ground meat preparations in the oven ".

The Code goes on to describe terrine as " pâté cooked in the oven " and " pâté of superior quality ". The definition of terrine goes on to include " numerous preparations made with meat and also fish and shellfish and vegetables. The terrine can be made of one major ingredient or a combination. Therefore a terrine is a superior quality product which can be made from a variety of ingredients. "

All of the terrines in this series, based on liver or not, follow the guidelines set forth by the Charcuterie Code. In abiding to the regulations, which are established to protect the work of the artisan charcutier, the terrines are assembled in molds. Therefore:

- the terrine is the product in the mold.
- a mold is used to assemble all terrines.

This chapter on liver-based pâtés and terrines covers the range from the most classic (liver pâté (" pâté de foie ")) to sophisticated (roquefort pâté). The modern selections offer new combinations that are interesting without being outlandish.

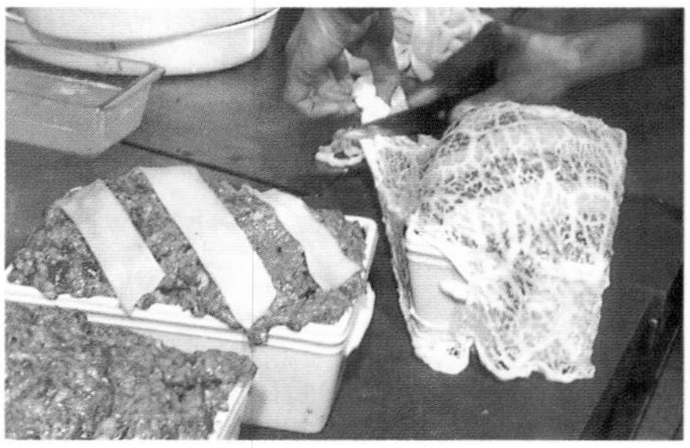

The classic liver pâté and the country pâté, were the " bread and butter " of the business in the first half of this century when they were consumed in large quantities by the working class. The manual laborer of yesteryear worked long hard hours and needed inexpensive high calorie foods.

Due to the recent campaign against fat consumption, the demand has dropped for these products and some charcutiers have adapted their recipes to conform to the new tastes of consumers.

But we advise the charcutier of today to remain calm despite the reports. The media often blow information out of proportion and the medical findings are always under constant research. Small recipe adjustments can be made without changing products completely.

The great French doctor Claude Bernard (1813-1878) spoke words of wisdom for all ages: " Everything is harmful and nothing is harmful, one should avoid excess. ".

The most important goal is to use the freshest, best quality ingredients possible to make products that are nutritious as well as delicious. This is a principle that we believe in very strongly and is stressed throughout this series. We hope that the readers of these volumes realize the importance as well.

*Note:* The French have long realized that a small portion of a highly flavorful dish is preferable to large portions of tasteless food, which in part explains why relatively rich foods remain a part of their diet. They are not among the overweight and the rate of heart disease is surprisingly low in France.

Our selection is based on products that appeal to the senses of sight, smell, feel and taste:

- ***The visual aspect*** of the dish triggers the first reaction and makes the consumer want to taste it.

- ***Odor*** is the second stimulus. The smell of a well-seasoned terrine certainly makes the dish more desirable.

- ***Taste*** is the most important sense to be satisfied. Working hand in hand with smell, the taste buds transmit messages of pleasure to the brain.

- ***Touch*** plays a lesser role, however the texture of the dish should not be overlooked and certainly contributes to the aspect as well as the taste.

This leads to the probing question " Do we eat to live or live to eat " The answer is a balance of the two as is true with so many situations in life.

**Classic liver pâté (p. 98)**

**Country pâté (p. 102)**

**Pâté " Grand-mère " (p. 107)**

**Country terrine with prunes (p. 112)**

**Chicken liver mousse (p. 116)**

**Duck " moussette " with morels (p. 120)**

**Rustic pâté with three peppers (p. 124)**

**Chicken liver pâté " Périgourdine " (p. 128)**

**Liver pâté with Roquefort (p. 132)**

**Venison liver pâté (p. 136)**

# Classic Liver Pâté

Classic liver pâté is an emulsified mixture of pork liver and fat. The meat proteins and eggs act to stabilize the emulsion.

**Equipment**

Horizontal chopper (fixed or rotating bowl), large mixing bowl, terrine mold, strainer, paring knife, thermometer

**Ingredients**

*For 10 kg (22 lbs)*

***Main Ingredients***

2.5 kg (5.5 lbs) pork liver
4.5 kg (10 lbs) soft pork fat
500 g (1 lb) egg whites or whole eggs
2.5 L (2.5 qt) whole milk
200 g (7 oz) onions
50 g (1 1/2 oz) garlic

***Seasonings***

42 g (scant 1 1/2 oz) curing salt (salt blended with sodium nitrite)
75 g (2 1/2 oz) fine salt
10 g (1/3 oz) white pepper
5 g (1/6 oz) chili powder (Jamaican)
5 g (1/6 oz) four spice powder
50 g (1 1/2 oz) mild paprika
10 g (1/3 oz) rosemary

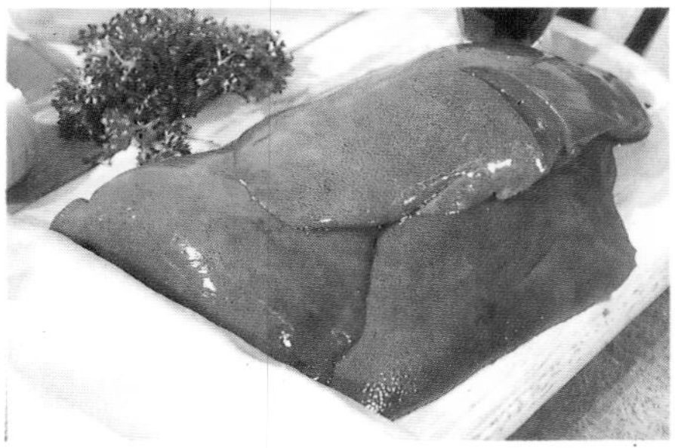

**Preparing the Ingredients**

***The Pork Liver***

It is of the utmost importance to select a top quality, perfectly fresh liver. Not only does the taste depend on it but the emulsion will not be successful if the liver is not fresh.

The mediocre taste of a second-rate liver that has been stored for several days after slaughter demands extra seasonings to compensate for the loss of flavor.

Remove the skin, nerves and vessels. Rinse the liver then sponge dry with paper towels.

Cut the trimmed liver into even-sized pieces, coat evenly with the curing salt, cover and refrigerate for 12-24 hours.

***The Fat***

The fat that is recommended for this recipe is " gras de mouille " which includes the fat from the shoulder, the ham, and the belly. Softer than fatback, it is moist yet does not melt easily.

***The Onions and Garlic***

Slice the onions thinly then cook in goose fat until soft but not browned. Set aside to cool.

Onions should never be used uncooked. Raw onions will ferment in the mixture and cause spoilage.

Remove the green sprout from the garlic (which is bitter) and poach or cook in fat so that it does not ferment.

**Procedure**

***Classic Method***

It is very important that the blades of the chopper be well-sharpened.

In the bowl of the chopper, place the seasoned liver, the fine salt and spices, the cooked onions and garlic (green sprout removed). Warm the milk and maintain at 60 °C (147 F) until ready to use.

Process these ingredients, without overheating, until the mixture is homogeneous, smooth and creamy. Tiny bubbles will be visible on the surface.

With the bowl turning slowly, add the egg whites or whole eggs and blend until incorporated.

Add the warm (60 °C (147 F)) poached fat and process until the mixture is very smooth and soft with no lumps at all.

Add the warmed milk and process until incorporated.

It is recommended to verify the temperatures with a thermometer:

- Liver and seasonings: 5-8 °C (45 F)
- Poached fat: 80 °C (175 F) when just poached; 60 °C (147 F) when added to the mixture
- Mixture in chopper: 50-55 °C (122-125 F)
- Milk: 50-55 °C (122-125 F)

Scrape down the sides of the chopper bowl and process a little more to blend perfectly.

Fill the molds immediately. Line the terrine with a thin sheet of barding fat or coat the sides and bottom with lard. Ladle the mixture gently to fill the mold.

***The Modern Method***

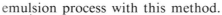

The guidelines for this method are the same as the previous method but the ingredients are added in a different order. The liver and the eggs do not play main roles in the emulsion process with this method.

Cut and season the liver as in the previous method, then process it with the eggs, onions and garlic until the mixture is very smooth and homogeneous. Note that the onions and garlic have been cooked in advance in goose fat and cooled.

Transfer to a stainless steel bowl, cover and refrigerate for 12-24 hours.

Just before finishing the mixture, poach the salted fat in milk, water or stock and keep it warm (50 °C (147 F)).

Warm the bowl of the chopper then process the fat with the warmed milk and herbs. When the fat mixture is smooth add the puréed pork liver (5-8 °C (45 F)).

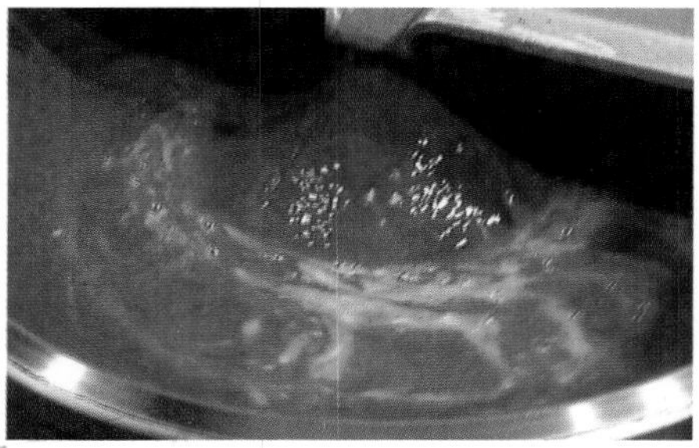

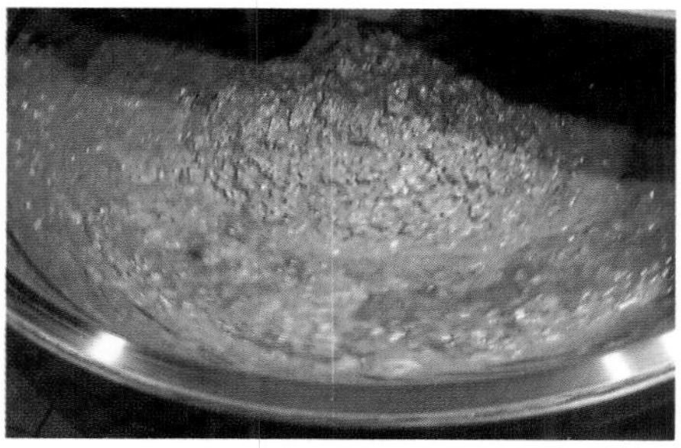

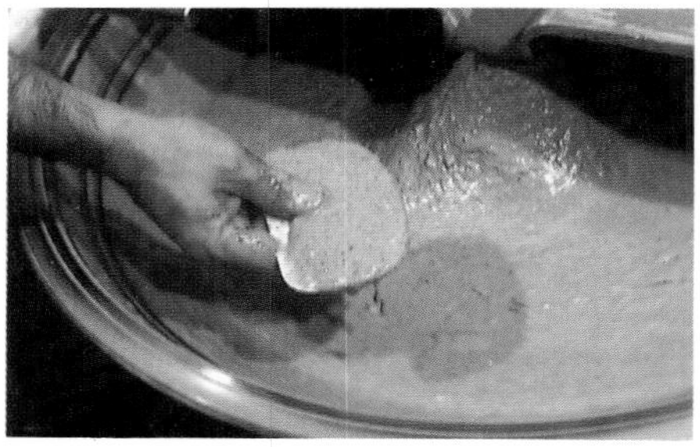

This procedure should result in a a very smooth, fine-textured

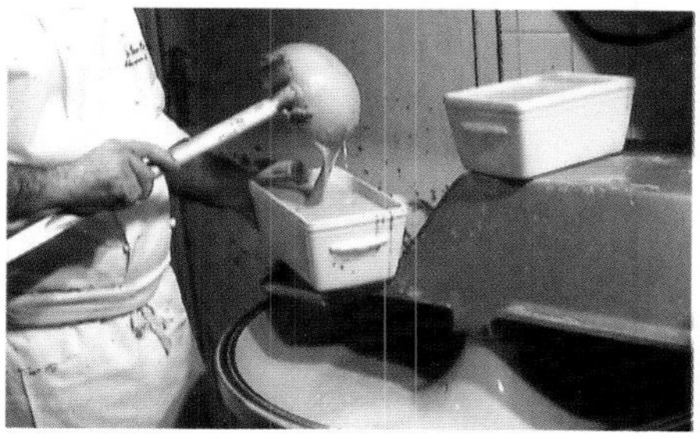

mixture that is perfectly homogeneous. Ladle the mixture immediately into prepared molds and cook right away.

*Note:* It is vital to stress the importance of cooking the vegetables (onions and garlic) in advance. Vegetables do not cook thoroughly until they reach a temperature of 90-100 °C (195-212 F). This liver pâté is cooked until the internal temperature is 72 °C (160 F) maximum.

Since onions and garlic added raw to the mixture would not completely cook they would ferment and also darken, making gray spots in each slice. The charcutier needs only to make one batch with raw onions and another with cooked onions and compare the results and be convinced that this step is obligatory for all charcuterie products.

**Cooking**

Set a branch of rosemary or other herb of choice on the top of the pâté (it is recommended to dip the herb in boiling water or steam it to sterilize). The aromatic herb will perfume the whole terrine.

Place the terrine in a water bath and put it into a 150 °C (275 F) oven to brown the top a little. Place the cover on the mold, turn the oven down to 95-100 °C (200 F) and cook until the internal temperature is 72 °C (160 F). (An electric probe thermometer enables the chef to monitor the temperature without opening the oven door.) A little fat will melt and form a layer on the top which will serve to keep the terrine fresh when cooled.

**Cooling**

Remove the cooked terrine from the oven and pour over a little full-flavored stock flavored with port or madeira.

Cool quickly then cover and refrigerate for at least 24 hours. To present the pâté, scrape any fat that has collected on the top, decorate and coat with a thin layer of aspic.

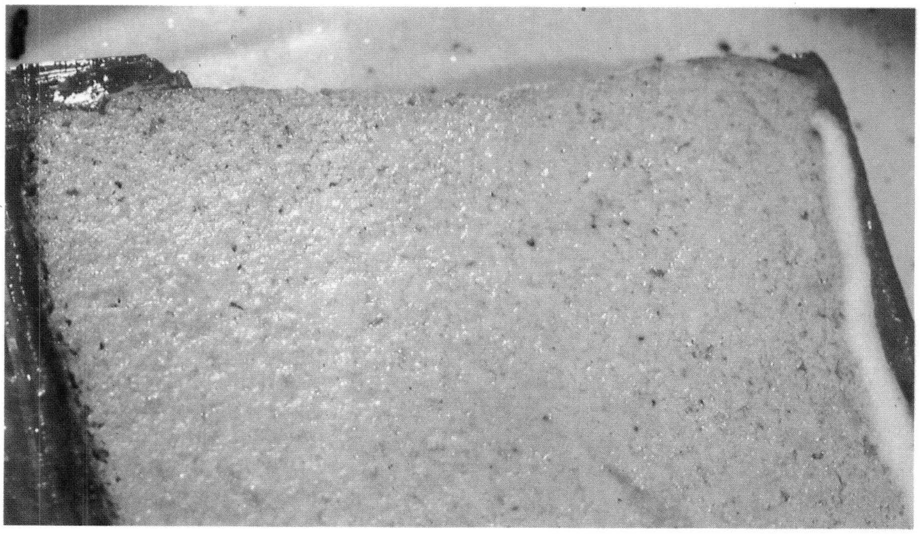

# Country Pâté

**Introduction**

The definition of a " pâté de campagne " in the French Charcuterie Code indicates that it is " a pure pork mixture of lean fat, pork jowl and the following variety meats: liver, heart, edible portions of the head and sometimes kidneys ".

The name given to this rustic pâté goes back many years and the origin is not known.

The Code specifies that the terms " pâté de ferme " or pâté fermier " (farm-made pâté) are not permitted. The label of a country pâté may indicate " recette fermière " (farm recipe) if certain standards are met (no polyphosphates).

The pâté described here is a coarsely ground mixture bound with eggs with an addition of milk and red wine. The technique involved is

known as "Parisienne" (not included in the Code) which incorporates 30% pork liver to bind the mixture.

It is cooked in a well greased earthenware terrine with strips of barding fat and caul fat on the top. The cooking is done slowly to fully develop the flavors.

Each year in Briare in the Loire region a competition is held to promote this well-loved product, a cornerstone of French charcuterie.

**Equipment**

Meat grinder or horizontal chopper, plastic scraper, stainless steel bowls, earthenware terrine, strainer, knives, probe thermometer, conical strainer, casserole, mixer.

**Ingredients**

***" Parisienne Method "***

3 kg (6.6 lbs) pork belly
2.5 kg (5.5 lbs) pork jowl
3 kg (6.6 lbs) pork liver
600 g (1 lb 3 1/2 oz) eggs
200 ml (scant cup) red wine
700 ml (scant 3 cups) milk

***Seasonings***

150 g (5 oz) curing salt
30 g (1 oz) fine salt
30 g (1 oz) sugar or dextrose
20 g (2/3 oz) polyphosphates (optional)
20 g (2/3 oz) ground pepper
10 g (1/3 oz) four spice powder
5 g (1/6 oz) nutmeg
500 g (1 lb) onions, cooked
30 g (1 oz) garlic
200 g (7 oz) parsley, chopped

**Preparing the Ingredients**

***The Liver***

The liver must be very fresh; the taste as well as the texture depends on it.

Trim the liver, removing all nerves and ducts and any green stains left by the bile sack.

Cut into even pieces and season with the corresponding amounts of salt and sugar. Cover and marinate in the refrigerator for 12-36 hours.

***The Pork Jowl and Belly***

The pork jowl must also be very fresh. This is a relatively simple preparation that depends on top quality ingredients.

Remove the skin from the jowl then trim all glands and blood spots. Cut into even pieces and season with the corresponding amounts of sugar and salt.

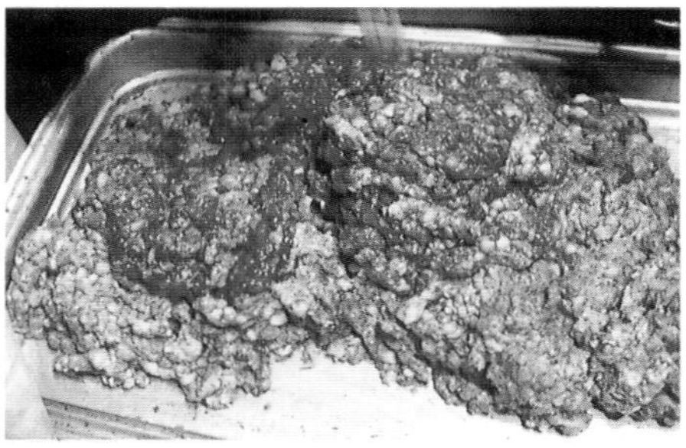

Trim the belly of all nerves, bones and cartilage. Cut into even pieces and season with salt and sugar.

Note that the spices are not added until the end so they will not lose their flavor while the meats are marinating in the refrigerator. However, if the meat is to be marinated in a vacuum pouch all of the seasonings can be added as they will penetrate into the meat evenly and the flavor cannot escape.

### *The milk*

Cook the onions in good quality lard until soft but not browned. Crush the garlic and add to the onions to cook a little.

Bring the milk to a boil, add the onions, garlic and chopped parsley, remove from the heat, cover and infuse for 15 minutes.

Pass the milk through a conical strainer, pressing on the vegetables to extract maximum flavor. Keep warm until ready to make the mixture.

### Procedure

Poach the pieces of pork jowl in very light bouillon for 10 minutes.

The jowl is very susceptible to bacteria because the animal is bled through this portion at the slaughtering house. The brief poaching will help to eliminate bacteria. Note that improper trimming or lack of poaching will sometimes result in dark greenish spots in the finished product.

The meats can be processed in a grinder or chopper. Working in the chopper requires extra attention to ensure that the meats are processed evenly. Tho grinder will give more consistant results because all the meats pass through a disk with holes that determine the " grain ".

In the chopper, the other ingredients can be added directly as the machine turns. The meats processed in the grinder are transferred to a mixer and the remaining ingredients are incorporated using the paddle attachment.

### *Grinder Method*

Grind the pork jowl and belly through a disk with 4-6 mm (1/4 in) holes. Pass the liver through a disk with 8 mm (about 1/3 in) holes.

Transfer the meats to a mixer. Add the spices and polyphosphates (optional) then incorporate the eggs one at a time. Lastly blend in the wine and warm milk.

Mix at low speed to blend and bind the various ingredients to obtain a mixture that is homogeneous.

### *Chopper Method*

In the bowl of the chopper, place the pieces of pork jowl, belly and half of the eggs and process briefly to obtain a " grain " of about 8 mm (about 1/3 in).

Add the spices, polyphosphates (optional), the remaining eggs, the

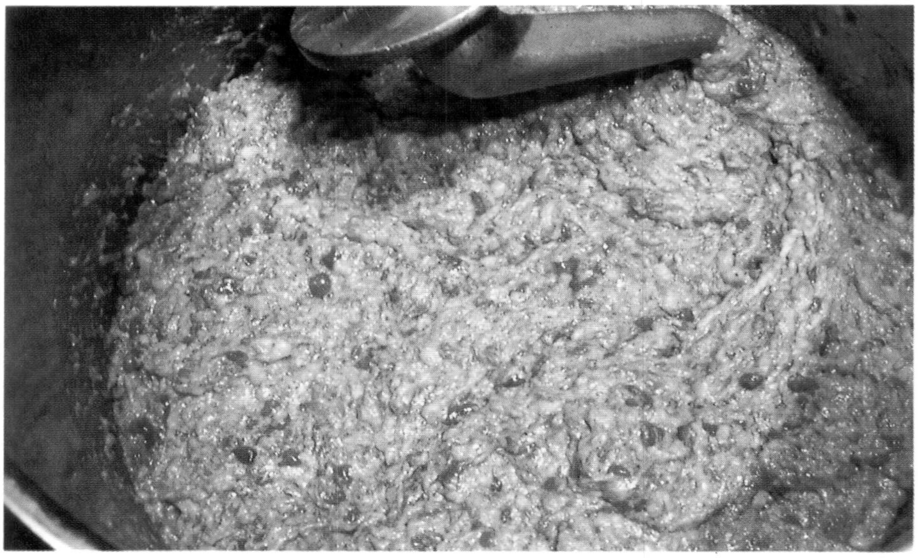

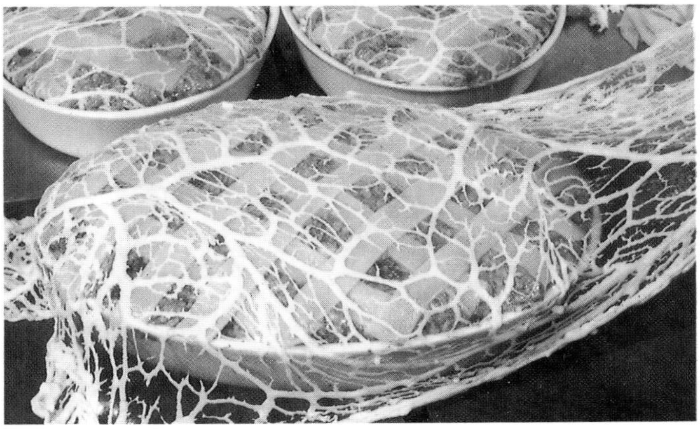
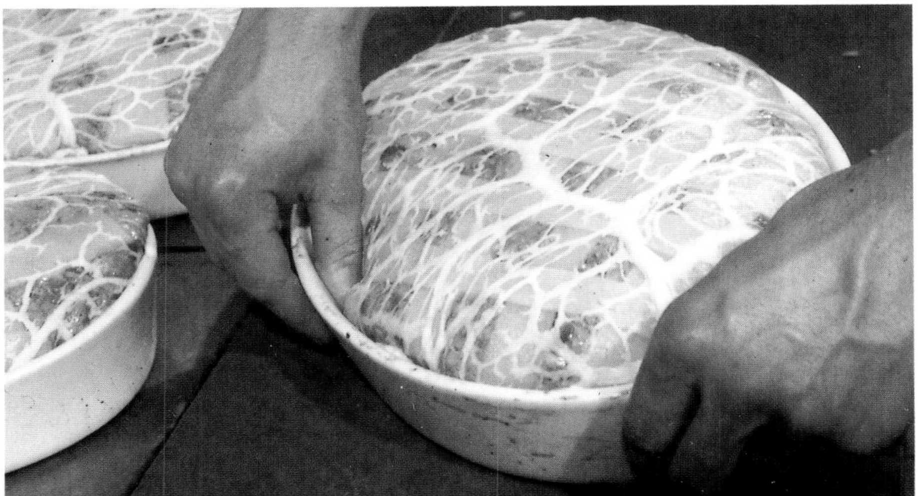

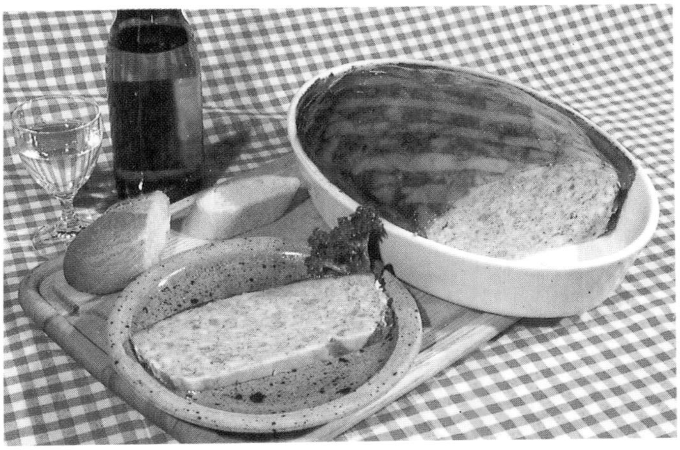

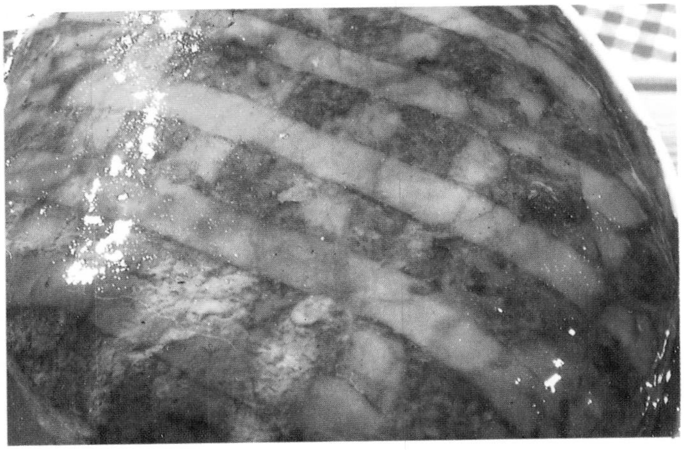

red wine and milk. Lastly add the pieces of liver.

Start the chopper at low speed. Gradually increase the speed to mix all the ingredients and obtain a mixture with a " grain " of about 4-5 mm (1/4 in). The mixture should be homogeneous.

**Assembly**

Country pâté can be cooked in different molds: oval terrines or rectangular or oval baking dishes.

Our choice is a glazed earthenware terrine for its rustic appearance.

Whichever mold is used, it must be generously coated with lard.

Fill the greased terrine, mounding the top a little.

Place strips of barding fat in a criss-cross pattern on the top then cover with caul fat. (The caul fat must be soaked 2 hours, rinsed and dried.)

**Cooking**

Cook the pâté immediately. Cook in a steamer or place the mold in a water bath and cook in the oven. The cooking enviroment must be humid.

Start the cooking at 150-170 °C (300-325 F) to brown the top then lower the heat to 90-100 °C (195-200 F) and continue to cook until the internal temperature is 76-78 °C (170 F).

**Cooling**

Drain the fatty juices rendered by the pâté during cooking and replace with full-flavered pork stock.

Place a baking sheet on top with a light weight to compress the pâté slightly and eliminate gaps. Cool rapidly in a convection cooling chamber or in the refrigerator.

**Storage**

To keep for up to 10 days, pour a thin layer of lard over the top of the cooled pâté. The storage time can be prolonged by placing the pâté in a vacuum pouch.

**Presentation**

To display the pâté, scrape off the layer of lard, decorate with a simple design or simply glaze with amber-colored aspic.

# Pâté " Grand-Mère "

## Introduction

Marc Coulon, the most distinguished " Meilleur Ouvrier de France " in the charcuterie profession, has strived for more than 50 years to maintain high quality in the industry.

A specialist in products from the Aquitaine, his native region, he shares one of his favorite recipes here, " Le Pâté Grand-Mère ". The name " grandmother's pâté, evokes the homestyle origin of this terrine.

On farms in the Aquitaine, the pig along with the goose, provide the base of meat cookery. As a result many charcuterie treasures have been developed in this region.

This is a variation on a classic country pâté with a coarser " grain ". The refined ingredients and techniques used to make this pâté groups it with more elegant products.

## Equipment

Knives, grinder or horizontal chopper (fixed or removable bowl), plastic scraper, stainless steel bowls and hotel pans, sauté pan, thermometer, mixer, terrine molds

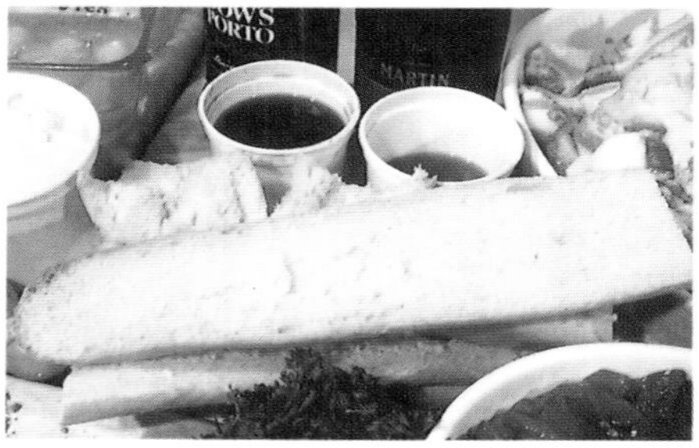

**Recipe " Marc Coulon "**

***Ingredients***

3.5 kg (7.7 lbs) chicken livers
3 kg (6.6 lbs) pork jowl
600 g (1 lb 3 1/2 oz) eggs
250 g (1/2 lb) goose fat
200 g (7 oz) shallots
100 g (3 1/2 oz) flat parsley
500 ml (2 cups) heavy cream
1 liter (1 qt) milk
500 g (1 lb) bread
(pullman loaf, crust removed)

*Seasonings*
100 ml (scant 1/2 cup) eau de vie
(distilled liqueur)
125 ml (1/2 cup) madeira
Fresh thyme, bay leaf
110 g (scant 4 oz) curing salt
(sodium nitrite with fine salt)
40 g (generous 1 oz) fine salt
18 g (generous 1/2 oz) sugar or
dextrose
12 g (generous 1/3 oz) pepper
6 g (generous 1/6 oz) nutmeg

**Preparing the Ingredients**

***The Chicken Livers***

The freshness of the livers is of the utmost importance. Chicken livers are often frozen then defrosted for sale. It is difficult to distinguish the two by sight so it is necessary to stress to the purveyor that only perfectly fresh livers are acceptable.

Trim the livers well, removing all the small nerves and all green stains from contact with the bile sack.

Rinse them in cold water and dry.

***The Pork Jowl***

Trim the pork jowl, removing the skin, glands and all blood spots. Cut into large even cubes.

The jowl for this recipe is not blanched (a security measure to destroy bacteria) so it is important to trim very thoroughly. Also, blood spots will darken during cooking and leave unpleasant grey areas in the finished product.

**Procedure**

***Marinating the Meats***

In separate stainless steel recipients, season the livers and pork jowl with corresponding amounts of the curing salt, fine salt, sugar, thyme and bay leaf. Note that fine salt is used in addition to curing salt to compensate for the unsalted cream, eggs and milk.

Sprinkle the meats with madeira, cover and refrigerate for 24-36 hours.

### *Making the Forcemeat*

Cut the shallots into slices or dice and cook over low heat in goose fat for 2-3 minutes.

Add 500 g (1 lb) of the marinated chicken livers.

Brown the livers on all sides but do not cook them; they should remain very pink on the inside.

Off the heat, flame the livers with " eau de vie " (a clear distilled liqueur made from aged wine).

When the flame is out, stir in the parsley (chopped coarsely).

Chill this mixture thoroughly in the refrigerator before grinding.

Soak the bread (crusts removed) in cold milk.

Note that this bread is close-textured " pain de mie " which is similar to pullman loaf.

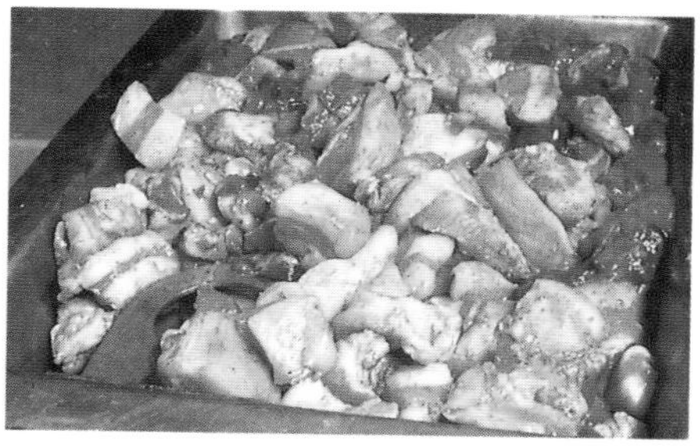

Grind all of the meats through a disk with 6 mm (1/4 in) holes. Remove the branches of thyme and bay leaf before passing the marinated meats (jowl and livers) through the grinder. Also grind the cooked livers and the soaked bread.

It is preferable to use a grinder and not a horizontal chopper. The livers become a purée very quickly in the chopper but in the grinder the " grain " is established by the size of the disk.

Transfer the ground ingredients to a mixer and blend in the eggs, one at a time, at low speed. Incorporate the cream.

The pepper and nutmeg are added last for maximum flavor. At medium speed, blend until the mixture is homogeneous.

Note that in this recipe the pork jowl is not blanched like in some country pâtés.

This is why the trimming process must be performed with care. Thorough trimming of blood spots, glands and skin reduces the risk of bacteria growth. Blanching destroys bacteria so when the meat is not blanched extra attention must be paid to the trimming process.

The appearance of the slice is better as well because there are no dark spots from blood or glands. The pâté is cooked to an internal temperature of 76-78 °C (170 F) which destroys bacteria.

Place the pâté in a moderate oven (150 °C (300 F)) to brown the top then turn the heat down to 95-100 °C (200 F) and continue cooking until the internal temperature is 76-78 °C (170 F).

Drain the fatty juices from the cooked terrine and replace with full-flavored chicken stock that has been boiled, skimmed and strained.

**Cooling and Storage**

Cool the pâté quickly, using a " cooling chamber " if available.

The pâté " Grand-Mère " will keep for 5-6 days in the refrigerator. This product is so easy to make that it is recommended to not make large batches.

**Assembling the Pâté**

Generously grease the earthenware molds with fresh goose fat.

Fill the molds with the forcemeat.

Cover the top with coarsely ground pepper (" mignonette "). It is recommended to crush the pepper just before using with a rolling pin or spice mill.

Decorate the top with thin strips of barding fat arranged in a criss-cross pattern.

Cover the top with caul fat that is tucked in around the sides.

For maximum flavor, cover and refrigerate the assembled pâté for several hours to allow the aromas to develop.

**Cooking**

The pâté is cooked in a water bath in a steamer.

**Presentation**

Coat the top of the pâté with amber-colored aspic and display with other terrines.

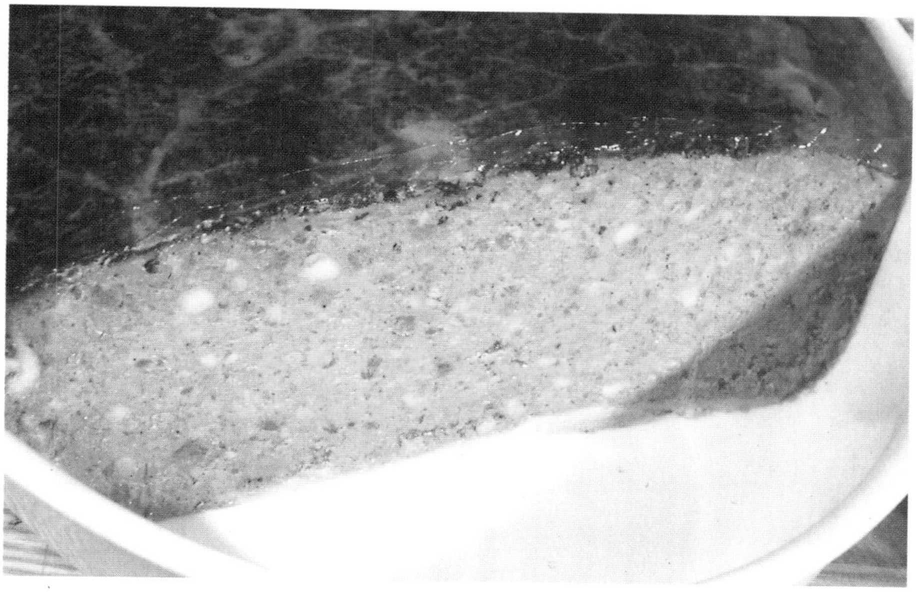

# Country Pâté with Prunes

**Introduction**

This pâté originated in the southwest region of France. The area around the city of Agen is particulary noted for its fine prunes. Armagnac from the southwest is another regional accent.

The addition of prunes gives this classic " pâté de campagne " a fresh and delicious dimension.

Other additions could be used in the place of the prunes in this standard recipe to reflect local ingredients.

Nuts for example--walnuts,

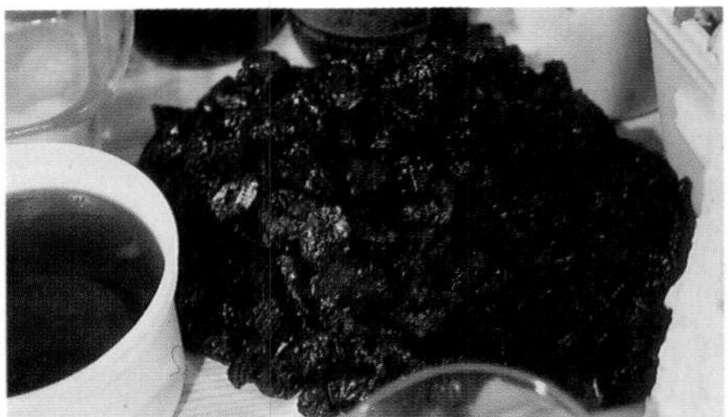

toasted hazelnuts or almonds, pistachios and chestnuts are all good choices to add character to this pâté. Other possibilities include exotic fruits like banana or mango, artichoke hearts or green or black olives.

The charcutier has a wide range of choices to personalize his product and express his imagination and creativity.

As long as he respects the natural harmony of flavors and the rustic character of this basic pâté, he can add any ingredient that he thinks his clients will enjoy. The opportunity for personal expression is one of the true joys of the charcuterie profession.

**Equipment**

Grinder or chopper (fixed or removable bowl), large bowl, plastic scraper, terrine mold, strainer, paring knife, thermometer, conical sieve, large pot, mixer

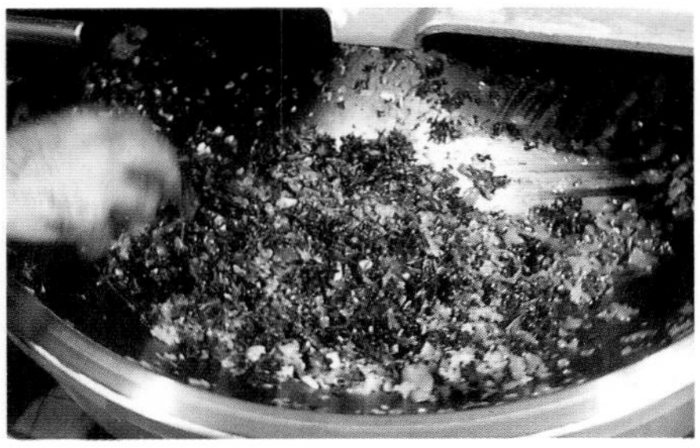

**Ingredients**

*For 10 kg (22 lbs) of mixture*
3 kg (6.6 lbs) sowbelly
2.6 kg (5.75 lbs) pork jowl
2.4 kg (5.25 lbs) pork liver
600 g (1 lb 5 oz) whole eggs
4 L (1 cup) dry red wine
1 L (1 qt) milk
50 cl (2 cups) Armagnac

***Seasonings***

140 g (scant 1/3 lb) curing salt (sodium nitrite with fine salt)
30 g (1 oz) fine salt
30 g (1 oz) sugar (or dextrose)
20 g (2/3 oz) polyphosphates (optional)
20 g (2/3 oz) freshly ground pepper
10 g (1/3 oz) four spice powder
5 g (1/6 oz) nutmeg
500 g (1 lb) cooked shallots
30 g (1 oz) garlic
200 g (7 oz) parsley
1 kg (2.2 lbs) pitted prunes

**Procedure**

For the preparation of the main ingredients and the mixing procedure, refer to the recipe for classic country pâté.

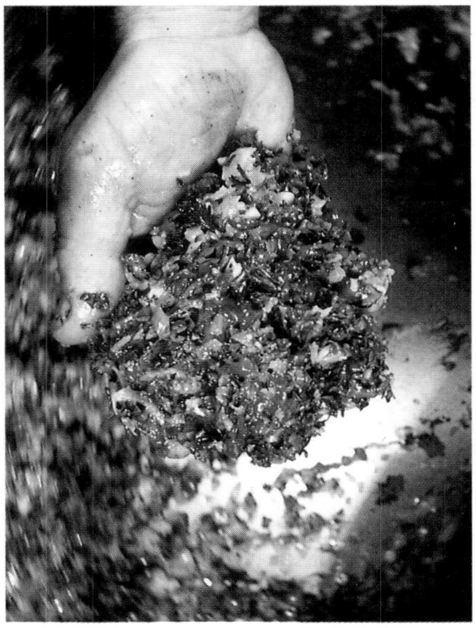

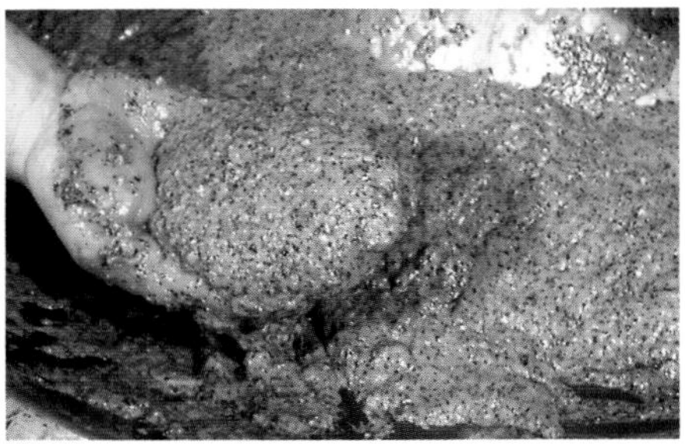

However in this recipe, note that the onions have been replaced by shallots which have a more subtle flavor.

The shallots are prepared in the same way--sliced and cooked in a covered pot with goose fat or lard until soft but not browned.

Prunes in France are available dried and " half dried ". Choose plump prunes for this preparation. For many recipes from this region the prunes are macerated in the Armagnac but not for this pâté.

The Armagnac is added to the livers when they are seasoned (with salt).

The prunes absorb juices from the pâté as it cooks. This is sufficient to make them moist. If they are soaked in advance they would be mushy in the final product, making it difficult to slice neatly.

Also the strong taste of the Armaganc tends to mask the delicious taste of the prunes with a strong alcohol flavor.

The cooking procedure is exactly the same as the classic country pâté.

When the pâté is cooked, drain off the rendered juices and replace this fatty liquid with a full-flavored stock perfumed with a little Armagnac.

The sweet and sour taste of this preparation is surprisingly delicious.

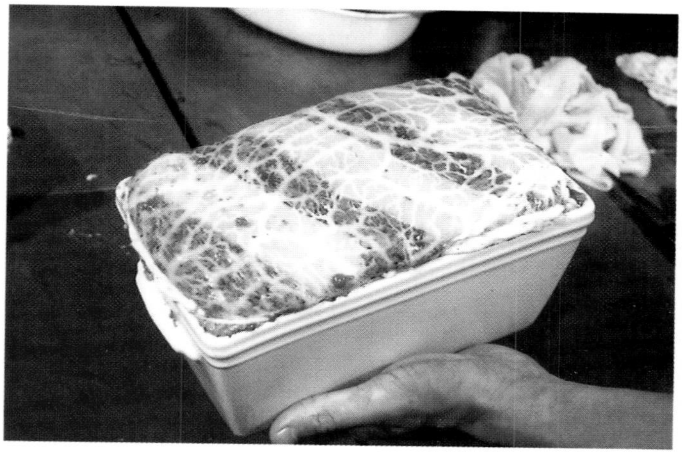

*Regulations*

The regulations concerning this type of pâté in the " Code de la Charcuterie " (Volume III, page 9, 1-222) specifies that additions such as nuts or dried fruits are considered to be decoration when they make up to 5 % of the weight of the product.

The correct labeling for this preparation would be " Country Pâté with Prunes " *10 % Prunes* (which is the quantity called for in this recipe).

# Chicken Liver Mousse

## Introduction

Chicken liver mousse (" La mousse de foies de volaille ") is part of the family of emulsified, finely-textured, spreadable products which includes liver pâté, " crèmes ", and purées made with liver.

This preparation is served on its own as an appetizer or used to make canapés. With a little crème fraîche and port, cognac or Armagnac the mousse becomes a creamy mixture that can be piped into ham " cornets " or molded aspics.

The mixture can be blended in one of two ways:

***" Classic Method ":*** First the liver is ground then the fat, cream and milk are incorporated.

"*Modern Method*": The livers are processed in advance but not introduced into the mixture until the end. This is the technique described here.

**Equipment**

Grinder, chopper (fixed or removable bowl), strainer, skimmer, large bowl, plastic scraper, terrine molds, paring knife, thermometer with electronic probe, conical sieve, pot

**Ingredients**

*For 10 kg (22 lbs) of mixture*

3 kg (6.6 lbs) poultry livers (1/2 chicken-1/2 duck livers)
3.5 kg (7.7 lbs) soft pork fat
1.5 L (6 cups) chicken stock
24 egg yolks
25 cl (1 cup) port
1.5 kg (6 cups) heavy cream

***Seasonings***

50 g (1 3/4 oz) curing salt (sodium nitrite with fine salt)
100 g(3 1/2 oz) fine salt
30 g (1 oz) sugar (or dextrose)
20 g (2/3 oz) ground white pepper
5 g (1/6 oz) ground nutmeg
20 g (2/3 oz) ground coriander
10 g (1/3 oz) four spice powder
5 g (1/6 oz) paprika
100 g (3 1/2 oz) lacto-proteins (optional)
10 g (1/3 oz) polyphosphates
30 g (1 oz) cooked shallots
50 g (1 3/4 oz) parsley

The addition of lacto-proteins (sodium caseinate) improves and stabilizes the emulsion. *Note:* Check manufacturers label for proper dosage as products will differ.

**Preparing the Ingredients**

***The Livers***

Choose perfectly fresh livers. Carefully trim the vessels and nerves.

All traces of bile (in the form of green stains on the liver) must also be removed. If any of the bile is left it will darken during cooking and also pervade the product with a very unpleasant bitter flavor.

Place the livers in the chopper with the curing salt, sugar and lacto-proteins. Process until smooth then gradually add the port.

Transfer the mixture to a stainless steel container, cover and refrigerate for 12-24 hours.

***The Fat***

The fat is cut into even pieces and poached in milk, water or chicken stock for about 10 minutes at 80 °C (175 F).

The preferred liquid is stock; water adds no flavor and milk will sometimes add a disagreeable taste and adhere to the fat.

**Procedure**

Drain the poached fat and place it in the chopper with the shallots (cooked in goose fat and cooled), and the parsley (washed thoroughly and chopped).

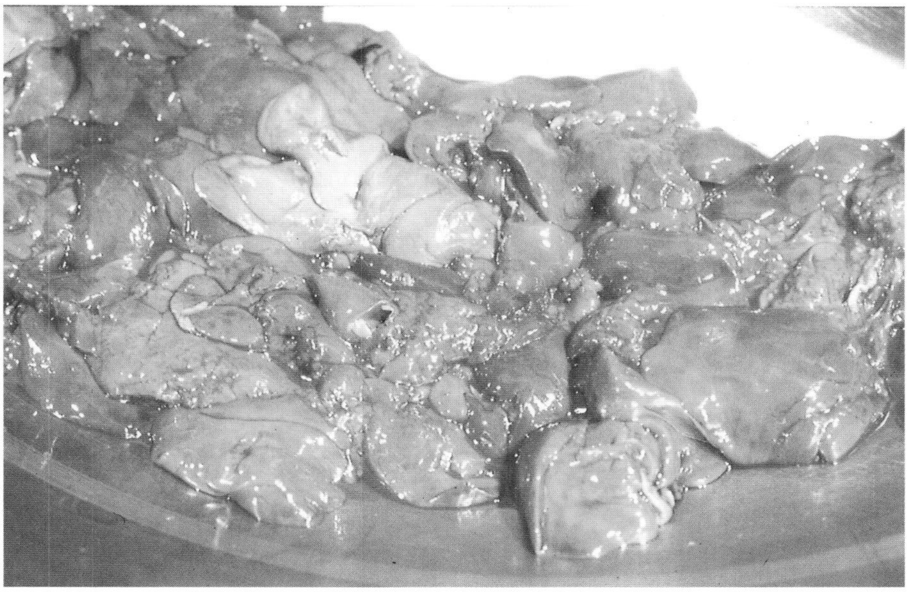

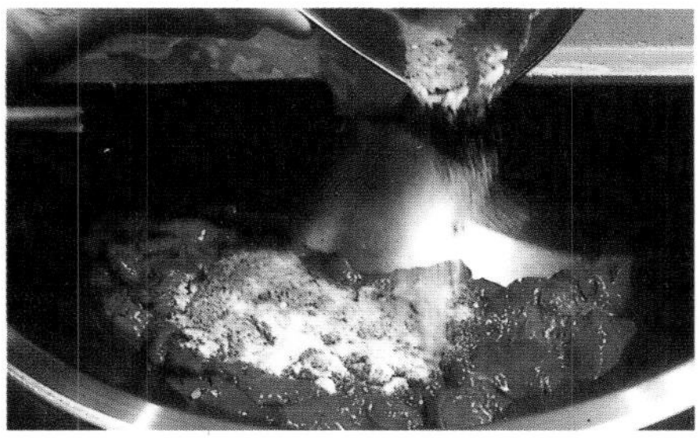

Process until smooth then add the egg yolks and continue processing until incorporated.

Then sprinkle the lacto-proteins into the mixture as it turns in the bowl.

*Note:* The chopper is operated at high speed for this operation and it is important that the blades be well-sharpened to purée without over-heating the mixture.

It is vital to remember the importance of maintaining all equipment (grinder, stuffers, ovens, cooling units...) in perfect working order.

An investment in top quality equipment will certainly pay off in the long run in the form of better products with a higher yield.

When the lacto-proteins have been absorbed, add the

seasonings; fine salt, pepper, sugar, and spices.

Heat the cream to 75 °C (167 F) and bring the chicken stock to a boil and skim all impurities that rise to the surface.

Add these ingredients gradually to the mixture.

The temperature of the mixture at this stage should be between 40-50 °C (104-122 F) which is the ideal temperature for the emulsion.

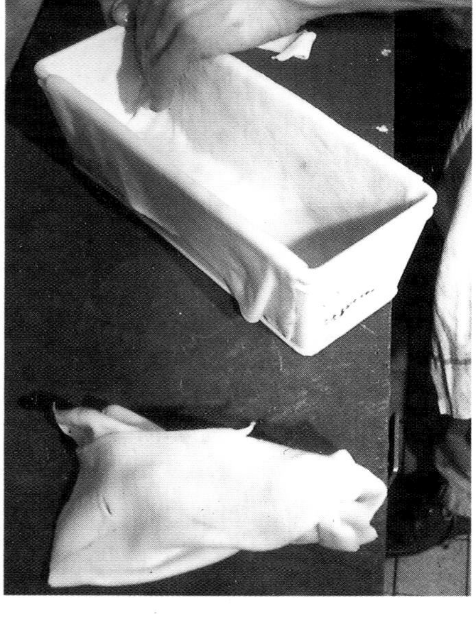

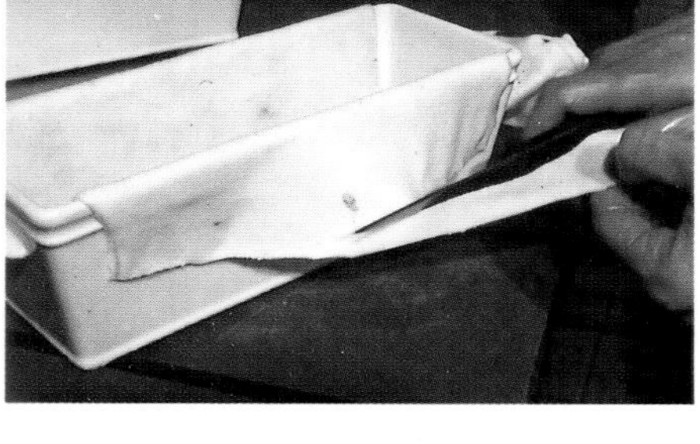

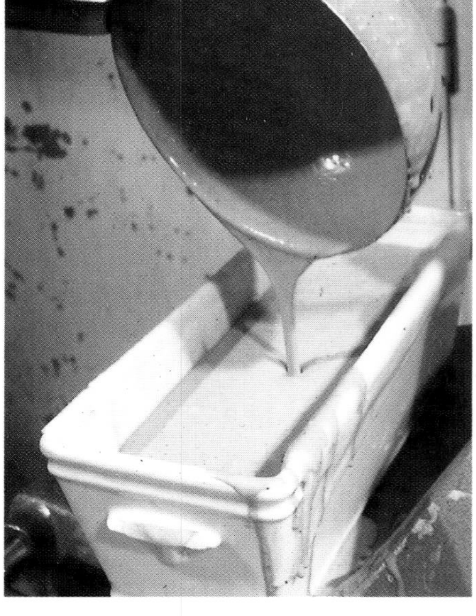

Lastly add the puréed liver mixture.

Process until the mixture is smooth and homogeneous.

**Molding**

Ladle the mixture immediately into molds that have been coated with goose fat or lard or lined with a thin sheet of barding fat.

**Cooking**

The pâtés should be cooked immediately.
The best method is to use a steamer.
Heat the oven to 200 °C (about 400 F) and cook the terrine until it browns a little.
Lower the temperature to 90-100 °C (195-200 F) and continue cooking until the internal temperature of the pâté is 72-74 °C (160-165 F).

**Cooling**

Cool the pâté quickly in the refrigerator or in a specially designed " cooling chamber ".
To store for 8-10 days place in a vacuum pouch (once it is completely chilled) and refrigerate.

**Presentation**

This rustic dish needs no fancy decorations. It is served cold, cut in medium slices.

# " Moussette " of Duck with Morels

## Introduction

The name " moussette " in French evokes the wonderful qualities of this terrine, creamy and light like a mousse with the intense taste of morels enhanced by a subtle blend of aromatics.

The cooking juices of the morels are reduced and concentrated and add a very elegant touch to this preparation.

" Moussette de Canard aux Morilles " is the perfect name for this refined dish which is appreciated by the most knowledgable gourmets.

## Equipment

Grinder, horizontal chopper, plastic scraper, large bowl, terrine mold, strainer, paring knife, thermometer with electronic probe, conical sieve, pot, saucepan

## Ingredients

*For 10 kg (22 lbs) of mixture*

3 kg (6.6 lbs) duck livers
3.5 kg (7.7 lbs) soft fat ("mouille")
750 g (1 1/2 lbs) duck fat
1.5 L (1.5 qt) chicken or duck stock
1.5 L (1.5 qt) cream (20% butterfat)
20 egg yolks

### *Seasonings*

50 g (1 3/4 oz) curing salt (sodium nitrite with fine salt)
90 g (3 oz) fine salt
20 g (2/3 oz) sugar or dextrose
20 g (2/3 oz) ground white pepper
10 g (1/3 oz) mild spice blend (vol 1)
5 g (1/6 oz) paprika
5 g (1/6 oz) ground nutmeg
20 g (1/16 oz) ground coriander
100 g (3 1/2 oz) dried morels
50 g (1 3/4 oz) shallots
50 g (1 3/4 oz) parsley
50 cl (2 cups) madeira

## Preparing the Ingredients

### *The Duck Livers*

Like the liver pâté and chicken liver mousse, it is of prime importance that the livers for this dish be perfectly fresh.

Trim away all nerves and vessels then rinse thoroughly in cold water and pat dry with a clean handtowel.

Divide the trimmed livers into two bowls and season half of the livers with the corresponding amount of curing salt.

Pass the seasoned livers through the fine (2 mm (about 1/16 in)) disk of the grinder. Transfer to a stainless steel recipient, cover with plastic wrap and refrigerate 12 hours.

Slice the shallots thinly and cook them in duck fat until just soft but not browned.

Over high heat, add the remaining duck livers and sauté them quickly, browning them on all sides (turn with a wooden spoon).

The livers should remain very pink inside. If they are overcooked, they lose their ability to bind the mixture and may leave gray spots in the finished product. They also become too dry if overcooked and the terrine will no longer be moist and unctuous.

Remove the browned livers and deglaze the pan with madeira (and reduce by half). Remove from the heat and add the parsley.

### *The Morels*

Sort through the morels to remove bits of twigs and dirt. Soak in water for at least 12 hours then rinse several times to remove all the sand and grit that are found in the crevasses.

Make a duck stock with chopped duck bones, aromatic vegetables and seasonings. Skim well and strain.

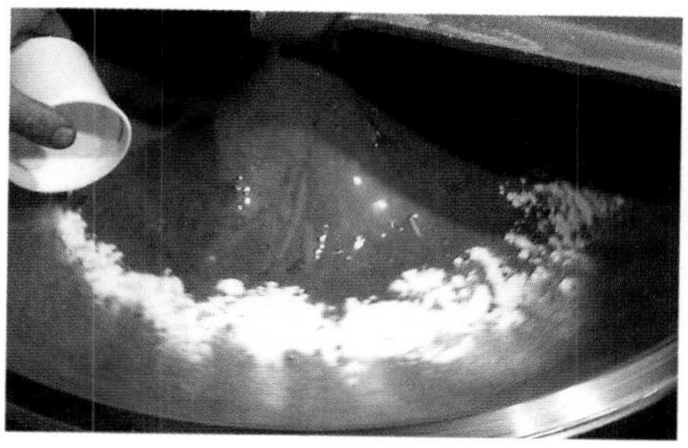

Cook the morels in the duck stock for about 1 hour. Strain, pressing down on the morels to extract all the liquid.

Reduce this cooking liquid by 3/4 to obtain a full-flavored stock.

The rinsing is important for the removal of the gritty substances and the lengthy cooking ensures a bacteria free ingredient.

Chop the morels coarsely and set aside.

### *The Fat*

Cut the fat into even pieces and poach in water, milk or better yet duck stock.

First bring the stock to a boil, skim then add the fat and cook over low heat (85 °C (185 F)) for 10 minutes. This operation facilitates grinding, destroys bacteria and eventually warms the other ingredients in the chopper so the mixture will emusify correctly. This gives the mousse a smooth, spreadable texture.

Strain the poached fat then pass through the fine disk of the grinder.

This procedure is done just before the mousse is made so that the fat is at just the right temperature to be blended into the mixture and create the emulsion.

### Making the Mousse Mixture

In the chopper, place the sautéed livers, egg yolks, and spices. Process at high speed until the mixture is smooth and creamy.

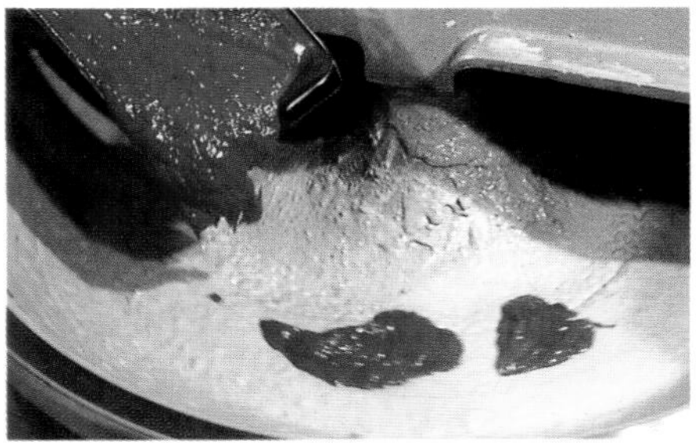

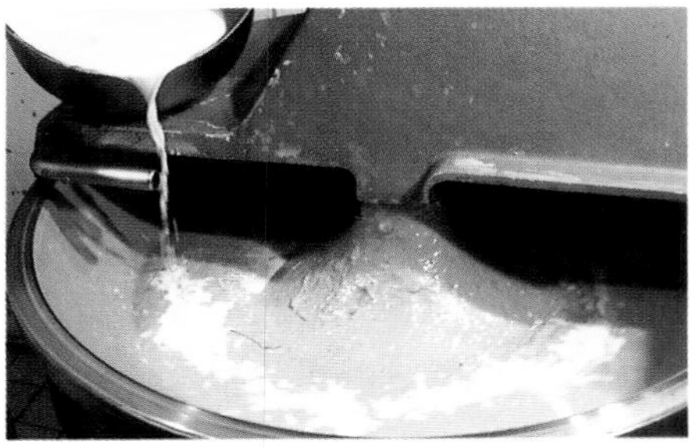

Warm the goose fat to about 60 °C (147 F) and the cream to about 70-80 (160-175 F). First add the fat to the mixture then the cream and process until smooth and homogeneous before adding the warm ground fat.

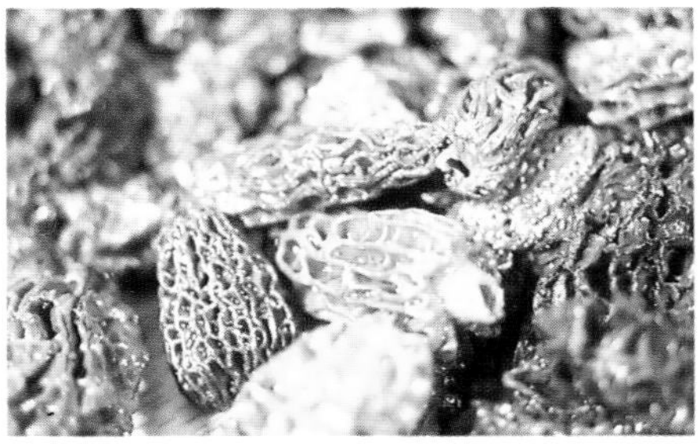

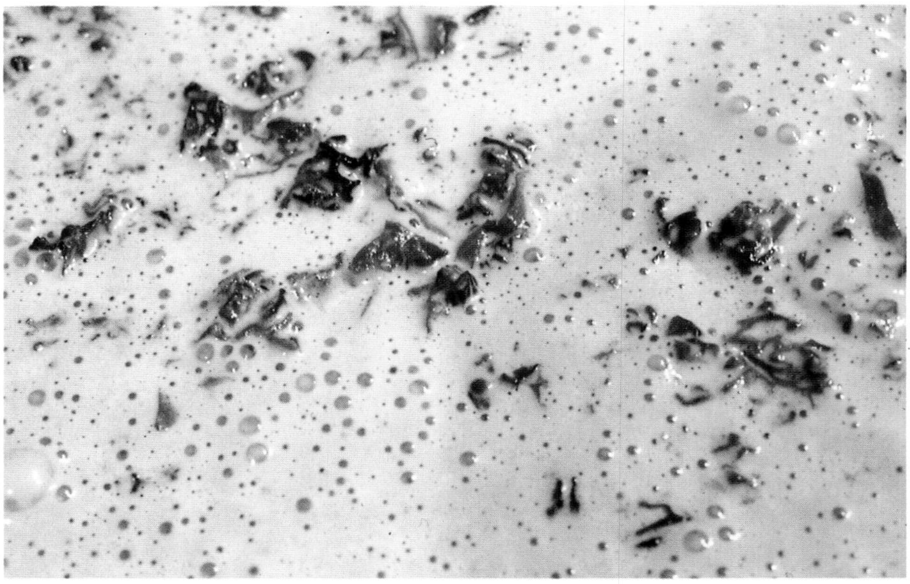

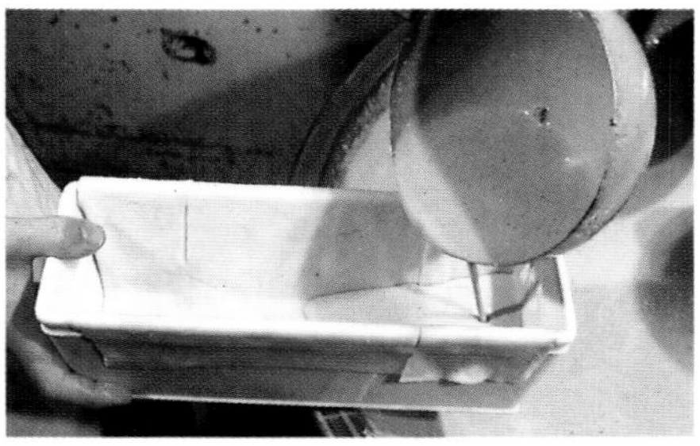

The temperature of the mixture at this stage should be about 40-45 °C (105-115 F).

Lastly, add the fine salt, remaining curing salt and sugar, process until very light then add the reduced mushroom liquid during the last few turns.

Gently fold in the chopped morels by hand.

Immediately ladle the mixture into molds that have been brushed with duck fat.

**Cooking**

The moussette is cooked right away in a water bath. Place in a 180 °C (350 F) oven, brown for a few minutes then turn the heat down to 120 °C (250 F).

Cook until the internal temperature is 72-74 °C (165 F).

Cool quickly in a " cooling chamber " or the refrigerator. Cover the cooled terrine and refrigerate for 12 hours before slicing.

**Presentation**

This elegant terrine deserves a lovely decoration. Morels or cut pieces of blanched vegetables arranged in the shape of a duck would signal to the customer that this is a special dish.

The moussette will keep for about 8 days.

To keep the terrine fresh, cover the top with a thin layer of lard or duck fat. After a full 12 hours of refrigeration, it can also be placed in a vacuum pouch.

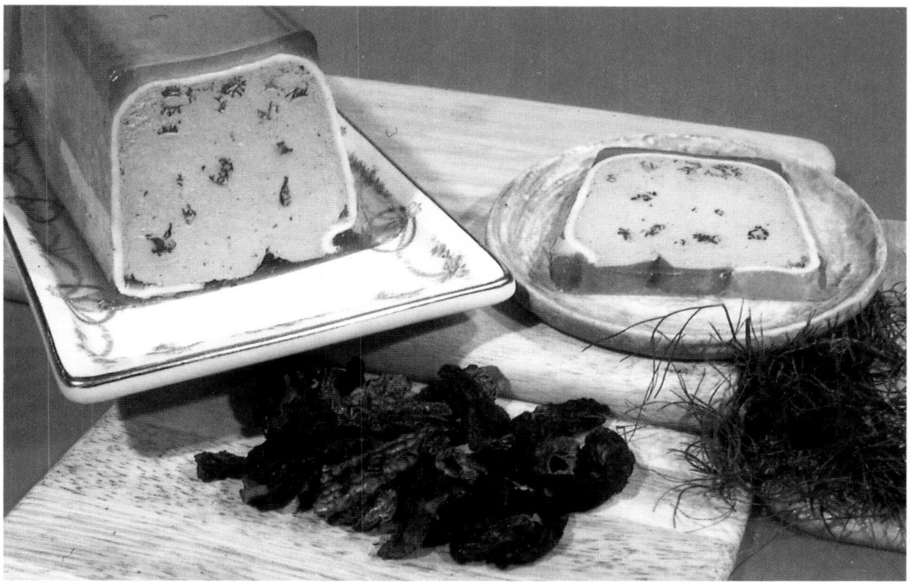

# Rustic Liver Pâté with Three Peppercorns

**Introduction**

" Le pâté rustique confit aux trois poivres " is an original dish whose spicy flavor would add just the right note to a warm weather picnic. The appearance as well as the taste is very agreeable.

This preparation is made with coarsely ground meats with a texture like a country pâté. But the method of preparation is different.

This variation on a classic pâté adds dimension to a selection of traditional products.

**Equipment**

Grinder, sauté pan, plastic scraper, large bowl, wooden spoon, terrine mold, thermometer (with electronic probe)

**Ingredients**

*For 10 kg (22 lbs) of mixture*

3 kg (6.6 lbs) pork liver
3 kg (6.6 lbs) chicken livers
2 kg (4.4 lbs) pork jowl
1.5 kg (3.3 lbs) sowbelly
500 g (1 lb) eggs

***Seasonings***

100 g (3 1/2 oz) curing salt (sodium nitrite with fine salt)
70 g (2 1/2 oz) fine salt
10 g (1/3 oz) white peppercorns
10 g (1/3 oz) green peppercorns in brine
10 g (1/3 oz) pink peppercorns
5 g (1/6 oz) ground nutmeg
10 g (1/3 oz) sugar
100 ml (scant 1/2cup) cognac
Coarsely ground black pepper
Duck or goose fat

**Preparing the Ingredients**

***The Livers***

The pork and chicken livers should be perfectly fresh. They are trimmed of nerves and vessels. The chicken livers must be trimmed of all traces of bile in the form of green stains on the livers.

Cut the livers into even pieces and toss with the curing salt and cognac. Place in a stainless steel recipient, cover with plastic wrap and refrigerate for 12-24 hours.

***The Meats***

Trim the nerves and skin from the pork jowl and sowbelly, cut into even pieces (5-6 cm (2 in)) and season with the fine salt.

Place in a stainless steel recipient, cover with plastic wrap and refrigerate for 12-24 hours.

**Making the Mixture**

Brown the pieces of pork jowl and sowbelly in goose fat. Lower the heat and cook for about 10 minutes until the meat is stiffened.

Add the pieces of liver and sauté briefy. The liver should remain very bloody pink on the inside.

The proteins should not be heated enough to coagulate so that they will later congeal and help bind the mixture.

Transfer the meat and liver to a grinder fitted with a large disk (6-8 mm (1/4 in)) and grind these meats into the bowl of a mixer.

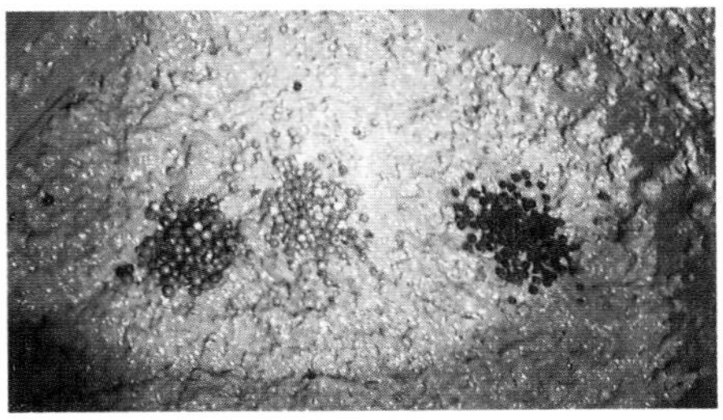

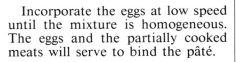

Incorporate the eggs at low speed until the mixture is homogeneous. The eggs and the partially cooked meats will serve to bind the pâté.

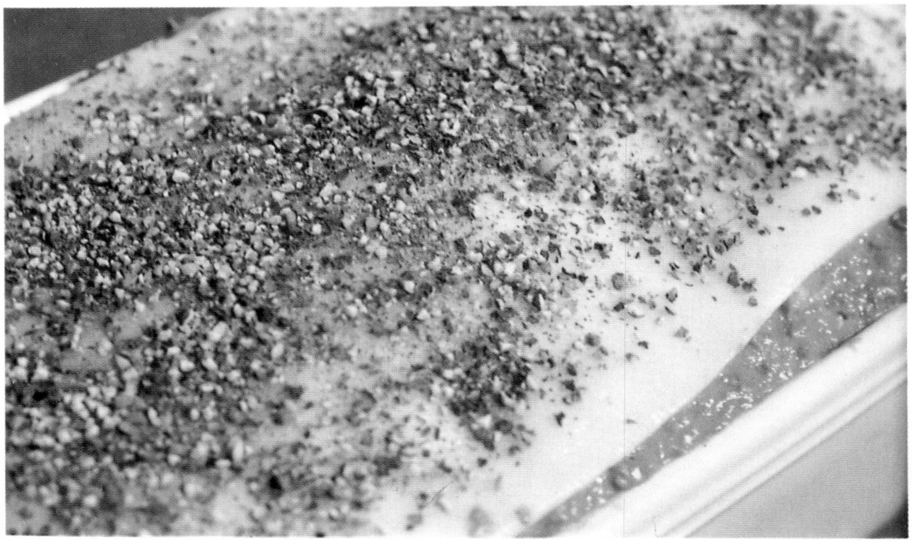

Add the peppercorns (and the brine from the green peppercorns) at the end so that they are not crushed. Mix at low speed to incorporate the peppercorns evenly into the mixture.

Brush a rustic porceline mold with goose fat and fill with the mixture. Sprinkle the top with the coarsely crushed black peppercorns (" mignonette de poivre ") and cover with a piece of caul fat that has been soaked to remove excess salt.

Cook immediately.

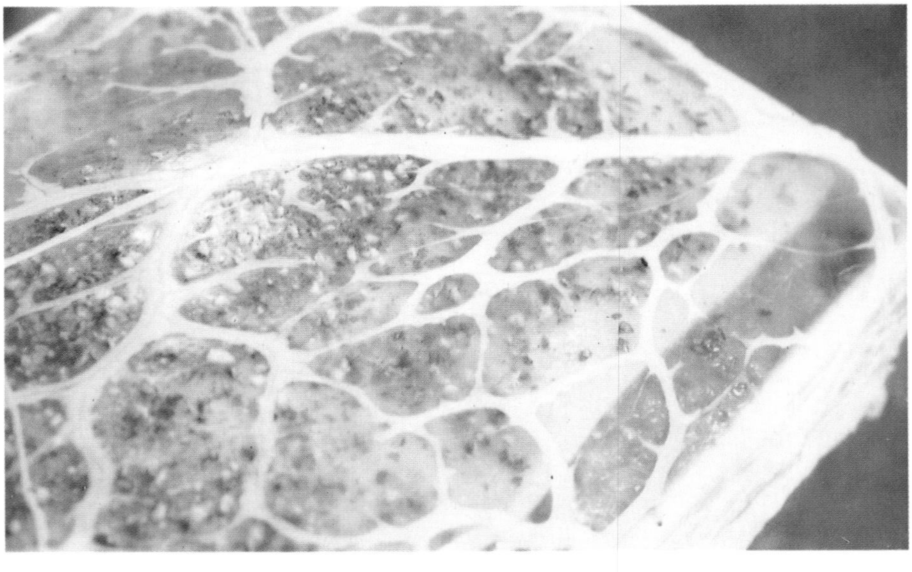

**Cooking**

Cook the pâté in a 180 °C (350 F) oven until the top is lightly browned.

Lower the temperature to 100 °C (about 200 F) and continue cooking until the internal temperature is 85 °C (185 F).

Pour off the juices rendered out of the pâté during cooking and replace them with a full-flavored stock. Place a light weight on the top.

Cool at room temperature for about one hour before placing the pâté in the refrigerator.

**Storage**

This rustic pâté keeps very well because it has been cooked to 85 °C (185 F).

It is best to seal it in a vacuum pouch or it can be covered with a thin layer of lard to keep it fresh.

It will keep for up to 2 weeks in the refrigerator.

***Note:*** The pink peppercorns called for in this recipe are not really peppercorns at all. They are the fruit of a " false " peppercorn plant which grows in warm climates (South America and the Island of the Réunion). Réunion is the former Bourbon island thus this peppercorn is sometimes marketed as " pink Bourbon berries " (" baies roses de Bourbon ").

The leaves and the fruits of this plant have proven to be medicinal as well as toxic. The use of these peppercorns is forbidden in some countries, Germany for example.

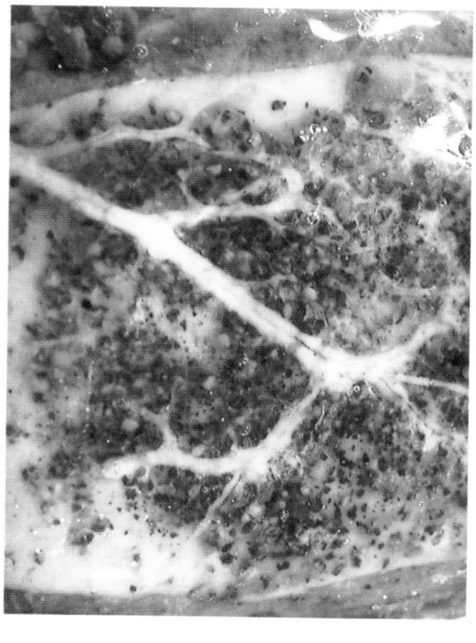

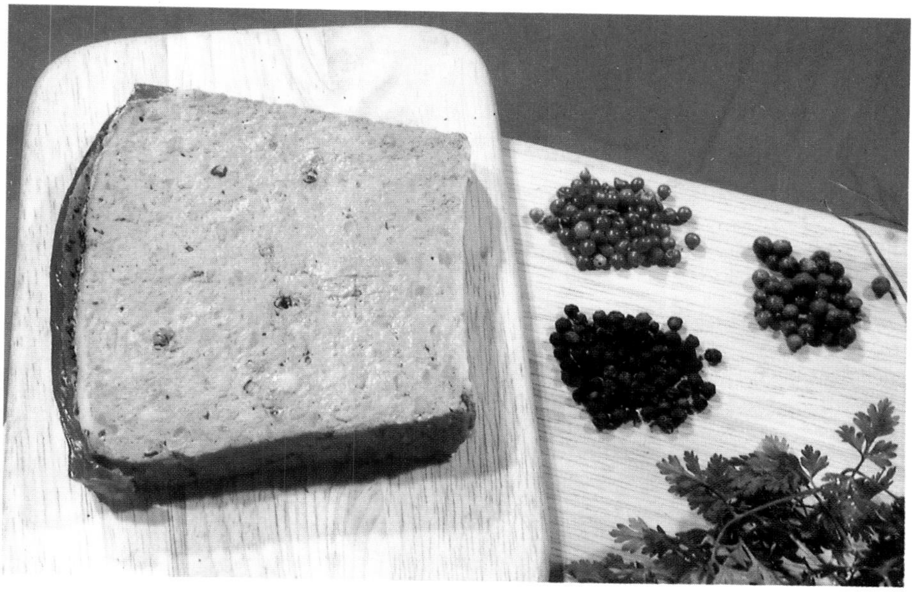

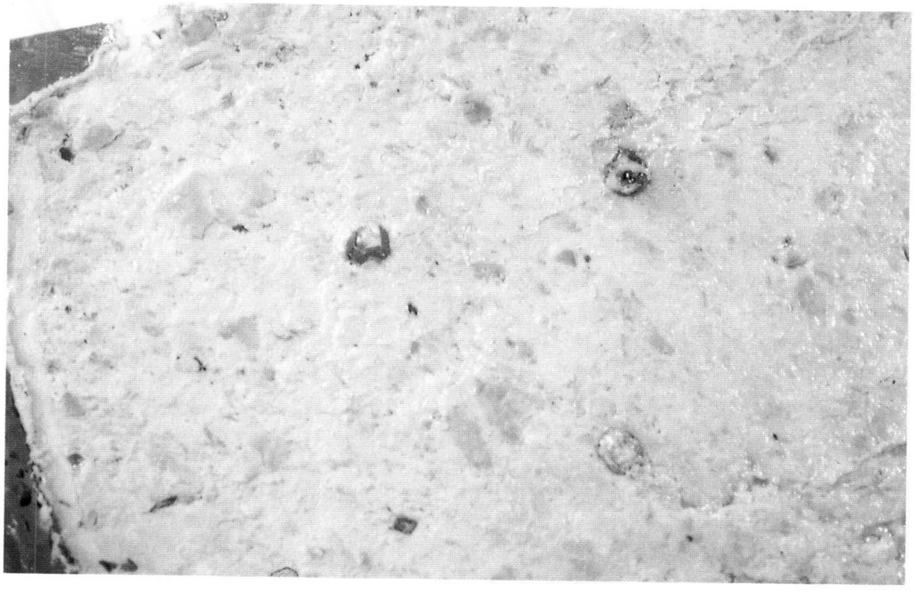

# Poultry Terrine " Périgourdine "

## Introduction

French dishes that are labeled " Périgourdine " always include foie gras and sometimes truffles as well. (Périgueux is a major city in the foie gras producing region in southwest France.)

" Terrine de Volaille Périgourdine " is a terrine of chicken livers with a roulade of goose foie gras in the center.

The subtle flavor of the foie gras permeates into the rest of the terrine as it is assembled and especially as it cooks.

This regional dish from southwest France can be made in many forms (terrines, in sterilized jars or cans...) and may be labeled by different names indicating its origin.

## Regulations

The French Charcuterie Code sets strict limitations concerning products labeled " pâté de Périgueux " (further specified with regulations referring to " Recette Périgourdine "). In order to comply with the " Services de Contrôle " this terrine contains the regulated amount of foie gras (30 %). (Regulations are the same for duck or goose foie gras.) If truffles are added, the government standards must also be met.

The regulations are very strict. The weight of foie gras must be 30 % of the final product with barding fat removed and before the aspic is applied.

In the chapter on foie gras it is stressed that the foie gras always loses a certain percentage of its

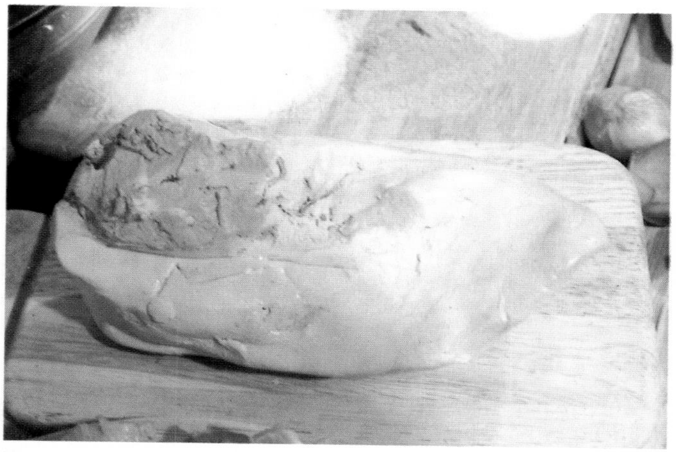

weight during cooking which is impossible to estimate in advance. To ensure that the percentage in the final product meets the standards, it is recommended to overestimate the amount of raw foie gras by about 15-20 % (based on the weight of the other raw ingredients). If the chef is absolutely sure that the foie gras he is using is top quality and therefore will melt less, he can reduce the " extra " amount.

Remember that duck foie gras tends to melt more than goose.

This refined preparation would be the ideal first course for a dinner featuring other soutwest specialties; confit and cèpes.

The region of Périgord is rich in many agricultural products (walnuts, truffles) but is especially known for its fattened geese and ducks which provide foie gras.

**Equipment**

Grinder, large bowl, plastic scraper, platter, long terrine mold, thermometer (with electronic probe), wooden spoon, sauté pan

**Ingredients**

*For 10 kg (22 lbs) of mixture*

1.25 kg (2.75 lbs) chicken livers
3.5 kg (7.7 lbs) fatty pork jowl
3.45 kg (7.6 lbs) goose foie gras
20 eggs
1/2 L (2 cups) heavy cream
600 g (1 lb 5 oz) chanterelles

***Seasonings***

150 g (5 oz) curing salt
(sodium nitrite with fine salt)
20 g (2/3 oz) sugar
20 g (2/3 oz) mild spice blend
5 g (1/6 oz) ground nutmeg
Sage
25 cl (1 cup) cognac
200 g (7 oz) shallots

**Preparing the Ingredients**

***The Chicken Livers***

As with all products using chicken livers, it is important to select fresh top quality livers.

Remove the nerves and vessels then rinse in cold water. Pat dry with a clean handtowel.

Season with half of the curing salt and the sugar. Toss with the cognac to coat evenly.

Grind the livers through a 6 mm (1/4 in) disk of a meat grinder.

Transfer to a stainless steel recipient, cover with plastic wrap and refrigerate.

### *The Pork Jowl*

Trim the nerves and skin from the jowl.

Cut into even pieces about 5-6 cm (2 in) and season with curing salt and sugar.

Transfer to a stainless steel recipient and refrigerate 12 hours.

### *The Foie Gras*

Choose a moist, supple foie gras of good quality which will not melt too much during cooking.

If the terrine is made with duck livers, use duck foie gras in the center. If chicken livers are used as the base of the mixture, use goose foie gras.

Refer to the chapter on foie gras for instructions on removing the vessels that run through the center of the liver. Season with curing salt and pepper.

Cover and refrigerate for 12-24 hours.

### *The Chanterelles*

Also known as girolles, chanterelles, like all wild mushrooms used in charcuterie must be carefully washed in several changes of water to rinse away all the gritty substances. (The soil that is often attached to wild mushrooms is a prime carrier of bacteria). It is recommended to add a little bleach or vinegar to the first basin of water. Lift the mushrooms out so that the sand will settle to the bottom then repeat the process until no sand remains in the bottom of the basin.

Drain and pat dry with paper towels then cut into small pieces.

Heat some goose fat in a sauté pan and cook the shallots (previously sliced thinly) until soft but not browned. Add the mushrooms.

Cover the pan and cook the mushrooms for 5-10 minutes.

Drain the chanterelles and set aside.

Reduce the liquid from the mushrooms to a glaze and set aside.

### Making the Mixture

Form the foie gras into cylinders that weigh about 20 % of the weight of the mixture for each mold. (refer to chapter 5 for the procedure for shaping the foie gras.) For a mold that holds 2 kg (4.4 lbs), use about 400 g (14 oz) of foie gras.

Any foie gras trimmings can be ground with the pork jowl and added to the mixture.

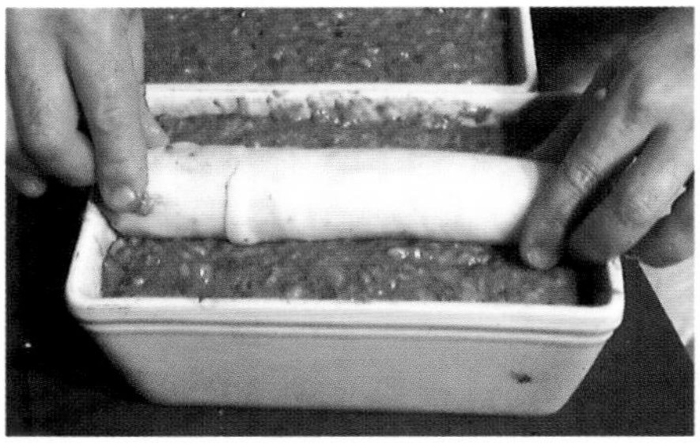

Roll each cylinder of foie gras in a thin sheet of barding fat, cover with plastic wrap and set aside in the refrigerator.

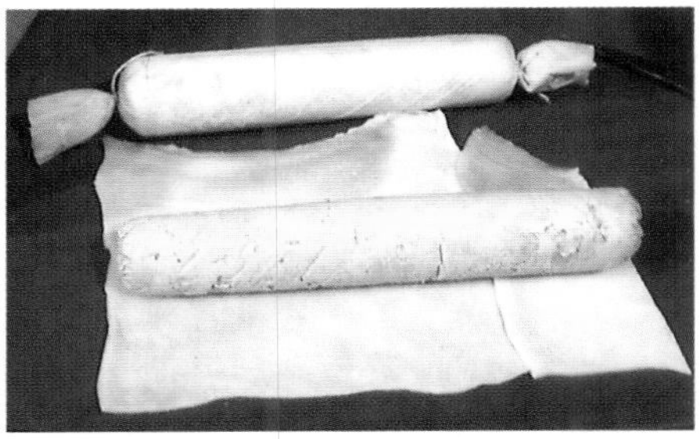

Grind the pork jowl through a medium disk (4 mm (about 18 in)) and transfer to the bowl of the mixer with the chicken livers and spices.

Blend these ingredients together then gradually add the eggs two at a time.

Lastly add the reduced mushroom glaze and the cream and mix at high speed to bind the mixture without overworking. Add the mushrooms at the end and blend just enough to incorporate evenly.

Line the molds with thin sheets of barding fat (leave a few inches hanging over the edge to later fold over the top of the terrine).

Fill each one half way with the mixture. Place a roulade of foie gras in the center then cover the roulade and fill each mold to the top with the mixture of chicken livers, pork jowl and foie gras.

Fold the barding fat over the top of the terrine and cook immediately.

**Cooking**

It is best to cook this terrine in a steamer.

Start the cooking at 180 °C (350 F). After a few minutes turn the oven down to 85 °C (185 F).

The presence of foie gras in this terrine demands that meticulous attention is paid throughout the cooking process. It is better to cook the terrine a little longer at a lower temperature than rapidly at a higher temperature.

The terrine is cooked until the center of the foie gras roulade reaches 60 °C (147 F). This temperature minimizes the loss of precious foie gras juices yet is hot enough to safely cook the outer layer of the preparation.

Remove the terrine when the probe of the thermometer registers 60 (147 F) and handle it very gently during the cooling process.

Place the terrine carefully into the refrigerator on a rack so air circulates around it. When it is no longer hot, cover with plastic wrap and keep in the refrigerator for 24-48 to allow the flavors to mellow.

**Storage and Presentation**

To keep the terrine up to 8 days, cover with a thin layer of lard or place in a vacuum pouch. As we have stated before customers prefer a product stored in a vacuum pouch to one that has been covered with fat.

For sale in the charcuterie, cover the top with a little aspic and cut in 1 cm (3/8 in) slices.

# Roquefort Pâté

**Introduction**

This is a delicious, original preparation which is greatly appreciated by discerning customers.

The marriage of meat with three cheeses, with the Roquefort as the dominant flavor, makes this unusual terrine a good example of " nouvelle charcuterie ".

Lovers of cheese will enjoy the taste of this product. But even those who have shyed away from the strong flavor of Roquefort in the past may be surprised by the subtle taste that the Roquefort gives this pâté.

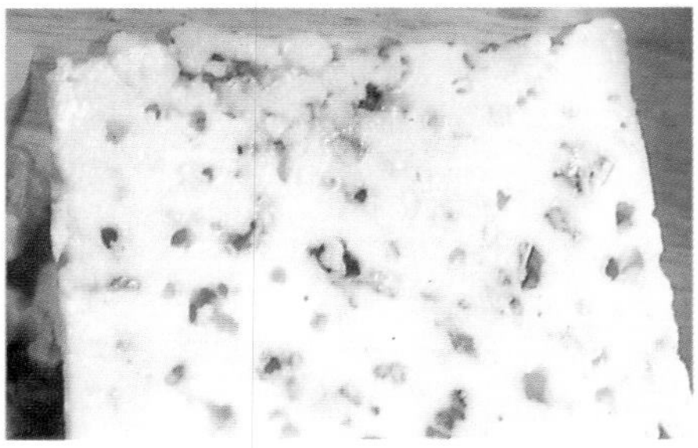

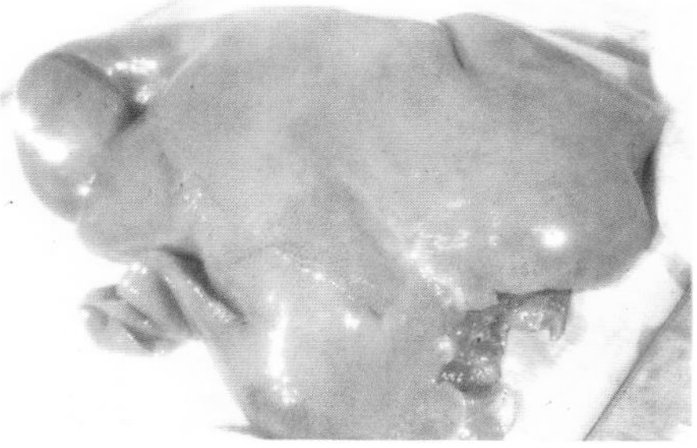

**Equipment**

Grinder, large bowl, plastic scraper, thermometer with electronic probe, sauté pan, wooden spoon, mixer

**Ingredients**

*For about 10 kg (22 lbs) of mixture*

4 kg (8.8 lbs) sowbelly
2 kg (4.4 lbs) pork liver
1.5 kg (3.3 lbs) " fromage blanc " (or cottage cheese)
1.5 kg (3.3 lbs) gruyère
750 g (1 1/2 lbs) roquefort
10 eggs
300 g (1 1/4 cup) heavy cream
30 slices smoked bacon

***Seasonings***

100 g (3 1/2 oz) curing salt (sodium nitrite blended with salt)
20 g (2/3 oz) ground pepper
5 g (1/6 oz) ground mace
125 ml (1/2 cup) " Marc " de Champagne
100 g (3 1/2 oz) shallots

Note that the recipe does not call for fine salt. The Roquefort and the gruyère are salted. The fresh cheese which is usually not salted should be seasoned with salt and pepper to taste. If using cottage cheese, press it through a fine sieve.

" Marc " is a strong alcohol made from the distilling of the stems and seeds of grapes. Cognac could be substituted.

**Preparing the Ingredients**

***The Sowbelly and Pork Liver***

Trim the sowbelly of skin, bones and cartilage and cut into 5 cm (2 in) cubes. Set aside in a stainless steel recipient.

Choose pork liver which is perfectly fresh and light in color. Trim all nerves and vessels. Rinse it under cold running water, pat dry with paper towels then cut into 3 cm (1 in) cubes. Set aside in a stainless steel recipient.

Season the sowbelly and liver separately with curing salt and " marc ".

***The Gruyère and Roquefort***

Cut the two cheeses into 1 cm (3/8 in) dice.

The roquefort tends to be crumbly. Any bits that are left after 750 g (1 1/2 lbs) of dice are made can be incorporated into the mixture when the meat is ground.

***The Shallots***

Shortly before making the mixture, slice the shallots thinly and cook in goose fat until soft but not browned.

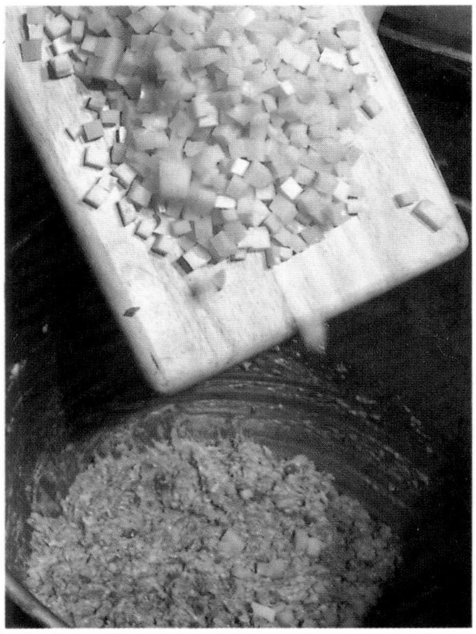

**Making the Mixture**

Pass the marinated sowbelly, liver, cooked shallots and roquefort trimmings through the medium (4 mm (about 1/8 in)) disk of the grinder.

Place these ingredients into the bowl of the mixer and incorporate the eggs two at a time. Process at medium speed until the eggs are absorbed into the other ingredients

Add the seasoned fresh cheese then the cream.

Scrape down the sides and mix until the mixture is homogeneous. Incorporate the cubes of gruyère then at low speed add the cubes of roquefort and mix very briefly to incorporate them evenly into the mixture.

The roquefort should not be crushed at this stage. You may prefer to fold the delicate cubes of cheese into the mixture by hand.

The roquefort can be placed in the freezer for 15 minutes to harden. However this dries the cheese and makes it more crumbly once it thaws. However this may be necessary depending on the quality of roquefort that is available to you.

The finished mixture has a medium-coarse texture with cubes of gruyère and roquefort evenly dispersed and clearly visible.

Brush the mold with lard or goose fat and arrange strips of smoked bacon on the bottom.

Fill the prepared mold with the mixture and cover the top with a piece of caul fat and tuck it in all around the edges of the pâté.

**Cooking**

Cook immediately in a steamer or in a water bath in the oven.

Set the oven at 180 °C (350 F), cook a few minutes to brown the top then turn down the temperature to 80 °C (175 F).

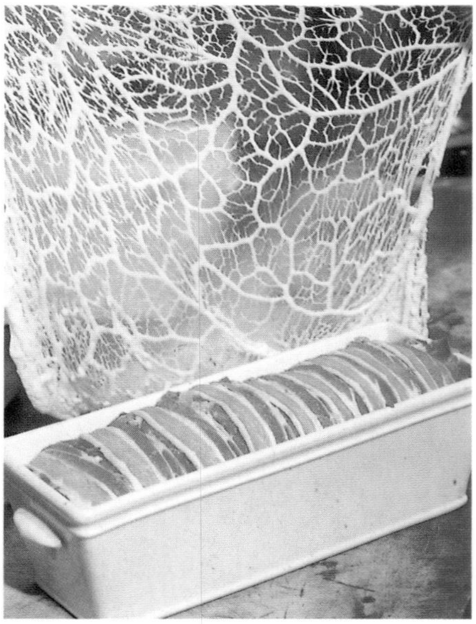

Cook until the internal temperature is 76 °C (170 F).

Drain the rendered fat and juices from the cooked pâté and replace with full-flavored stock that has been brought to a boil and skimmed.

Chill for 12-24 hours before slicing.

**Storage**

This pâté will keep for 8-10 days if covered with a thin layer of fat or better yet placed in a vacuum pouch.

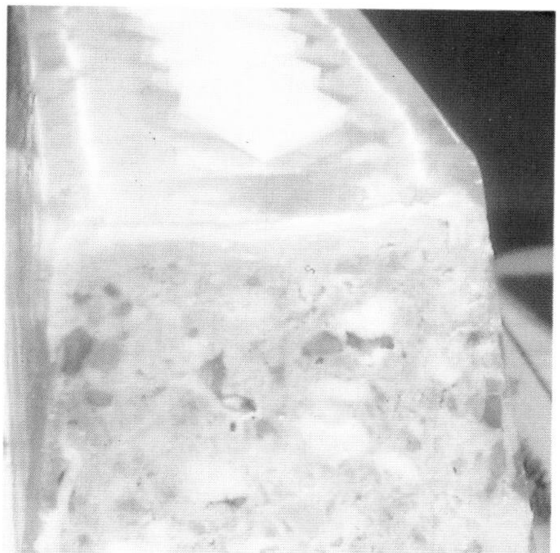

**Presentation**

Decorate the top with small dice of gruyère and roquefort, then glaze with aspic.

Note that this product is not included in the French " Code de la Charcuterie ". Therefore the recipe can be adapted by the charcutier to suit his personal tastes.

# Venison Liver Pâté " à l'Ancienne "

**Introduction**

This is one of the most flavorful preparations made with game. The straight-forward procedure makes this an easy dish for all cooks with basic culinary knowledge.

This is a country pâté (" pâté de campagne ") with a coarse texture and rustic appearance. The old-fashion, traditional aspect gives it the name " Le pâté de chevreuil a l'ancienne ".

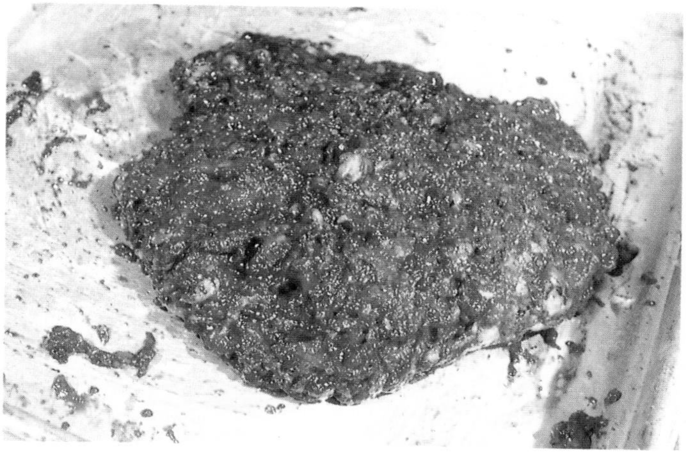

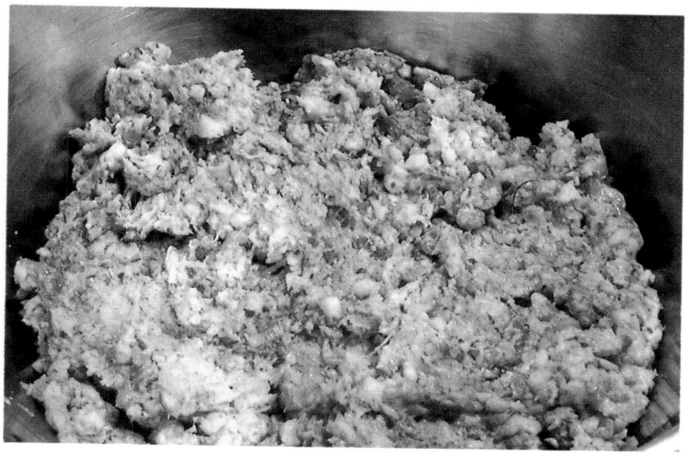

## Equipment

Knives, grinder, mixer, hotel pan, mold

## Ingredients

1 kg (2.2 lbs) venison liver (with heart if possible)
3 kg (6.6 lbs) pork jowl
250 g (1/2 lb) shallots
1 garlic clove
8 eggs
Chopped parsley
Caul fat
Cognac
Madeira
Stock made with game

*Seasonings (per kg (2.2 lbs))*

18 g (generous 1/2 oz) curing salt (sodium nitrite with fine salt)
2 g (1/16 oz) pepper
2 g (1/16 oz) sugar or dextrose
0.5 g (1/64 oz) four spice powder
Pinch dried sage

## Preparing the Ingredients

### *The Liver and Heart*

Order the venison liver and heart from a purveyor of game meats.

Trim and wash the liver very carefully. Sometimes the organs have been damaged by the hunt and are usually removed " on the spot " in less than ideal conditions.

Remove all traces of bile in the form of green stains on the liver. Wash then dry the liver.

The heart should have been emptied of blood when the animal was slaughtered. Cut it open and wash it thoroughly and dry.

Set aside 300 g (10 oz) of liver to make the " gratin ".

Marinate with curing salt, sugar and cognac. Refrigerate for 12 hours.

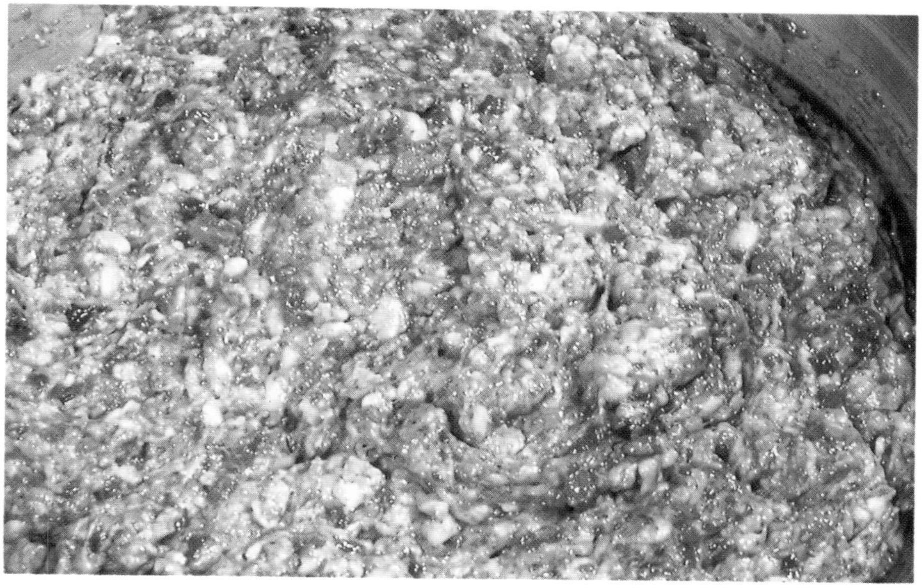

***The Pork Jowl***

Trim the jowl, removing the skin and glands. Cut into even cubes (2 cm x 2 cm (3/4 in). Marinate with curing salt, sugar and cognac. Refrigerate for 12 hours.

***The " Gratin "***

Make a gratin with the reserved venison liver:
Slice the shallot.
Chop the parsley.
Cut the liver in large cubes.
Cook the shallots in goose fat (or butter and oil).
Add the liver and brown lightly on all sides and season with salt and pepper.
Add the chopped parsley and madeira.
Cook for a few minutes. Very important! Do not overcook the liver; it should remain very rare. (Cut in large cubes which will take longer to cook.)
Cool quickly. Cover and refrigerate for 12 hours.

**Making the Forcemeat**

Reduce 1 liter (1 qt) of stock (made with venison bones if possible) to a glaze.

Grind the marinated meats (liver, heart and jowl) through a disk with 6 mm (1/4 in) holes.

Grind the gratin through a 2 mm (1/16 in) disk.

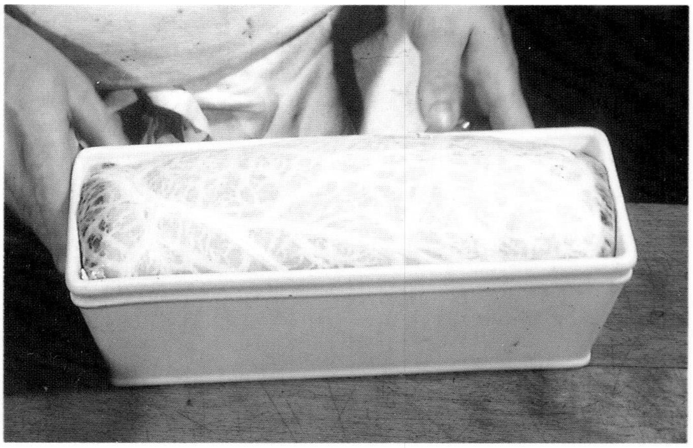

Place the ground meats into a mixer. At low speed, incorporate the eggs two at a time then the meat glaze.

Blend until the mixture is homogeneous.

**Assembly**

Line the mold with barding fat.
Fill the mold with the forcemeat and fold over the barding fat to cover the top.

Cover the top with a piece of caul fat and tuck it in around the edges.

**Cooking**

Cook the pâté in a water bath.
Start the cooking at 180-190 $^0$C (375 F). Brown the top a little then turn the oven down to 110-115 $^0$C (225 F).

Cook until the internal temperature is 76-78 C (170 F) registered on a probe thermometer.

Pour off the fatty juices rendered during cooking and replace these juices with full-flavored game stock that has been boiled, skimmed and strained.

Place a light weight on top and cool quickly.

**Storage**

This pâté will keep in the refrigerator (2-4 $^0$C (35 F)) for 10-12 days.
The storage can be prolonged if the cooled pâté is placed in a vacuum pouch.

**Presentation**

The pâté can be glazed and sliced directly from the mold.

To present the pâté unmolded like in this example, line the bottom of the clean mold with aspic. Arrange a decoration on the bottom then pour in a little more thickened aspic.

Slide the pâté back into the mold and refrigerate for at least 6 hours to completely set the aspic. Unmold onto a platter.

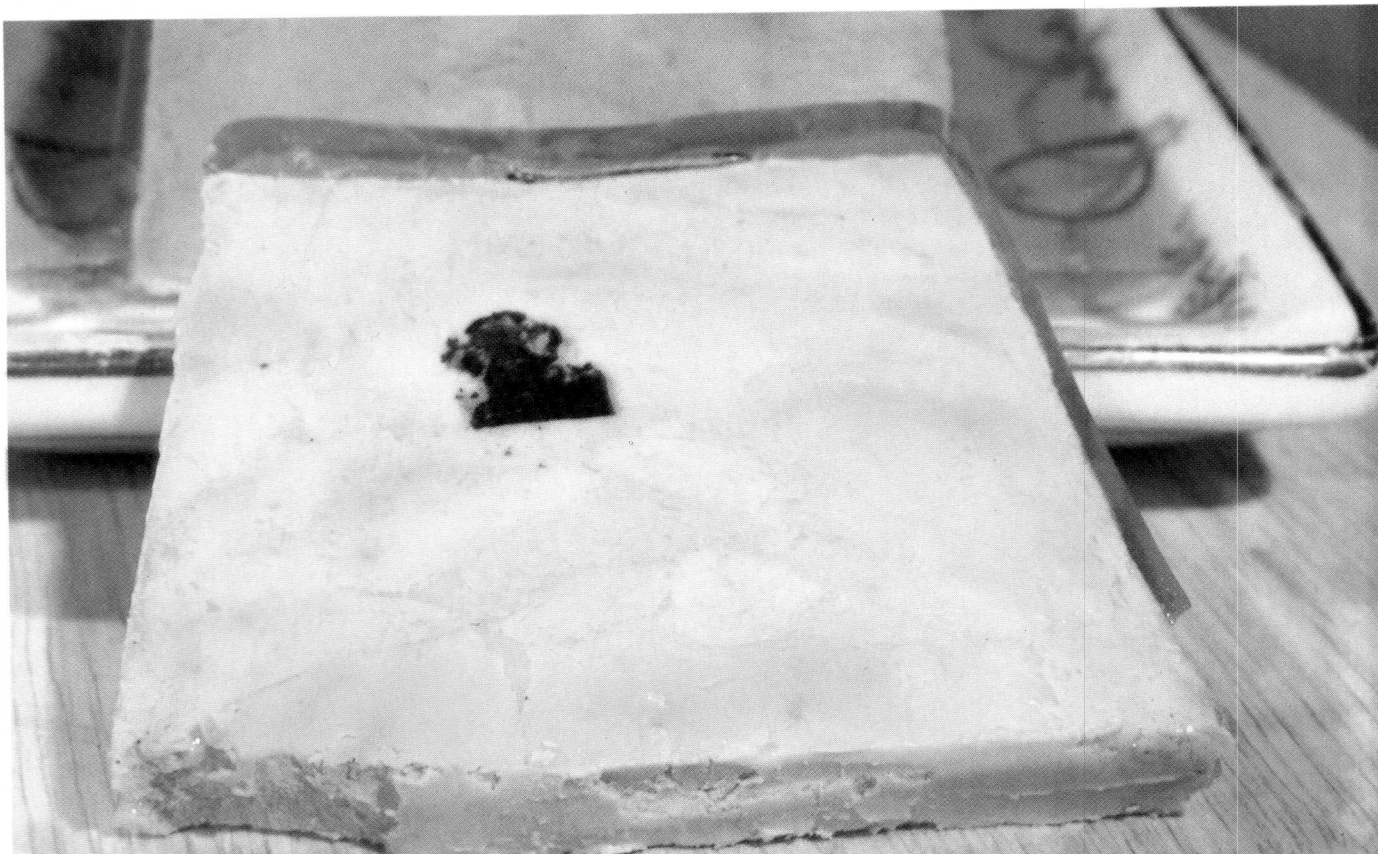

# Chapter 5
# Foie gras

## The Most Luxurious Product of French Charcuterie

*Foie gras adds an elegant touch to many top quality products. A chef's creativity and talent is often judged by his use of this versatile yet delicate ingredient.*

*Consumers who enjoy foie gras should discover the variety that the charcutier has to offer and include these products on menus for many occasions.*

*The authors present their best recipies here and hope that charcutiers everywhere will share their enthusiasm for foie gras.*

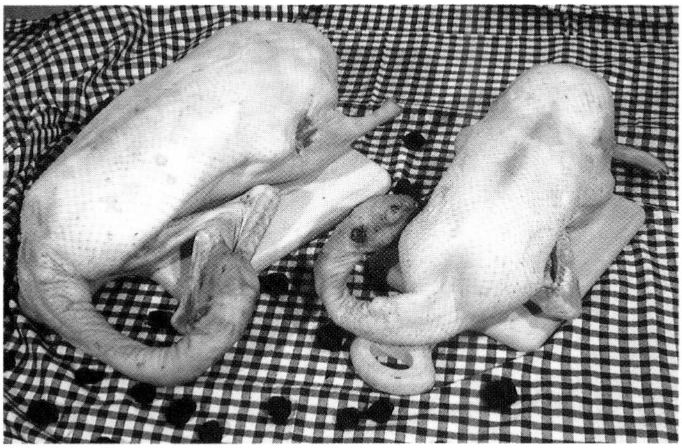

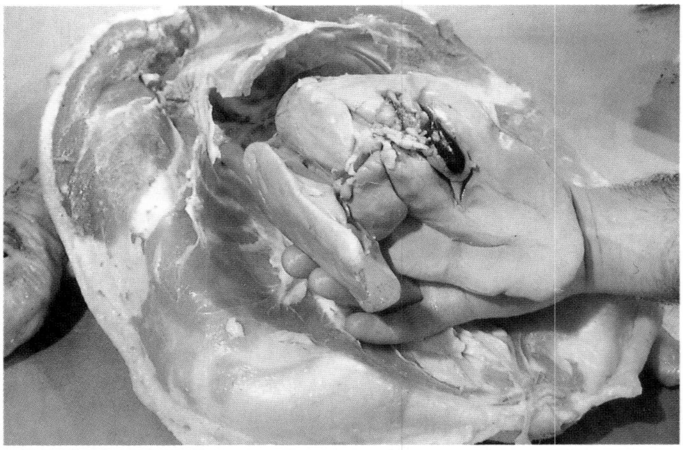

# Presentation

**Goose and Duck Foie gras** can be prepared in many ways. The authors present a wide range of possibilities. We also include information about the **truffle**, which complements foie gras and is often used as a garnish.

## Truffles: regulations

Furthermore, the word " truffé " on the label of products made in France is allowed only in the following cases:

- When the product includes 3% or more truffles by weight the label can state simply " truffled ".
- Between 1-3% the label must indicate the exact percentage of truffle (" truffé à 2% " for example).
- Below 1% the word truffle cannot appear on the label.

It is important to remember that the percentage of truffle is calculated on the net weight of the cooked product (without barding fat or aspic). The loss in weight of the truffle and the other ingredients during cooking must be taken into consideration so that the final product meets regulations.

As stated, " truffé " on the label allows for only " tuber melanosporum " and " tuber brumale ".

**Uses**

The charcutier-caterer will usually stock truffles of several qualities and sizes to use in the full range of his products.

The truffles are then cut into four shapes depending on the product:

- Thin slices
- Sticks of different sizes
- Dice of different sizes
- Chopped

Slices are used for decoration. They are cut from whole, large truffles with a special tool: truffle slicer or " coupe-truffe ". The slices are used " as is " or cut into a variety of shapes with small truffle cutters. The slices can also be cut into very this strips that are pieced together end to end to make pictures (called " decoration au fil de truffe ").

The four sided sticks (" bâtonnets) cut from large truffles are primarily used to add a core of truffles in the center of a product, the best known is of course " foie gras truffé ". The " bâtonnettes " can be large or small depending on the price of the final product.

Dices of truffles are most often used to flavor the forcemeat of galantines, ballotines and terrines. The dice are an important aspect of the slice so the dice should be very regular (2 cm × 2 cm (3/4 in) is a good size). Truffle pieces or the trimmings from " bâtonnettes " can be used to make the dice.

Chopped truffles are used in the same type of products as the diced truffles when the aspect of the slice is not as important. Individual sausages such as " boudin blanc " or white sausage can be made with chopped truffles. Peelings and broken pieces are well suited to being chopped.

There is yet another product that offers the flavor of truffles: " jus de truffe " or truffle juice.

The liquid that is rendered by the truffle when it is sterilzed in the can or jar is very flavorful and can be used to enhance and reinforce the truffle taste of a product.

In some cases a small amount of water and/or wine has been added to the can and this liquid absorbs flavor from the truffle.

The " jus " is also available in bottles on its own; a by-product of the sterilizing process of truffles that are cooked before canning. The quality of " jus de truffe " is also regulated by the authorities.

The French Charcuterie Code includes a detailed description of the regulations concerning truffles.

**Truffles**
**(p. 145)**

**Breeding Ducks and Geese**
**(p. 146)**

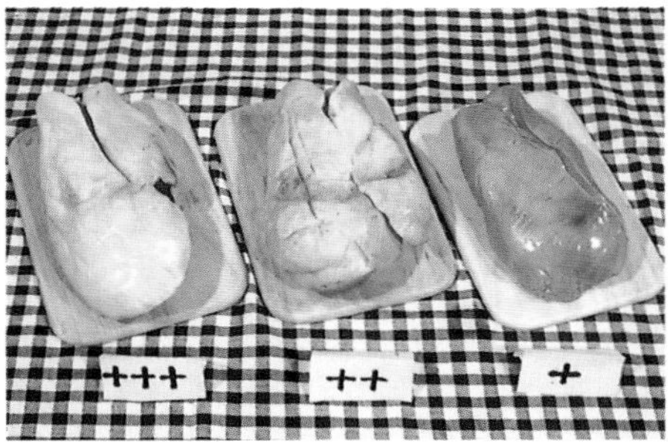


**Selecting and Grading Foie Gras**
**(p. 150)**

**Preparing and Cooking Foie Gras**
**(p. 158)**

**Terrine of Whole Goose Foie Gras**
**(p. 164)**

**" Bloc " of Goose Foie Gras**
**with Truffles (p. 168)**

**" Rouleau " of Goose Foie Gras**
**(p. 172)**

**" Rouleau " of Goose Foie Gras**
**with Truffles (p. 176)**

**" Lucullus " of Foie Gras**
**with Truffles (p. 178)**

**" Kouglof " of Goose Foie Gras**
**(p. 180)**

**Terrine of whole Duck**
**Foie Gras (p. 184)**

**Terrine of Duck Foie Gras**
**(p. 186)**

**Terrine of Duck Foie Gras**
**with Truffles (p. 188)**

**Small Terrine of Duck Foie Gras**
**with Truffles (p. 190)**

**Foie Gras in Brioche**
**(p. 192)**

# The Origin and History of Foie Gras

*Jean Rougié, the largest producer of foie gras products in France, declares that much information is published about the mystery of foie gras and truffles which is not always objective.*

*Here we present the origin and history of foie gras as presented in well documented sources.*

The earliest records of foie gras are found in the bas-reliefs of ancient Egypt dating back 5 000 years. The Egyptians force fed geese with figs to obtain very succulent fattened livers.

The civilizations of Greece and Rome also practiced the art of force feeding. Our ancestors the Gauls probably learned force feeding techniques from the Romans.

But it is not until the grand royal feasts of Louis XV and Louis XVI that foie gras was prepared by great chefs and given its noble status. In 1760 in Nérac, in Landes, the great chef Taverne created the " Foie gras terrine of Nérac ". At the same time, terrines were being developed in Périgueux in the southwest. In Strasbourg, the chef to the " Marechal des Contades " created a foie gras in pastry which quickly became very popular in Paris.

Therefore it is the foie gras producers of Landes, Périgord and Alsace that claim to have the best foie gras and the best recipes. The rivalry that began many years ago persists today.

At the beginning only geese were force fed. About twenty years ago France was the first European country to produce duck foie gras and it has developed into an important industry.

How and why are certain webfooted birds capable of producing a liver filled with fat after force feeding?

Domestic geese and ducks are descendants of wild migrating birds. Over time, these migrating birds developed the capacity to store fat in their livers which would provide nourishment during the long voyages from Scandinavia to Africa. It is this heritage that is put into play to produce fattened livers in domesticated geese and ducks. For these birds, however, the trip ends at the slaughtering house.

The foie gras is obtained after a closely monitored term of force feeding with the grain of choice being corn.

The French production of goose foie gras is centered in the southwest and Alsace. Small-scale production is taking place in Brittany and Normandy but the procedure with geese is a delicate one so is not widespread.

However ducks have proven to be robust and easier to force feed. Duck foie gras is produced in all regions where goose foie gras is found and is also produced to some degree throughout France.

But even with production of duck foie gras, France still imports livers to fulfill its needs. In 1988, 5,095 tons of foie gras was marketed in France, 2,020 tons of which was imported. The imported livers came mostly from eastern Europe; Hungary, Czhechoslovakia, Bulgaria, Poland and also Israel. Even before the war in 1914, France had been importing foie gras from these countries.

Geese have been fattened in the Israel region for many years. The strict dietary laws of the jewish faith permits the consumption of goose and its fat. One can imagine that the Alsatian foie gras industry grew from the traditions of the many jewish people who came to settle there.

The production in Israel grew as more people from the eastern European countries came to live in the new state.

The progress that has been made in transportation and refrigeration has enabled producers to maintain constant temperatures and get their foies gras to the wholesale markets in just a few hours. (This also facilitates the importation of more foie gras.) In many cases the manufacturing plants are just miles away from the breeding farms.

With more imported livers coming into France, the competition Israel, Hungary, Poland, Bulgaria and Czhechoslovakia.

We do not favor the foie gras of one region over another. Recent blind tastings have shown that the imported livers measure up favorably to the top quality French foie gras. Expert judges, including chefs, caterers, charcutiers, and canners have been surprised to find that the imported livers compared well with the best French livers.

We feel that excellent foie gras is produced in each area and that it is the trained cook who uses his skill to choose the best livers and prepare them well.

# Truffles

The truffle has been a misunderstood ingredient for centuries. Scientific research (by the French National Institute for Agricultural Research) is slowly unraveling the mystery.

The search for information was underway in the time of the ancient Greeks and Romans.

Up until the fourth century truffles were believed to be minerals when Théophraste discovered the molecular makeup and classified them with vegetables.

Written information on the truffle does not exist from the Middle Ages, they reappeared in the 16th century. At this time they were not marketed, only consumed by the nobles and upper classes of the regions where they were found.

In 1729, the botanist Micheli confirmed the studies of Théophraste and further classified the truffle as a fungus or mushroom.

Truffles became a business in the middle of the 19th century when the phylloxera virus attacked the vineyards of France. Tens of thousands of hectars (1 hectar = 2.47 acres) of medium quality vines were destroyed in southwest France.

Many winemakers chose to replant their land with the " truffle oak " and by 1890, 75,000 hectars (5,000 acres) had been planted. 60,000 hectars (4,000 acres) produced truffles within a short period. The remaining land developed its " crop " more slowly, with " harvest " starting at the beginning of the 20th century.

The chalky/clay soil of the southwest and the temperate climate proved to be ideal for the growth of the truffle.

The truffle is a " mycorhize ", a fungus that thrives in symbiosis with the roots of certain trees. All mushrooms posess filaments or " mycelium " which support the portion that we consume. In the case of truffles, these filaments exist but the " mushroom " remains underground and during the course of development, the mycelium detach and the truffle completes its growth without visible means of nourishment. This puzzling phenomenon makes the sowing of truffles impossible.

Research has been underway for several years with " truffle oaks " impregnated with mycelium with the hopes of " harvesting a crop " within five years. But this risky venture means an investment of large sums of money with no guarantee of return.

This research has become necessary because the yield has been low in recent years as the following statistics show:
1870: 1,600 tons; 1890: 1,800 tons; 1940: 250 tons; 1958: 150 tons; 1970: 33 tons; 1980: 45 tons; 1984: 11 tons.

In just one century the harvest has greatly decreased by. This explains why the price has become so high, leading many manufacturers to reduce the amount of truffle in their products or eliminate it all togehter.

***30 Varieties***

There exists about 30 varieties of truffles but we will describe only the major ones.

- ***The black truffle of Perigord*** comes in two varieties, " tuber Melanosporum " and " Brumale ". They are black inside and out with a spiny outer covering and a strong characteristic odor and taste. They are harvested from November to March.
- ***White truffles from Piedmont or Italy*** which are a creamy yellowish color on the inside and the outer covering looks like a Jeruselem artichoke. The odor and taste have a slight accent of garlic.
- ***White truffles with black covering*** with a honeycombed covering and neutral taste. They are harvested in the summer and are sometimes called " summer truffles " (" truffes d'été ") or " truffles Saint Jean ".
- In the regions of Champagne and Burgundy is found a truffle called ***the " grey autumn " (" grise d'automne ")*** and is similar to the summer truffle.

All of these varieties are edible but only the black truffle qualifies for the mention of " truffled " (" truffé ") on the label of French products.

The black truffles (" melanosporum " and " brumale ") are sold in three forms:

- ***Fresh*** still covered in soil. They are sorted for size and quality and lightly brushed to remove excess soil.
- ***Fresh and cleaned*** thoroughly to remove the soil in all the crevasses.
- ***Sterilized*** in cans or jars. After thorough cleaning the truffles are sorted according to size and quality and sterilized.

The canning process in France is called " appertissement " named after the scientist from Champagne, Nicholas Appert, who perfected the technique. In 1810 he wrote " Taité de Conservation en Boîtes " in which he devoted an entire chapter to truffles.

Five grades or " qualités " are available:

- " Truffes surchoix ": top-quality whole truffles (usually large), peeled and brushed.
- " Truffes premier choix ": whole truffles (smaller, lower quality), peeled and brushed.
- " Morceaux de truffes ": truffle pieces.
- " Pelures de truffes ": truffle peelings.
- " Brisures de truffes ": broken pieces of truffle.

The canned truffles are processed in two ways:

***" Truffes première cuisson ":*** the truffles are placed uncooked in the can or jar after thorough cleaning and brushing. They are then sterilized directly in the recipient which preserves a maximum of aroma and flavor. During the sterilizing process the truffles lose about 25% of their weight. This loss is impossible to estimate in advance so the net weight of the truffle is hard to control. This method sacrifices yield for flavor.

***" Truffes deuxième cuisson ":*** the truffles are cooked first then placed in the cans and jars with a samll portion of the cooking liquid and undergo a second cooking when they are sterilized in the recipient. The net weight of the truffle can therefore be guaranteed. This method produces a higher yield but the flavor is not as good as the first method.

# Foie Gras Production and Marketing

## A Large Production

The French wholesale market sells about 8,500 tons of foie gras. Of this 6,000 tons are produced in France and 2,500 tons are imported.

The breakdown of the various products is as follows:

- 4,700 tons sold fresh to restaurants, charcutier, caterers.
- 3,800 tons are made into preserved products (cans and jars).

*1,100 tons are exported:*

- 850 tons are exported as preserved products in cans or jars.
- 250 tons are exported fresh.

As a general trend over the last 10 years, duck liver consumption is rapidly increasing.

### The Labeling is Very Strict

In France, the regulations governing the labeling or " appellation " of all foie gras products are very strict.

The words " foie gras " can appear on the label only if the strict standards are met as shown in the chart.

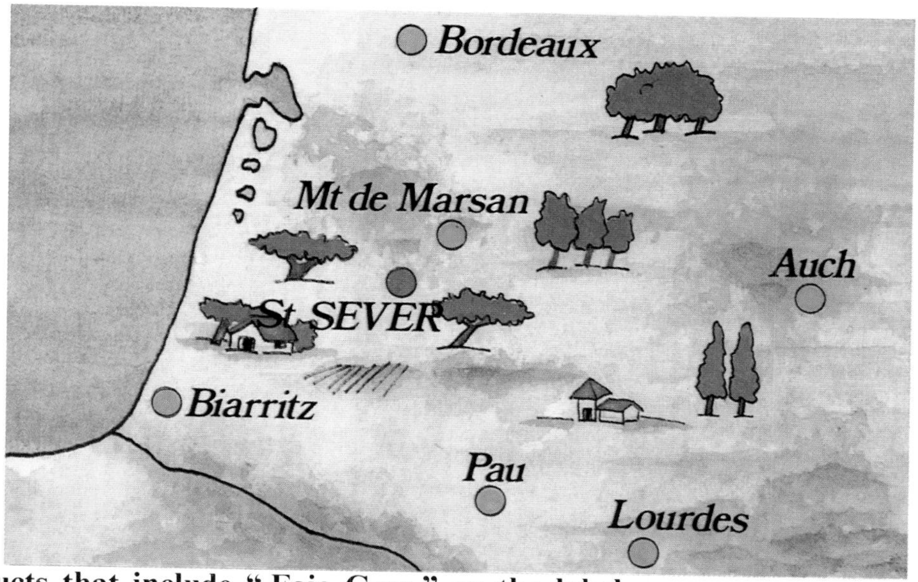


**French products that include " Foie Gras " on the label**

| Name on the label | Principle Characteristics of the Product | Ingredients and Seasonings |
|---|---|---|
| a) *" Foie gras d'oie entier "* *(Whole goose liver)* *" Foie gras de canard entier "* *(Whole duck liver)* | **– One or two whole lobes, molded – A portion from a whole lobe if the preparation is less than 200 g (7 oz) In both cases, it is permissable to add a small piece of a lobe to make up the required weight.** | **Foie gras** Seasoning possibilities: Truffles (3 %) Additives |
| b) *" Foie gras d'oie "* *(Goose liver)* *" Foie gras de canard "* *(Duck liver)* | **Large pieces of goose liver pressed together Large pieces of duck liver pressed together Large pieces of duck liver bound with purée of foie gras The pieces of foie gras must be visible in the slice.** | **Foie gras** Seasoning possibilities: Truffles (3 %) Additives |
| c) *" Bloc de foie gras d'oie " (*)* *(" Bloc " of goose liver)* *" Bloc de foie gras de canard " (*)* *(" Bloc " of duck liver)* | **Foie gras preparations formed mechanically with pieces of foie gras visible in the slice.** | **Foie gras** Seasoning possibilities: Truffles (3 %) Additives |

(*) The name " bloc d'oie (ou canard) avec morceaux " (bloc of goose (or duck) liver with pieces) is not allowed unless the product includes a minimum of pieces visible in the slice (50 % for goose and 30 % for duck).

# Raising Geese and Duck in Southwest France

The majority of the force-fed geese and ducks are raised in the southwest region of France. The mild climate (warm and humid), and grassy prairies have made the southwest the preferred region for the raising of force-fed birds since the 15th century.

Another important factor is the availability of corn in the region which is the staple diet during the force feeding process (" gavage ").

This extensive industry influences the economy of the region in many ways:

- Creates business for small-scale farmers.
- The southwest is the center for many societies for animal farmers.
- Distributing center for food products.
- Large-scale construction of buildings for raising animals and production.
- Internships for young artisans.
- Hygiene equipment much in demand.
- Large market for refrigeration and air-conditioning equipment.
- Center for slaughterhouses, production houses, and laboratories.
- Preserving industry is extensive.
- Packaging industry is extensive.

**Raising the Birds**

The first step for raising geese and ducks is the incubation of the eggs of selected breeds which lasts for three weeks.

The birds then grow for a minimum of twelve weeks before force feeding begins. (12 weeks is necessary to obtain the " label rouge ".)

Ducks are force fed twice a day for two weeks and geese three times a day for three weeks.

The fattened liver (foie gras) is removed when the animal is slaughtered. The average weight of the liver ranges from 300-800 g (10 oz-1 lb 10 oz) for an animal weighing 5-6 kilos (11-12 lbs).

The foie gras represents 55-60% of the revenue received for the animal. The " magret " or breast meat is a product that is also much in demand.

Other popular products include " confit ", most often made with the legs and " rillettes " made from the meats that adheres to the skin and carcass.

Following slaughter, the livers are placed in a cool room to chill slightly for two hours.

They are kept under constant refrigeration until graded for different uses.

A large portion of the livers are sold fresh to be transformed by charcutiers. The demand for fresh products however is concentrated at the end of the year when foie gras is featured for many holiday meals.

To relieve the problem created by this high seasonal demand, research has been done in the field of quick freezing using liquid nitrogen (– 70 °C (– 86 F)). The results have been very good; the frozen livers retain the taste and creamy texture of the fresh foie gras.

Duck livers have become more popular in recent years. Due to the shorter " gavage " they are less expensive than goose foie gras and many connoisseurs prefer the stronger flavor.

## The Labeling

In addition to the preparations that are pure foie gras, there are three other categories that carry " foie gras " on the label:

***1. Products made with a minimum of 75% foie gras :***

*Name on Label*

- " Parfait " of goose foie gras
- " Parfait " of duck foie gras
- " Parfait " of goose and duck foie gras
- " Parfait " of duck and goose foie gras

***2. Products containing a minimum of 50 % foie gras (with barding fat removed) :***

*Name on Label*

- " Parfait " of goose foie gras
- " Parfait " of duck foie gras
- " Parfait " of goose and duck foie gras
- " Parfait " of duck and goose foie gras
- Galantine of goose foie gras
- Galantine of duck foie gras
- Galantine of goose and duck foie gras
- Galantine of duck and goose foie gras
- Purée of mousse of goose foie gras
- Purée of mousse of duck foie gras
- Purée of mousse of goose and duck foie gras
- Purée of mousse of duck and goose foie gras

***3. Preparations containing a minimum of 20 % foie gras:***

*Name on Label:* The label can include " foie gras " but must also include the exact percentage of foie gras used in the product.

# Selecting Foie Gras

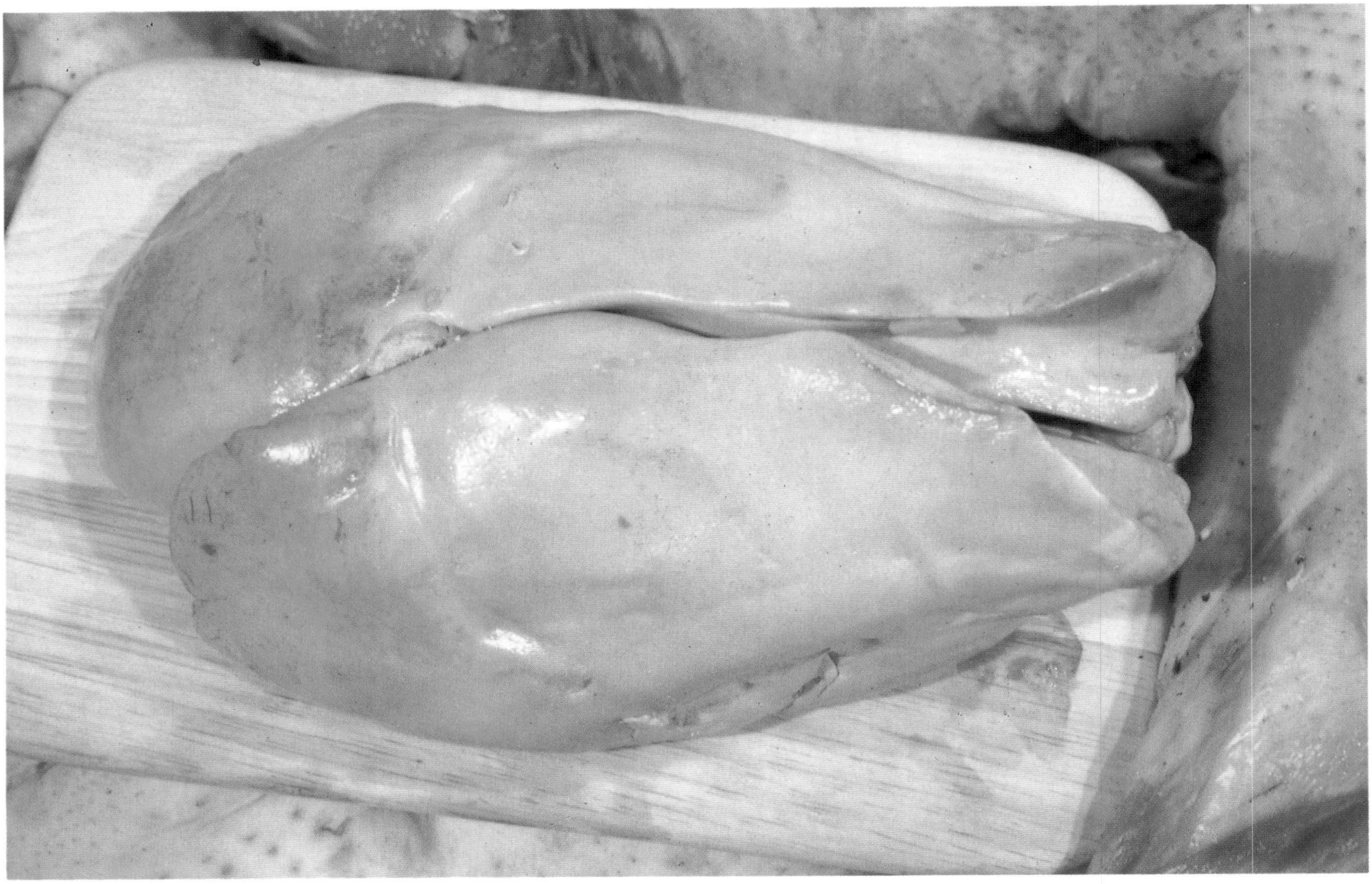

Determining the quality or grade of fattened livers is a very important and delicate step. The taste and texture of top-of-the-line products based on whole livers depend on selecting the best quality livers. From an economical standpoint, inferior foie gras renders more fat during cooking resulting in a lower yield.

This step is more difficult than it seems for the French charcutier-caterer. Only 10-15% of the foie gras marketed is of the superior quality necessary for the most refined preparations.

Through experience, the charcutier develops the skill to determine the various grades. However, even the most experienced will make errors up to 25% of the time.

To simplify the procedure somewhat, there are two criteria that help to narrow the choice:

***Weight:*** The desirable weight of a goose foie gras ranges between 600-900 g (1 lb 4 oz-1 lb 14 oz) and 300-600 g (10 oz-1 lb 4 oz) for a duck foie gras. Within this weight range, the livers will fall into three categories--non-melting (" non fondant "), intermediate (" intermédiare "), and melting (" fondant ").

***Texture*** This is the most important test and requires the most skill. When the liver is pressed with a finger (which in high quality livers will leave an imprint), the experienced professional can determine the texture and unctuosity of the foie gras. If the foie gras cracks rather than " giving " a little with an elastic feel to the touch it is not of the best quality.

Foie gras that is dry to the touch

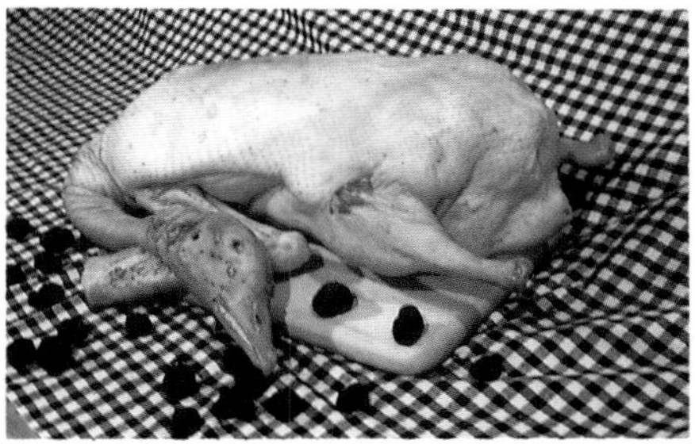

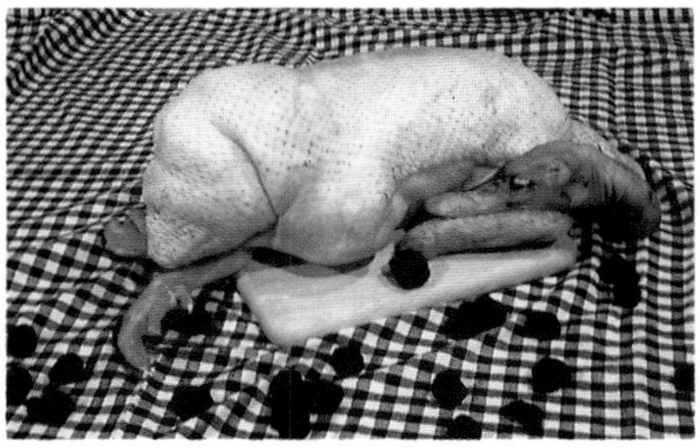

and cracks often melts more during cooking. These livers are chosen to make " parfaits ", purées and mousses. They are also acceptable for the making of galantines where the fat that melts out of the liver is absorbed by the forcemeat and surrounding meat and therefore actually improves the final product.

A scientific advancement has been developed in the form of a tool that can determine how much of the fat in the liver will melt during cooking. This electric tool is outfitted with two small electrodes which are inserted into the liver. The resistance to the electric current is measured and the " melting factor " can be estimated.

Unfortunately, this apparatus is expensive and out of the reach of most artisinal charcutiers. Often, several small scale charcuteries will invest in one machine and use it alternately.

In addition to estimating the " meltability " of the foie gras it is also important to determine the freshness. After slaughtering and cleaning the bird, the foie gras will keep at 2 °C (35 F) for 8-10 days.

Foie gras stored longer than 8-10 days and/or at temperatures higher than 2 °C (35 F) often develops a bitter and acid flavor as well as an undesirable odor.

*Note:* The use of vacuum packing in France prolongs the storage time. It is advised to check the packaging and labeling closely.

## How does goose foie gras differ from duck foie gras?

In addition to the difference in size (although a small goose liver will be similar to a large duck liver) the shape of the lobes differ.

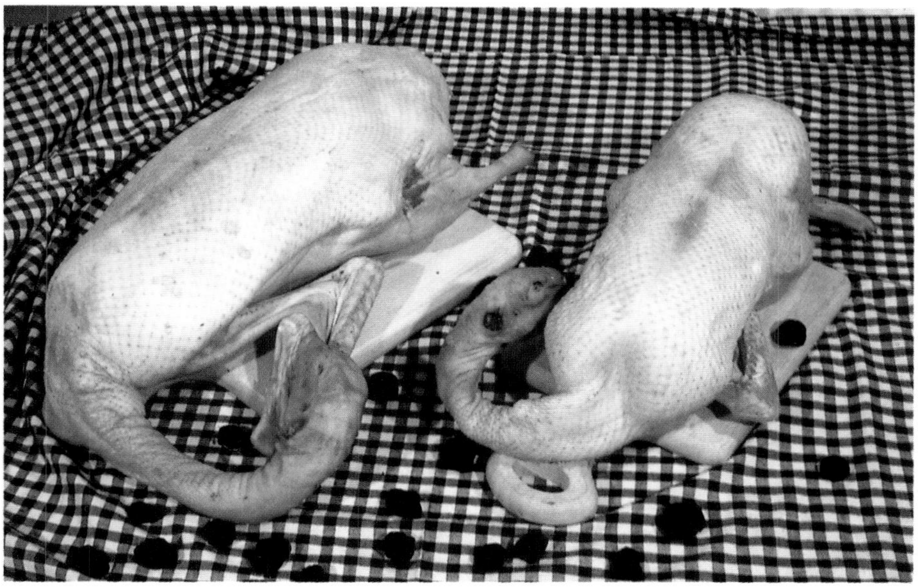

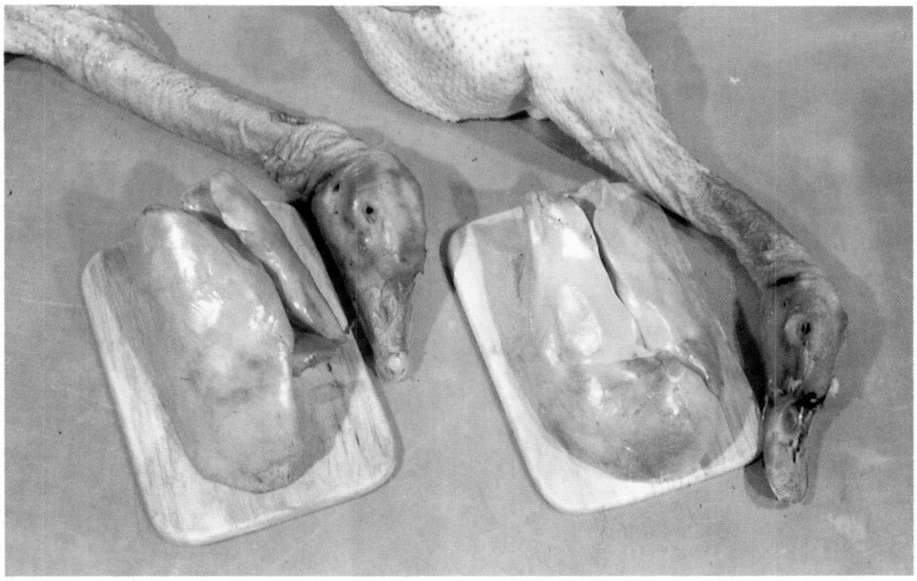

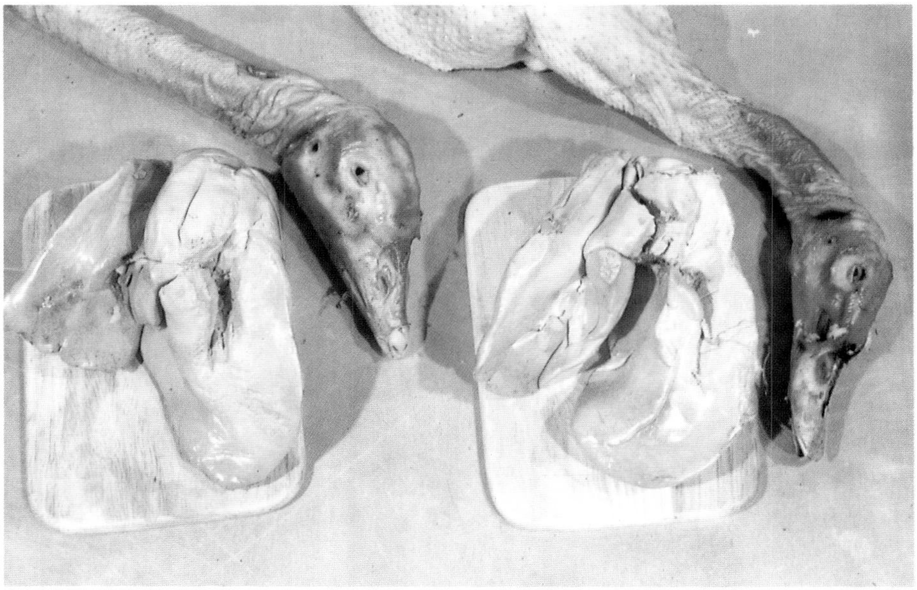

# Selecting Foies Gras (continued)

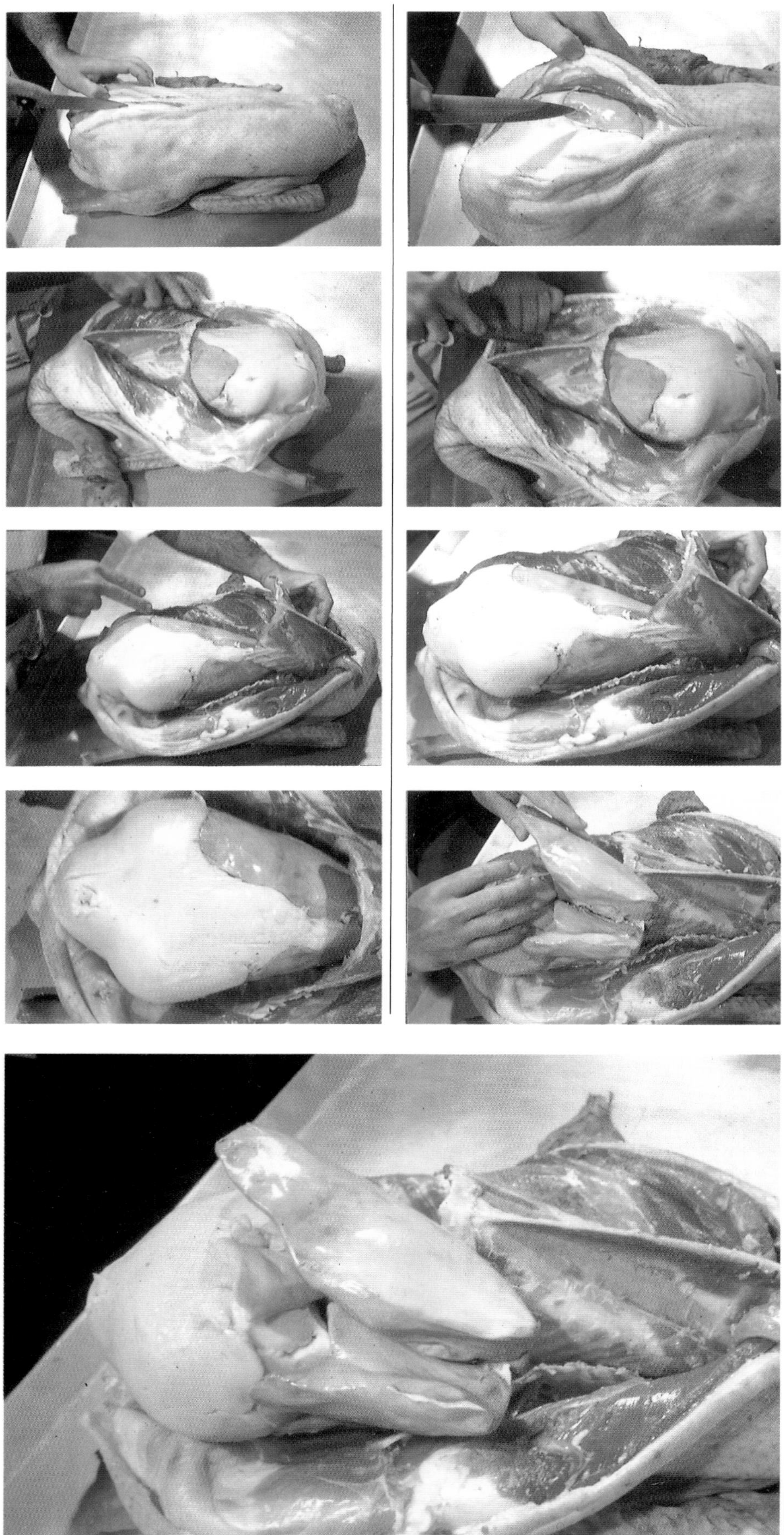

Both types have two lobes--one larger than the other, but the large lobe of the duck foie gras is rectangualar while the large lobe of the goose liver is triangular.

### Color

Another factor to be noted is the color of the foie gras. In most cases, the color is not an indication of the taste or meltability of the liver. The birds from various regions in France and other countries will have been fed a different diet which influences the color. Foie gras from Israel and central Europe range from ocre to pale gold in color. Fattened livers from the Landes region of France are usually creamy white to pale pink. Naturally the finished product will be the color of the raw liver.

It is advised to avoid mixing livers of different colors in one preparation. A marbled appearance in the finished product is undesirable.

A dark (bloody) or uneven color can indicate that the foie gras is from a bird that was not bled properly. This is an inferior product with a texture and appearance that is unsuitable for the preparation of refined products.

### Refrigeration, Packaging and Storage

Wholesale merchants in France often display fresh foie gras on a bed of crushed ice. However a fattened liver left too long on ice will absorb moisture therefore changing the texture and flavor.

The preferred method of display is vacuum packaging. Although this protects the delicate liver from drying out or absorbing moisture or flavors, it is still imperative to maintain the product at a constant cold temperature to ensure freshness.

A few years ago a new method of quick-freezing was developed which uses liquid nitrogen (– 50 °C (– 23 F)). This allows foie gras to be processed during the off season and frozen for sale during the holidays. The quality of these livers is so good that even the experts cannot tell the difference.

Purchasing fattened livers when the wholesale prices are low for use when the finished products are most in demand generates profits that pays for the equipment needed to freeze the foie gras.

Foie gras in France that has been quick-frozen must indicate this on the label.

### Slaughtering

Traditionally the slaughtering of the geese and ducks was done on the same farm where the birds were raised. However, legislation has been passed that requires all meat destined for public consumption to be slaughtered in government inspected facilities.

Private and cooperative slaughtering houses have been constructed that ensure better hygeine and therefore better foie gras.

Most of the foie gras on the market in France is processed in these government approved slaughtering houses. The farm production of yesterday is disappearing except for private consumption and special orders that the farmer/producer fulfills directly for a client. Even in these cases, hygeine regulations are being enforced.

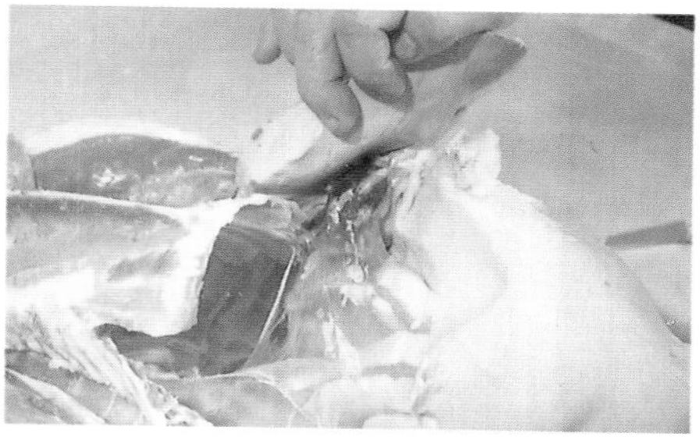

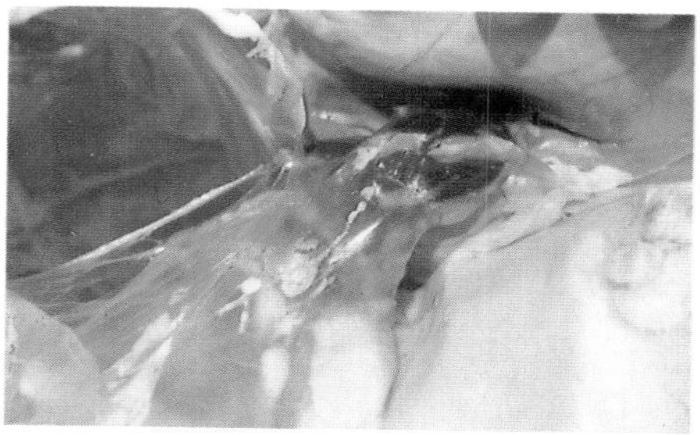

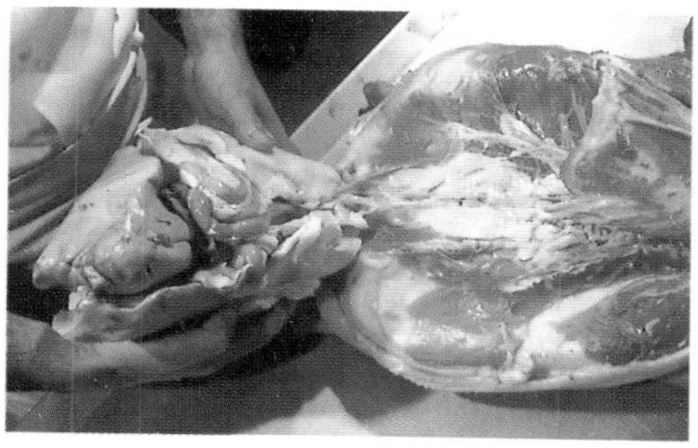

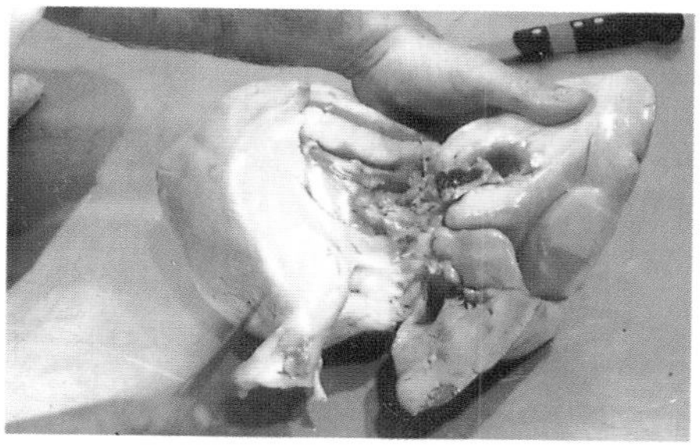

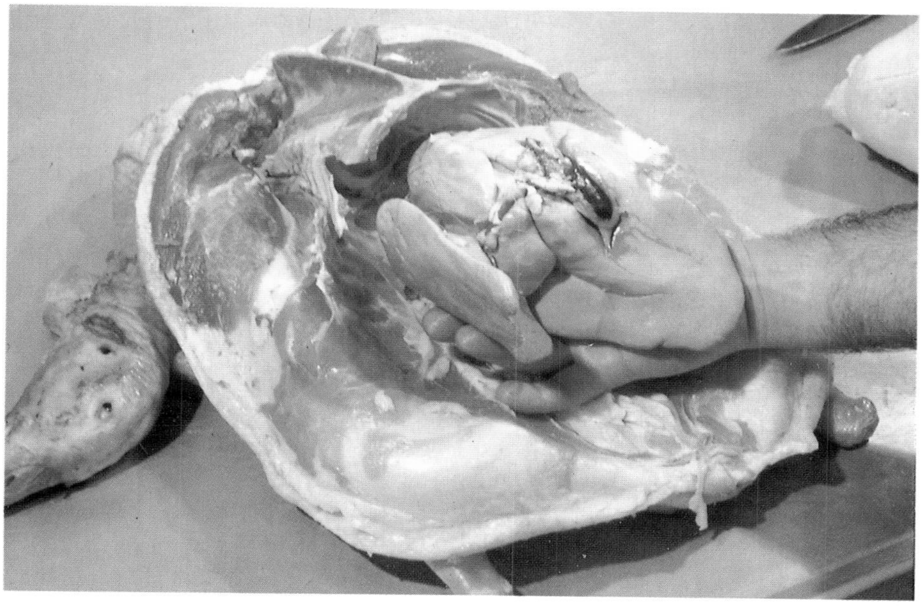

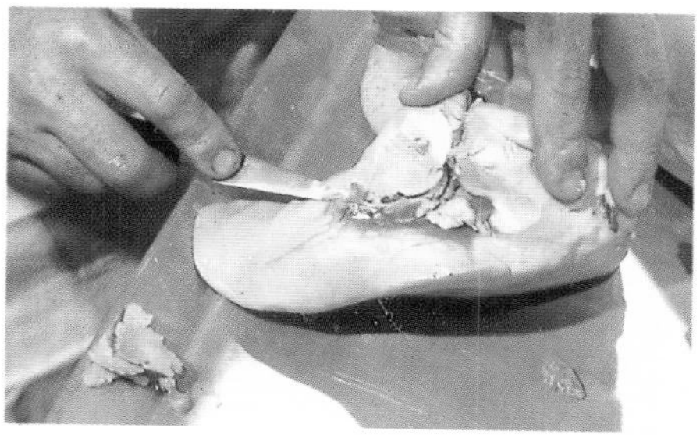

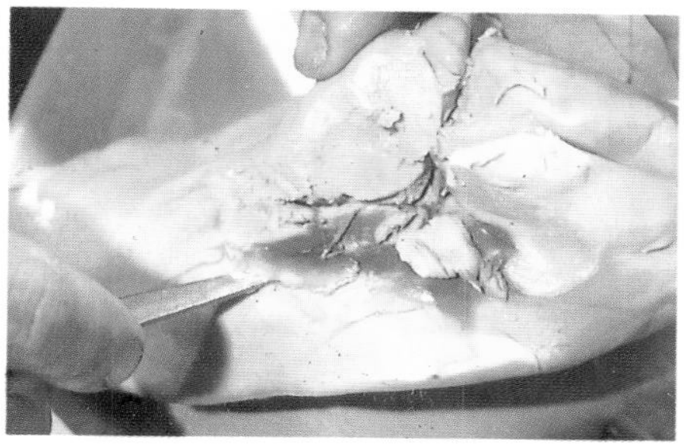

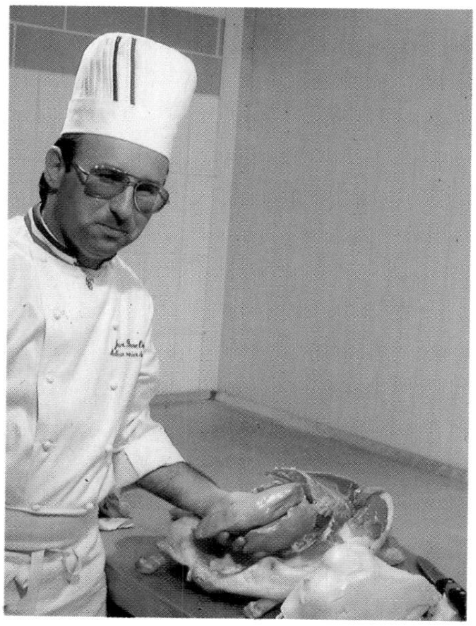

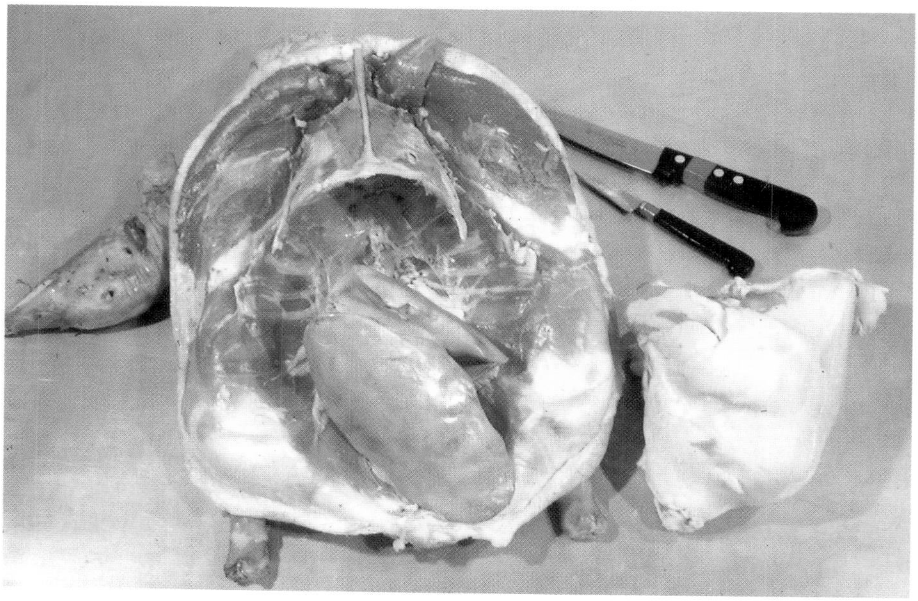

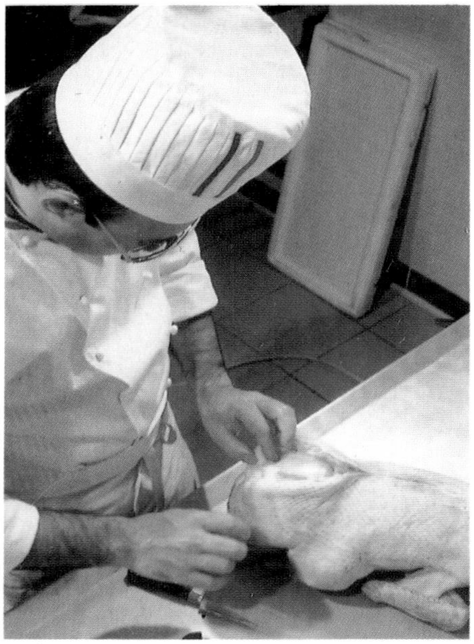

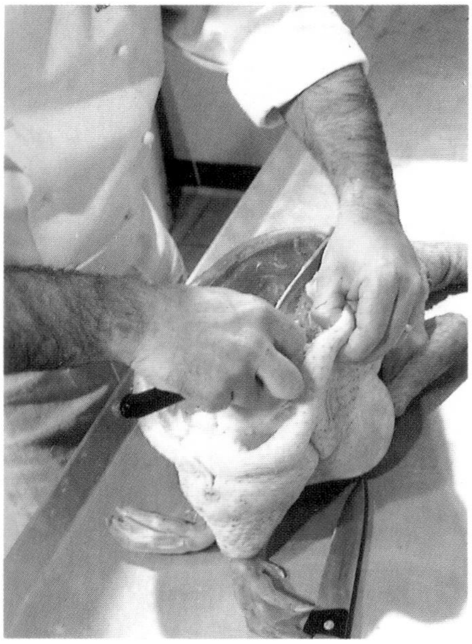

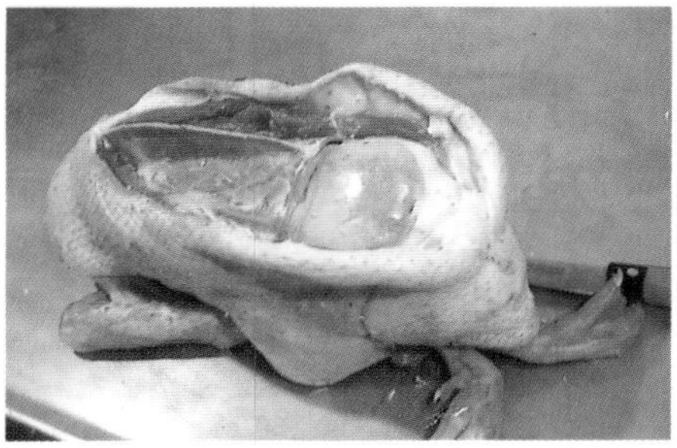

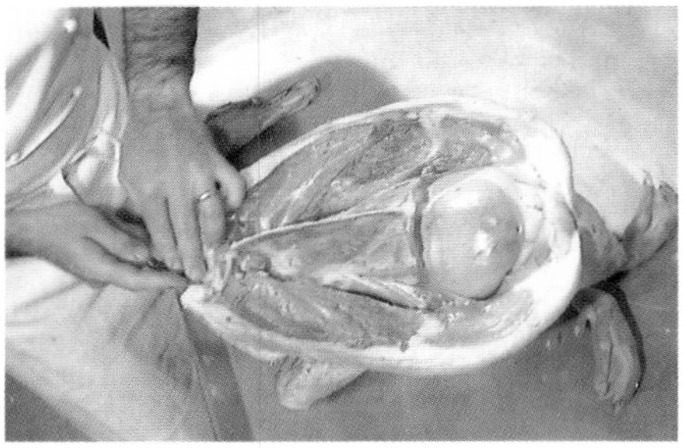

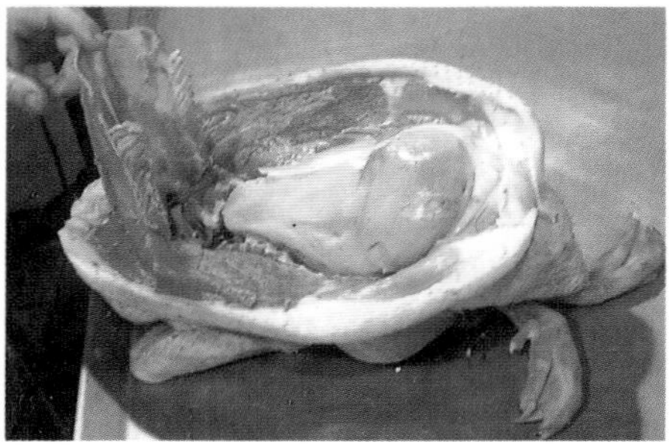

## Marketing Foie Gras

Sale of the whole bird; slaughtered but not cleaned, represents about 10-12% of the market. This too is a fast-disappearing tradition.

Spoilage begins from the moment the bird is slaughtered and it usually takes at least 24 hours for the product to reach the wholesale market.

The bird is then sold which accounts for another 24 hours during which spoilage continues.

It is preferable to remove the foie gras at the time of slaughter and chill immediately and keep it at a constant temperature through each step of marketing.

This ensures the freshness of the liver.

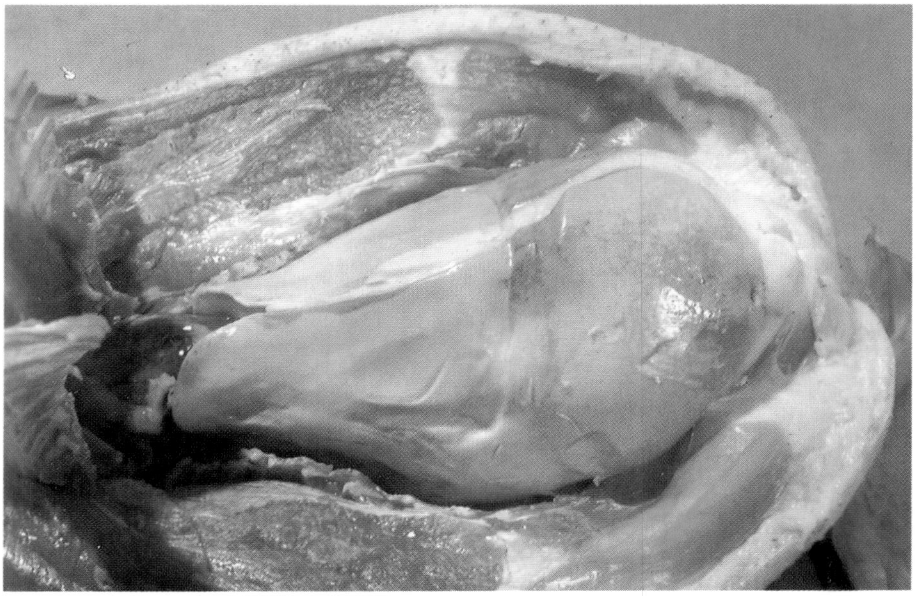

## The Remainder of the Bird

Although the fattened liver is the most important part of the force-fed goose or duck, the remainder of the bird should not be overlooked.

When the liver and bones are removed, leaving all the meat attached to the skin this is known as the " paletot " or " overcoat ".

The rich breast and leg meat of the force-fed goose or duck make the excellent rillettes described in Volume 1 of this series.

The legs are also sold on their own for confit and the meaty breast, known as " magret " is marketed separately for roasting and grilling--a popular dish in the best restaurants.

These by-products of the force-fed goose and duck are delicious and are very much in demand.

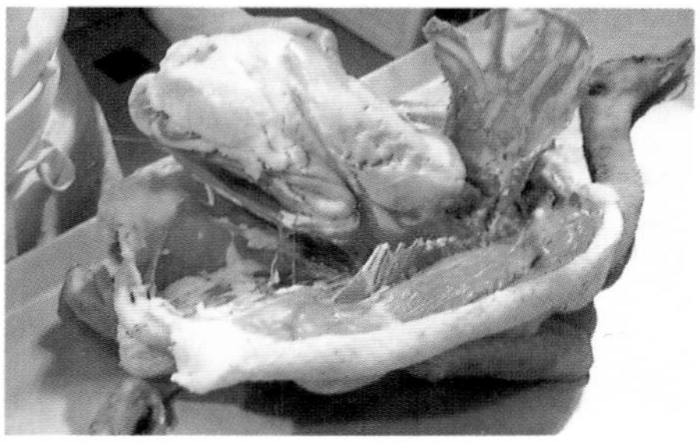

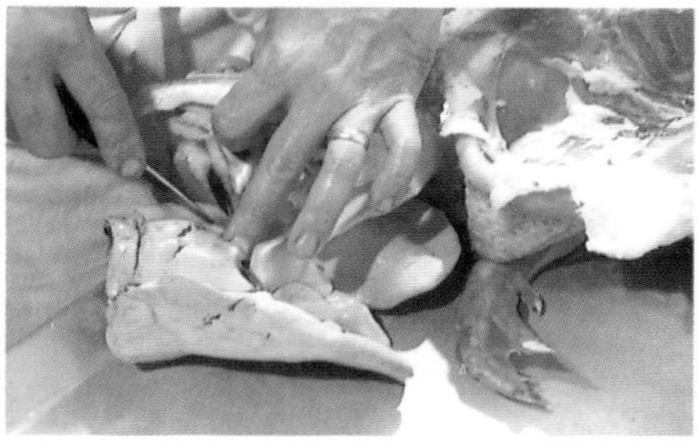

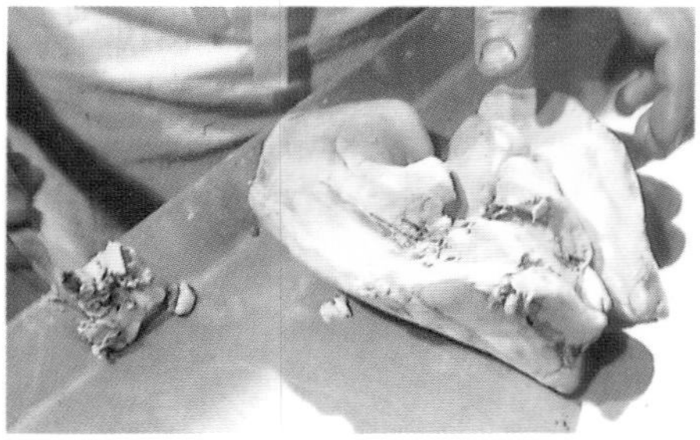

# Grading Foie Gras

According to the product that is being made, the livers are selected according to grade.

**A Grade Suitable for each Product**

***Foie gras " extra ":*** The best foie gras is used for products demanding the whole lobe such as " roulades " and " Marie Stuart ".

***Foie gras " 1st choice ":*** The next grade is suitable for terrines (demanding lobes and large pieces) with or without truffles.

***Foie gras " 2nd choice ":*** These livers may be partly bloody and dry to the touch. They are appropriate for " parfaits ", mousses and " blocs ". The puréed liver can also be added to meat terrines (" duck terrine with foie gras ").

**Large Scale Industry**

The three categories just described include the range of foie gras used by the charcutier-caterer. Certain foie gras products in cans and jars produced on an industrial scale use the remaining livers which fall into two categories.

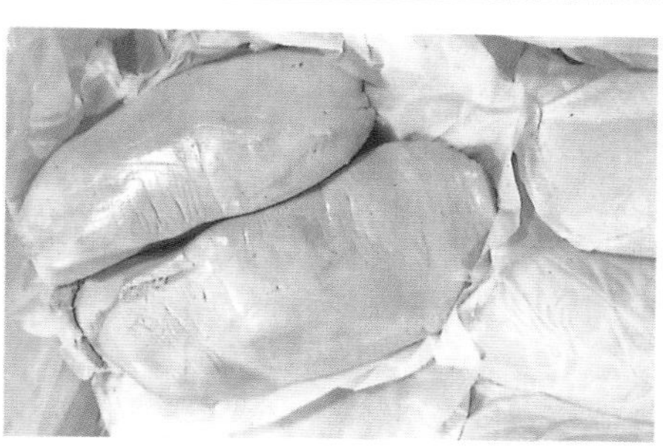

***Foie gras " 4th choice ":*** This category includes small livers that are often dry and bloody. They are used for canned purées and " crèmes ".

***" Tout venant " (" the rest "):*** As the name indicates, these are the inferior livers that are not included in the above categories. They are used only in large industry and not by the charcutier-caterer.

*Note:* The foie gras available in the U.S. is available in three grades--A, B, and C. Since this is not an extensive industry like in France it is difficult to compare the grading procedures. Wholesale suppliers can advise their clients on selecting the right grade for their particular preparations.

### Testing by Touch and Appearance

The three different fattened goose livers pictured below show varied levels of quality.

On the left we see a top quality, " three star " foie gras which weighs about 850 g (about 1 3/4 lb), is of a uniform creamy white color and moist consistency. When pressed with a finger the liver feels a bit elastic like calking cement. The imprint left by the " touch test " remains and does not disappear (it should not " give " like an inflated balloon).

This all important test should be performed on foie gras that is refrigerated (about 10 °C (50 F)).

The liver pictured in the center weighs about the same (850 g (about 1 3/4 lb)) but is not of uniform color.

This factor places it in a " two star " category. Pressing a finger lightly into the liver also leaves an imprint but the feel of the liver is not as " elastic " resulting in slight cracking which indicates a dryer foie gras. This liver would be suitable for the preparations described for " 2nd choice " foie gras.

On the right we see a dark liver with a bloody appearance. This is an indication that the bird was not slaughtered and bled correctly. The appropriate use for this liver cannot be determined until it is denerved.

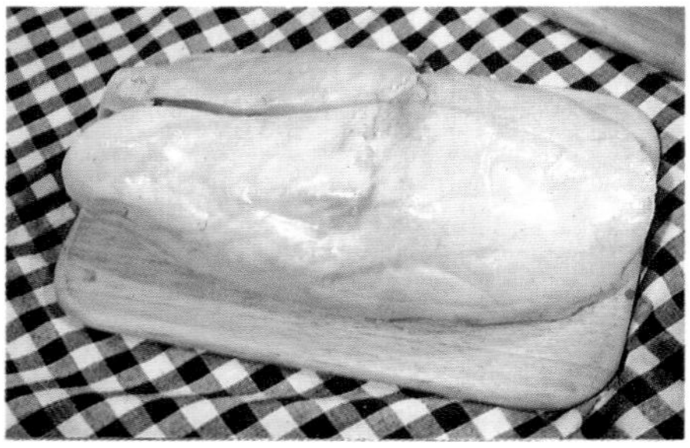

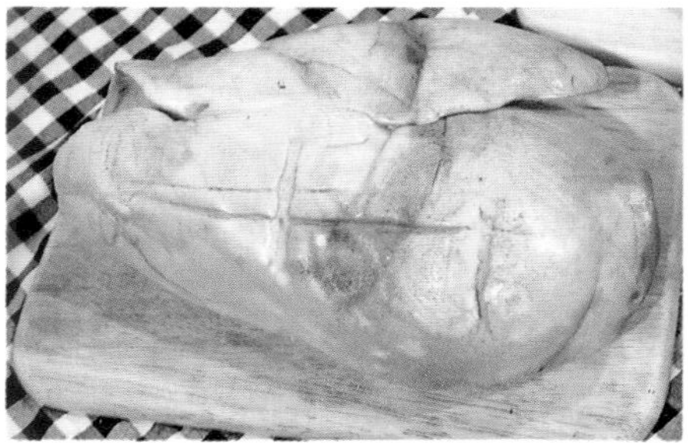

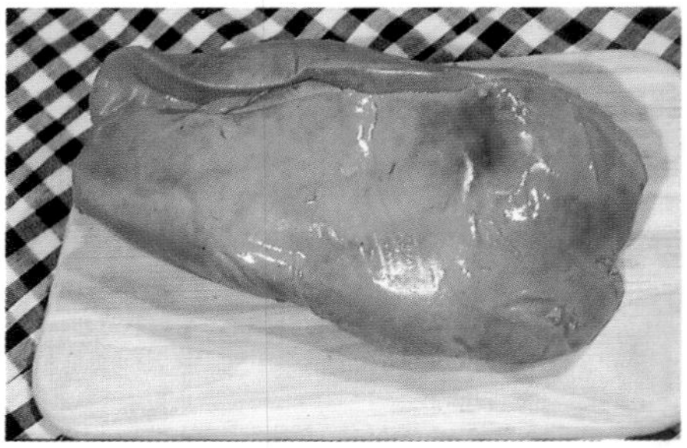

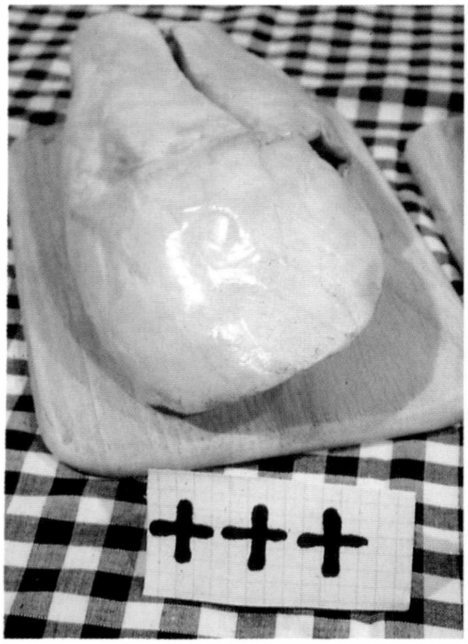

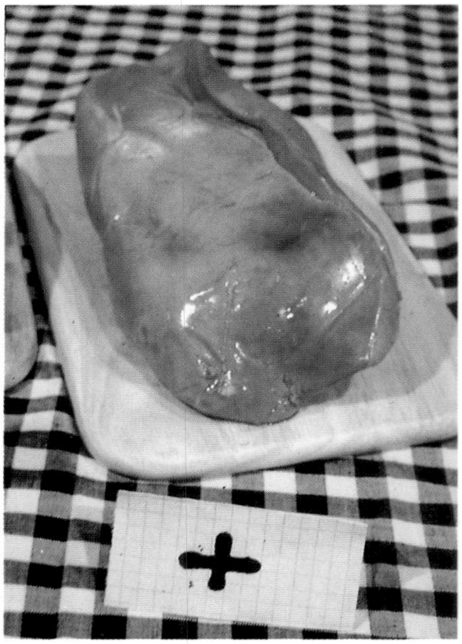

## Foie Gras from Different Origins

The French foie gras production accounts for only 10% of the total fattened livers needed for the products that are made in France.

As mentioned in the beginning of this chapter, good quality foie gras is produced in many countries throughout Europe. However the livers differ according to the climate and type of feed.

The charcutier should avoid mixing different types of livers in one preparation which would result in a marbled appearance. (Note that the textures of the various livers may vary as well.)

It is important to remember that although the foie gras from different origins may vary slightly in color and texture, it is the skill and technique of the chef that makes the preparation top-quality or not.

### *French or Imported*

The foie gras pictured on the left is from the Landes region in southwest France and weighs exactly 860 g (1 3/4 lb).

The outstanding quality of this fattened liver is apparent in the enlarged picture below, left.

The foie gras pictured to the right and above is from Israel and the two livers pictured side-by-side are from Bulgaria.

Note that the imported livers are smaller (550-700 g (about 1 lb-1 1/3 lb)) but are also of a very good quality (even though the color is not as light and creamy).

The French are naturally proud of the excellent foie gras produced in their country and our personal preference is for the foie gras from Landes.

However, blind tastings have shown that the imported livers measure favorably and are often indistinquishable from top-quality French foie gras.

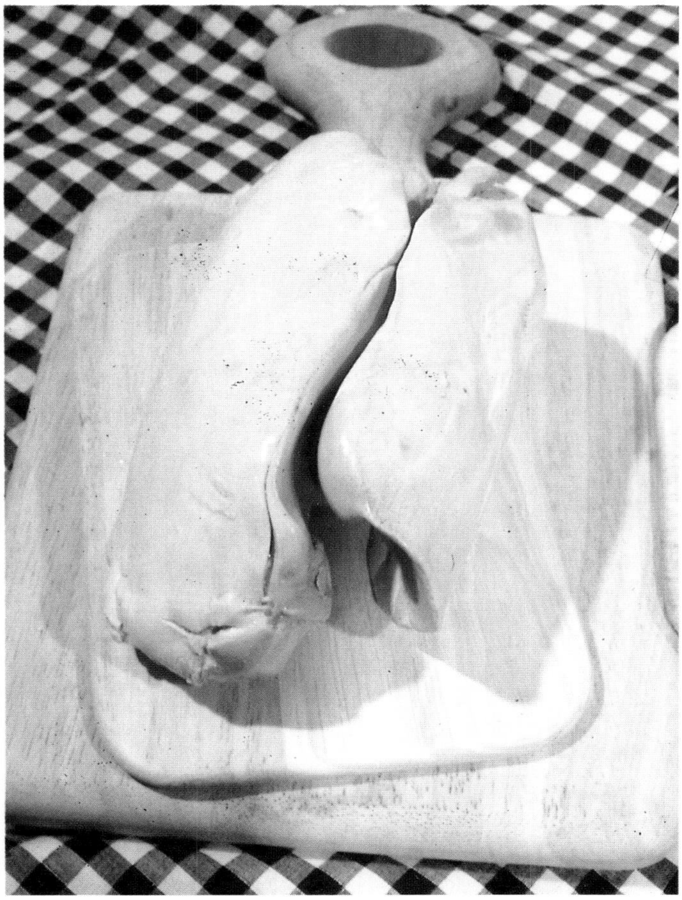

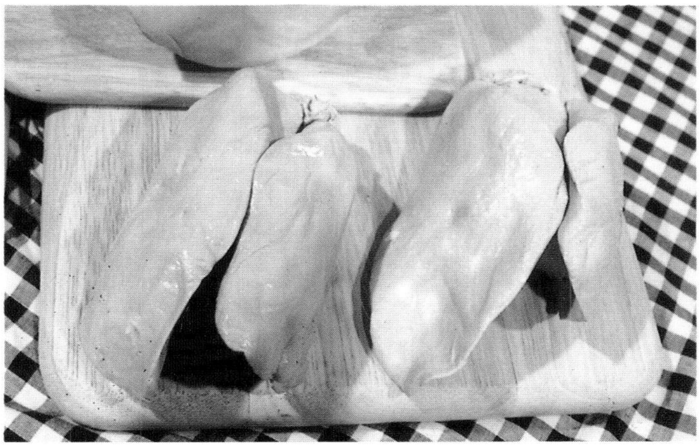

# Preparing Goose and Duck Foie Gras

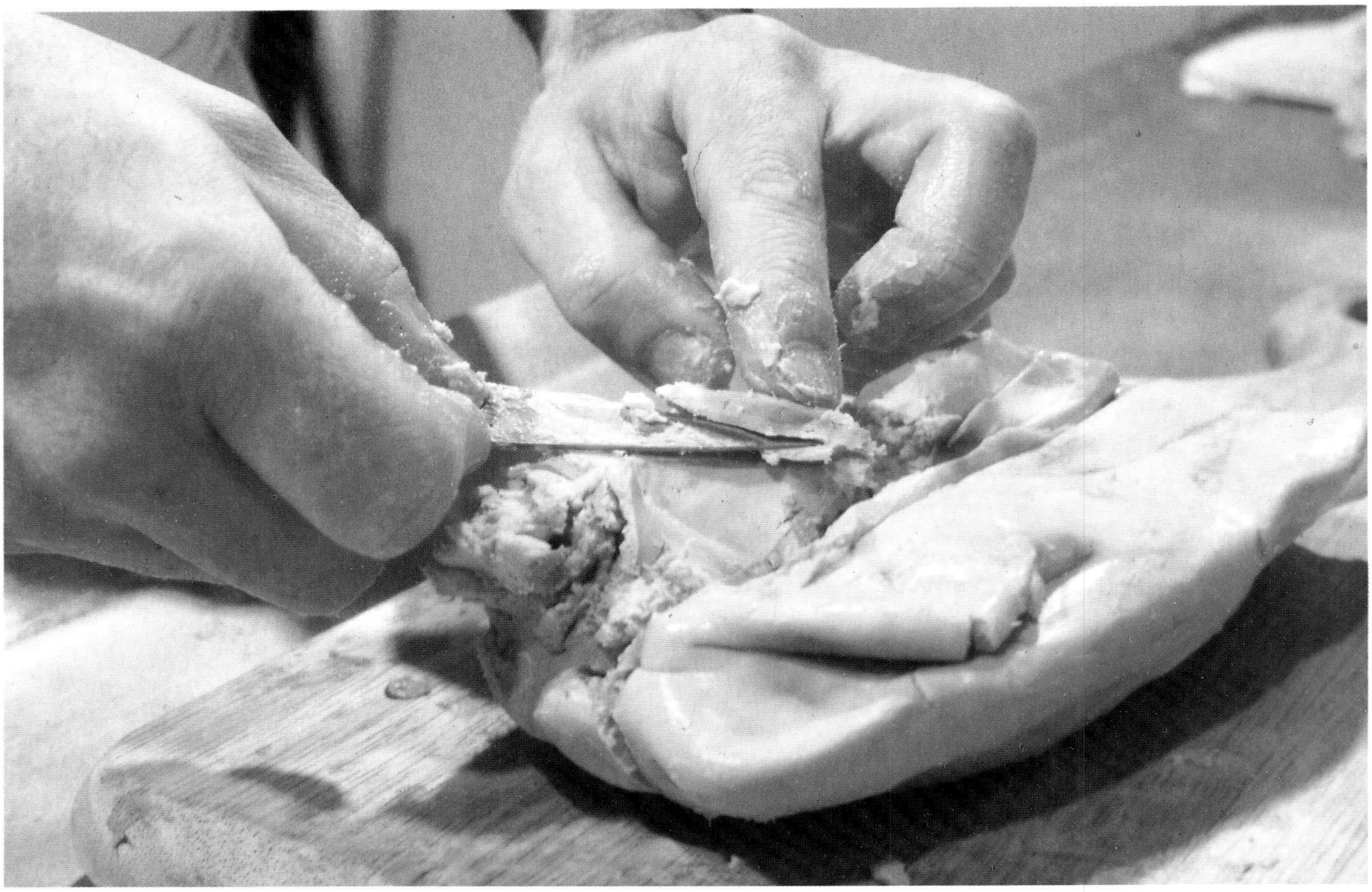

**Preliminary Preparation**

From the time of purchase until preparation, the foie gras must be kept at a constant cold temperature (2-3 °C (35 F)) and covered with plastic wrap or a perfectly clean, moistened handtowel.

Before the denerving procedure, it is immersed in lightly salted water or milk (or a 50/50 blend) for up to two hours. A longer time in the liquid may result in absorption of the water or milk.

The liver is then drained and dried with paper towels.

**Deveining**

***The Large Lobe***

First the two lobes are carefully pulled apart. Using a well-sharpened thin-bladed knife, a cut is made to expose the veins that lie below the surface. Starting at the top where the main artery is visible, the surface of the liver is cut down the center then pulled open to expose the lacy web of veins. By working down the liver a little at a time and following the vein, the entire network can be exposed then pulled out carefully in one piece without further cutting of the foie gras.

If any small vessels which carry bile through the liver remain, they

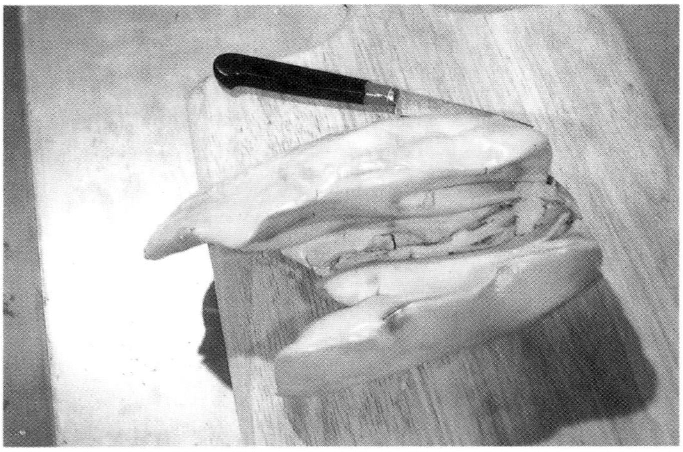

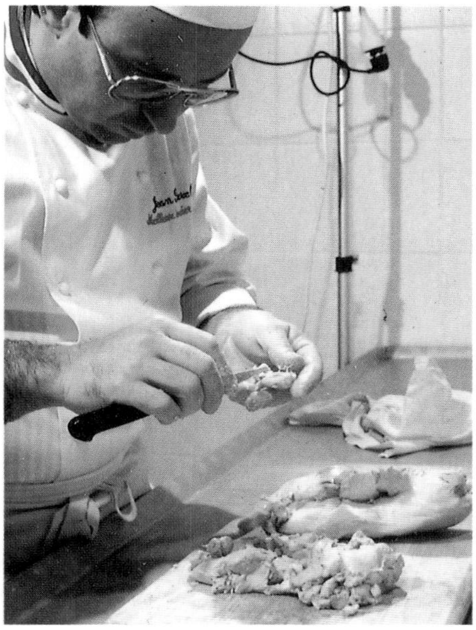

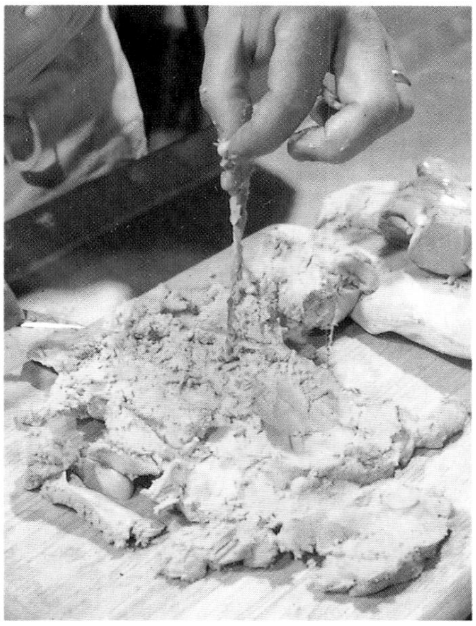

should be removed. These are usually emptied at the time of slaughter and are not easy to locate.

The vein network branches out into tiny vessels in the bottom portion of the liver. It is practically impossible to remove all the vessels without breaking the liver apart. Many professional chefs choose to cut off the tip of the foie gras and use it in puréed products.

All of the small vessels left in the foie gras will be visible in the cooked liver in the form of tiny blood spots.

### *The Small Lobe*

As with the large lobe, the deveining process starts at the top where the large vein comes out of the liver.

The vessels in the small lobe spread out like a spider's web making it difficult to remove more than the large central vein. A delicate hand is demanded for this operation.

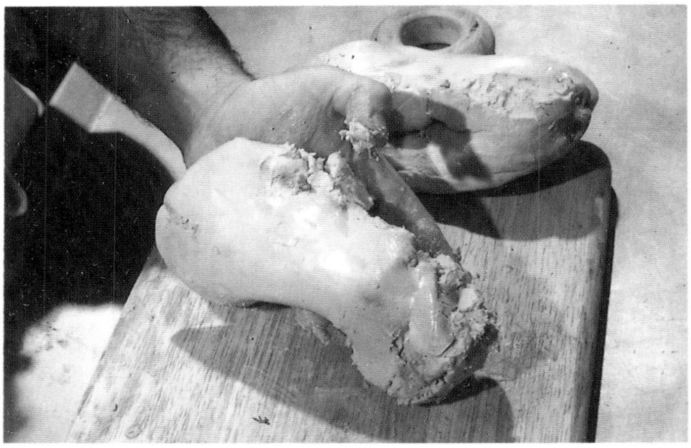

## Preparing Goose and Duck Foies Gras (continued)

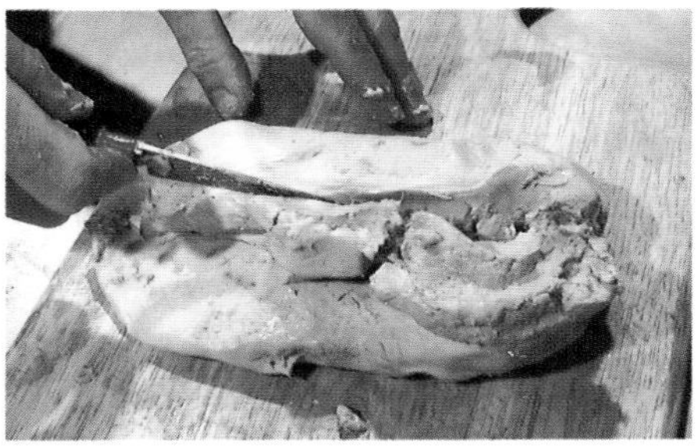

In both lobes it is imperative to remove all green spots that are stains from the bile sac. This substance has a very bitter taste which could ruin the finshed product if not thoroughly removed. The blood spots may not be attractive, but they do not have an unpleasant flavor. A small amount of the bile left on the liver could prove catastrophic.

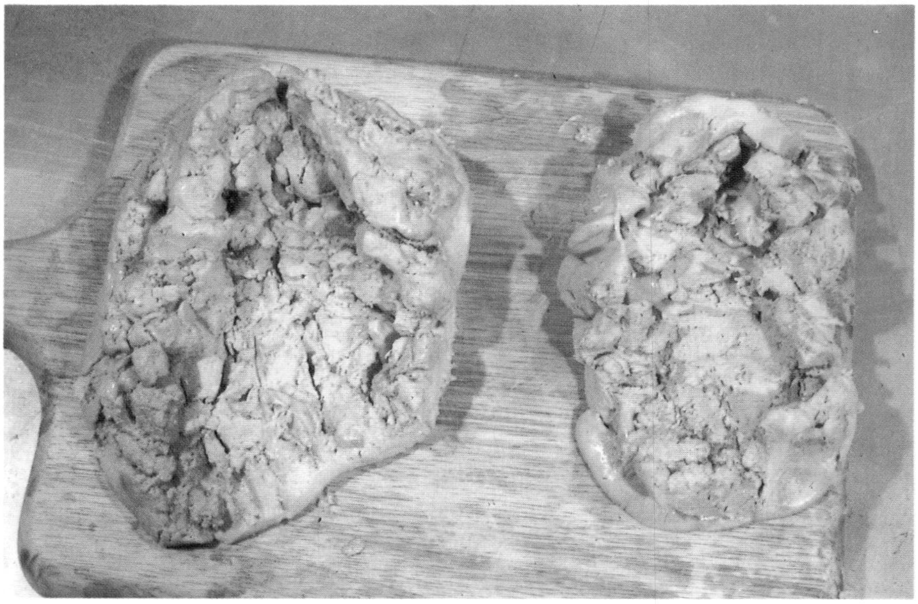

Removing the thin layer of skin which covers the foie gras is not obligatory. The portions of skin that are visible around the edges can be be easily pulled off with the aid of a small knife.

The meticulous work of deveining requires dexterity, using the tips of the fingers along with a small knife to not break apart the liver any more than is necessary. When working with this delicate product, hands should be kept impeccably clean.

Foie gras that is going to be vacuum packed demands an even stricter compliance with cleanliness regulations. It is recommended to wear surgical gloves when handling the livers and to routinely clean and disinfect the work surface.

To further ensure purity, the work surface can be covered with dampened sheets of parchment paper.

The denerved foie gras should be arranged on clean stainless steel platters, covered and refrigerated until ready to be seasoned.

## Seasoning

Blend 2 is better for small batches to avoid an error when weighing the small amount of saltpeter.

***Blend 1***

(For 1 kilo (2.2 lbs) foie gras)

16 g (1/2 oz) fine salt
0.5 g (1/64 oz) saltpeter
1g (1/8 oz) sugar
1 g (1/8 oz) paprika (optional)
15-20 cl (about 3/4 cup) port

***Blend 2***

17 g (generous 1/2 oz) curing salt (sodium nitrite blended with salt)
1 g (1/8 oz) ground white pepper
0.5 g (1/64 oz) ground nutmeg
1 g (1/8 oz) paprika (optional)
15-20 cl (about 3/4 cup) port

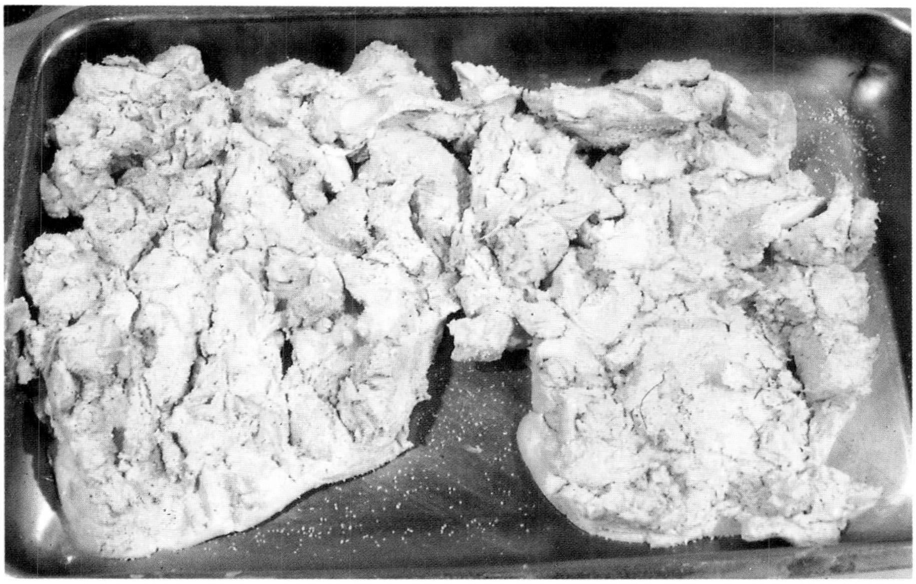

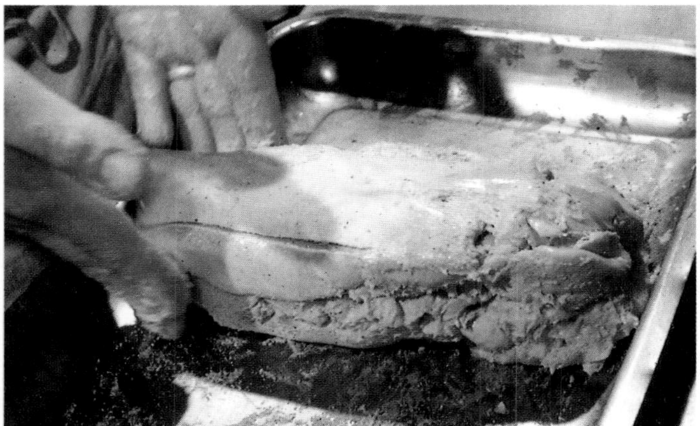

**Seasoning**

The denerved livers are spread out on a clean work surface or a sheet of parchment paper and the dry seasonings are evenly distributed over the surface then the port is sprinkled over the liver.

The foie gras is then tossed gently to coat it evenly then arranged neatly in a stainless steel container.

Make several layers of the foie gras if necessary to save space. Press down to eliminate air pockets and cover the surface with plastic wrap to keep the foie gras from drying out.

***Vacuum Seasoning***

Foie gras can be seasoned in the vacuum pouch and this method is highly recommended. The seasonings are drawn into the liver and penetrate so efficiently into the liver that the amounts should be reduced to 15 g (1/2 oz) curing salt, 0.5 g (1/64 oz) white pepper, 0.24 g (1/120 oz) nutmeg, 10 cl (6 tbls) port (per kilo (2.2 lbs).

***Marinating***

The seasoned foie gras is then placed in the refrigerator to marinate. In the vacuum pouch 10-12 hours is enough and up 20-24 hours if not vacuum packed.
In the vacuum pouch there is no evaporation of the seasonings at all.

In both cases, the temperature should be 2-3 C (35 F).

## Duck Foie Gras

The procedure for denerving duck foie gras is identical to the steps described for goose foie gras.

Duck foie gras however is even more fragile than goose so that it is of the utmost importance to maintain cold temperatures during preparation.

It is recommended to work on a chilled work surface (marble is best) and to handle the liver as little as possible as the heat from the hands can cause the liver to melt and spoil.

The dry seasonings used for duck foie gras are identical to the blend for goose foie gras.

The wine can be port as with goose foie gras or Sauternes as suggested by Jean-Francois Deport.

Many purists prefer to not add any wine at all so to not mask the flavor of the liver in any way. It is up to the chef to decide what is best for his style of preparation.

# Cooking Foie Gras in Vacuum Pouch

Cooking foie gras in a vacuum pouch has become so prevalent in France that this chapter would not be complete without describing this recent innovation. There are many advantages with this style of cooking which are winning over more professionals each year.

George Pralus, the French chef who has led the field in vacuum techniques in the kitchen perfected the procedure for marinating and cooking foie gras " sous vide " over ten years ago. This method can be used for all foie gras products at all stages of production.

*Note:* For charcutiers outside of France, it is recommended to consult the local health department about legislation concerning vacuum processing.

Vacuum cooking demands impeccable working conditions:

- Equipment must be in perfect working order.
- Use of approved plastic sheets and pouches is required.
- Personnel must observe rules of hygiene.
- The raw foie gras must be absolutely fresh and of the highest quality.
- Each step in the production must be carried out exactly as outlined.

Following these guidelines ensures products that are:

- Extremely flavorful because the seasonings and juices are sealed in the pouch.

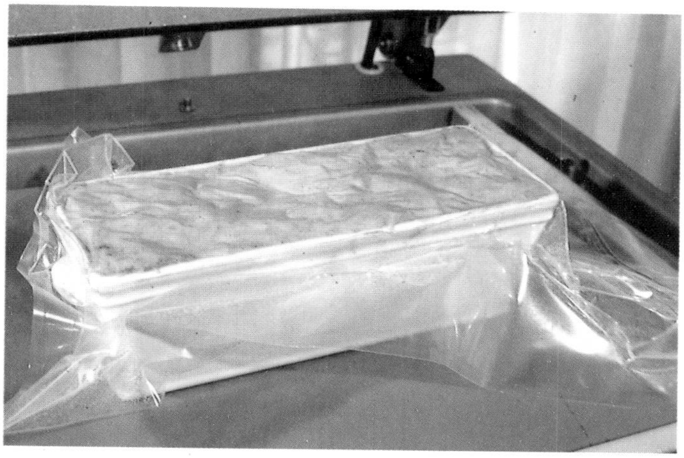
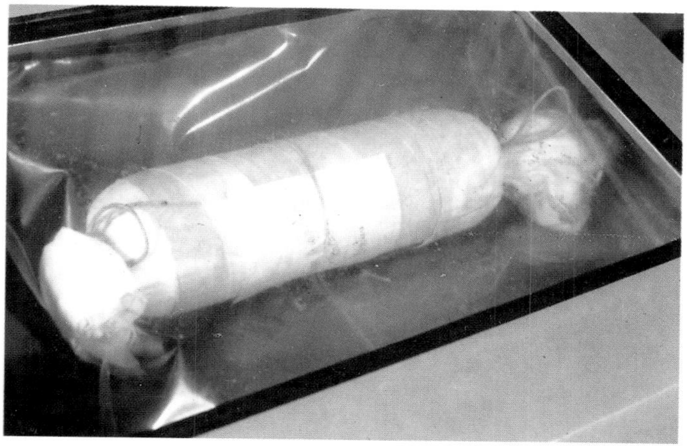
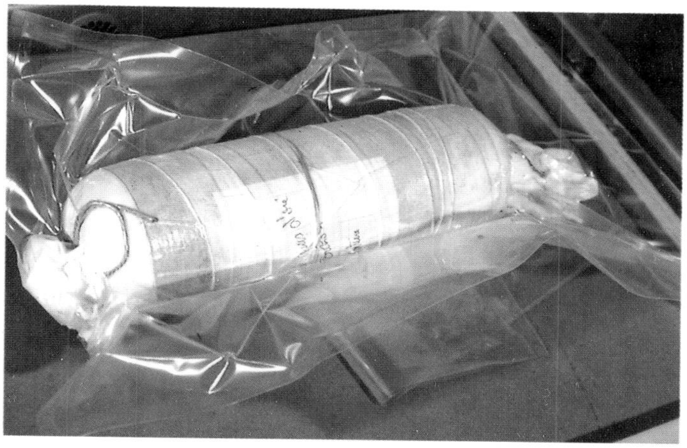

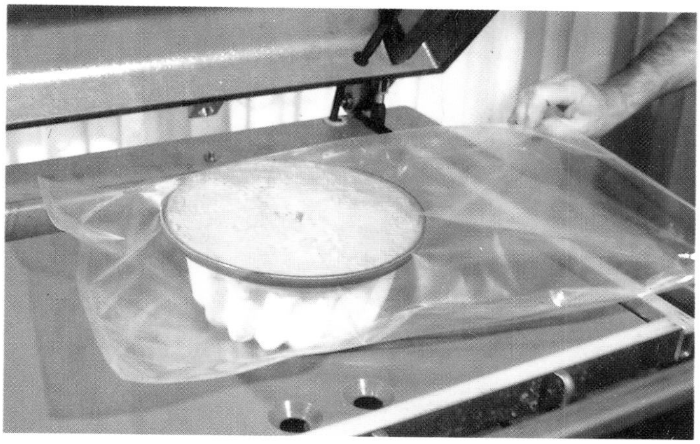

- Sterilized and protected until use if temperature guidelines are heeded.
- Easy to transport therefore facilitating marketing and storage.

**Vacuum Cooking Procedure**

***Terrine of Goose Foie Gras***

Place the prepared terrine immediately into a vacuum cooking pouch that is large enough to allow for shrinkage.

Attach the pouch to the vacuum machine and process for 5 minutes. Shrink the sack by plunging it into 90 °C (195 F) water then remove it immediately.

Immerse the terrine in 75 °C (167 F) water. (Stock is unnecessary as the plastic pouch blocks all osmosis).

Maintain a constant temperature throughout cooking.

The terrine is cooked until the internal temperature reaches 68 °C (155 F). Special thermometers (with electronic probes) have been developed for use with vacuum packages.

Transfer the cooked terrine immediately to an ice bath to cool it quickly, then store in the refrigerator.

After it has thoroughly cooled for 24 hours, it is recommended to place the cooked terrine in a second vacuum pouch for storage.

***Terrine of Duck Foie Gras***

The technique is identical however the duck terrine is cooked to 65 °C (150 F).

***Advantages of Vacuum Cooking***

Duck terrines that are cooked in the oven will lose up to 30-35% of their weight in rendered fat. Vacuum cooking reduces this to 10% or less.

Goose terrines fare even better, with as little as 2-3% loss when vacuum-cooked.

There is no doubt that cooking the foie gras without contact with the direct heat of the oven or the liquid when poaching produces a product that retains more of its flavors and aromas. This technique has greatly enhanced the overall quality of the foie gras products in France.

# Terrine of Whole Goose Foie Gras

This product is one of the most refined of all foie gras preparations. The procedure is relatively simple as long as top quality raw materials are used.

## Using Truffles

French regulations indicate that if a product is labeled " truffled " that it must contain at least 3% truffles. Therefore the recipes here call for 30 g (1 oz) of truffles per kilo (2.2 lbs) of foie gras.

The truffles used in these recipes are fresh which are available in France at the wholesale market. There are many " false " truffles sold that do not compare to the genuine " Tuber Melanosporum ". When a product in France has " truffled " on the label this type of truffle must be used.

Fresh truffles must be handled carefully and with a certain level of expertise. At the wholesale market they are usually sold with a reddish soil attached which keeps the truffles' aromas more or less intact until they are sold. Straight out of the ground the perfume is quite strong. Once they are removed from the ground and the soil is brushed away, the perfume and taste becomes less intense.

Truffles must be meticulously brushed to remove the grit and soil from between the crevasses.

They should be processed in the same way as vegetables with the

same precautions to prevent harmful growth of bacteria (Clostridium Botolinum).

Therefore uncooked truffles are never used in charcuterie products unless the internal temperature is brought to 80 °C (175 F) and maintained for 10 minutes. This of course is out of the question for foie gras preparations which would melt at such a high temperature. This would decrease the yield as well as the overall quality of the foie gras.

### Cooking Fresh Truffles

After the fresh truffles are thoroughly washed and brushed they are marinated for two hours in madeira with salt, pepper and four spice powder.

Remove the truffles and bring the madeira to a boil then return the truffles to the liquid. Lower the heat, cover and cook gently for about 10 minutes depending on the size. Leave to cool in the liquid.

Left in the liquid, the truffles will keep well for several days in the refrigerator.

Fresh truffles are available only in the cold months (December-March). Therefore when fresh truffles are not available, it is recommended to use truffles in cans or jars. In this case the chef is assured of having truffles that are sterilized.

The charcutier must beware of truffles " put up " by individuals who may not follow the strict standards of government regulated canners. One bad truffle could have disastrous results.

## Assembling the Terrine

There are several ways to assemble the terrine of goose foie gras. All can be successful if the guidelines are followed closely.

### A - Assembling and Marinating

This method entails placing the seasoned livers directly into the terrine and leaving to marinate for 24 hours in the refrigerator before cooking.

The mold can be lined with a sheet of barding fat or not lined at all. The lobes of seasoned foie gras are placed on the bottom with the smoothest side of the liver on the bottom to form a layer that fills the mold halfway. With the tip of a finger or better yet a sharpening steel that has been washed in boiling water, form an indentation down the center of the layer of foie gras about 1 cm (3/8 in) deep.

Weigh the truffles (3% of the weight of the foie gras), cut into large matchsticks and arrange them in an even row in the indentation.

Place another layer of the seasoned foie gras on top with the smooth side of the lobes on top. Press down the livers to eliminate air pockets and stick the two layers together.

Remember that the amount of truffle used is based on the weight of the raw foie gras. Since the liver always loses a little weight during cooking, the final product is assured of having enough truffles to comply with regulations.

The truffle also renders some of its weight during cooking. It should be noted that products that are cooked to a temperature of 78-80 °C (175 F) should be made with a little more than 3% truffle to compensate for possible loss in weight.

The assembled terrine is then covered tightly with plastic wrap and left to marinate in the refrigerator (2-4 °C (35-37 F) for 24 hours.

**Assembling after Marinating**

For this terrine the lobes of denerved foie gras are left to marinate in the stainless steel container as previously described.

After 24 hours, the livers are then placed in the terrine as explained in the first method. An indentation is formed in the same manner and the same amount of truffles are cut in large matchsticks and arranged envenly down the center.

The assembled terrine is then compressed slightly (with your hands) to eliminate air pockets.

Once assembled, this terrine made with fully marinated foie gras can be cooked immediately.

**Assembling with Purée**

The third method uses a little foie gras purée to hold the terrine together. The purée is made from the tips of the lobes that are filled with tiny blood vessels which are difficult to remove.

The amount of purée does not exceed 10% of the total weight of foie gras. The purée is made by processing the pieces of foie gras in a chopper or food processor until smooth. Great care is needed to not overheat the liver while processing (temperature should not exceed 6-8 °C (45 F)).

This purée serves to " glue " the two layers of livers together and also serves to fill the small spaces between the pieces of foie gras.

The livers used for this terrine should be already marinated. The procedure for assembling and adding the truffle is identical to the the terrines already described.

This terrine however should not be labeled " whole goose liver terrine " (" terrine de foie gras d'oie

entier") but rather "goose liver terrine" ("terrine de foie gras d'oie").

**Cooking**

The terrine is cooked in a water bath in the oven or in a steamer.

The temperature of the oven is 78-80 °C (175 F) and is carefully maintained throughout cooking. The terrine is cooked when the internal temperature is 64-68 °C (150-155 F). The thermometer used for this procedure has a long tube that extends out of the oven door. The probe is inserted in the terrine at the beginning of cooking and the temperature can be read from outside the oven.

After the terrine is cooked, it is weighted to compress it slightly and chilled (2-4 °C (35-37 F)) for at least 24 hours before serving.

The equipment used to cook foie gras products must be well-maintained because the exact temperature of the cooked preparation is crucial to the quality. One or two degrees too high can cause a substantial loss of weight of the final product.

When purchasing equipment, make sure that the thermostats and thermometers have the capability of indicating the temperature down to the degree. Some equipment is made to be accurate within 5 degrees which is not good enough for these preparations.

If the financial gains made by proper cooking are added up, the charcutier will quickly replace any machinery that does not function perfectly.

**Storage**

To keep the terrine for several weeks, pour a thin layer (4-5 mm (1/6 in)) of goose fat or lard (or a 50/50 blend) over the top to seal out air.

To serve immediately, the terrine needs only a simple decoration of a slice of truffle and a thin layer of full-flavored aspic perfumed with port (5%).

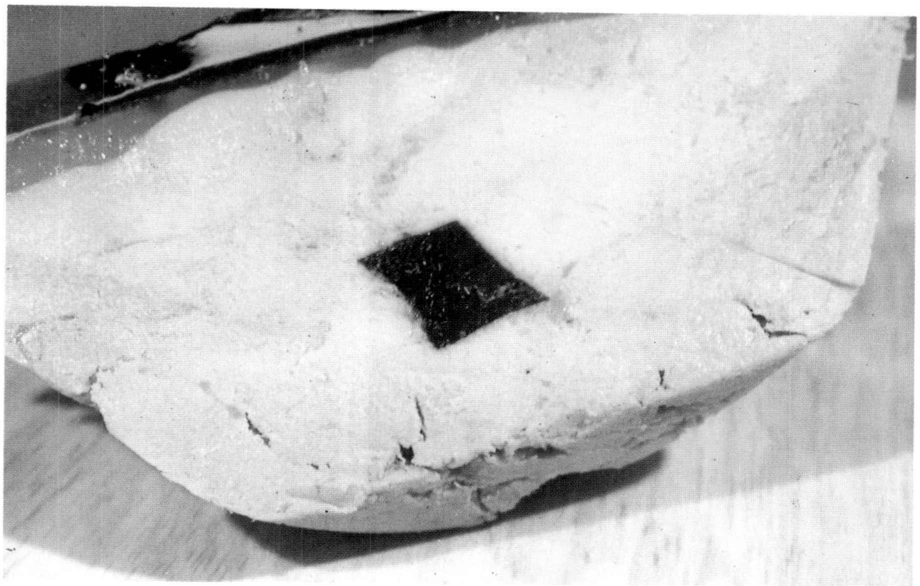

# " Bloc " of Goose Foie Gras with Truffles

**Regulations Concerning Labeling**

In France, preparations made with foie gras are labeled with very specific names that are regulated by the government.

In the previous recipe the term " entier " or " whole " means exactly that--the product is made with the entire lobe in one piece.

The variation with a little purée to hold the terrine together cannot bear this prestigious label.

This preparation for " bloc " or " block " requires by law (" Code de la Charcuterie-Decembre 1988 ") that there be pieces of foie gras apparent in a slice of the finished product but it can be composed of purée and pieces formed together.

The " Code " specifies that for a goose " bloc " 50% of the product be made up of pieces (rather than purée) and 30% for " bloc " of duck foie gras.

As with the terrine, the percentage of truffle must be 3% by weight in the finshed product in order to be labeled " truffled ".

**Procedure**

The preparation of the foie gras (selecting, denerving, seasoning) does not differ from the previous recipe for the terrine.

However the pieces for this product can be small trimmings or broken parts of the lobe.

The portions of the lobe with the tiny blood vessels (as well as other dark spots) can be used to make the purée.

Since we strive for the best possible product, this version contains 80% large pieces with 20% in purée made from the bloodier parts of the foie gras.

The purée is made in a food processor or horizontal chopper using well-sharpened blades which will purée without warming the mixture.

The temperature should be kept below 6-8 $^{0}$C (45 F) during processing.

***Mixing***

The marinated pieces of foie gras and the purée are mixed by hand in a chilled stainless steel bowl until evenly blended.

The temperature should remain cold but otherwise this procedure presents no difficulties.

**Assembling**

The mold is a classic porceline terrine.

Remember that the % of truffle must be in the proper proportion (3%) in each " bloc " and in each slice if the product will be sold by individual portions.

The chef must know how much foie gras each different mold holds so the right amount of truffle can be prepared.

The mixture of foie gras pieces and purée is placed in an even layer that fills the mold halfway.

An indentation is made to hold the truffle which has been cut into large pieces as shown.

The mold is then filled to the top with more of the foie gras mixture. The terrine must be knocked on the work surface and pressed to eliminate air pockets.

Since the foie gras was thoroughly marinated the terrine is ready to cook. It can be placed in a vacuum pouch and cooked as previously described. Traditional cooking methods also work well for the preparation.

**Cooking**

The cooking procedure for the " bloc " is identical to the terrine of whole goose liver. Cooking can be done in the oven in a water bath or in a steamer at 78-80 °C (170-175 F).

This temperature is maintained throughout cooking until the internal temperature of the product reaches 64-68 °C (150-155 F).

The internal temperature is verified with a thermometer.

The best method is with an electric probe that is placed in the terrine at the beginning of cooking and can be read from outside the oven.

As with the other preparations, it is very important to use equipment that is well-maintained and reliable to cook the product to exactly 64-68 °C (150-155 F).

After cooking, the " bloc " is drained of excess fat then compressed slightly with a light weight. It is cooled immediately.

**Storage**

As with all terrines of foie gras the shelf life can be prolonged if chilled thoroughly then covered with a thin layer (4-5 mm (1/6 in) of goose fat or lard (or 50/50 blend) which seals out air.

It is also possible to place the cooked terrine in a vacuum pouch in which case the product can be kept 3-4 weeks before sale.

**Presentation**

To prepare the " bloc " for serving or sale by the slice, unmold by running a thin-bladed knife around the edge, dip the mold in hot water then turn the mold on the diagonal and shake to release the terrine.

Clean and dry the mold and in the bottom pour a thin layer of aspic with port (7 mm (1/4 in) maximum).

When the aspic has set, pour a little more partly set aspic over this layer then slide the unmolded terrine back into the prepared mold.

The " bloc " is quite easy to slice due to the purée which " cements " the pieces together.

To facilitate slicing, use a thin-bladed knife and run it under boiling water just before cutting each slice.

This product is usually served unmolded on a platter. But it can also be sold by the slice from the terrine.

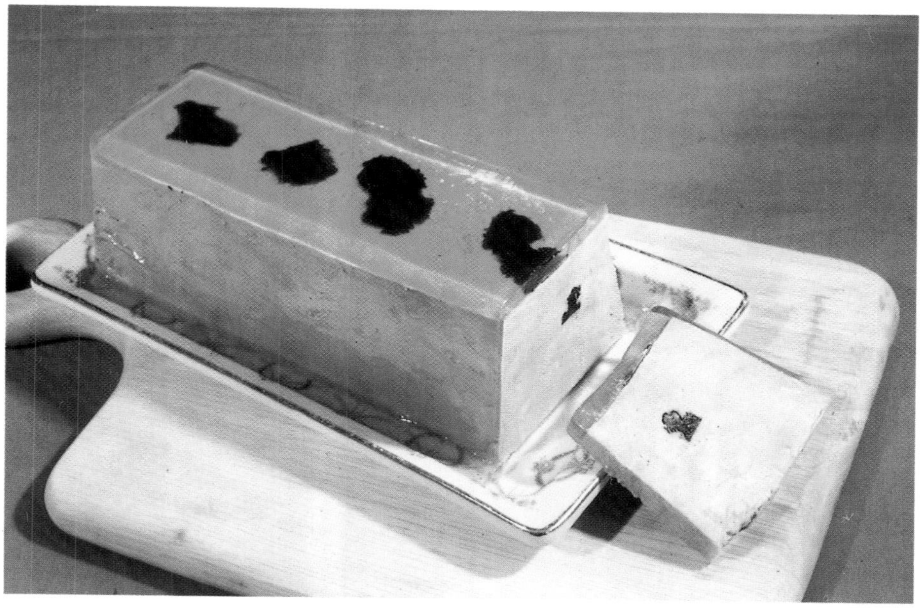

# " Rouleau " of Foie Gras " au Torchon "

### Terminology

The " rouleau " is a cylinder similar to the size and shape of a rolling pin. Cooking products " au torchon " entails wrapping them in clean handtowels and a strip of cloth to hold the shape and compress the livers to ensure a firm texture.

This product is not listed in the official " Code de la Charcuterie ". However it is a refined preparation which calls for whole lobes of foie gras.

### Procedure

As with all foie gras products that are cooked to be eaten cold, the preparation of the raw livers must be thorough and performed under ideal conditions. The quality of the final product depends on it.

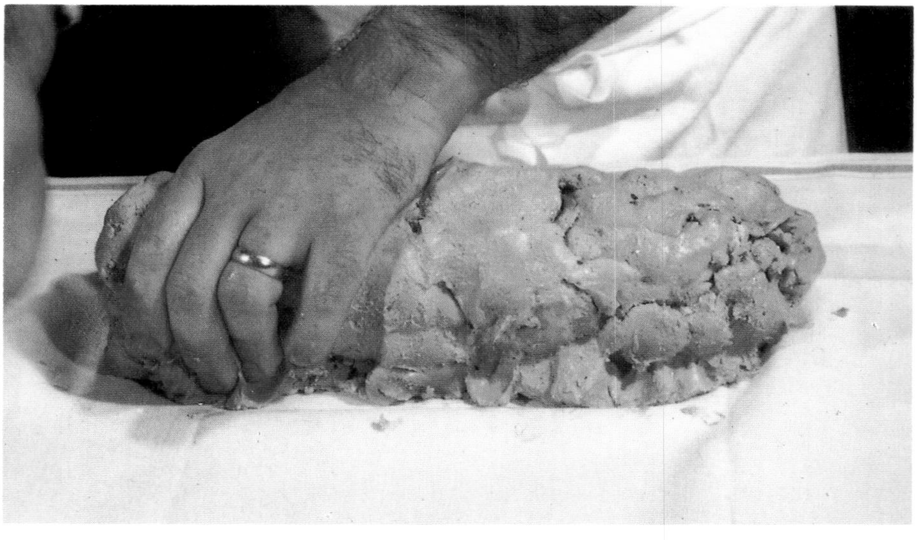

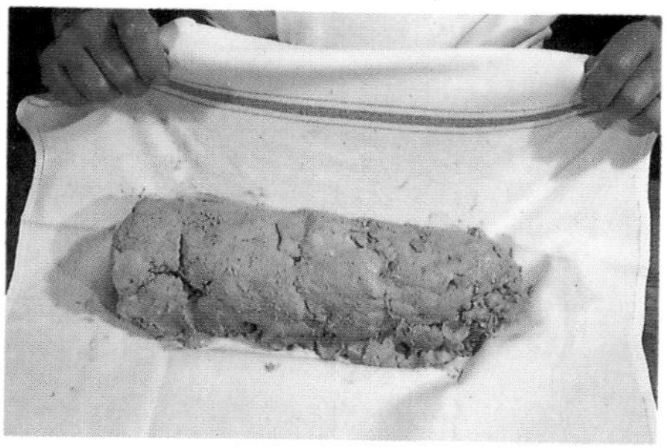

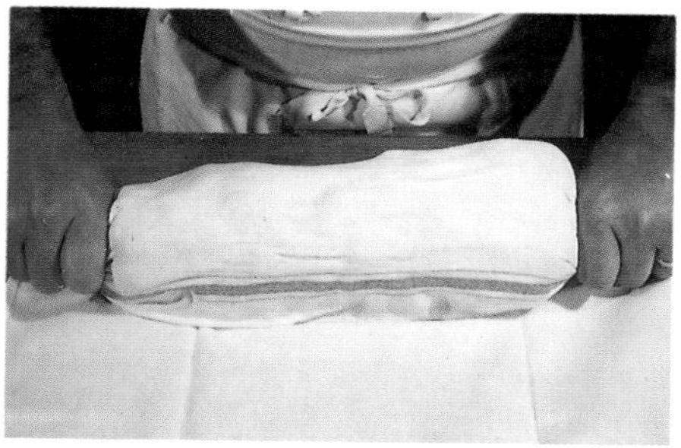

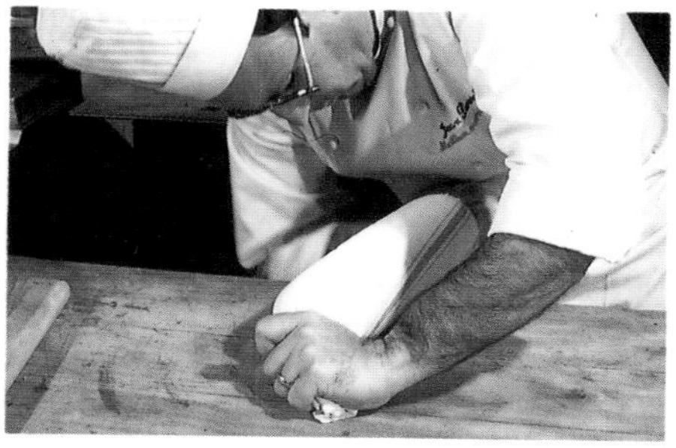

The procedure for soaking, deveining, and marinating does not differ from the terrines that have already been described.

Layer the seasoned foie gras and leave to marinate then proceed with the assembly.

**Assembling Methods**

There are two methods for forming the " rouleau ". The first method demands more dexterity with the same results as the second method.

***Method A***

*Making the Rouleau Form*

Lay a moistened sheet of parchment paper on the work surface. The paper must be 10-15 cm (4-6 in) longer than the rouleau and large enough to wrap around several times.

Arrange the prepared lobes and pieces of foie gras in a wide strip about 7-9 cm (about 3-4 in) across down the middle of the paper.

Place them with the pointed ends toward the center.

The diameter can be smaller or larger depending on how big across the rouleau will be.

Large slices are attractive but the price of each portion is of course much higher.

Next, the foie gras is rolled firmly to form the cylinder shape. It is then wrapped tightly in the sheet of parchment paper and rolled to cover the rouleau with several thicknesses of paper.

Twist the ends shut.

Smooth out the cylinder so that it is a perfectly even shape from one end to the other.

Tighten the ends by twisting and secure with kitchen string.

Although the parchment paper facilitates the forming of the rouleau it can be easily damaged with a knife and it sometimes sticks to the pot during cooking.

It is therefore recommended to cover the cylinder with plastic wrap or better yet with a clean handtowel that is secured with kitchen string.

*Note:* Plastic wrap is used more and more in French kitchen for items that are poached or steamed.

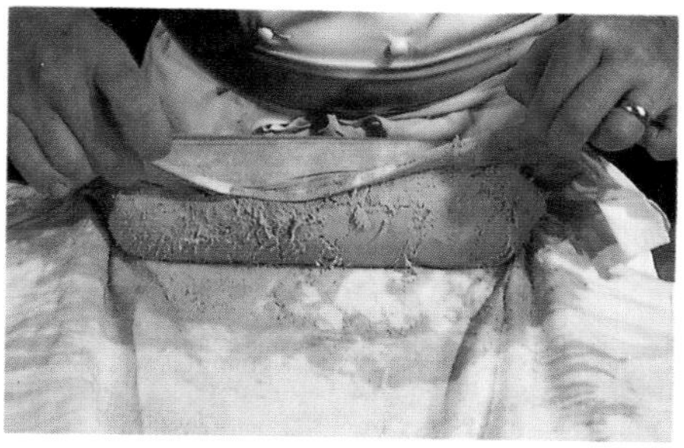

Jean-Pierre Odeau uses the handtowel method as shown here.

The rouleau can actually be formed directly in the handtowel. It should be moistened as well and the procedure is identical.

*Wrapping*

The final wrapping and tying is very important because it assures the shape and texture of the final product.

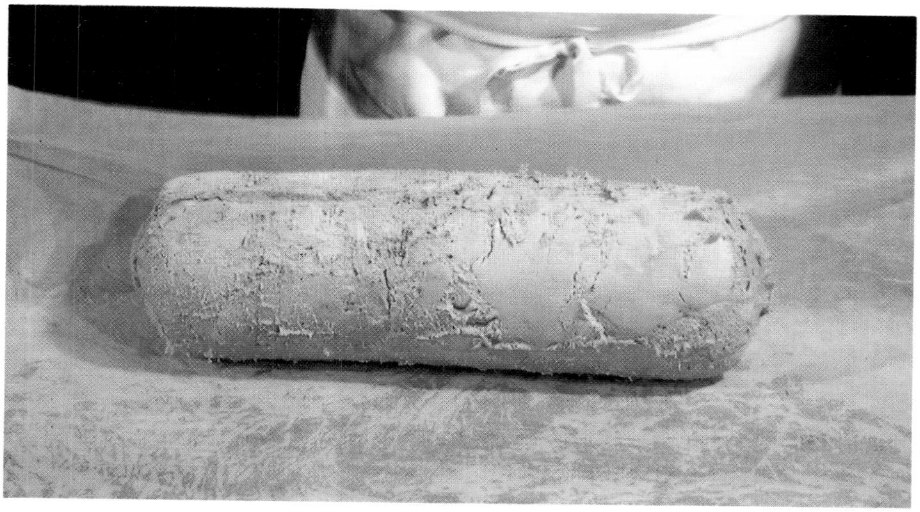

The rouleau is wrapped in a linen strip sometimes referred to as a galantine " bandage " which is traditionally used in France to wrap pigs' feet.

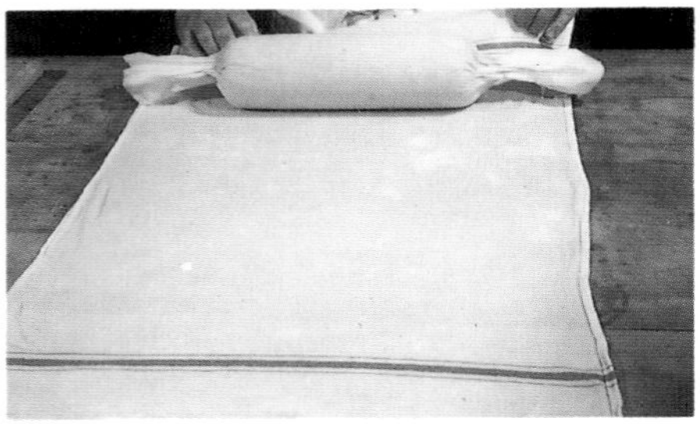

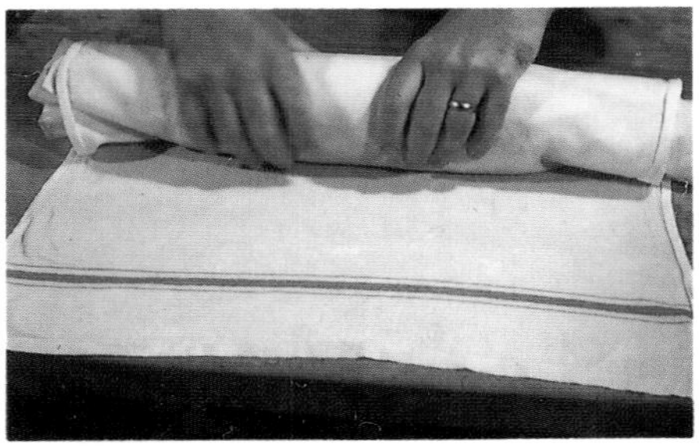

The cloth strip is wrapped evenly and tightly around the cylinder, pulling it snug with each wrap around the rouleau.

The rouleau is then chilled for 12 hours before cooking.

*Method B*

This method uses a hinged cylindrical mold that is used for baking the rich, finely textured bread-" pain de mie ".

Only half of the mold is needed as it is used simply for the forming of the rouleau.

Place a piece of moistened parchment paper in the bottom of the cylindrical mold.

Press the lobes of foie gras into the mold and flatten the top.

Turn the half rouleau out onto a large sheet of moistened parchment paper or handtowel. Replace the small piece of parchment paper in the mold and repeat the process to form the second half of the rouleau.

To form an even cylinder, the two halves are simply stuck together. The rouleau is then rolled, wrapped and tied just like the previous method.

As with the first method, the rouleau is placed in the refrigerator for 12 hours before cooking.

**Cooking**

The classic cooking method is to gently poach the rouleau in full-flavored, gelatinous stock.

The stock is brought to a boil, the impurities are skimmed from the surface then the temperature is brought to 75 °C (167 F).

The chilled rouleau is immersed in the stock and is gently cooked for 80-100 minutes (for the size shown here) at 75 °C (167 F).

As with all foie gras preparations, the internal temperature should reach 65-67 °C (150-154 F) and not higher.

An electronic probe is recommended which is inserted into the rouleau at the beginning of the

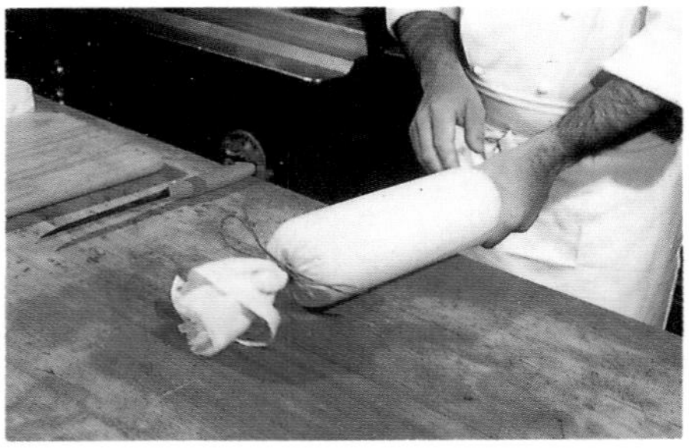

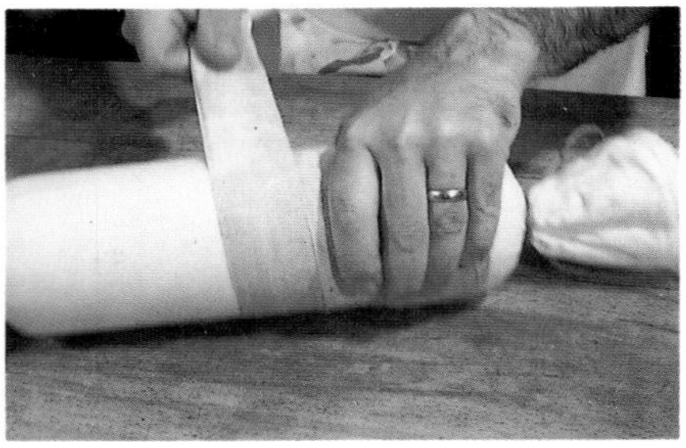

cooking process and therefore monitors the temperature throughout cooking.

Using a probe enables the chef to lower the temperature to 70 °C (160 F) and cook the rouleau even more gently. It may take up to 2 1/2 hours to achieve the 65-67 °C (150-154 F) internal temperature.

It is important to check the temperature of the cooking liquid at regular intervals throughout cooking to verify that the stock in all parts of the pot (top, sides, bottom and center) is of the correct temperature.

**Cooling**

The cooked rouleau is carefully lifted out of the pot and the stock is brought to a simmer for 8-10 minutes and the surface is skimmed of all impurites.

The rouleau is placed in a deep recipient, the stock is drained, cooled and poured over to cover. The rouleau is then cooled as quickly as possible in an ice bath or special cooling chamber which circulates cold air to chill before refrigerating.

Many chefs leave the wrapping intact at this stage. Marcel Cottenceau unties the ends and drains off the excess liquid then reties the ends.
Draining the rouleau in this fashion eliminates all traces of rendered fat.

**Presentation**

The rouleau should chill for at least 24 hours before serving. It however will keep for 2-3 weeks when covered with stock and stored in the refrigerator.

To prepare the rouleau for service or sale, lift it out of the stock and carefully remove the wrapping and pat dry.

Decorate with thin slices of truffle. Stir aspic (with 5% port) over ice to thicken slightly and brush a layer over the rouleau. Dip the pastry brush in boiling water to assure that the aspic is brushed on smoothly. The rouleau can also be immersed in thickened aspic, chilled to set then immersed again.

The presentation platter can also be coated with a thin layer of aspic to "frame" the rouleau on the platter. To facilitate slicing, dip the knife in boiling water.

# " Rouleau " of Foie Gras with Truffles

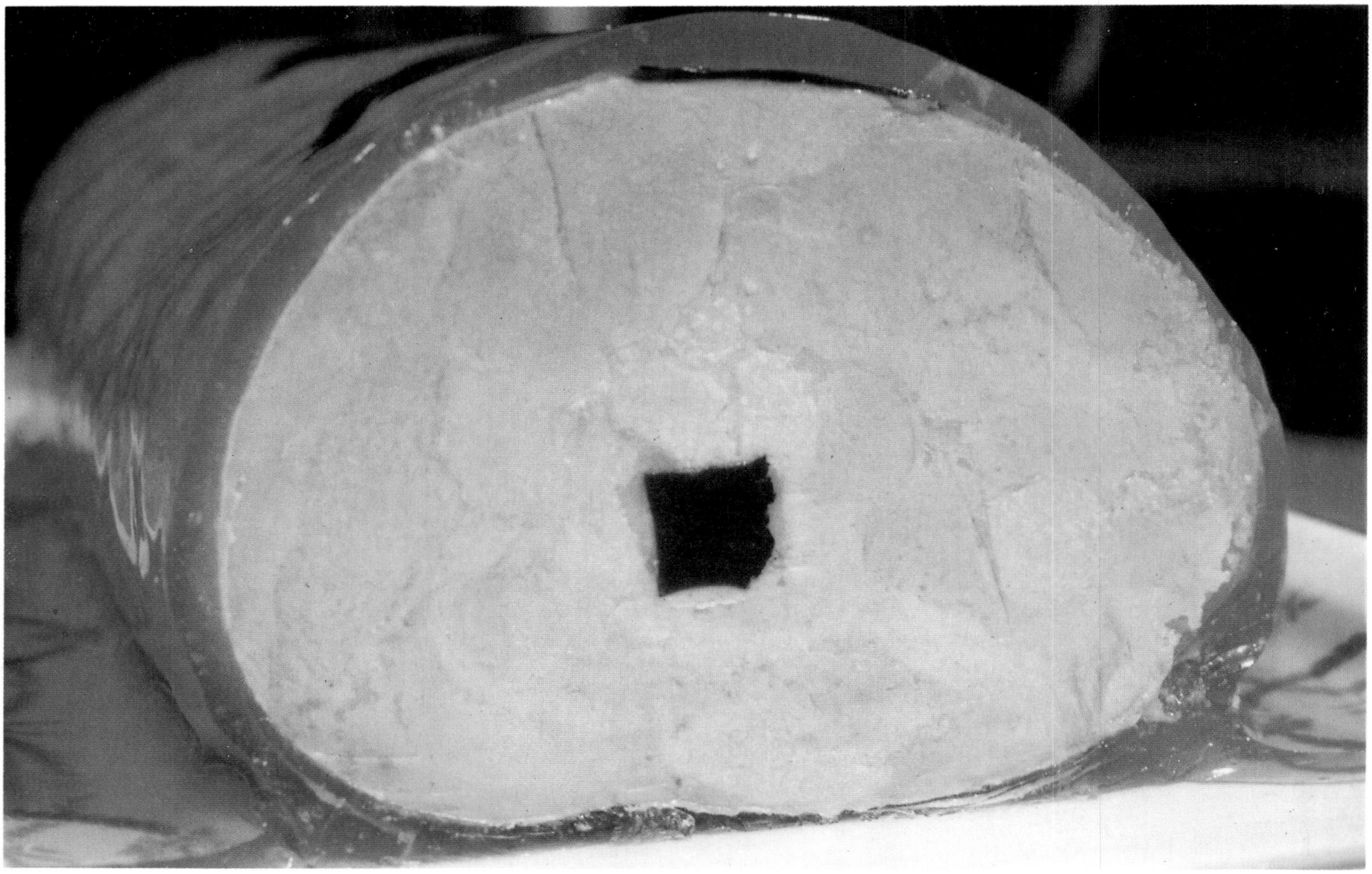

**Procedure**

The preparation of the foie gras is identical to the previous rouleau.

This version contains an addition of truffle which changes the procedure for assembling.

For information on selecting and cooking fresh truffles, refer to the description of the terrine of goose foie gras with truffles. When fresh truffles are not available, preserved truffles can be used.

Remember that products labeled " truffled " must contain at least 3% truffles. A top-quality product may contain up to 5% truffles. However if less than 3% is used to lower the cost of the product, the label must then indicate the exact percentage.

**Assembling Methods**

***Method A***

When the cylinder has been shaped, weigh it to determine the amount of truffles to be used. As previously stated, we recommend using the weight of the uncooked foie gras as a reference for the weight of the truffles since it is difficult to estimate how much weight the truffles will lose during cooking. With this method, the percentage of truffles is always within the regulated amounts.

With a well-sharpened paring knife, make a neat slit down to the center of the rouleau and place the prepared truffles in a row from one end to the other.

Close the rouleau making sure that the truffles remain exactly in the center of the rouleau. The truffles can be easily pushed out of place with the risk that a few slices may have the truffle off center or have no truffle at all.

The wrapping of the rouleau is identical to the previous recipe.

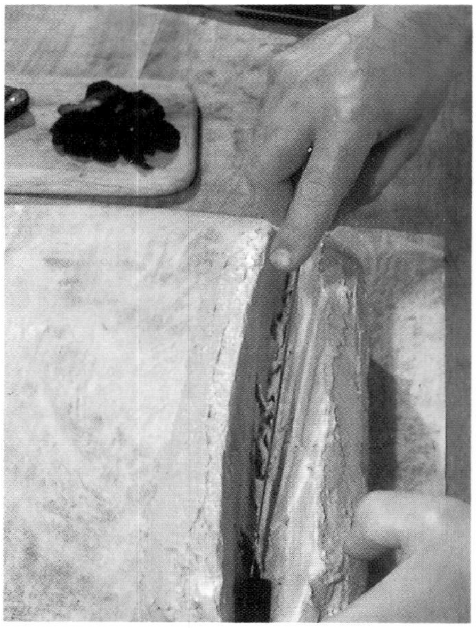

*Method B*

Using the bread mold described in the previous recipe enables the charcutier to easily place the truffles in the center.

without upsetting the arranged truffles.

The procedure for forming and wrapping is identical to the previous recipe.

**Cooking and Cooling**

The procedure is identical to the previous recipe.

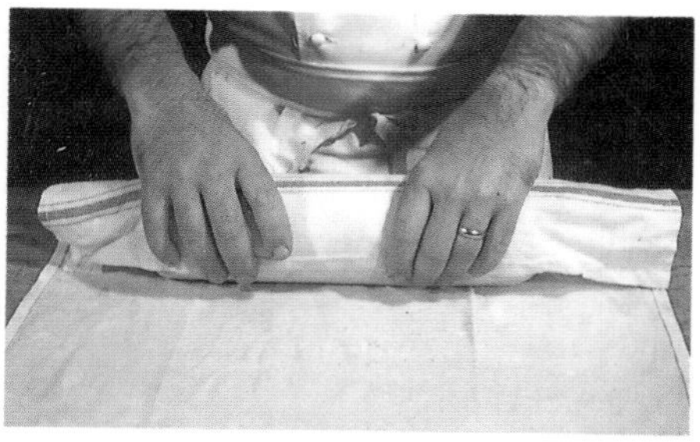

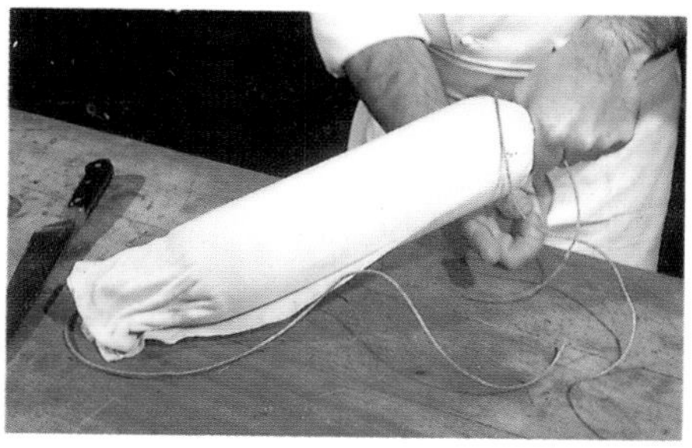

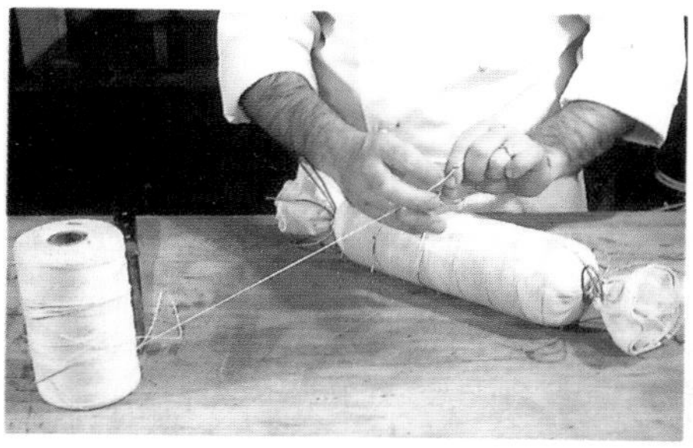

After the lobes are packed tightly, form an indentation down the center of one half of the rouleau with your finger or a cleaned sharpening steel.

Place the truffles in a neat row from one end to the other. The truffles are secured in place and the second half can be placed on top

# " Lucullus " and " Marie Stuart "

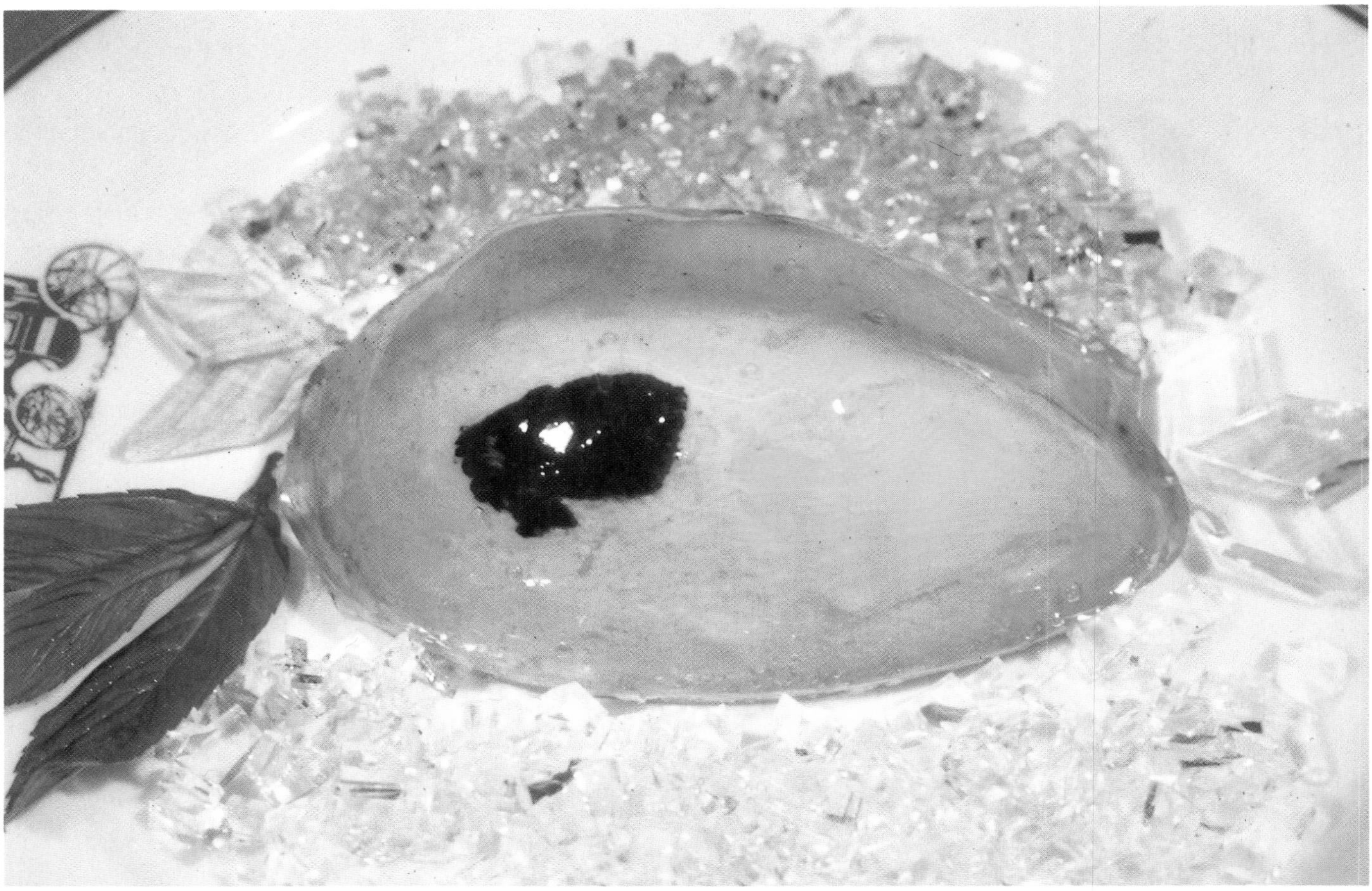

The two preparations are the same form but made in different ways.

The mold used for both is called a " Lucullus " which is the form of the two lobes of a foie gras. The molds are available in graduated sizes (holding 25-500 g (1 oz-1 lb)) to make individual servings or larger presentations. The " Lucullus " is usually an individual serving made with small pieces of foie gras. The " Marie Stuart " is larger and is a more " noble " preparation made with whole lobes or large pieces of liver.

## " Lucullus "

The procedure is identical to the other preparations up until the marinating. This product is usually made with the tips of the lobes and trimmings from the denerving process. Set these pieces aside and season separately.

The special molds are filled to the top with the marinated foie gras and knocked on the work surface to force out air pockets. The molds are covered tightly with aluminum foil and arranged in deep containers with baking sheets on top to weigh down the contents. Several layers of the molds can be stacked on top of one another.

### Cooking

The " Lucullus " are cooked like the " rouleau ". Full-flavored stock is brought to a boil and poured over the molds to cover. The temperature of the cooking liquid is maintained at a steady 75-78 °C (167-172 F) throughout cooking until the internal temperature is 64-65 °C (150 F). The length of cooking will

differ with large and small molds.

As soon as the molded foie gras is cooked, it is cooled as quickly as possible then refrigerated (2-4 °C (35-37 F)).

**Presentation**

The chilled Lucullus is unmolded, the mold is washed and lined with aspic. The foie gras is decorated with truffle slices (the size of the slice in rapport with the size of the mold) then the foie gras is replaced into the prepared mold. It is possible to add truffles to the center of the preparation during assembly.

## " Marie-Stuart "

The mold used is the same shape as the Lucullus but is larger (holding 800 g (1 lb 10 oz)) to accomodate entire lobes of foie gras.

The foie gras for this preparation is whole lobes of the highest quality. After it is marinated, the lobes are placed in the mold following the contour, placing the large rounded end at the top and the pointed end at the base of the mold.

For this top-of-the-line product a row of truffles is usually added in the center (follow the directions in the terrine recipe).

**Cooking**

These larger molds are cooked in the same way as the smaller Lucullus. The internal temperature must be carefully monitored.

Cool the cooked Marie-Stuart as quickly as possible then refrigerate.

**Presentation**

The decoration with truffle slices and the remolding with aspic is the same as for the Lucullus.

These preparations can be made with goose or duck foie gras as long as the final product is clearly labeled to indicate which was used.

# Kouglof of Foie Gras with Truffles

## Introduction

Kouglof is a pastry from the Alsace region in eastern France. It is a leavened dough rich in eggs and butter with currants in the bread itself and sliced almonds baked on the outside. It is baked in an fluted earthenware mold known as a Kouglof mold. (Other spellings include Kougelhopf or Gougelhof.)

Jean-Pierre Odeau proposes to use this lovely mold to give an attractive shape to another Alsatian specialty--foie gras.

## Procedure

This is a top-of-the-line product which requires high quality foie gras. The volume of the mold will determine the amount of truffles needed (3% of the weight of the foie gras minimum; 5% is recommended). The truffle is cut into large pieces as shown.

## Assembly

The bottom of the mold is packed tightly with foie gras to form a layer about 3 cm (about 1 in) high. A circle of truffle pieces is arranged in the center of this layer.

A second layer of foie gras (lobes and pieces) is arranged on top and packed down well without disturbing the row of truffles. (An indentation for the truffles will keep them in place.) The mold is now 2/3 full and this wider layer receives two rows of truffles arranged in neat circles equidistant from each other and the edges.

Fill the mold to the top with a third layer of foie gras.

Like most of the preparations in this chapter, it is recommended to chill the Kouglof thoroughly (for 12 hours) before cooking.

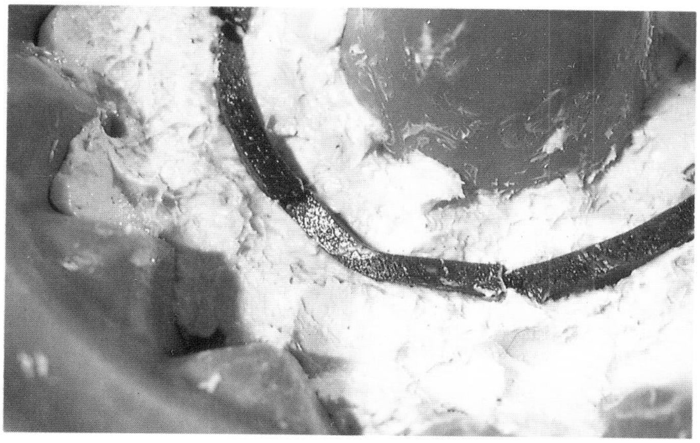

# Kouglof of Foie Gras with Truffle (continued)

**Cooking**

The method for cooking the Kouglof is identical to the cooking of the terrine of foie gras.

The mold is covered tightly with aluminum foil and placed in a water bath with hot water covering 1/3 of the mold.

It is placed in a 70-75 °C (160-167 F) oven and cooked until the internal temperature of the Kuglof is 64-65 °C (150 F).

The internal temperature must be monitored carefully. The use of an electronic probe is highly recommended.

Chill the cooked Kouglof as quickly as possible with a light weight on top to compress it slightly. (A ring mold filled with rice would work well.)

Refrigerate the chilled Kouglof and leave in its mold for 24 hours before serving.

**Storage**

The Kouglof can be stored in its mold under the same conditions as described for the terrines.

To prolong the shelf life a thin layer of goose fat can be poured over the top to seal out air. Better yet, place the mold in a vacuum pouch which protects the foie gras from all oxidation.

**Presentation**

To unmold, dip the mold in very hot water and shake to release.

Wash and dry the mold and pour a thin layer of thickened aspic (with 5% port) in the bottom.

Coat the sides of the mold with aspic and chill to set.

Decorate the unmolded Kouglof with slices of truffles, spacing them evenly in the fluted parts of the foie gras. Add a little thickened aspic to the chilled mold then slide the Kouglof back into the mold and chill to set.

The Kouglof is an attractive and original presentation for foie gras which will add sparkle to any buffet table.

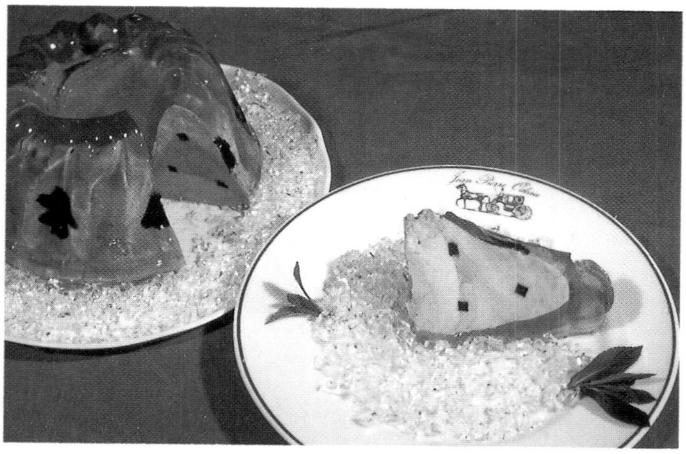

# Terrine of Whole Duck Foie Gras

**Introduction**

The methods used to make preparations with duck foie gras do not differ substantially from dishes made with goose foie gras.

The fattened liver of the duck however is more fragile which makes it unappropriate for some products that require more handling to assemble.

For example the Lucullus and the rouleau are not made with duck foie gras because they would probably lose too much fat during cooking and therefore not keep their shape. Duck foie gras is used almost exclusively for products that are assembled in terrines or other molds.

## Procedure

The livers are seasoned in the same way and left to marinate. They are then placed in the terrine (smoothest sides of the lobes and the largest pieces on the bottom and the top to give a smooth exterior to the terrine). Press down on the terrine to eliminate air pockets.

As with goose foie gras, the prepared terrine is refrigerated for 12 hours before cooking.

Jean-Francois Deport recommends taking the terrine out of the refrigerator 1 hour before cooking and leaving at room temperature to take the chill off.

## Cooking

The best way to cook this terrine is in the steamer.

The terrine is covered with foil and placed in a water bath, and steamed at 75 °C (167 F) until the internal temperature is 64-66 °C (150 F). Verify the internal temperature with a thermometer or electronic probe placed in the terrine at the beginning of cooking.

The cooked terrines are cooled as quickly as possible without a weight on top or any other manipulation. They can be placed directly into the refrigerator and chilled for 24 hours.

Cooking in a vacuum pouch is well suited to this terrine of duck foie gras. A separate section describes this process in detail.

## Storage

The chilled terrine should be covered with a thin layer of duck fat mixed with lard (to harden). It can then be kept in the refrigerator (2-3 °C (35 F)) for several weeks.

Also effective is a vacuum pouch which seals out air and makes the product easier to store.

## Presentation

To prepare the terrine for sale in a charcuterie, remove the layer of fat from the top and wipe the surface. Arrange a few truffle slices down the center and pour a layer of thickened aspic over the top.

The regulations governing the labeling of duck foie gras is the same as for goose foie gras. The word " entier " (whole) can be used only if the entire lobe and large pieces are used with no purée added.

# Terrine of Duck Foie Gras

### Introduction

This is a variation of the previous preparation but is assembled in a different type of terrine.

Therefore the procedure is the same until the terrine is cooked.

### Cooking

The best cooking method for this terrine is steaming. The procedure is identical to the previous recipe.

The cooking time for this larger terrine will be longer than the previous recipe.

It is also very important to monitor the cooking very closely.

The use of an electronic probe is recommended which is placed in the terrine at the beginning of cooking. The temperature is read from the

outside of the oven which enables the chef to keep the oven door closed throughout cooking to maintain an even temperature.

When the terrine is cooked (internal temperature of 65 °C (150 F)) the terrine is cooled as quickly as possible following the directions in previous recipes.

**Presentation**

In an identical terrine pour in a thin layer of aspic and chill to set. Arrange a row of truffles on this aspic.

Unmold the terrine then chill to harden the exterior that was softened during unmolding. When ready to insert into the prepared mold, add a little more aspic then slide the terrine into the mold.

**Storage**

This preparation can be stored in the same manner and for the same length of time as the other terrines in this chapter.

The client must be informed of how to properly transport, store and serve the foie gras. The charcutier should print instructions on a small card which is included with all foie gras products. This gesture is very good publicity, showing the client that the charcutier is thorough and proud of his products.

**Service**

Whether at a seated dinner or on a buffet, the terrine can be sliced using a thin-bladed knife dipped in boiling water or scooped out with a silver spoon dipped in hot water.

The slices should be " medium "--too thin, they could break apart; too thick a slice would provide too large a portion of this rich dish.

The ideal temperature to fully appreciate the aroma and taste of foie gras is between 10-15 °C (50-60 F). It is recommended to take the terrine out of the refrigerator a little in advance to take the chill off. This is a small gesture that can make a big difference in the final result.

# Terrine of Duck Foie Gras with Truffles

## Introduction

This terrine is a variation of the previous preparation with an addition of truffles. The basic method is the same as the other terrines.

For this refined product it is important to use the best quality foie gras available.

## Procedure

To determine the amount of truffle to be used the amount of foie gras that the terrine will hold must be determined. For this "truffled" terrine 3% truffles is the minimum. If the food cost allows, it is recommended to use 5% of the weight of the foie gras in truffles.

When denerving the duck foie gras remember that it is more fragile than goose foie gras. Seasoning and chilling is identical to the goose foie gras terrine with truffles.

## Assembly

Place the marinated lobes and large pieces of foie gras in the terrine with the smoothest side on the bottom. Fill halfway and press down well to compact the liver.

Make an indentation down the center and arrange the truffles in a neat row.

Fill the mold to the top with more foie gras and press down to eliminate air pockets.

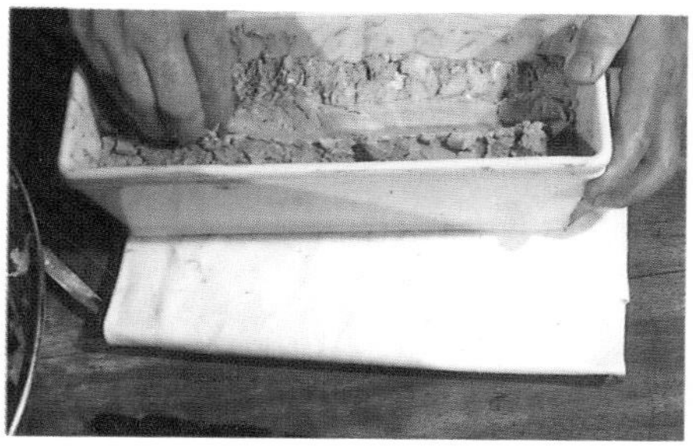

Chill the prepared terrine in the refrigerator (2-3 $^{0}$C (35 F)) for 12 hours before cooking.

**Cooking**

The cooking of this terrine is identical to the other duck foie gras terrines in this chapter. As with all foie gras products, it is important to closely monitor the cooking.

Storing and serving this terrine is the same as the others as well.

**Presentation**

The classic decoration, as for most of the molded foie gras preparations, is a simple glaze of crystal clear aspic.

It is imperative that this aspic be flavorful and of good quality. It would be a shame to ruin a wonderful and expensive slice of foie gras with inferior aspic.

" Real " aspic (as opposed to powdered aspic) is made from full-

flavored stock rich in natural gelatin, achieved through slow cooking of meat and bones. Careful skimming and draining is necessary for an uncloudy stock that is easy to clarify. The gelatin content is tested before using to coat the mold. Additional information on aspic is available in chapter 1.

The procedure for coating the mold with aspic is the same as the other terrines in this chapter.

# Small Terrine of Duck Foie Gras with Truffle

**Introduction**

This preparation requires the same techniques that have been described for the larger terrines.

It is the marketing of this terrine that distinguishes it from the others in this chapter.

The objective is to offer the client a terrine suitable for the number of his guests. So rather than purchasing slices, the client transports the terrine in its attractive mold and slices it fresh or serves it directly from the mold.

The charcutier-caterer can offer this service to his clients by having molds in a variety of sizes to suit different occasions. Molds vary in size from 250 g (1/2 lb) to 1,000 g (2.2 lbs). The average portion is 80 g (2 1/2 oz) of foie gras per guest. It is a good idea to have a little more on hand for the extra-hungry guest.

The elegant presentation makes this product suitable for fancy occasions but the size makes it just right for an informal gathering of good friends.

The charcutier must choose his molds with care (porcelaine is recommended) as this is a reflection on the style and quality of his business. The name of the business, attractively printed on the mold, is effective publicity. The molds can be purchased or returned by the client (deposit is collected in advance).

**Procedure**

The duck foie gras is denerved and marinated for 24 hours. Truffles are added (3% of the weight of the foie gras). The method for assembly is identical to the other terrines in this chapter.

## Cooking

It is recommended to cook these terrines in a steamer. The temperature is the same as the other terrines.

Since several terrines will be cooked at once, it is advised to cook only one size at a time. The smaller ones would obviously be done before the larger ones. Opening the oven door would lower the temperature and offset the cooking of the remaining terrines.

Duck foie gras is particularly sensitive to slight changes in temperature.

The cooked terrines are cooled rapidly as with the other terrines.

## Storage

This product is destined to be purchased by the client and consumed, in some cases, several weeks later.

To ensure proper freshness, for several weeks, the charcutier should cover the top of the cooled terrine with a thin layer of duck fat mixed with lard to seal out air. Not all clients like having this layer of fat and as a result vacuum packing has become a popular method for storing foie gras for long periods.

The protective plastic film seals out all air and makes the product easier to handle. The terrine is vacuum packed without its lid which is placed on top of the package when the terrine is sold.

In all cases it is imperative that the client is advised to store the terrine in the refrigerator until serving.

For the perfect gift, the terrine is placed in an insulated box and wrapped with elegant paper.

# Foie Gras in Brioche

## Method A

This is the more difficult of the two methods but the taste is superior. The uncooked foie gras is rolled in the center of the brioche and after the dough has risen the two elements cook together.

During the cooking, the foie gras permeates the delicate brioche with its marvelous taste and aroma. However foie gras usually renders fat and juices during cooking which could result in a soggy final result which would be unacceptable for a preparation of this status.

The choice of the fattened liver is therefore of the utmost importance. Goose foie gras, which tends to render less fat during cooking, should be used.

**Ingredients**

1 kg (about 2 lbs) uncooked foie gras (trimmed and marinated)
1 kg (about 2 lbs) brioche dough:
500 g (1 lb) sifted flour – 5 eggs
250 g (1/2 lb) unsalted butter
10 g (1/3 oz) cake yeast
10 g (2 tsp/1/3 oz) fine salt
10 g (1/3 oz) sugar
100 ml (scant 1/2 cup) warm water
Aspic with port

**Procedure**

***The Foie Gras***

Trim and marinate (12-24 hours) the foie gras following the classic method outlined in this chapter.

Form the foie gras into a cylinder (see " roulade of foie gras ") slightly shorter than the mold that it will be baked in. Roll the cylinder tightly in a clean handtowel and refrigerate for 12 hours. This chilling process accounts for part of the marinating time.

***The Brioche***

The brioche dough is also prepared a day in advance.

Allow the dough to double in volume in a warm (35 °C (95 F)) moist place (" étuves " are used in France which are equipped with shelves and automatic temperature and humidity controls).

Punch down the dough (can be done in the mixer) and repeat the rising process two more times.

After the third rising, punch down the dough, cover and leave to rest and chill overnight in the refrigerator (2-4 °C (35 F)).

Roll out the chilled dough with a rolling pin or sheeter (" laminoir ") to a thickness of 1 cm (3/8 in).

Brush the surface of the dough with egg glaze. Remove the chilled foie gras from the handtowel and place it on the dough and roll to form a cylinder of brioche with the foie gras in the center and seal the edges of the dough. Lightly butter the mold and carefully insert the brioche. Brush the top with egg glaze and set aside to rise for 1 hour.

**Cooking**

Place the foie gras in brioche in an oven preheated to 220 °C (425 F). When the top has browned a little, lower the heat to 180-190 °C (375 F) and continue cooking for about 45 minutes.

Using a probe thermometer, verify that the internal temperature of the foie gras has reached 68-70 °C (155-160 F). Transfer the cooked brioche to a cooling rack and leave to cool at room temperature for about two hours then cover and refrigerate (2-4 °C (35 F)).

**Presentation**

Make a small hole in the top of the brioche (this can actually be done before it is cooked). Stir the aspic flavored with port (10 % maximum) over ice to thicken slightly. Pour the aspic into the hole in the brioche to fill the space created between the foie gras and the crust.

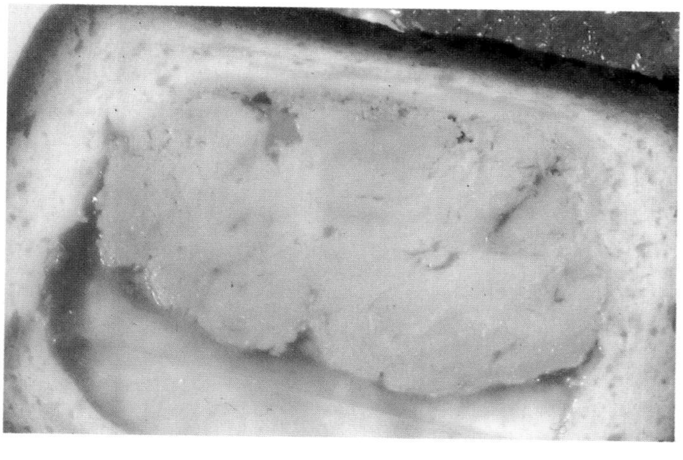

# Foie Gras in Brioche: Method B

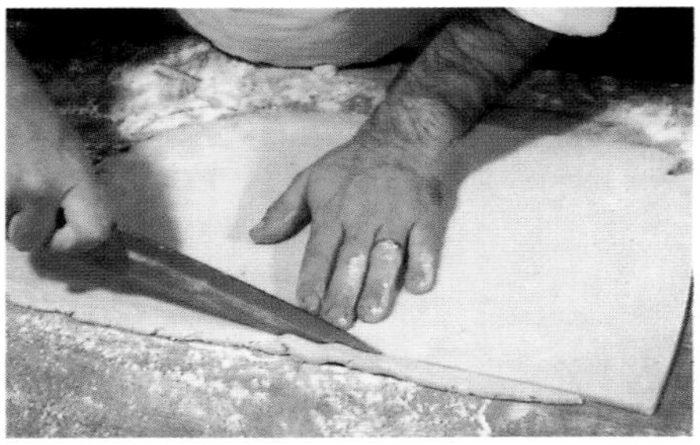

This method is much less risky than the first because the brioche and foie gras are cooked separately which eliminates all chances of the foie gras making the dough soggy.

Even though the shape of this product may be neater, it is obvious that the taste cannot compare to the first version of the recipe.

**Ingredients**

1 kg (about 2 lbs) foie gras (uncooked, marinated)

1 kg (about 2 lbs) brioche dough:
500 g (1 lb) sifted flour – 5 eggs
250 g (1/2 lb) unsalted butter
10 g (1/3 oz) cake yeast
10 g (1/3 oz) fine salt
10 g (1/3 oz) sugar
About 100 ml (scant 1/2 cup) warm water

*Note:* The presence of sugar in the brioche does not make it sweet but is a basic ingredient in the recipe to make it brown better during baking.

**Procedure**

For the preparation of the foie gras refer to the section on " roulade of foie gras ". It is trimmed and marinated in the classic way. The vacuum method can used for marinating.

The cooking of the " roulade " can also be done in a vacuum pouch. We

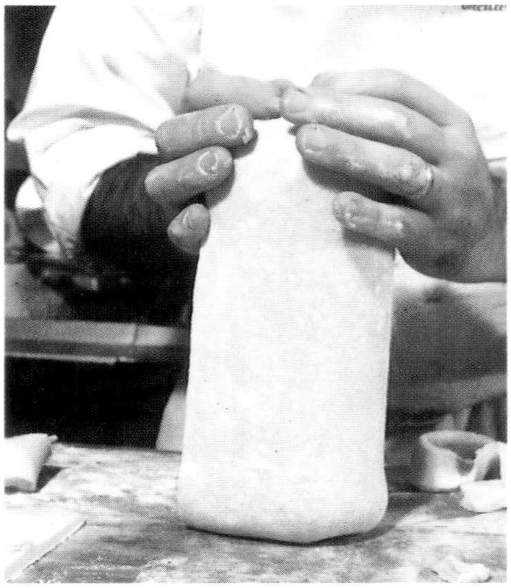

recommend this method for the best results in this preparation.

The foie gras must be prepared well in advance (at least one day) so it is thoroughly chilled before it is assembled with the brioche.

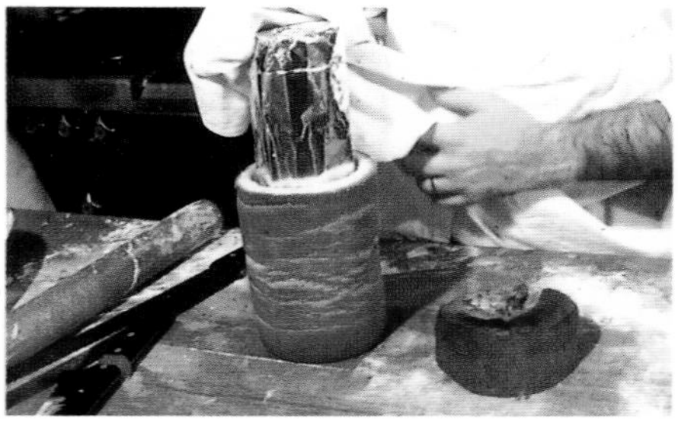

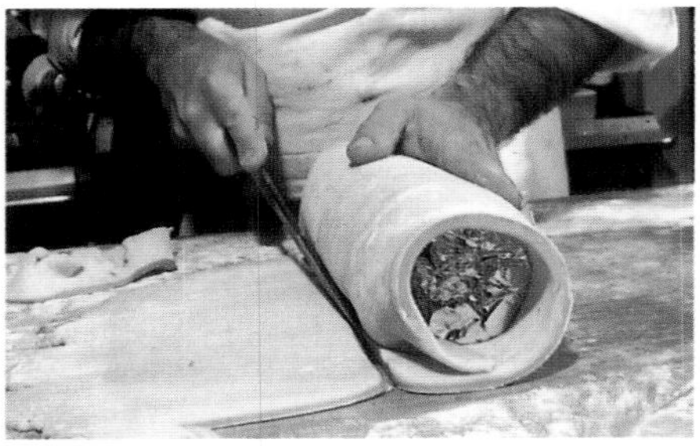

The brioche is shaped around a " false roulade ". For example an empty can of the right proportions can serve as the smaller mold to create a hole for the cooked cylinder of foie gras to slide into after baking.

Roll the brioche to a thickness of 1 cm (3/8 in). Cover the can with aluminum foil. Brush the sheet of dough with egg glaze to stick it to the mold then roll it around the smaller cylindrical form and seal the edges.

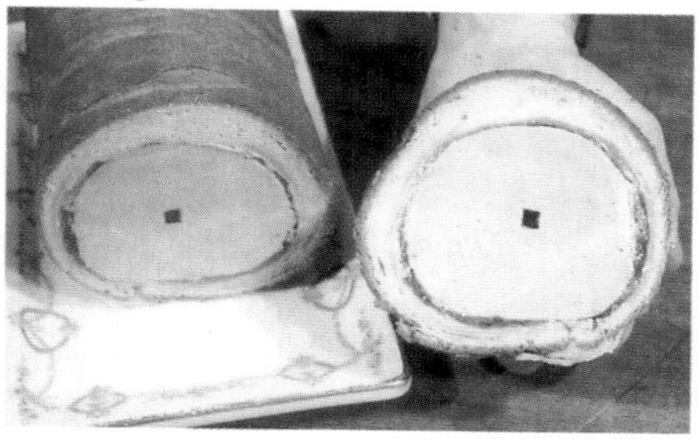

Lightly butter the larger mold and slide the brioche into it. Cover the end with a circle of dough and seal the edges. Brush with egg glaze and set aside to rise for about 1 hour.

Bake the brioche at 200 ⁰C (425 F) for a few minutes then lower the heat to 180-190 ⁰C (375 F) until done.

Refrigerate the baked brioche for 12 hours.

Remove the brioche from the mold.

Cut around the top third of the brioche. Brioche is very buttery which facilitates this operation. Remove the form in the center.

Remove the foie gras from the vacuum pouch (or torchon) and verify that it will fit in the space provided in the brioche. Flavor a little aspic with port like for method A.

Place the foie gras in the " lid " and pour aspic over until it comes to the top edge of the brioche and chill to set. Repeat the process in the other portion and chill to set.

The aspic will form an even layer around the foie gras whereas with the first method the foie gras has cooked onto the base leaving a large spoon on top. The uniform aspect of each slice of the foie gras in brioche using method B is stunning and is a compensation for its slight lack in flavor.

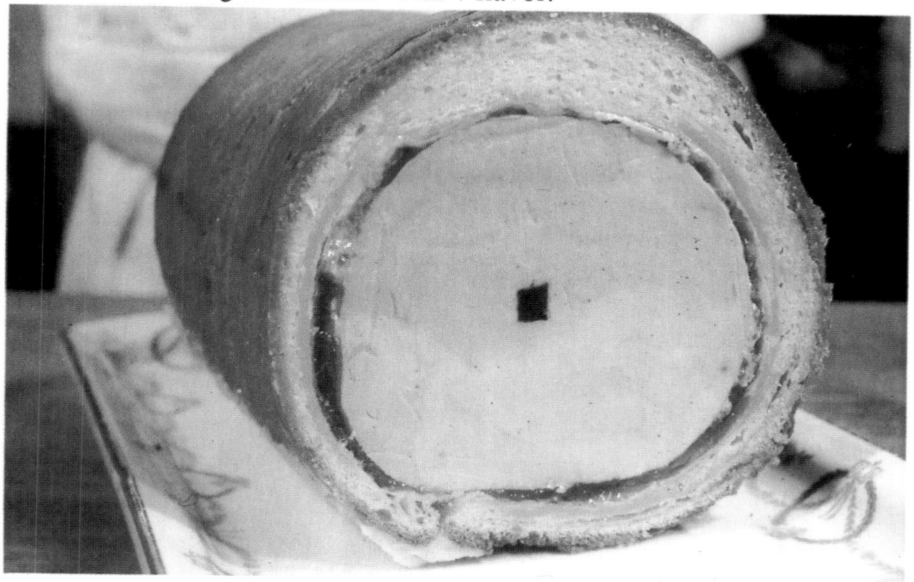

# Chapter 6

# Terrines, Galantines and " Roulades " made with Veal or Pork

## Finesse in a Variety of Products

*Pork and veal are meats that are light in color. The taste is not as pronounced as beef and lamb and therefore pork and veal marry well with a wide variety of ingredients.*

*The chef needs only to respect the natural harmony of flavors to create subtle combinations.*

*Forcemeats featuring pork or veal can be cooked in a mold or used fillings for galantines and roulades.*

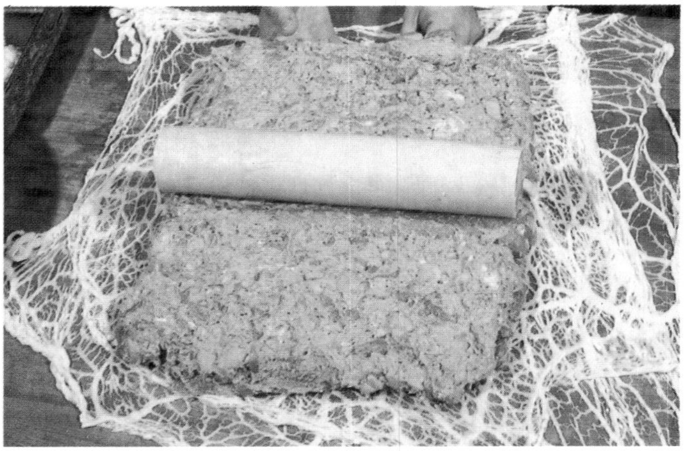

# Introduction

The products in this chapter, like the two previous chapters, are representative of the great variety of products offered by the French artisinal charcutier.

The selection here spans the range of veal and pork forcemeat preparations, illustrating just a few of the exciting flavor combinations that are possible.

The skill and creativity of the charcutier rivals that of the great chefs in this domain. Indeed terrines are served in practically every French restaurant, making this category of products a common bond between charcutier and chef.

Although both restaurants and charcuteries offer terrines, galantines and roulades, the preparation differs in several ways.

The major difference is the use of curing salt (sodium nitrite or saltpeter) by the charcutier.

The charcutier, who is usually producing larger batches of these products, uses additives for two reasons:

- To maintain a desirable rosy color.
- A security measure to inhibit bacterial growth.

Terrines made in restaurants are usually seasoned with fine salt which results in a gray color. Curiously the French diner does not object to being served a slice of a dull colored terrine in a restaurant but consistently rejects the " natural " color when the terrine is displayed on the shelf at the supermarket or charcuterie.

The preparations in this chapter range from a simple pork terrine with pistachios to an elaborate whole young pig with a flower-shaped " rosace " in the center. The latter requires skill and knowledge to prepare.

The seven products in this chapter have one point in common: forcemeat is used to hold the elements together. This ground mixture, made of marinated meats often flavored with a meat glaze and " gratin " serves to " cement " the varied ingredients for neat slicing and is seasoned to augment the overall taste of the product.

It is important to stress that high quality products are possible only if the ingredients are perfectly fresh. Not only does flavor suffer when foods are stored too long or in bad conditions, but the risk of bacterial contamination increases.

Unfortunately the growing demand for food products has created the need for ingredients produced on an industrial scale. The mass produced meats and vegetables are less expensive but the taste of veal and pork today does not compare with the delicious meat marketed 50 years ago.

To compensate for this decline in flavor, we have investigated techniques to augment the taste of the main ingredients. Playing a major role in this effort are the stocks, reductions and meat glazes which reinforce the natural taste of the meat. Also adding a dimension of flavor and texture is the " gratin " which is an ingredient in many forcemeats.

As with all the presentations in this series, the dishes in this chapter have been chosen for their appeal to sight and smell as well as taste.

The visual aspect is particularly important. The techniques and " tricks of the trade " used to create the stunning patterns in each slice do not require fancy equipment. For example, the stuffed pig with the elaborate " rosace " in the center requires only a freezer to harden the cylinder.

Some ingredients add color and contrast like pistachios in a forcemeat which is wrapped around a rosy filet of meat. No artificial colors are added to these products even though the government regulations would allow certain ones.

Symmetry is also important so that the slice of the final product is attractive.

The decoration on the top is an expression of the creativity and artistic talents of the chef. In choosing among the myriad of colorful fruits and vegetables, it is recommended to include something in the decoration which signals to the customer the contents of the preparation (for example a " bouquet " of wild mushrooms on top of a terrine " forestière ").

With so many food products becoming mundane in appearance and taste, it is the objective of the artisan charcutier to keep the imagination and creativity alive in his work and offer his clients preparations with a personal, original touch.

## Our selection

**Pork terrine with pistachios (p. 200)**

**Veal terrine with artichoke bottoms (p. 204)**

**Stuffed veal breast (p. 208)**

**Terrine of sweetbreads with morels (p. 212)**

**Veal loin with sweetbreads (p. 216)**

**Terrine of pork filets with broccoli mousse (p. 220)**

**Stuffed young pig " en rosace " (p. 224)**

# Pork Terrine with Pistachios

### Introduction

This simple, rustic terrine is an appropriate first course or hors d'œuvre suitable for many menus.

This product which marries the delicate tastes of pork and pistachios can be sold year-round.

### Equipment

Paring knife, large bowl, horizontal chopper, terrine mold.

### Ingredients

(for about 5 kg (11 lbs) of mixture)
3 kg (6.6 lbs) top quality lean pork
1.5 kg (3.3 lbs) forcemeat
(1/2 lean (belly), 1/2 fat (jowl))
3 eggs
250 ml (1 cup) heavy cream
450 g (about 1 lb) peeled pistachios

*Seasonings (per kilo (2.2 lbs))*

18 g (generous 1/2 oz) curing salt
(fine salt with sodium nitrite)
2 g (1/16 oz) sugar or dextrose
2 g (1/16 oz) white pepper
Port (aged)

**Preparing the Ingredients**

***The Meats***

The lean pork should be top quality meat that is light in color. After trimming cut in large dice (1.5 cm (1/2 in)).

The meats for the forcemeat are selected from the belly and the jowl. The overall mix should be about 2/3 lean and 1/3 fat. Cut in large dice as well.

Place the meats in separate stainless steel recipients and season with the corresponding amounts of curing salt and sugar and add a little port.

Note that when a sweet wine is used, the sugar can be eliminated from the recipe.

Cover and refrigerate (2-4 $^0$C (35 F)) for 12 hours.

***The Pistachios***

Pistachios are the fruit of a tree that grows in Turkey and Italy. Shelled pistachios are available in two forms:

- with the skin

- without skin – the papery covering of the nut is removed mechanically and the pistachios are cleaned.

As with all ingredients that are peeled in advance, pistachios lose much of their flavor when the skin is removed. Even nuts that are placed in a vacuum pouch immediately following the peeling process are not as flavorful as ones that are marketed with the skins attached.

Removing the skins is not difficult but is time consuming. The pistachios are immersed in boiling water a few seconds to loosen the skins then they are rubbed in a handtowel to remove them.

The chef has the choice to buy peeled pistachios which will save time but the final product will not be as good or to peel the pistachios just before using to ensure that they are full-flavored.

As always, we recommend the method that produces the most delicious results.

## Procedure

### *The Forcemeat*

To prepare, simply place the marinated belly and jowl in the bowl of a chopper. Process until smooth, adding the eggs then the cream as the blade rotates. Lastly add the corresponding amount of spices and blend until homogeneous.

The mixture should be cold throughout processing. This can be achieved by chilling the bowl and blade of the machine in the freezer and keeping the meats well chilled until just ready to make the forcemeat. The temperature should never exceed 4 °C (37 F).

### *The Meat Mixture*

Transfer the forcemeat to the chilled bowl of a mixer or a large stainless steel bowl.

Add the marinated cubes of lean pork and turn until incorporated evenly. Lastly add the pistachios and blend until homogeneous.

*Note:* The taste can be improved by adding the pistachios to the lean cubes of meat when they are marinated. This is especially recommended if the assembled terrine is to be cooked immediately (rather than being chilled and allowed to " mellow ").

## Molding

Line the terrine molds with barding fat with a little hanging over the edge to cover the top of the terrine. Spoon the mixture into the molds, pressing to eliminate all pockets of air.

Fold the barding fat over the top and pierce a few holes in the fat which will keep the fat from contracting and curling up during cooking.

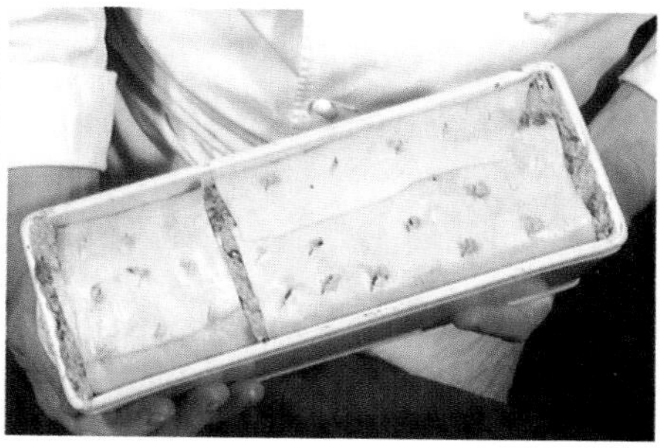

**Cooking**

The terrine can be cooked as soon as it is assembled. However if the pistachios were added at the last stage of mixing it is recommended to refrigerate the terrine (up to 12 hours) and allow the flavors to " mingle ". The pistachios and meat continue to exchange their flavors up to the point when the terrine reaches 45-50 °C (120 F) which coagulates the proteins.

Place the terrine in a water bath. Start the cooking in a 200 °C (400 F) oven. When the top has browned a little, turn the temperature down to 100-110 °C (200 F) and continue to cook until the internal temperature is 75-78 °C (170 F) (measured with a probe thermometer).

The cooked terrine is drained to remove the fatty liquid rendered during cooking which is then replaced with a " jus " or stock of pork which is gelatinous and reduced to make it full-flavored.

Place a weight (500 g (1 lb)) on top and cool as quickly as possible.

**Storage**

This terrine will keep in the refrigerator for up to 8 days.
The storage time is longer if the chilled terrine is placed immediately in a vacuum pouch.

**Presentation**

The terrine can be simply glazed with aspic and decorated with pistachios and sold directly from the mold. It can also be unmolded and coated with aspic by first coating the cleaned mold and reinserting the terrine then unmolding again.

# Veal Terrine with Artichokes

### Introduction

Veal, pork and artichokes combine to make a subtle marriage of flavors in this original terrine. The delicious taste of this dish makes it an excellent selection for any menu.

### Equipment

Knives, sauté pan, braising pan, stainless steel bowls, grinder, horizontal chopper, pots, molds.

### Ingredients

1 kg (2.2 lbs) lean veal
1 kg (2.2 lbs) lean pork
1 kg (2.2 lbs) forcemeat (jowl, belly)
250 g (1/2 lb) calves' liver
6-8 artichoke bottoms
200 ml (scant 1/2 cup) heavy cream
2 eggs
Port (aged)
150 g (5 oz) chopped parsley
Barding fat

*Seasonings (per kilo (2.2 lbs))*

18 g (generous 1/2 oz) curing salt
2 g (1/16 oz) sugar or dextrose
2 g (1/16 oz) white pepper
1 g (1/32 oz) four spice powder

### Preparing the Ingredients

#### *The Veal and Pork*

Choose lean veal and pork from a top-quality cut that is pale in color.

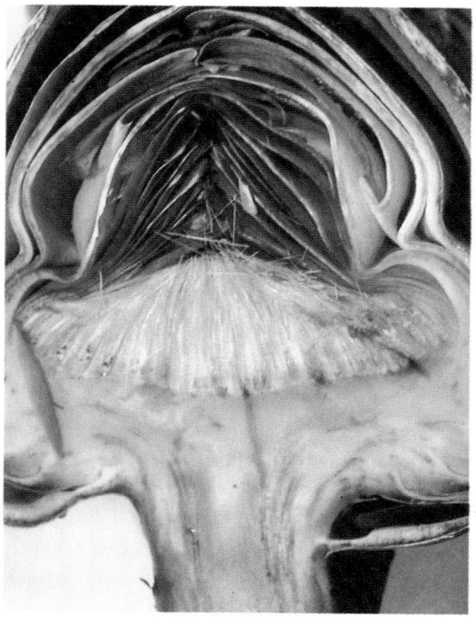

The trimmed weight of each should be 1 kg (about 2 lbs) which is then cut into small cubes or strips (lèches).

***The Forcemeat***

The forcemeat is the standard blend of fat and lean (from the lean part of the belly and the jowl). It is trimmed, boned, and skin is removed before cutting in small pieces.

***The Liver***

Remove all remaining vessels from the liver and cut all traces of bile (green stains on the liver). Cut in pieces.

***The Marinade***

The pieces of lean pork and veal can be marinated together in one recipient and the forcemat ingredients and liver in another. Season with the corresponding amounts of curing salt and sugar and sprinkle with port. Cover and refrigerate for 12-24 hours.

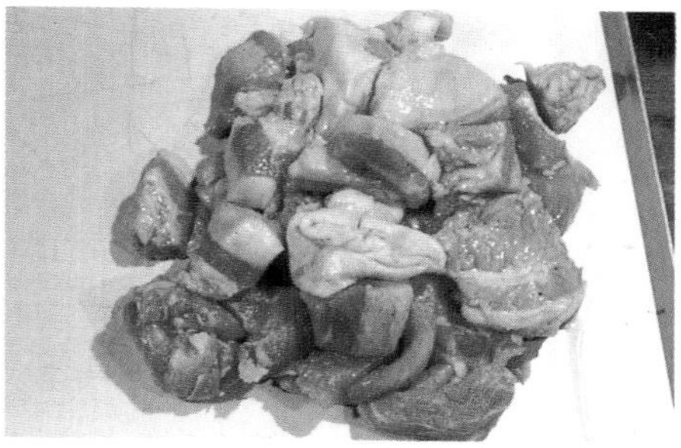

***The Artichokes***

Break off the stem of the artichokes. Cut off the leaves using a sharp paring knife, scoop out the choke and rub with lemon. Alternatively, remove the leaves and choke from the cooked artichoke.

Cook the artichokes in salted boiling water until tender then stop the cooking by plunging in cold water with lemon juice added. When cooled, drain on paper towels.

*Note:* When fresh artichokes are not available, canned or frozen artichoke bottoms can be used in this dish. The slice will look the same but the taste will not be as good.

**Making the Mixture**

Grind the liver and the forcemeat ingredients through the 2 mm (about 1/8 in) disk.

Transfer to the mixer, add the eggs then the cream and lastly the chopped parsley.

Add the remaining seasonings and blend until homogeneous.

At low speed blend in the strips of lean meat or stir in by hand.

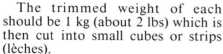

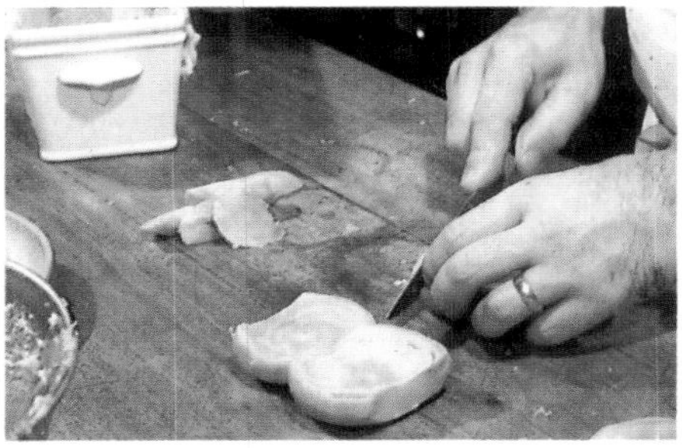

**Assembly**

Line the mold with a sheet of barding fat.

Square off the edges of the artichoke bottoms so that they can be lined up in the terrine (so that each slice is the same).

The artichoke trimmings are blended into the filling.

Fill the bottom third of the mold with the meat mixture.

*Note:* For a more attractive slice, the strips of lean meat in the filling can be lined up as much as possible.

Arrange a neat row of artichoke bottoms down the center.

Add a second layer of filling. Arrange another row of artichokes.

Fill the mold to the top with the remaining filling and fold over the edges of the barding fat to cover the top.

**Cooking**

This terrine is cooked in the classic manner.

First brown the top in an oven preheated to 180-200 °C (400 F) then lower the temperature to 110-115 °C (225 F).

Cook until the probe thermometer inserted into the center registers 76-78 °C (170 F).

Remove the cooked terrine from the oven and pour off the fatty juices rendered during cooking.

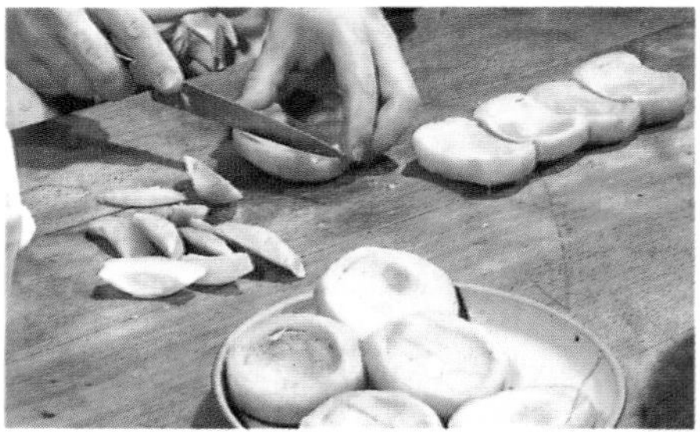

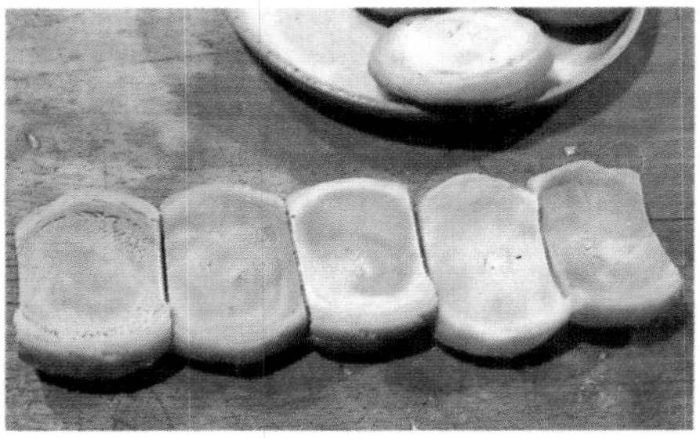

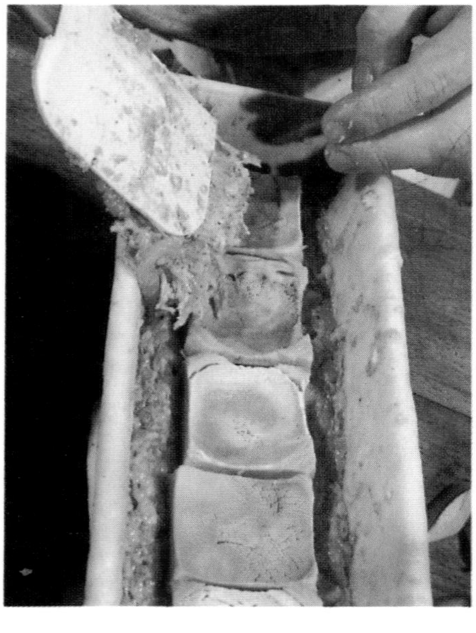

Replace these juices with pork stock that has been previously brought to a boil, skimmed and strained.

Place a weight on top (500 g (1 lb)) and cool as quickly as possible.

**Storage**

This terrine will keep in the refrigerator (2-4 °C (35 F)) for up to 8 days.

The terrine can be stored for 15 days if it is placed in a vacuum pouch after being completely chilled.

**Presentation**

This terrine can be cut in slices directly from the mold.

In this case the sides of the mold are cleaned and the top of the terrine is decorated with cut-out pieces of cooked vegetable (artichoke is a good choice) and brushed with aspic.

The terrine can also be presented unmolded.

Clean the mold, coat with aspic and arrange a decoration on this layer of aspic.

Pour in a little thickened aspic then slide the terrine back into the mold and chill to set the aspic. Dip the mold in hot water and unmold onto a platter.

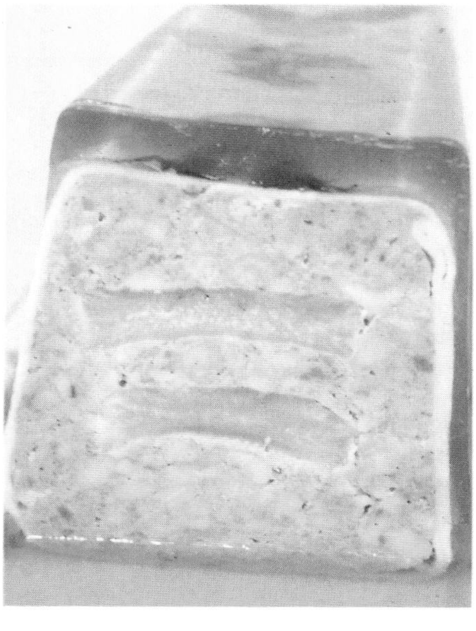

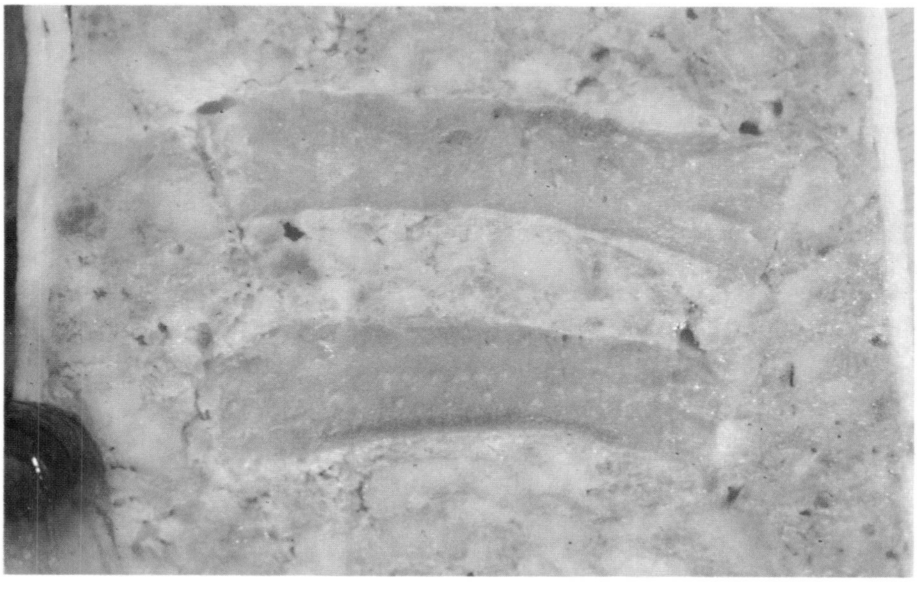

# Stuffed Breast of Veal

## Introduction

For this preparation a breast of veal is completely boned and rolled around a filling of finely ground forcemeat (1/2 fat, 1/2 lean) blended with sausage meat and " gratin ". The stuffed breast of veal is braised using pork juices to moisten the meat as it cooks.

The " roulade " can be shaped in two ways:

• Filling spread in a thin layer with the veal rolled in a spiral.
• A cylinder of filling with the boned veal breast around the outside.

Here we show the second method.

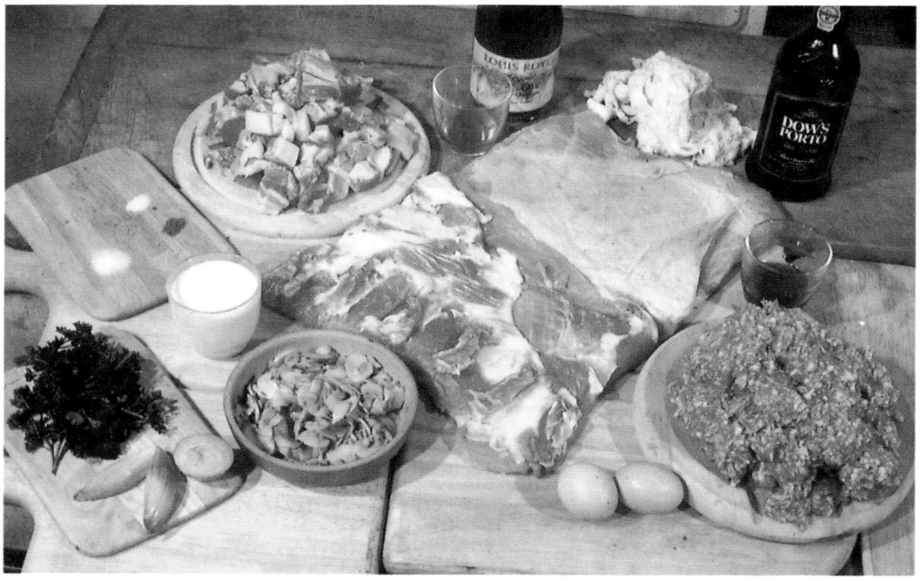


## Equipment

Knives, horizontal chopper, stainless steel bowls, kitchen string, large braising pot, platter.

## Ingredients

Breast of veal
1.5 kg (3.3 lbs) sausage meat (volume 1)
1 kg (2.2 lbs) belly and jowl (forcemeat)
300 g (10 oz) mushrooms
150 g (5 oz) shallots
250 g (1/2 lb) chicken livers
200 g (7 oz) parsley
2 eggs
150 ml (3/4 cup) heavy cream
Port
Cognac
Caul fat

*Seasonings (per kg (2.2 lbs))*

18 g (generous 1/2 oz) curing salt (sodium nitrite with fine salt)
2 g (1/16 oz) sugar or dextrose
2 g (1/16 oz) ground with pepper
1 g (1/32 oz) four spice powder
0.5 g (1/64 oz) ground nutmeg

**Preparing the Ingredients**

***The Veal Breast***

Remove the bones and all cartilage from the veal breast. Trim all nerves and fat.

Immerse the boned and trimmed veal in brine (same as for hams) for 12 hours. Drain in the refrigerator and allow the flavors to develop for 12 hours.

Soak in a basin of cold water to remove excess brine, drain thoroughly and pat dry.

It is also possible to season the bones veal with standards amounts of curing salt and cognac. It is rolled, wrapped and refrigerated for 24 hours.

Brining assures an even color but the seasoning method makes the products more flavorful.

***The Filling***

*The " Gratin "*

Finely chop the shallots and cook in goose fat until soft.

Slice half of the mushrooms, add to the shallots and cook until tender.

Trim the chicken livers and brown them quickly; they should remain very pink in the center.

Add half of the parsley (trimmed, washed and chopped) and a little port. Bring quickly to a boil then cool as quickly as possible.

Grind coarsely in a meat grinder.

*The Forcemeat*

Trim the belly and jowl, cut into pieces and marinate overnight. Grind the meats coarsely in a meat grinder.

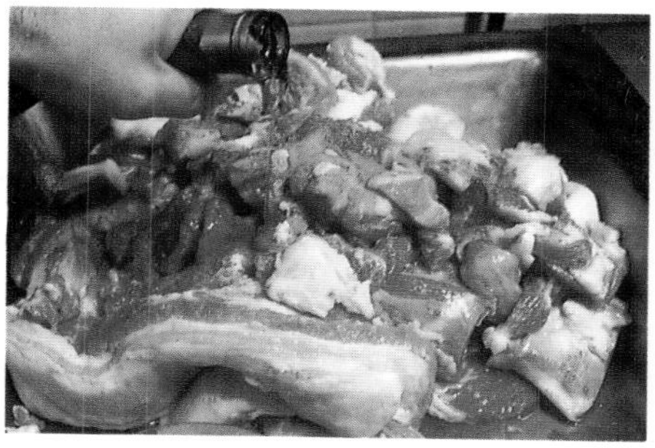

*Making the Filling*

*Note:* The filling mixture may also be called a " forcemeat ".

Place the ground gratin and forcemeat in the horizontal chopper.

Add the eggs then the cream and process until finely textured.

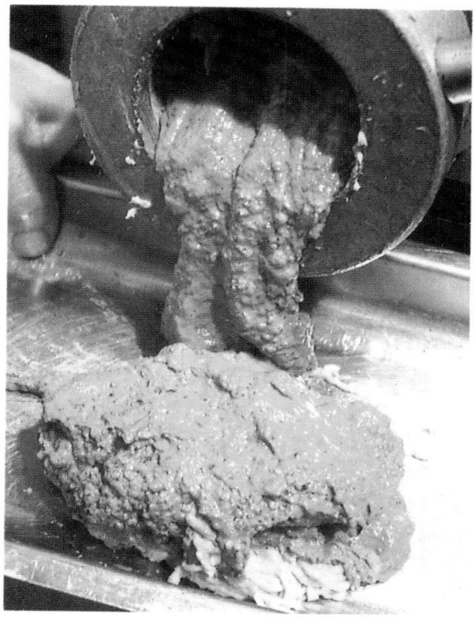

Transfer to a mixer (or mix by hand) and blend in the remaining parsley (chopped finely) and mushrooms (sliced, sautéed).

Blend until the parsley and mushrooms are incorporated and the mixture is smooth.

Add the sausage meat and blend until homogeneous.

**Assembly**

Soak the caul fat and rinse thoroughly and dry. Spread it flat on the work surface.
Place the veal breast, boned side up, on the caul fat.

Place the filling in an even mound down the center of the veal and roll the meat around it to form a cylinder.

Wrap the caul fat around the veal " roulade " to cover completely.

Tie the rolled veal like a roast. However it should not be tied too tightly because delicious juices would be squeezed out of the meat as it expands at the beginning of cooking.

**Cooking**

Cooking is done in two stages:
First the veal is placed on a baking sheet and browned in a hot oven (180-190 °C (375 F)).

The veal is then transferred to a deep pot and cooked with full-flavored pork stock (or cooking liquid from brined pork).

The cooking liquid is brought to 85 °C (185 F) and all fat and impurities that rise to the surface are carefully skimmed.

The veal is then returned to a moderate oven and cooked until the probe thermometer registers 76-78 °C (170 F) in the center.

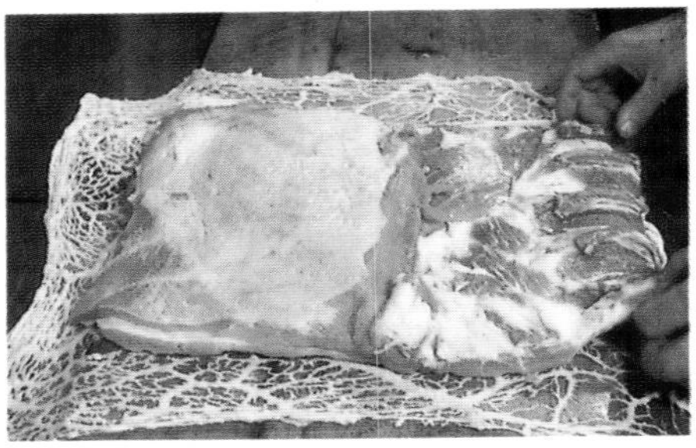

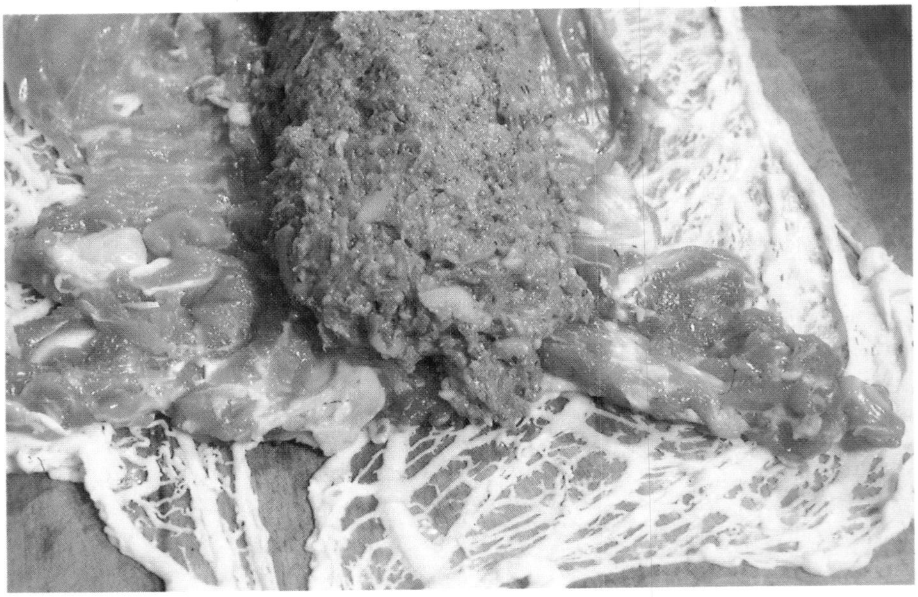

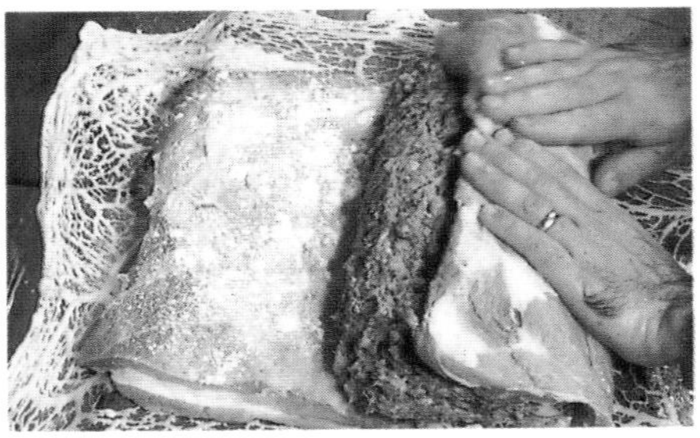

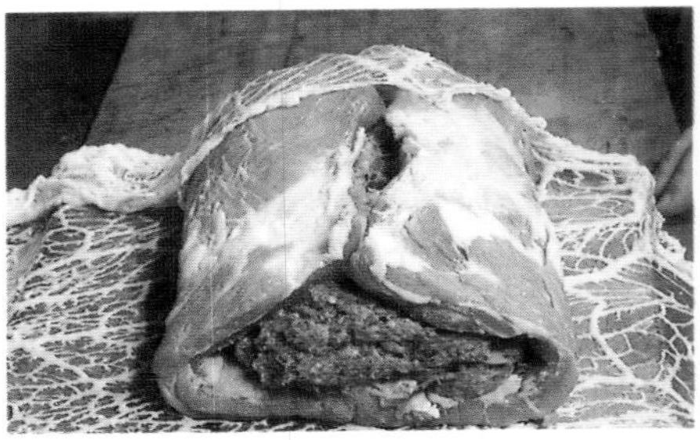

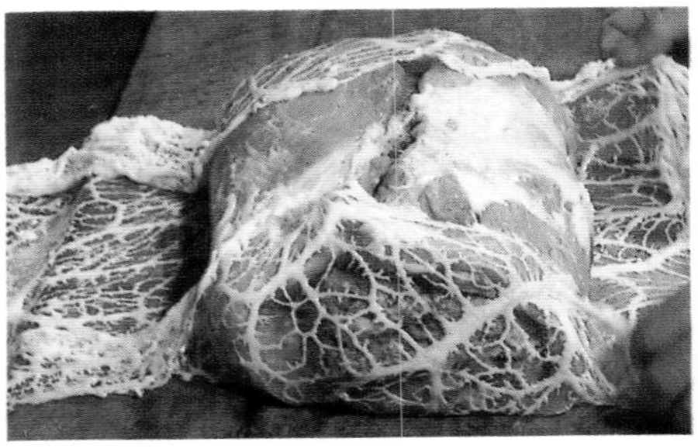

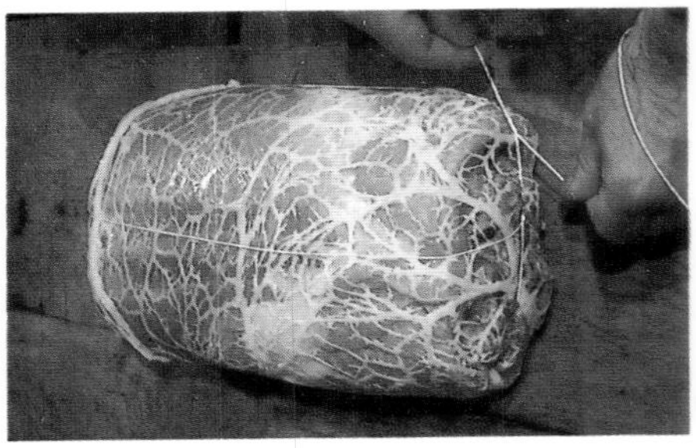

Transfer the veal to a deep recipient, bring the cooking liquid to a boil and skim. Strain over the meat and cool in the liquid as quickly as possible.

**Storage**

Stored in the refrigerator covered with the cooking liquid, the stuffed veal will keep for 6-8 days.

**Presentation**

Lift the veal out of the cooking liquid and remove the string.

Wipe off the stock that adheres to the meat and pat dry.

Decorate the top with an assortment of colorful fruits and /or vegetables cut in attractive shapes.

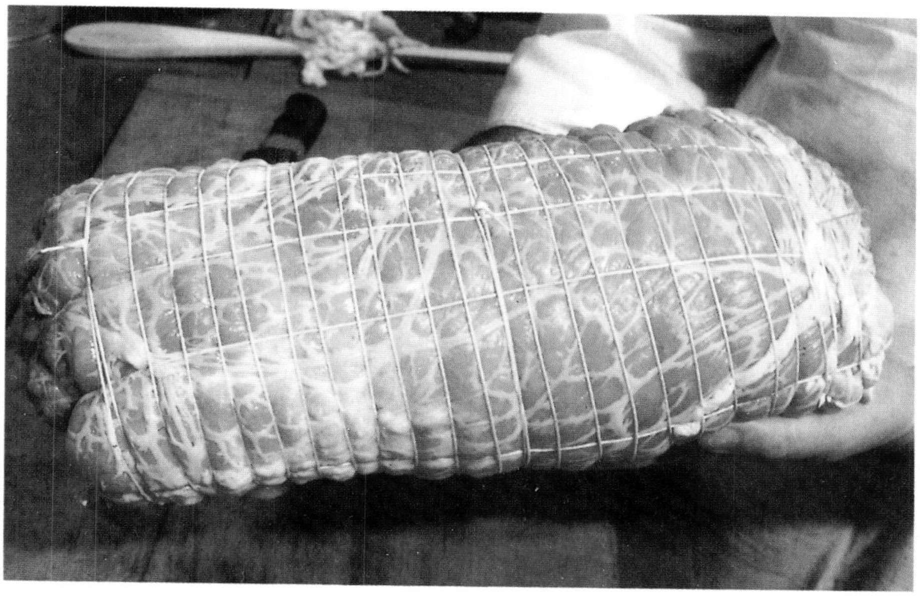

Glaze with aspic either by dipping the veal roulade several times in a large pot of aspic or by brushing with slightly thickened aspic.

The veal is served sliced accompanied by mustard, olives and tart pickles (cornichons).

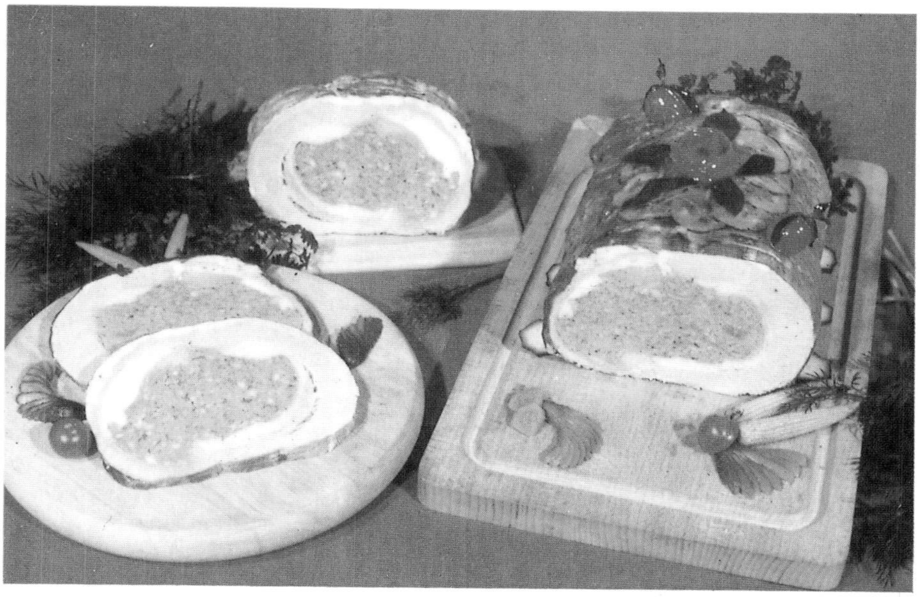

# Terrine made with Sweetbreads and Morels

**Introduction**

All of the dishes made with sweetbreads in this series are very flavorful preparations.

Braising enhances the wonderful flavor and texture of the sweetbreads and reducing the braising liquid further intensifies the taste.

The morels add a sophisticated, woodsy accent which makes the dish special.

**Equipment**

Knives, horizontal chopper, terrine mold, platter, large bowl, pot, gratin dish, wooden spoon.

**Ingredients**

1 kg (2.2 lbs) sweetbreads (untrimmed)
1 kg (2.2 lbs) pork jowl
200 g (7 oz) dried morels
" Gratin " made with:
50 g (1/2 lb) chicken livers, carrots, shallots, mushrooms, parsley and slab bacon
Aromatic vegetables
2 eggs
Chicken stock
Madeira
Cognac

*Seasonings (per kilo (2.2 lbs))*
18 g (generous 1/2 oz) curing salt (sodium nitrite with fine salt)
2 g (1/16 oz) sugar or dextrose
2 g (1 1/16 oz) white pepper
0.5 g (1/64 oz) nutmeg

**Preparing the Ingredients**

***The Pork Jowl***

Remove the skin from the pork jowl and cut in cubes (2.5 cm (1 in)). Coat evenly with the corresponding amount of curing salt (by weight) and sprinkle with madeira.

***The " Gratin "***

Make a " gratin " with the chicken livers (refer to page 259 for amounts):

Chop shallots and carrots.

Peel and slice mushrooms.

Trim, wash and chop parsley.

Cut the slab bacon into small strips (" lardons ") and blanch.

Cook the shallots, carrots and bacon in goose fat until lightly browned.

Add the mushrooms and cook for 3-4 minutes.

Add the chicken livers (trimmed) and brown quickly. Do not cook them through; they should remain very pink in the center.

Add chopped parsley and sprinkle with madeira, bring quickly to a boil then cool quickly.

Refrigerate the seasoned jowl and gratin for 12 hours.

***The Sweetbreads***

Trim the sweetbreads and remove the pockets of fat.

Blanch in boiling salted water then refresh immediately in cold water. Drain then dry thoroughly.

Prepare the aromatic vegetables, (2 carrots, 1 onion, celery, parsley stems, bay leaf and fresh thyme).

Place the vegetables in the gratin dish with some goose fat and place the blanched sweetbreads on top.

Season the meat with salt and pepper and place a nugget of goose fat on the top.

Brown the meat in a hot oven. Turn the meat and add chicken stock to cover the vegetables in the bottom of the pan.

Return to the oven and cook a little more to brown on all sides without cooking the sweetbreads through; the sweetbreads should remain very pink in the center.

Transfer the meat and cool quickly. Strain the cooking liquid and reduce to a glaze, skimming all fat and impurities that rise to the surface.

*The Morels*

Soak the morels in water and rinse several times to eliminate all dirt and grit.

Drain the cleaned morels and squeeze dry in a clean handtowel.

Cover with cold chicken stock, bring to a boil and cook for a few minutes.

Drain the mushrooms and refrigerate. (Chop coarsely if too large.)

Reduce the cooking liquid to a glaze and combine with the reduced braising liquid.

**Making the Forcemeat**

Grind the marinated jowl and gratin then place in the chopper.

Add the eggs and process until finely textured.

Add the reduced meat and mushrooms glaze and process until smooth and homogeneous.

The temperature of the mixture should never exceed 15 °C (60 F) during processing.

**Assembly**

Cut the chilled sweetbreads in large dice (1.5 cm (1/2 in)).

Transfer the forcemeat to a large stainless steel bowl and add the diced sweetbreads and morels and stir gently to blend. (This can be blended in the mixer at low speed.) This is a delicate procedure because the sweetbreads and morels should be evenly distributed but not crushed.

Line the mold with barding fat.

Fill the molds with the mixture, pressing a little so that there are no air pockets. Fold the barding fat over the top.

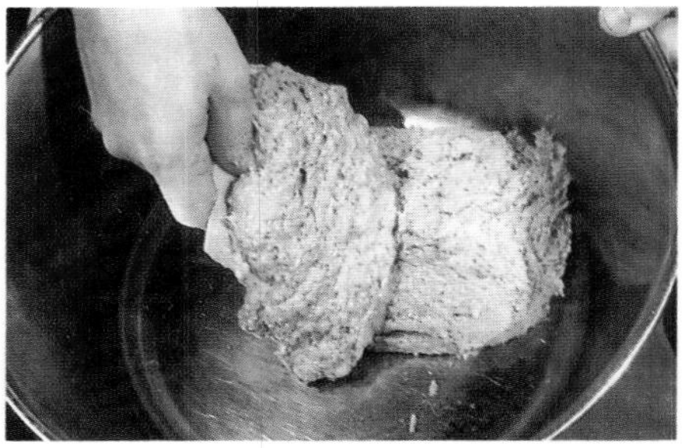

**Cooking**

The terrine can be cooked immediately or refrigerated for 3-4 hours to allow the flavor to develop.

Brown the top of the terrine in an oven preheated to 180-200 °C (375-400 F). Lower the temperature to 110-115 °C (225 F) and cook until the internal temperature is 76-78 °C (170 F).

Drain the fatty juices from the cooked terrine and replace with full-flavored veal or chicken stock that has been boiled, skimmed and strained.

Place a weight on top (300 g (10 oz)), cool quickly then refrigerate.

**Storage**

This terrine will keep in the refrigerator for 8-10 days. The storage time can be doubled if the chilled terrine (24 hours in refrigerator) is placed in a vacuum pouch.

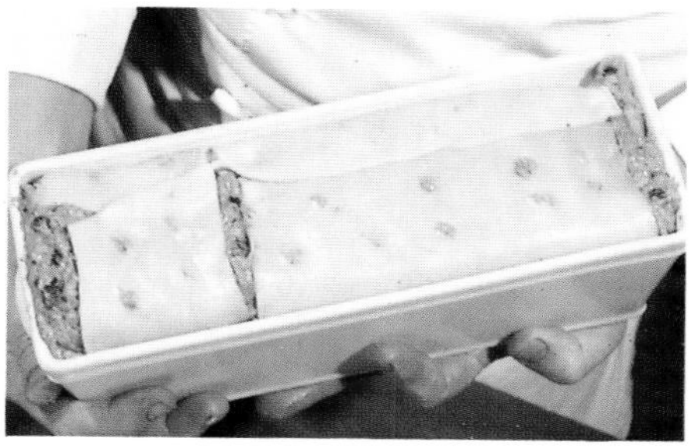

**Presentation**

Like other terrines, this one can be presented two ways:
- Decorated with fruits and/or vegetables then coated with aspic and sliced directly from the mold.
- Unmolded: the cleaned mold is lined with a little aspic, the decoration is arranged in the mold. Another layer of slightly thickened aspic is added then the terrine in replaced in the mold and chilled to set the aspic.

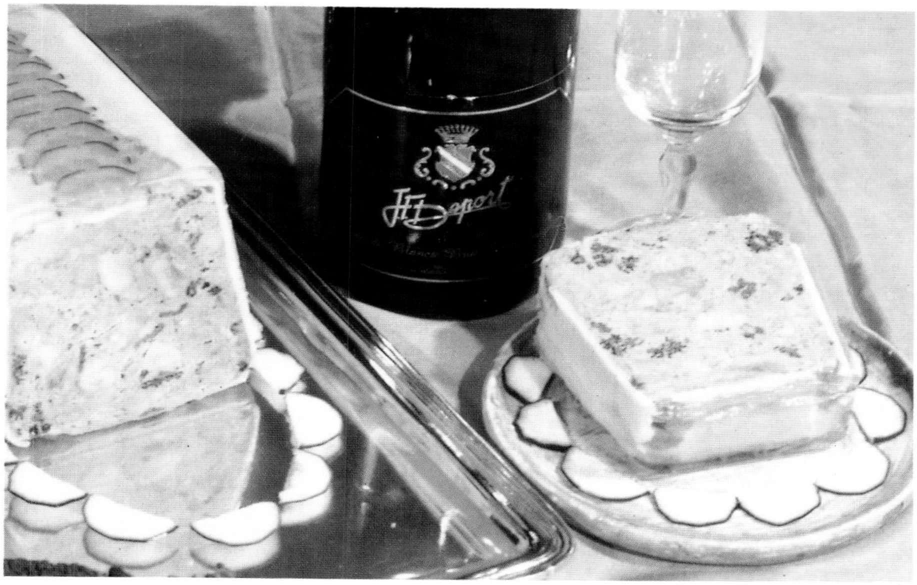

# Veal Loin with Sweetbreads and Brains

**Introduction**

This elegant preparation is the creation of Jean-Pierre Odeau.

The combination of sweetbreads and calves' brains blended with a finely textured pork forcemeat makes a unique and delicious filling for the veal loin.

**Equipment**

Knives, horizontal chopper, stainless steel mixing bowls, larding needle, roasting pan, platter

**Ingredients**

Veal loin
700 g (1 lb 7 oz) lean veal (trimmings)
1 kg (2.2 lb) pork jowl (trimmed)
500 g (1 lb) veal trimmings
200 g (7 oz) calves' liver
50 g (1 3/4 oz) chicken livers
2 kg (4.4 lbs) sweetbreads (untrimmed)
1 calves' brain
200 g (7 oz) peeled pistachios
2 eggs
250 ml (1 cup) heavy cream
Caul fat
Cognac – Port (aged)
Shallots – Parsley
Aromatic vegetables
Chicken or veal stock

*Seasonings (per kilo (2.2 lb))*

18 g (generous 1/2 oz) curing salt (sodium nitrite with fine salt)
2 g (1/16 oz) sugar or dextrose
2 g (1/16 oz) ground pepper
0.5 g (1/64 oz) nutmeg
18 g (generous 1/2 oz) saltpeter w/food color (for the forcemeat)

**Preparing the Ingredients**

***The Veal Loin***

Completely bone the veal and trim all the fat. Trim some of the lean from the wider section so that the loin is a uniform cylinder and butterfly as shown.

Season with salt and pepper and roll with the aromatic vegetables (which will be used for the cooking). Sprinkle with cognac and port, cover and marinate in the refrigerator for 12-24 hours.

***The Sweetbreads***

Trim and remove fat from the sweetbreads. Blanch in boiling salted water then refresh in cold water.

Braise briefly on a bed of aromatic vegetables with stock (see previous recipe). The sweetbreads are cooked just a little at this stage; they should remain very pink inside.

Chill the sweetbreads. Strain the cooking liquid, skim the fat and reduce to a glaze.

***The Forcemeat***

The forcemeat is a blend of pork jowl and the trimmings from the veal loin mixed with " gratin ".

Trim the pork jowl, cut in pieces and marinate with the veal trimmings (24 hours).

Make a " gratin " with the chicken livers (see " gratin " pages 259-260).

***The Calves' Brain***

Trim and soak in cold water to degorge excess blood. Poach in

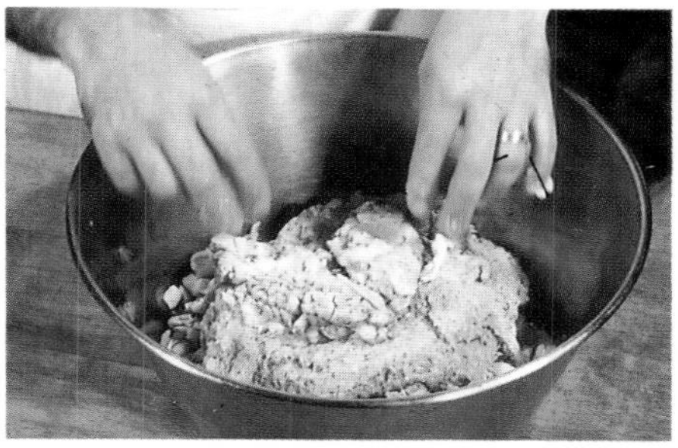

salted water with a bouquet garni and a little vinegar. Cool quickly and completely in the cooking liquid.

***The Meat Strips (" Lèches ")***

Marinade the meat strips in the

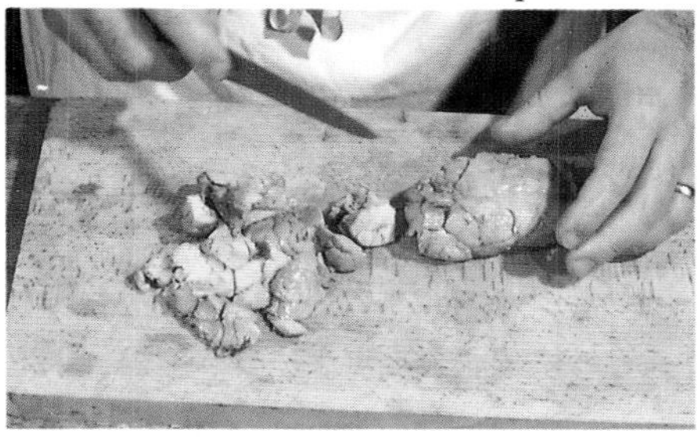

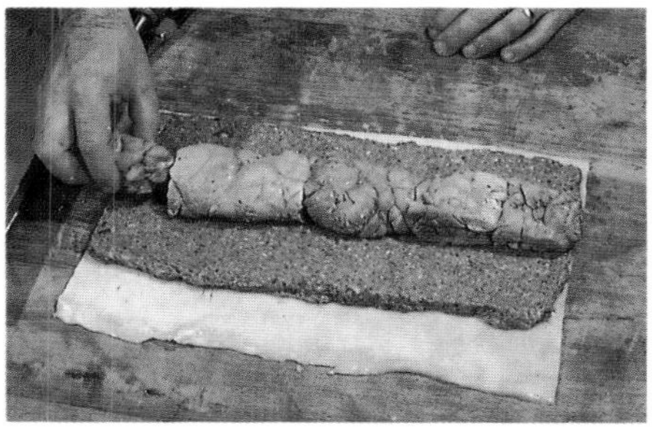

corresponding amount of curing salt with a little cognac.

**Procedure**

***Making the Forcemeat***

Chop the marinated forcemeat

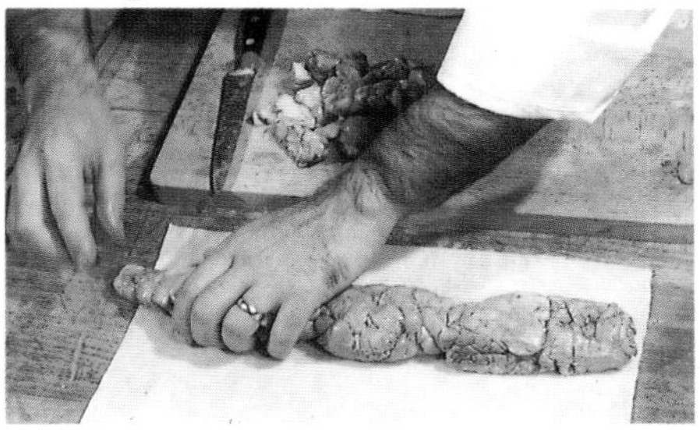

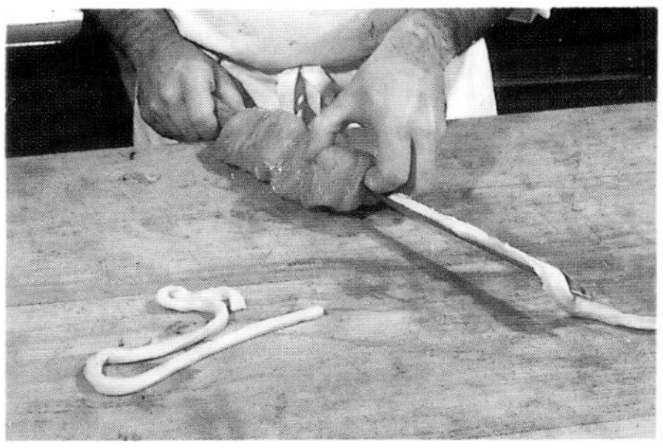

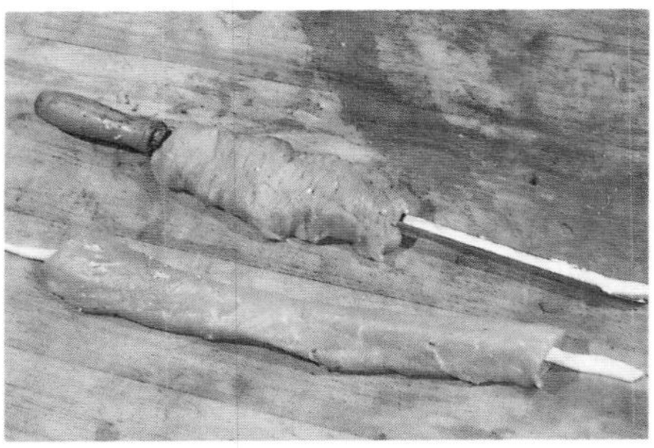

ingredients (jowl and "gratin") in the chopper, add the eggs, the reduced braising juices and cream.

Process until smooth and finely textured. Set aside 300 g (10 oz) of the mixture to blend with the pistachios (this portion will be studded with the lovely green nuts).

***The Sweetbreads***

Cut strips of fat the same length as the veal. Using a larding needle, thread the strips of fat into the sweetbeads. Spread a sheet of barding fat (the same length as the veal) on the work surface. Spread the forcemeat with pistachios on the barding fat. Arrange the sweetbreads evenly down the center and roll to form a uniform cylinder.

Place in the freezer for about 15 minutes to stiffen slightly and make the cylinder easier to handle.

Mix the remaining forcemeat with the marinated strips of lean meat.

Cut the chilled brain into large cubes. Very carefully fold the cubes of cooked brain into the forcemeat (cooked brain is very fragile).

**Assembly and Cooking**

Spread a sheet of clean caul fat on the work surface and place the veal on top. Spread the veal with the forcemeat in an even layer. Place the "roulade" made with sweetbreads in the center and roll the veal around it. Wrap in the caul fat to cover completely. Tie the veal like a roast. Do not tie it too tightly; the meat

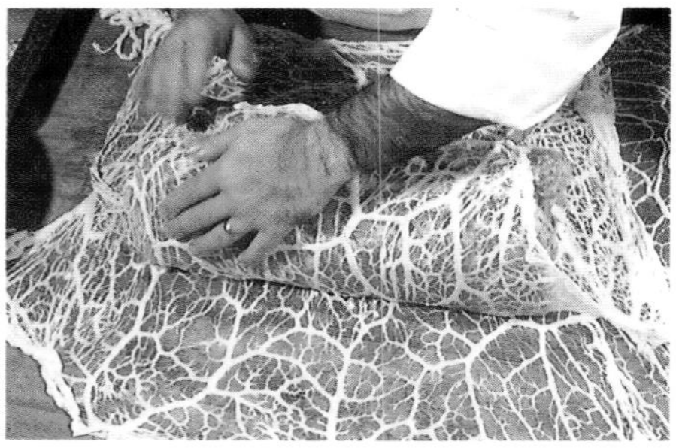

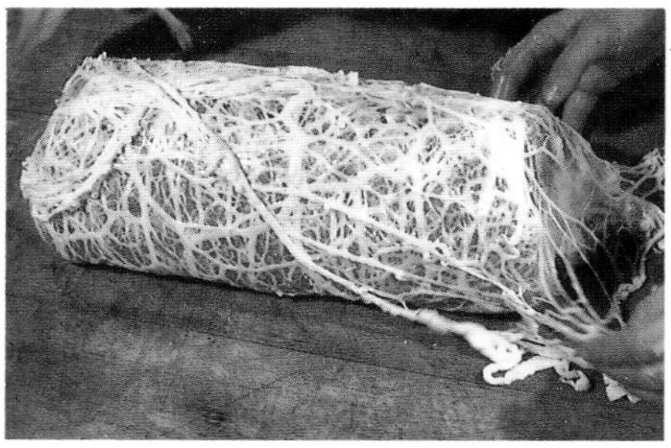

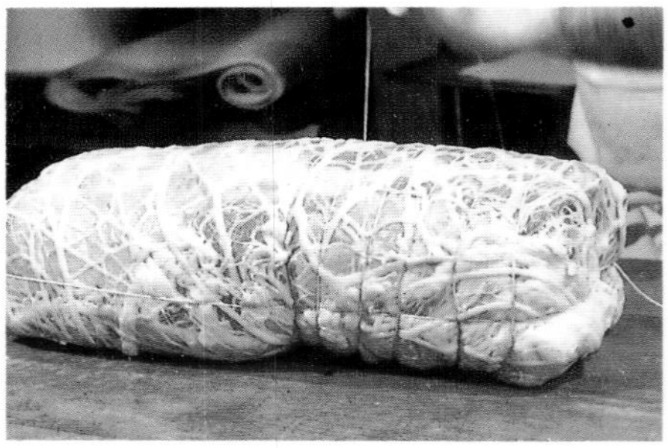

expands slightly when cooked and juices would be squeezed out of the meat.

Place the vegetables used in the marinade on the bottom of roasting pan and place the veal on top.

Brown on all sides in a hot oven (180-200 °C (375-400 F)).

Pour chicken or veal stock into the pan to cover the vegetables.

Continue to cook, basting often to keep the meat moist.

Cook until the internal temperature is 76-78 °C (170 F).

Cool the cooked meat quickly.

**Presentation**

This stunning preparation is decorated with pieces of fruits and/or vegetables cut in attractive shapes then coated with clear aspic (for best flavor use the cooking liquid to make the aspic.)

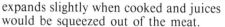

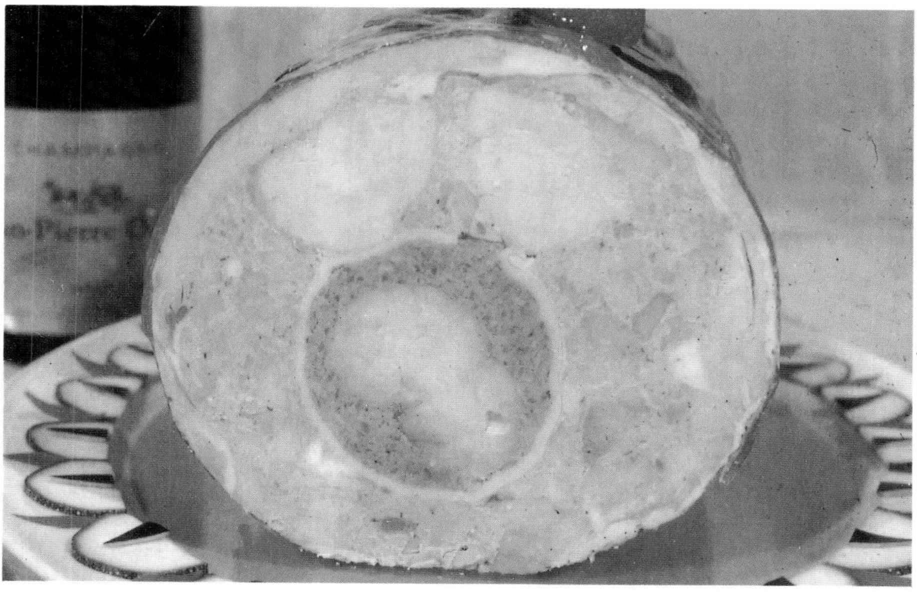

# Pork Tenderloin Terrine with Broccoli Mousse

**Introduction**

This is an original combination of flavors and colors which results in a perfect marriage of taste and a slice of this terrine is very attractive.

The procedure is quite simple however care must be taken when making the forcemeat.

Mediterranean in character, this is a wonderful dish to serve during the warm months of the year.

**Equipment**

Chopper (fixed or removeable bowl), large bowl, terrine mold, plastic scraper, stainless steel saucepan, thermometer with electronic probe, strainer, larding needle, conical strainer

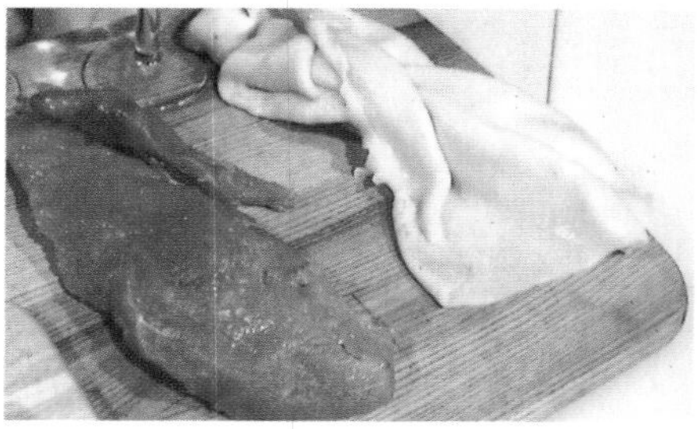

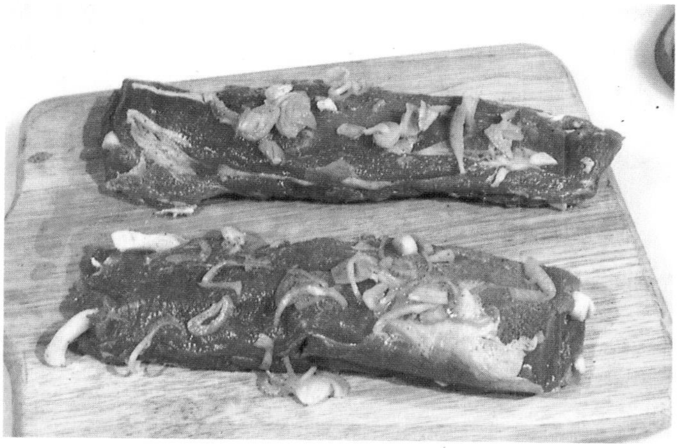

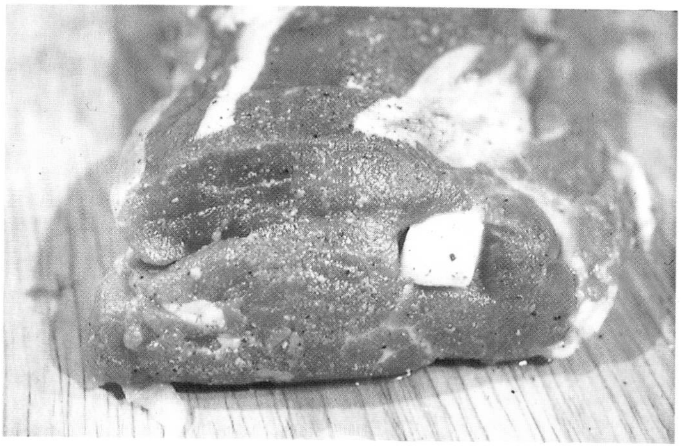

**Ingredients**

*For one 2 kg (4.4 lbs) terrine*

850 g (1 lb 11 oz) trimmed pork tenderloin (1 kg (2.2 lbs) untrimmed
350 g (11 oz) cooked broccoli
250 g (1/2 lb) turkey breast and pork tenderloin trimmings (pointed end)
4 eggs
30 cl (1 1/4 cup) heavy cream
1 slice (1 cm (3/8 in)) of top-quality ham
4 strips of bacon
Barding fat

***Seasonings***

18 g (1/2 oz) curing salt (sodium nitrite blended with salt)
2 g (1/16 oz) freshly ground pepper
5 g (1/64) ground nutmeg
2.5 cl (1/8 cup) dry white wine
Pinch four spice powder
1 shallot
Armagnac

**Preparing the Ingredients**

***The Pork Tenderloin***

Cut the pointed ends off the tenderloins, set aside. With a larding needle, thread the strips of fat through the tenderloins.

Place the tenderloins and trimmings in a stainless steel hotel pan and season with curing salt, pepper, nutmeg, dry white wine, spices, chopped shallot, and a little Armagnac.

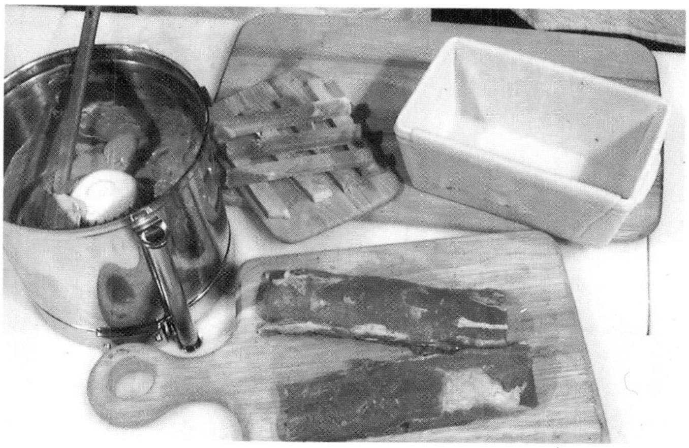

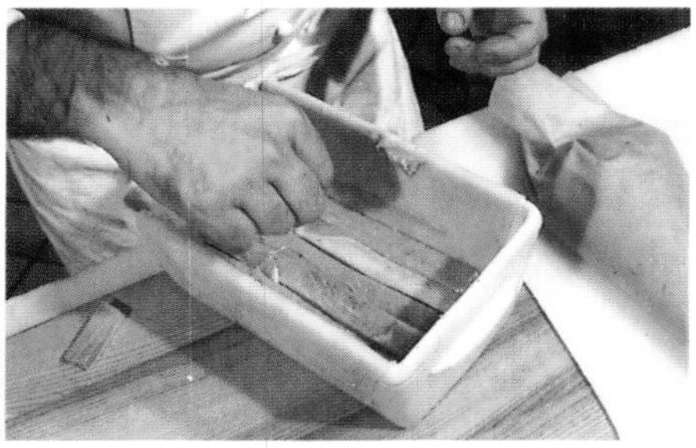

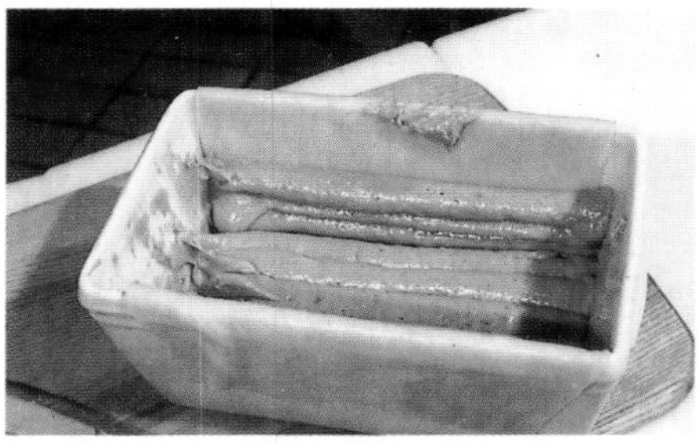

Turn to coat evenly, cover with plastic wrap then leave to marinate in the refrigerator for 36 hours.

***The Broccoli***

Bring a large pot of salted water to a boil and add a little baking soda.

Add the broccoli to the boiling water and cook until tender (about 15 minutes). Drain then plunge into ice water to stop the cooking.

*Note*

The baking soda serves to preserve the bright color of the vegetable. The same technique is used with carrots, spinach, green beans, peas...

Plunging the cooked vegetable into ice water stops the cooking and sets the color.

Drain the cooled broccoli then place in a clean handtowel and squeeze to eliminate all excess liquid. (*Note:* Weight of broccoli in recipe is for squeezed broccoli). Set aside.

***The Ham***

Cut the slice (1 cm (3/8 in)) of cooked ham into strips about 2 cm (3/4 in) across.

Set aside in the refrigerator.

**Making the Forcemeat**

Place the broccoli, the turkey breast cut in cubes and the marinated trimmings of pork tenderloin in the bowl of the food processor.

Process until the mixture is smooth.

Incorporate the eggs two at a time then the cream.

The forcemeat at this stage should be very smooth and not shiny which would indicate that the fat was warmed by the processing (and later would melt too quickly during cooking resulting in a dry texture). To avoid this situation, chill the bowl of the processor and the ingredients in the freezer for 15 minutes before processing.

Forcemeats (meat, fish or vegetable) differ from the emulsified liver-based mixtures in chapter 4 in that they must be mixed at a cold temperature for the binding process to be effective. The ingredients and equipment should be 1-2 °C (35 F) to ensure proper mixing. If the fat is warmed, the finished product is often difficult to slice.

**Molding the Terrine**

Line the mold with thin sheets of barding fat (enough to cover the top).

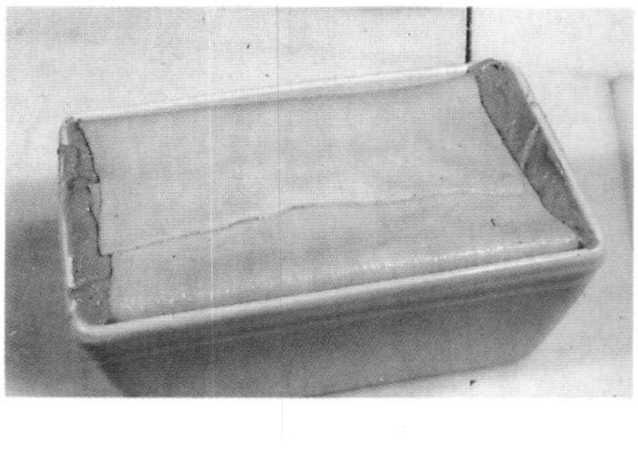

Make an even layer of the green forcemeat in the bottom of the mold.

Arrange three strips of ham on this layer then cover with more forcemeat.

Place the two tenderloins on this layer with a little space between them.

Cover with forcemeat, smoothing the layer to fill the space between the tenderloins.

Arrange the three remaining strips of ham and cover with the remaining forcemeat.

Smooth the top with the back of a spoon.

Fold the barding fat over the top and cover with aluminum foil and set a baking sheet on top to lightly weigh down the contents.

Tie a string around the terrine to further compress it and refrigerate for 3-4 hours before cooking.

**Cooking**

Cook in a water bath in a moderate oven.

Start the cooking at 150 °C (275 F), turn the oven down to 100 °C (210 F) and cook until the thermometer registers an internal temperature of 74 °C (170 F).

Pour off the rendered fat and juices and replace with full-flavored stock.

Place a light weight on top, cool rapidly.

**Storage**

It is recommended to make this easily assembled terrine weekly so that it is always fresh tasting and colorful.

**Presentation**

Coat the top of the terrine with aspic and arrange on a platter with chopped aspic.

Cut this terrine in slices about 1/2-1 cm (1/4-3/8 in) thick.

***Transporting***

All of the terrines in this volume are fragile once sliced. Also they rapidly lose thier aroma and flavor if not properly wrapped. It is recommended to instruct the sales staff on how to tightly wrap the slices.

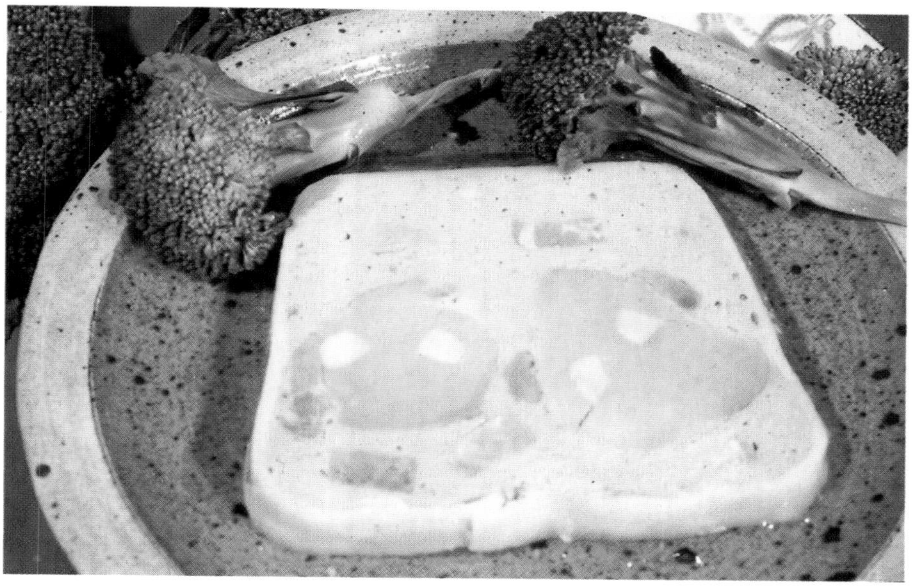

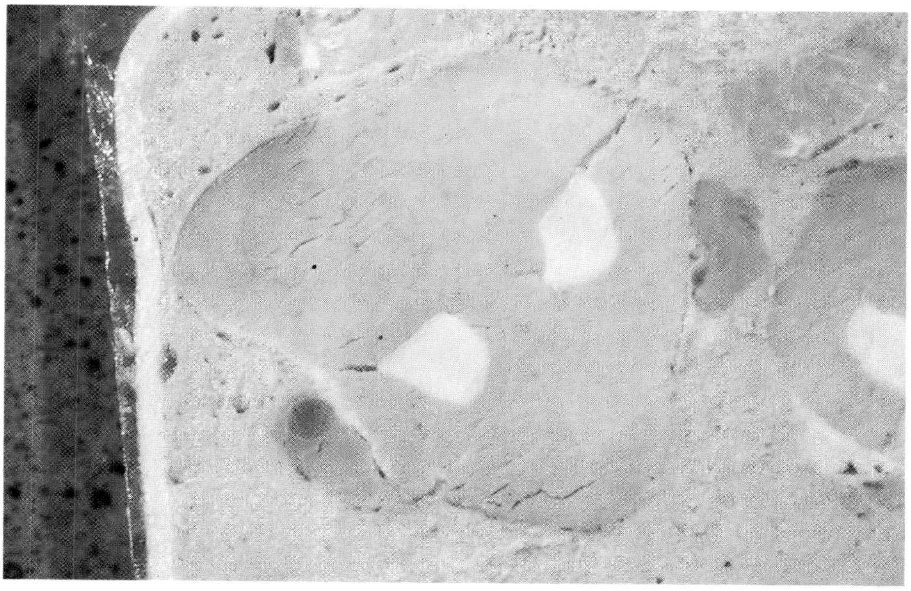

# Young Pig with Rosette Garnish "Le Porcelet en Rosace"

**Introduction**

Since early times, particularly in ancient Rome, young pigs (and suckling pigs) have been stuffed, roasted and presented whole as the highlight of the feast.

The taste as well as the endless possibilities for presentation have made the whole young pig a popular subject for culinary competitions and fancy banquets for many years.

**Ingredients**

Young pig about 7 kg (15 lbs)

4 kg (8.8 lbs) lean pork (from carcass) (cut in strips (" lèches "))
2 kg (4.4 lbs) forcemeat (1/2 lean, 1/2 fat)
500 g (1 lb) " gratin "
5 eggs
Cognac
Madeira
Reduced stock

*Seasonings*

(per kilo (2.2 lbs))

18 g (generous 1/2 oz) curing salt (fine salt with sodium nitrite)
2 g (1/16 oz) sugar or dextrose
2 g (1/16 oz) ground white pepper
Tomato paste
100 g (3 1/2 oz) peeled pistachios
Barding fat

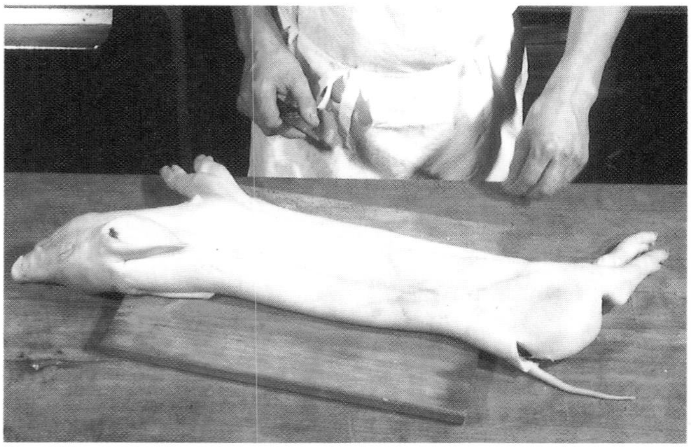

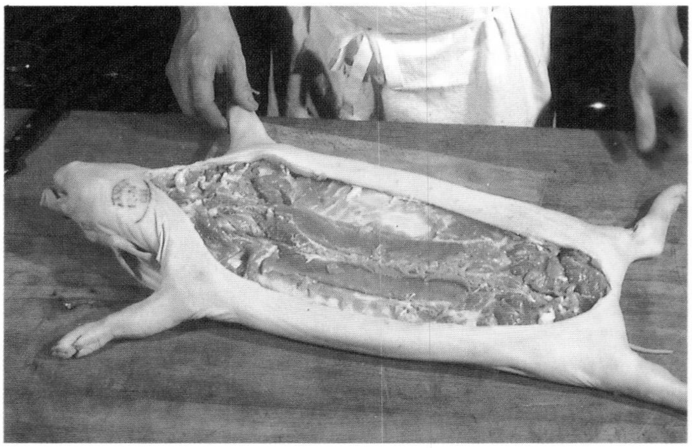

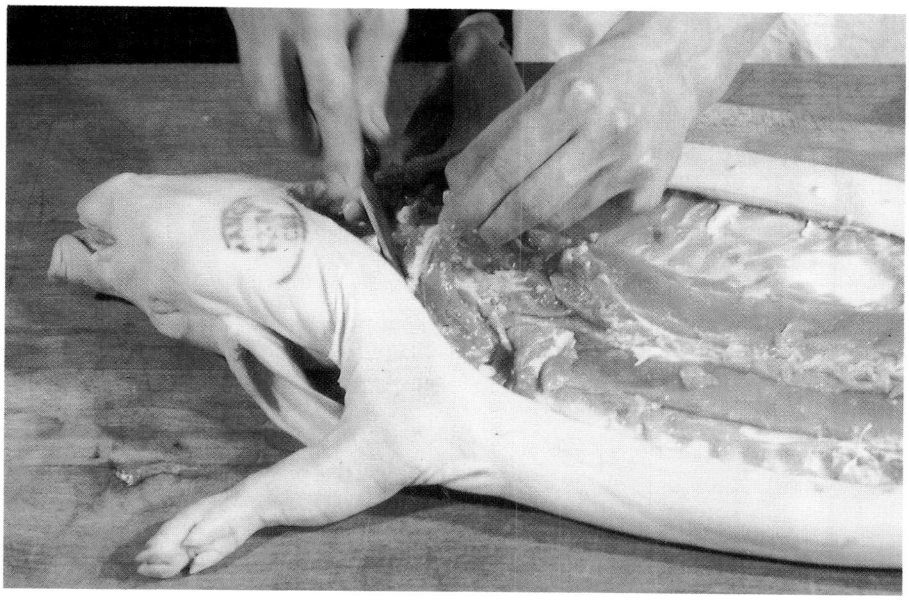

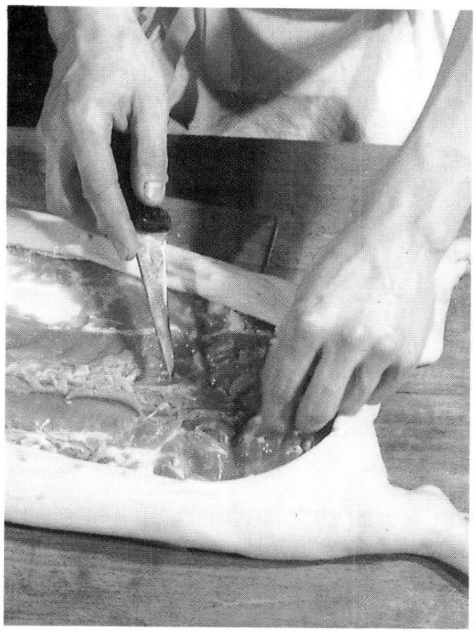

## Equipment

Paring knife, handtowel, linen galantine band, horizontal chopper, sauté pan, jacketed kettle or steam oven.

## Preparing the Ingredients

### *The Young Pig*

Clean the skin of the pig thoroughly, scraping with a knife or razor. Take care to clean all around the snout and the ears.

Remove all the bones leaving the feet and head intact. This must be done very carefully so that the skin is not pierced or damaged. The pig will weigh about approximately 4 kg (about 9 lbs) after this operation.

Cut away portions of lean meat from the legs (hams), shoulder, and back so that the meat remaining attached to the skin is all about the same thickness (the thickness of the belly meat). Trim the belly fat.

Cut the lean meat into strips (" lèches "). The belly fat will be used in the forcemeat.

Inject the head with brine then immerse the whole carcass into brine for 12 hours.

Soak the cured pig in cold running water to remove excess brine, rinse, drain and dry the interior.

Coat the inside with a little pepper and nutmeg and refrigerate for 12 hours to mellow.

Make a full-flavored stock with the bones. Add aromatic vegetables and use light stock to cover the bones. Skim several times during cooking, strain then reduce to a glaze.

### *The Stuffing*

The weight of stuffing is about equal to the weight of the pig before it was boned. Therefore approximately 7 kg (15 lbs) of forcemeat and garnishes are prepared to stuff a pig that weighed 7 kg (15 lbs) untrimmed.

Weigh the strips of lean pork obtained from the carcass and add top quality lean to bring the weight up to 4 kg (about 9 lbs).

The trimmings from the belly and other portions of the pig should weigh 2 kg (4.4 lbs). This mixture of fat and lean will be later ground to make the forcemeat.

Use the pork liver (or chicken livers) to make the " gratin " following the classic method.

Season the strips of lean with the corresponding amount of curing salt and sugar and sprinkle with cognac.

Season the forcemeat and sprinkle with madeira (the gratin is also flavored with madeira).

Marinate these meats in the refrigerator for 12 hours in covered stainless steel recipients.

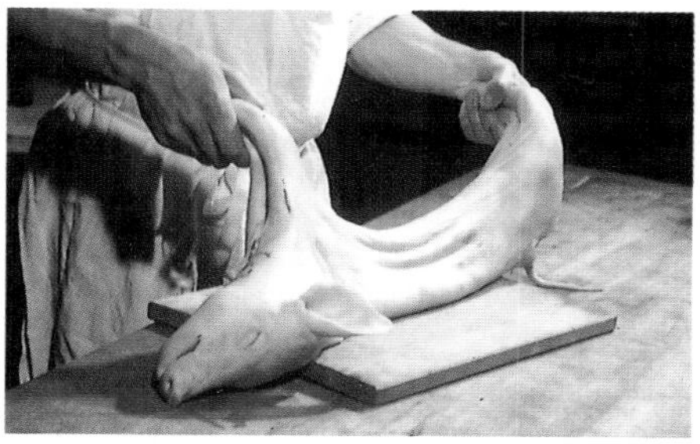

## Procedure

### *Making the Forcemeat*

Process the marinated forcemeat ingredients in the chopper, add the eggs and meat glaze and process until smooth.

The temperature of the mixture should not exceed 14-15 °C (58-60 F) during processing. (Chill the bowl of the chopper if necessary.)

Set aside 1.5 kg (3.3 lbs) of forcemeat (divided in three equal portions) for the rosette (" rosace ").

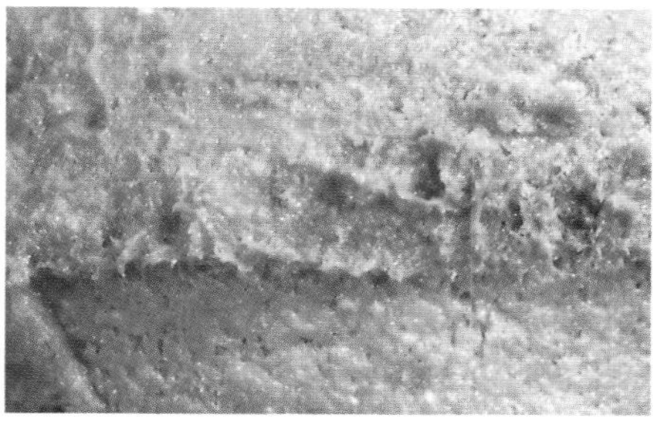

The first portion is left as is (and therefore will be pink after cooking).

The second portion is colored and flavored with pistachios. The peeled pistachios are blended into the forcemeat in a small food processor until the forcemeat in green. Chill the food processor if necessary to maintain cold temperatures during processing. This forcemeat will be green after cooking.

The third portion is blended with tomato paste to obtain a red forcemeat. The same precautions are respected during blending.

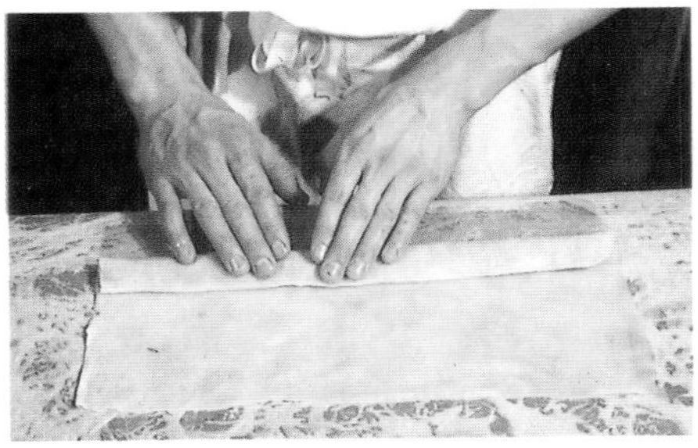

Wrap and freeze until ready to assemble the stuffed pig.

**Assembly**

Mix together the marinated strips of lean pork and the remaining forcemeat.

Place the boned pig on the work surface. Spread the forcemeat evenly over the interior of the pig. This even layer of forcemeat will hold the rosace in place. Place the rosace in the center and close the body of the pig carefully around it. Secure the opening with a trussing needle (about every 7-8 cm (3 in) then truss between to close the opening completely.

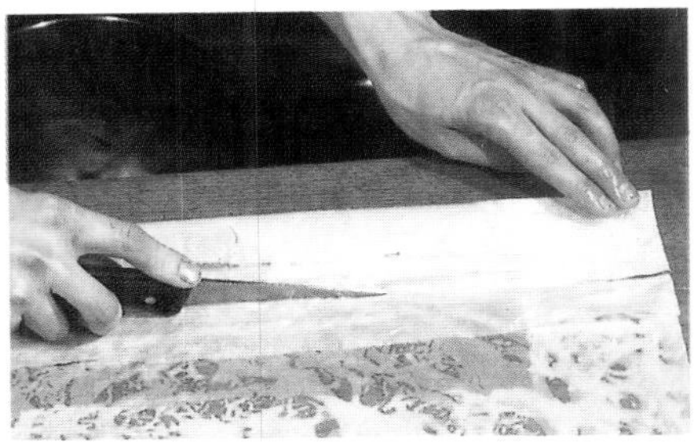

Wrap a sheet of moistened parchment paper around the pig then wrap in a handtowel or cheese-cloth. Make sure that the feet are evenly placed under the pig as you wrap.

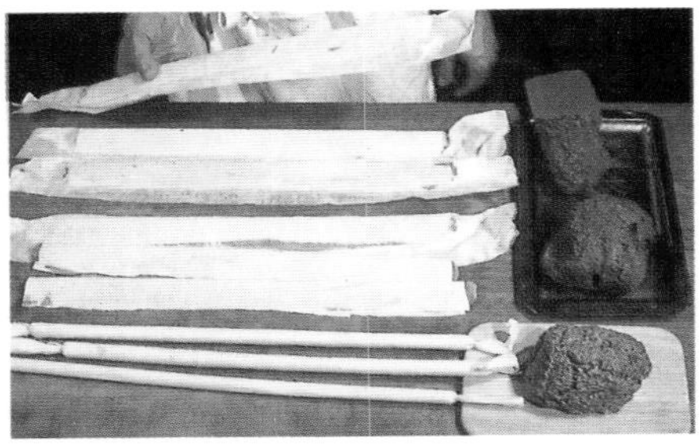

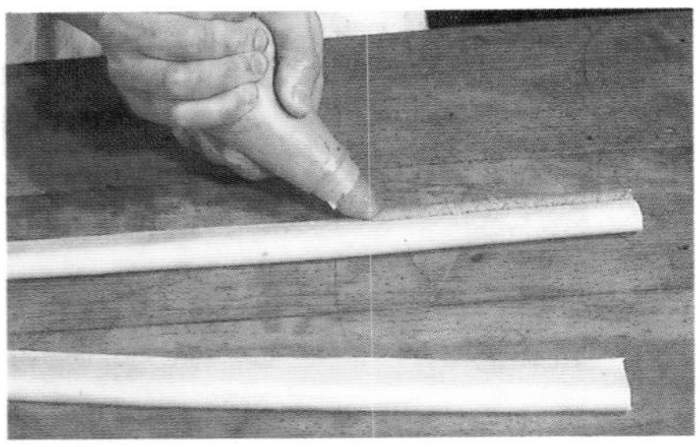

***The " Rosace "***

Select extra thin sheets of barding fat to make the rosace.

Fill three pastry bags with large tips with the three forcemeats. Cut the barding fat in long strips the same length as the body of the pig.

Pipe three strips of green and three strips of red forcemeat on the barding fat. Fold the fat over to form teardrop-shaped " petals ".

Pipe some of the neutral forcemeat on a strip of barding fat and roll into a cylinder. Place these preparations in the freezer for 15-20 minutes to stiffen.

Form the rosace with the colored petals surrounding the cylinder using the remaining neutral forcemeat to " glue " the petals together.

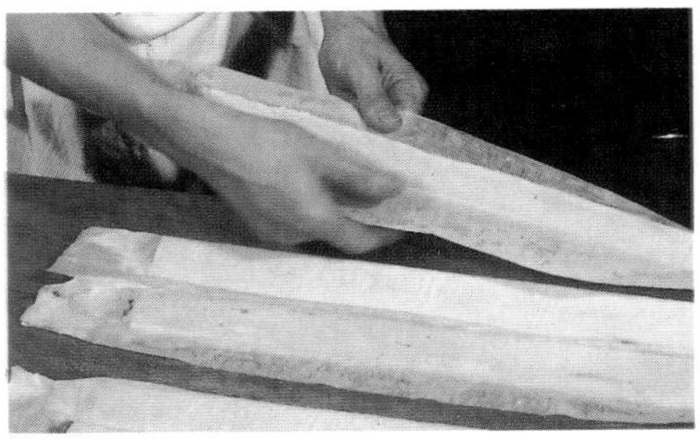

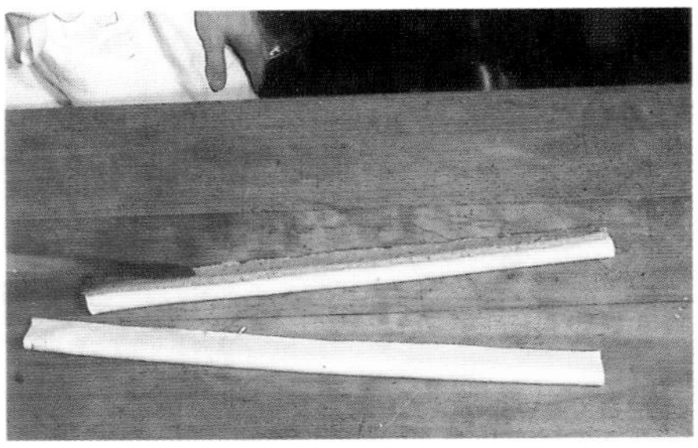

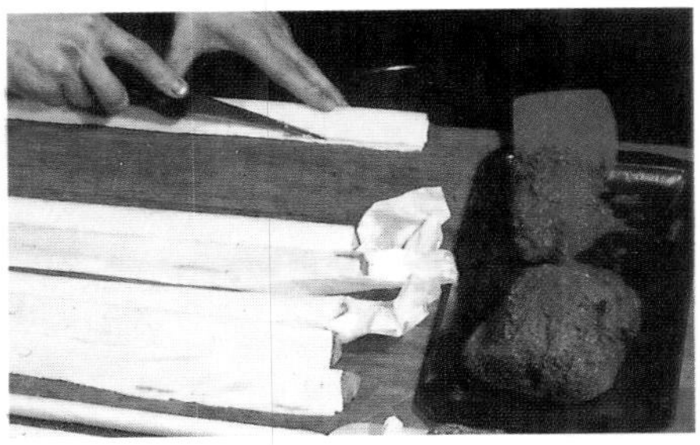

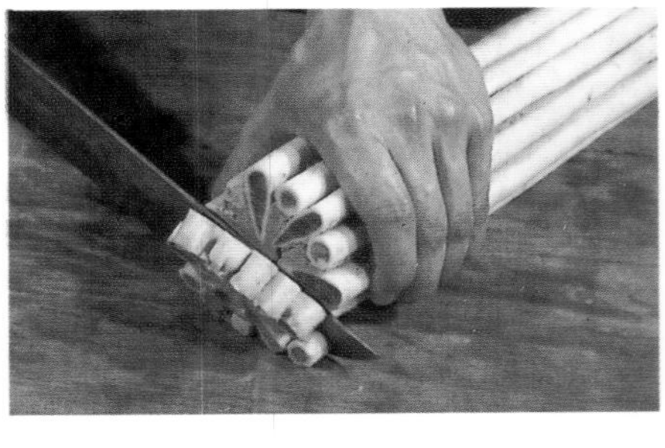

Leave the ears exposed then secure the ends with kitchen twine.

Next wrap the pig in a long strip of cloth (linen strips for wrapping pig's feet are available for this – sometimes called galantine bands or bandages). The band of cloth should be fairly tight and evenly " snug " around the pig.

To keep the ears standing straight up, cover with aluminium foil and prop them up with sturdy tooth-picks.

Before cooking allow the pig to " mellow " and " mature " at room temperature for 2-3 hours or over-night in the refrigerator.

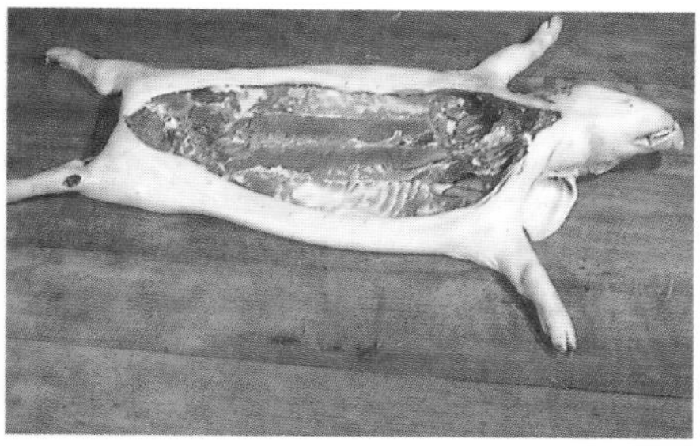

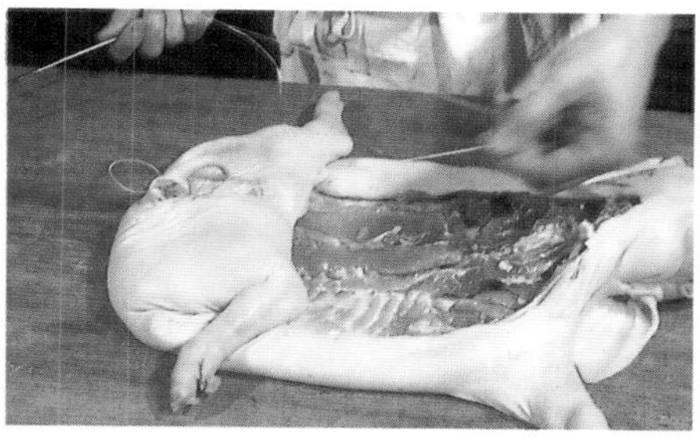

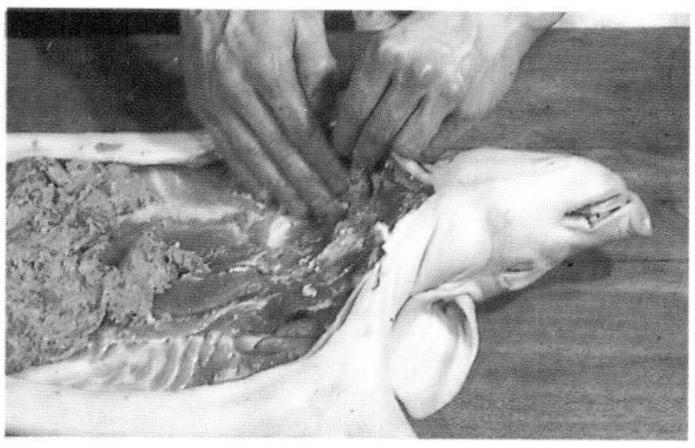

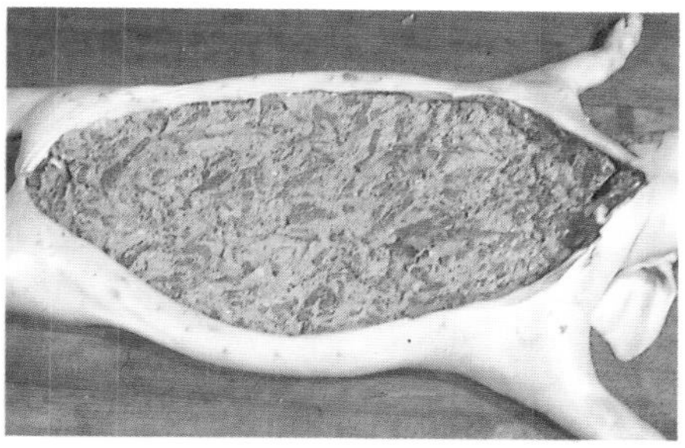

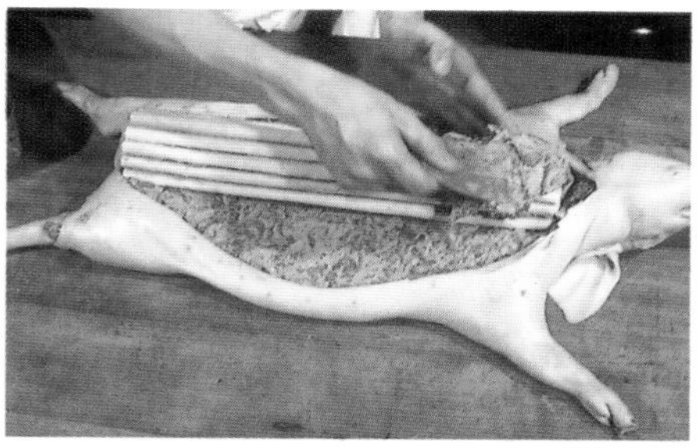

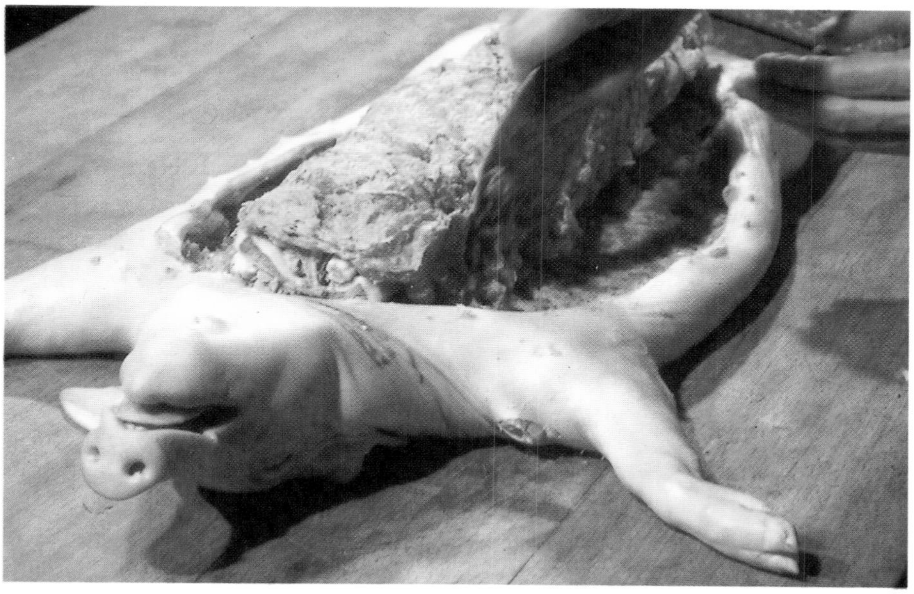

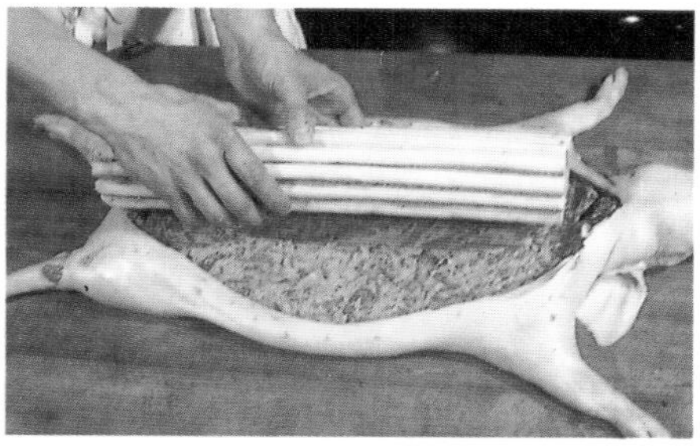

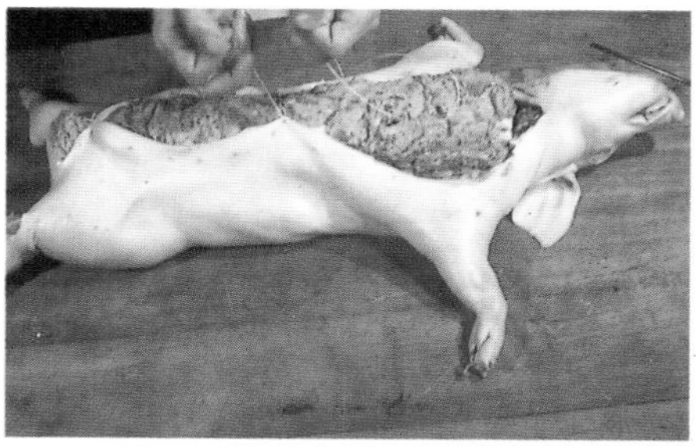

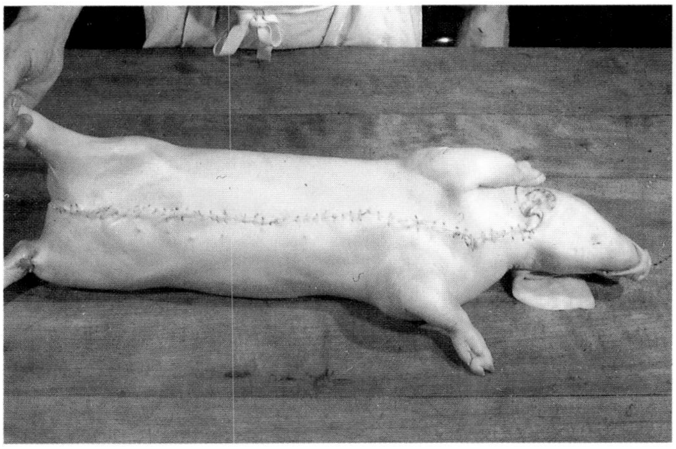

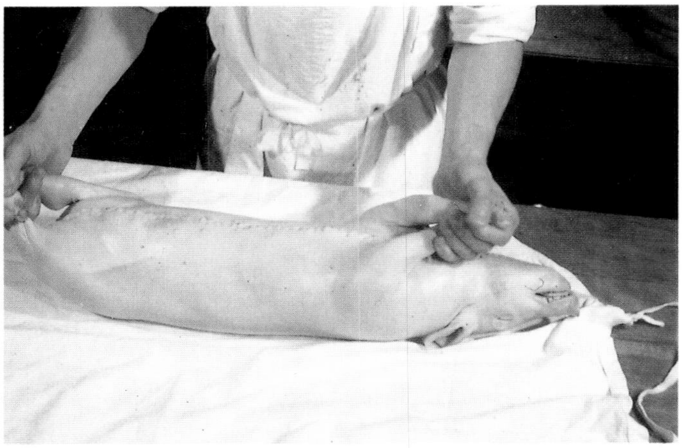

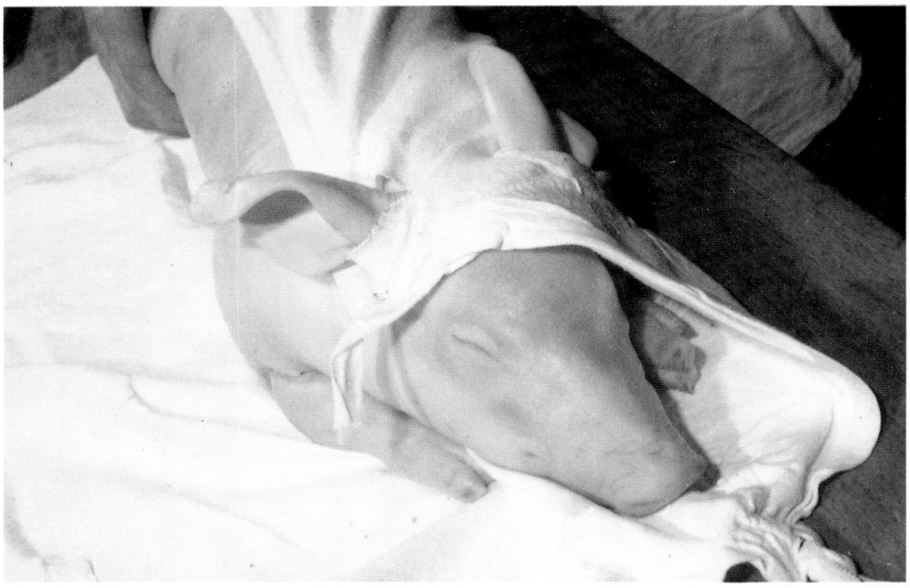

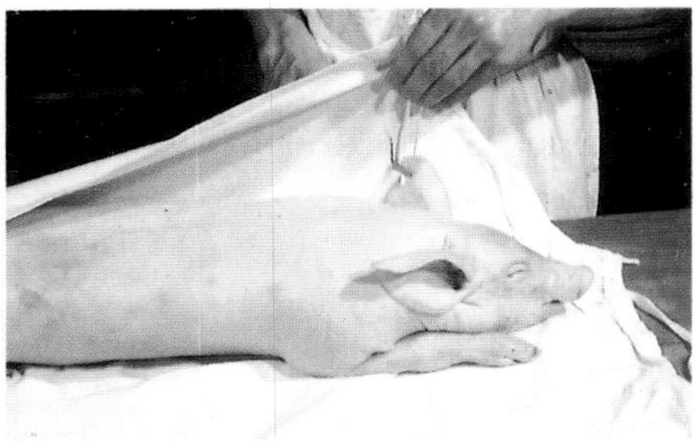

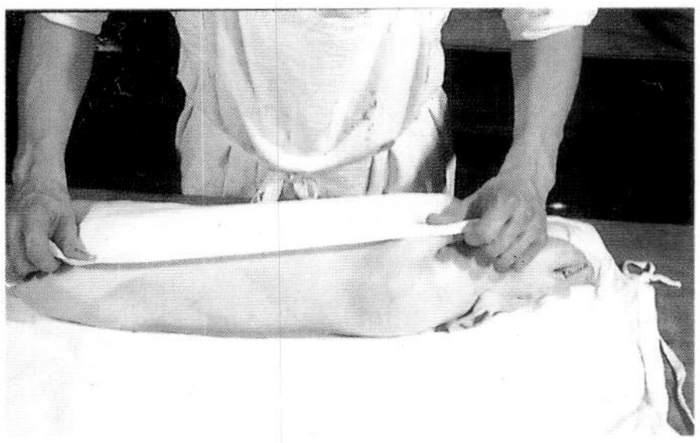

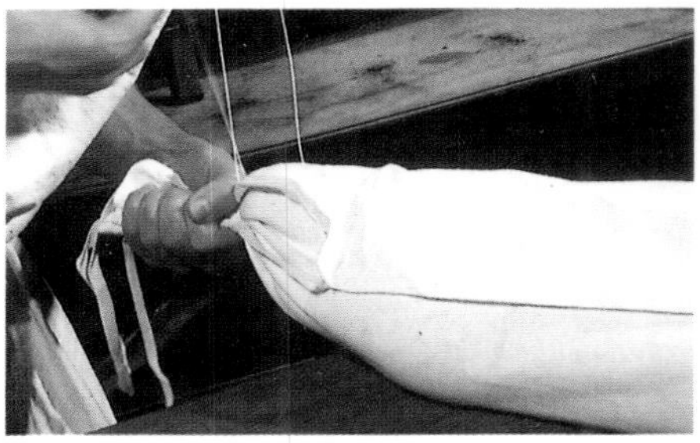

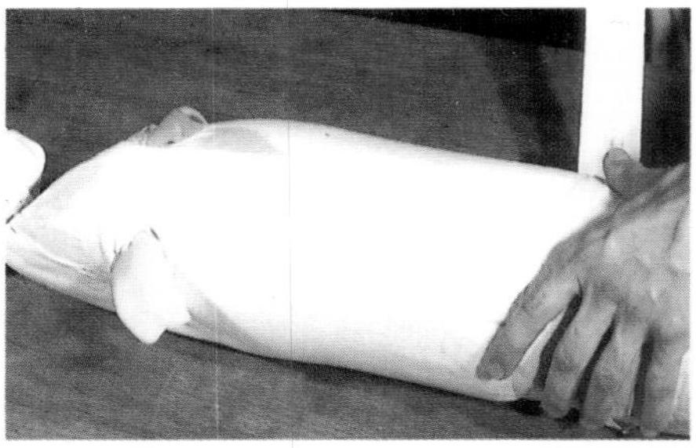

**Cooking**

It is best to cook the stuffed pig in pork stock if a large enough kettle or fish poacher is available. Otherwise the pig can be cooked in a steamer with some stock in the pan.

We recommend the first method if the equipment is available.

Bring the stock to a boil and skim all impurities that rise to the surface. Regulate the temperature to 78-80 °C (175 F) and cook the pig until the internal temperature is 70-72 °C (160 F).

Strain the cooking liquid, pour it back over the pig and cool as quickly as possible. If cooked in the steamer, the pig must also be cooled quickly.

This large preparation (12-14 kilos (28 lbs)) needs to chill at least 48 hours in the refrigerator (2-4 °C (35 F)) before serving.

**Presentation**

Remove the wrappings and rinse the pig under warm running water then again under cold running water to remove all traces of cooking liquid. It is then glazed with aspic that has been chilled over ice to thicken it slightly.

The pig can be decorated and arranged on the platter in a variety of ways.

For a simple presentation in the shop of the charcuterie, surround the glazed pig with colorful fruits and vegetables. Slices of the pig are sold from the hind portion keeping the front third intact.

For an elegant buffet, the stuffed pig can be decorated (inside and out) with truffles. The truffles not only provide a lovely contrast of color but add a delicious flavor as well.

The body provides a " canvas " for recreating any number of interesting designs using cut-out fruit and vegetables. Nature scenes and caricatures are among the popular choices.

The range of decorations is limited only by the level of imagination and creativity.

If the budget allows, the rosace can be made with a row of truffles. Remember that products in France that indicate " truffles " on the label must contain 3% truffles. Between 1-3% the exact percentage must be on the label and under 1% the word truffle cannot appear on the label.

Another elegant and costly addition is foie gras. It could be added as a garnish (rosace or roulade) in the center and/or as an ingredient in the forcemeat. The regulations governing the addition of foie gras is the same as for galantines.

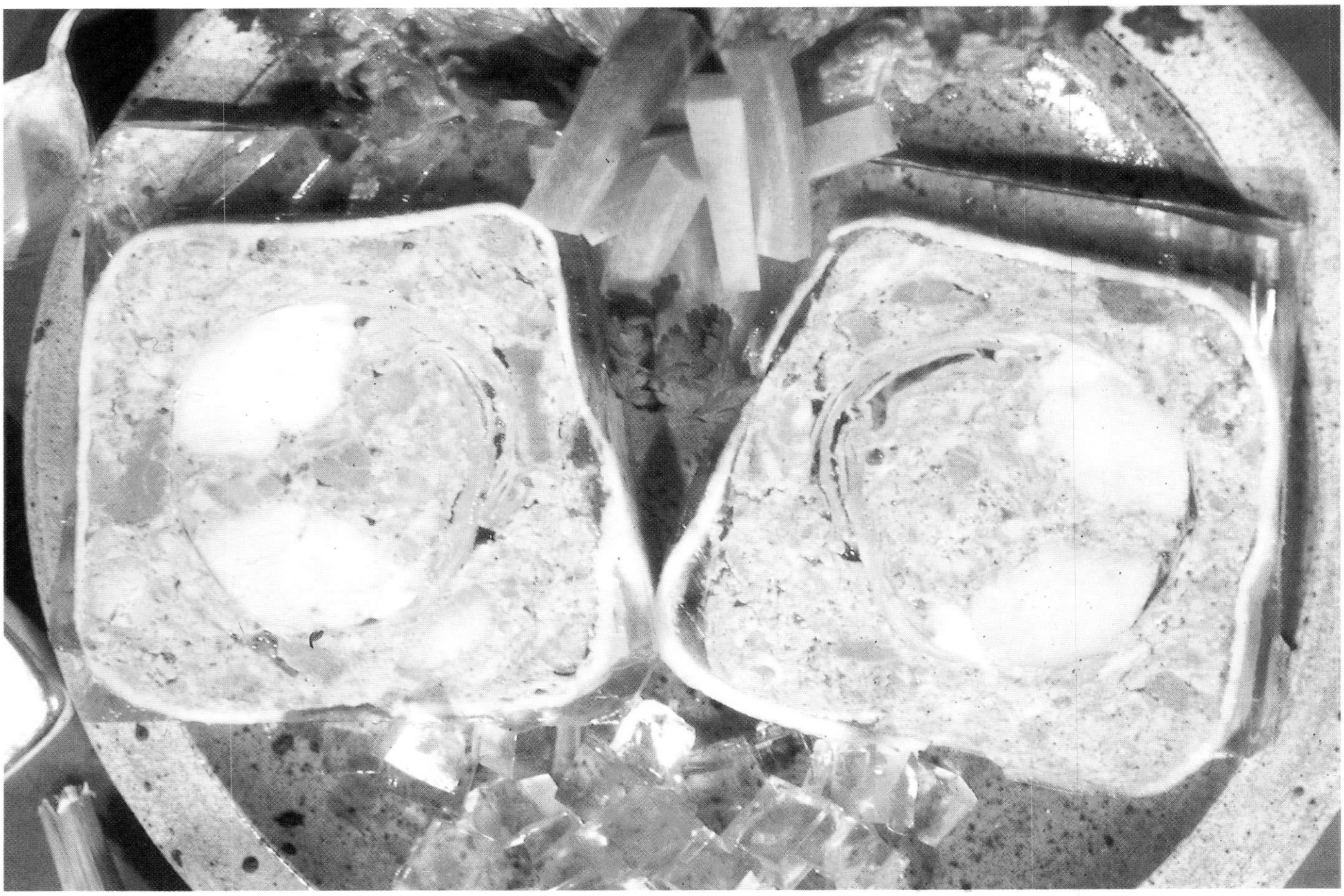

# *Chap. 7*

# *Pâtés and Terrines made with Poultry*

## *When " Charcuterie " Becomes " Fine Cooking "*

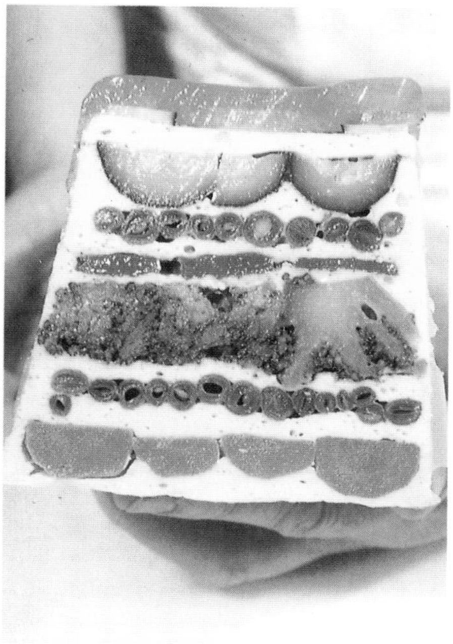

*The pâtés and terrines presented in this chapter are culinary masterpieces.*

*Poultry and game are used in countless preparations in charcuterie.*

*The range of different meats in this category is vast and each one brings its characteristic taste and texture to the product.*

*The delicious flavors of these meats marry well with many ingredients. New and interesting combinations can be made to add dimension to your selection.*

*The quality of the final product depends on the perfect freshness of the ingredients.*

# Introduction

Poultry is used in a large variety of delicious charcuterie preparations.

Many different types of birds are used which have characteristic flavors, giving the final dish a particular taste. The variety ranges from chicken and turkey, ducks and geese to game birds such as quail, pheasant and guinea hen. In France rabbit is grouped with poultry because the meat is used in similar dishes.

To enhance the flavor of the meat, flavorful marriages are made with interesting ingredients (raisins and quail, orange and duck, morels and guinea hen...).

A small portion of the poultry in France is still raised in the traditional way, which cannot be said for charcuterie's mainstay--pork. Birds that are grain fed are marketed with government-approved tags indicating exact origin and age . The use of these high quality birds is recommended when available. Wild game in France is sold wholesale and retail during hunting season. The regulations concerning the sale is strict and the availability and price vary.

In the U.S. and France game birds such as quail and pheasant have been domesticated and mass marketed. The taste is not as pronounced as their wild cousins but they are available year round at an affordable price. As a result, French consumers have lost their taste for the strong flavor of game which has to be hung for extended periods to tenderize the flesh (resulting in a " mature ", slightly rotted taste). To tenderize and mimic to some degree the taste from this hanging process, game is usually marinated with wines and spices.

These ground meat products are essentially the same as the preceding chapters; strips or cubes of meat and/or vegetables held together with a flavorful forcemeat. The techniques for preparation and assembly are therefore similar.

Among the selection are a few " ballotines " which are formed in the skin of the boned bird rather than in a mold. This method is used here primarily for the small birds which are perfect single servings. Even though we have chosen to present most of the dishes in terrine form, the recipes certainly can be adapted to make ballotines. The assembly is of course different and the terrine is cooked in the oven while the ballotine is poached in stock (usually in rapport with the animal; guinea hen stock for a guinea hen ballotine...).

The 18 products presented in this chapter are a just few of the many charcuterie dishes featuring poultry, rabbits and game. The charcutier needs only to respect the harmony of flavors in creating original dishes featuring poultry with different fruits, vegetables and aromatics.

**Terrine of Duck Breast with Prunes (page 234)**

**Ballotine of Bresse Chicken with Crayfish (page 238)**

Terrine of Duck Confit with Parsley (page 242)

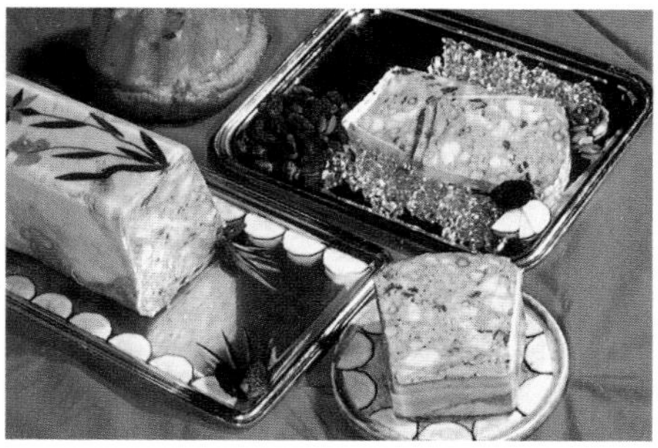

Terrine of Guinea Hen with Sweetbreads and Morels (page 246)

Chicken Terrine " à l'Ancienne " (page 250)

Duck Terrine " à l'Orange " (page 254)

Duck Terrine with Rosemary (page 258)

Chicken Terrine with Lemon (page 262)

Quail Terrine with Sweetbreads (page 266)

Turkey Mousses with Vegetables (page 270)

Saddle of Rabbit with Garlic (page 274)

Rabbit Terrine with Mushrooms (page 278)

Rabbit Terrine with Olives (page 282)

Squab with Foie Gras (page 286)

Stuffed Quail with Raisins (page 292)

Stuffed Rabbit " Bordelaise " (page 296)

Guinea Hen Terrine " Forestière " (page 300)

# Terrine of Duck Breast with Prunes

### Introduction

This special terrine combines three products of southwest France; duck breast, foie gras and prunes from Agen. The marriage of these rich and elegant ingredients creates a dish suitable for holiday menus.

### Equipment

Knives, hotel pan, terrine mold

### Ingredients

6 Duck breasts
800 g (1 lb 10 oz) goose foie gras
500 g (1 lb) prunes
Armagnac
Barding fat
Powdered gelatin

*Seasonings (per kilo (2.2 lbs))*

18 g (generous 1/2 oz) curing salt (sodium nitrite with fine salt)
2 g (1/16 oz) sugar or dextrose
2 g (1/16 oz) white pepper

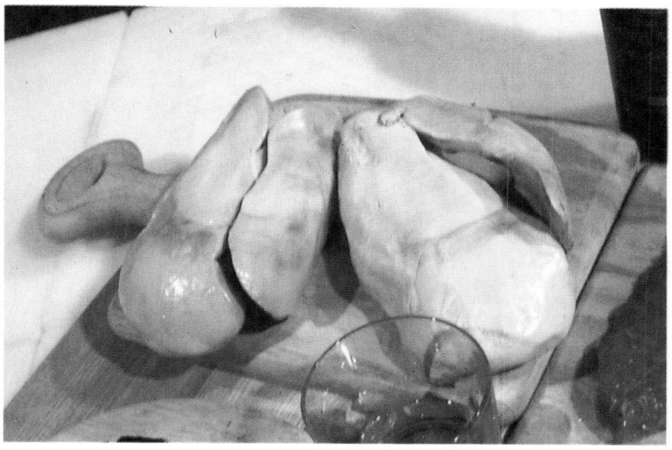

**Preparing the Ingredients**

***The Duck Breast***

The duck breast used here is from force-fed birds. These meatier breasts are called "magrets" in France. Although the word "magret" is often used for breast meat from duck and geese that have not been force fed, this is incorrect.

A decree in 1986 established that the word "magret" *"can be used exclusively in reference to the pectoral muscles of ducks and geese that have been force fed".* The magret does not include the thin filet or "aiguillette" found on the underside. The magret is presented with the fat and skin attached which covers the top. When packaged for sale the label should always indicate if the magret is duck or goose.

Duck breast has become such a popular item in France that meat from "lean" birds is sometimes sold as "magret" but the taste does not compare with the real magret.

This recipe calls for the authentic magrets, if the breast meat from a lean duck is used the flavor and texture will be quite different.

*Note:* Duck "magrets" are available in the U.S. from the same purveyors that market fresh foie gras.

Trim the thick layer of skin leaving a very thin layer of fat attached to the meat to moisten it during cooking.

Place the magrets in a stainless steel recipient and season with the corresponding amount of curing salt and sugar and sprinkle with armagnac. Cover and marinate in the refrigerator for 12 hours.

***The Foie Gras***

Goose foie gras is used here because it will usually melt less during cooking. Top quality duck foie gras can also be used.

Trim the nerves and vessels from the liver as described in chapter 5.

Be sure to remove any green stains from the bile sack.

Season the foie gras and sprinkle with aged port.

Cover and refrigerate for 12 hours.

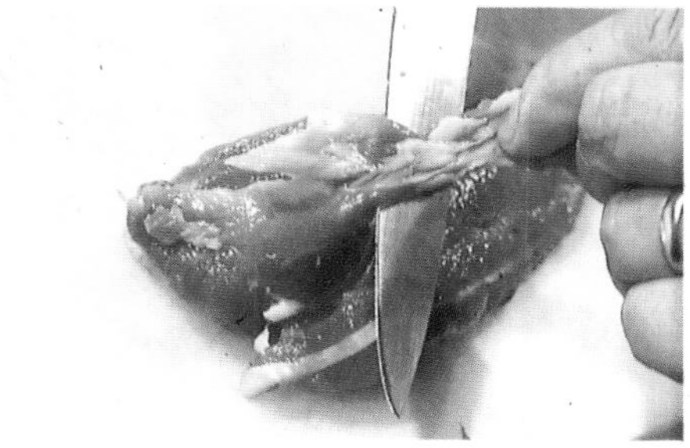

***The Prunes***

The prunes used in this recipe are the outstanding product from the city of Agen which are reputed to be the best.

California produces dried fruits that are certainly acceptable for this terrine.

In France, prunes are sold dried and "half-dried"; for this recipe the drier ones are used. (Note that they are pitted.)

In France, prunes are used in many savory dishes and desserts.

Often they are macerated in advance to moisten and flavor them (with armagnac for example).

However in this recipe, macerated prunes would soak into the meat and foie gras. Through osmosis, the wetter ingredient transfers its moisture to the drier ones around it.

It is more desirable for the prunes to absorb flavor from the foie gras and the duck and not the other way around.

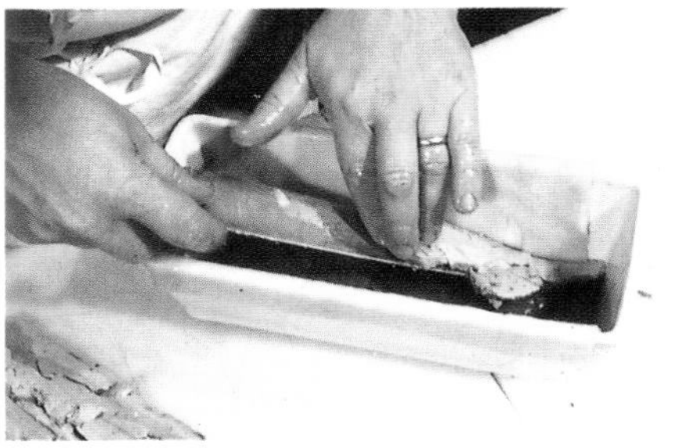

**Assembly**

There is no further preparation so we pass directly to the assembly of the terrine.

Line the terrine molds with barding fat.

Fill the bottom of the mold with a thin layer (1 cm (3/8 in)) of marinated foie gras, pressing down to eliminate all air pockets.

Arrange a row of prunes, pushing them into the foie gras.

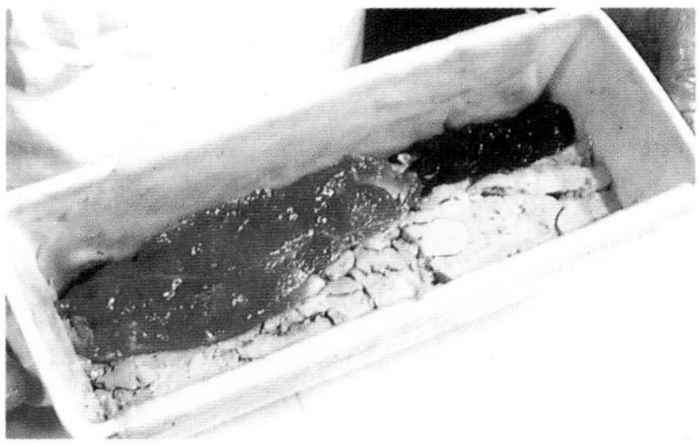

Place a layer of duck breast in the center then repeat the prune and foie gras layers to fill the mold.

To eliminate crevasses in the foie gras layer, all the foie gras can be pressed tightly into a mold, unmolded then sliced to fit into the mold for this recipe. (The molded foie gras can include the prunes arranged in neat rows.)

When the terrine is assembled, fold over the edges of the barding fat to cover completely.

*Note:* To help hold the layers together, since there is no binder of foie gras purée or forcemeat, it is recommended to sprinkle each layer with powdered gelatin. When the terrine is cooked, the gelatin will melt and stick the layers together then set when the terrine is chilled.

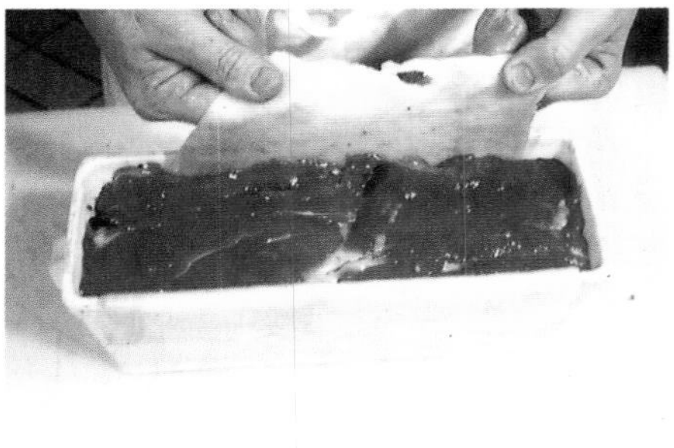

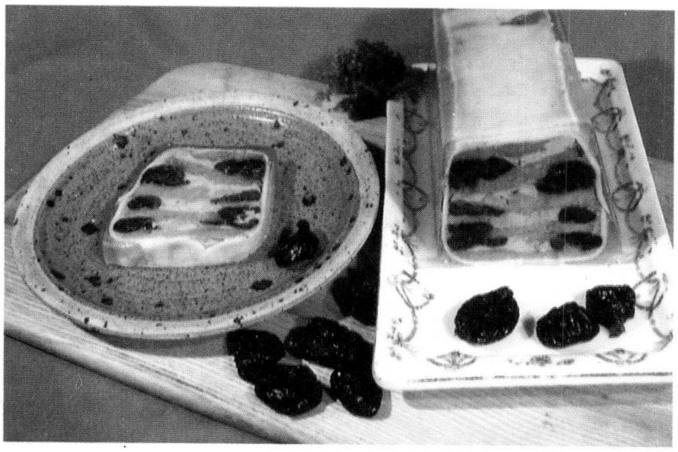

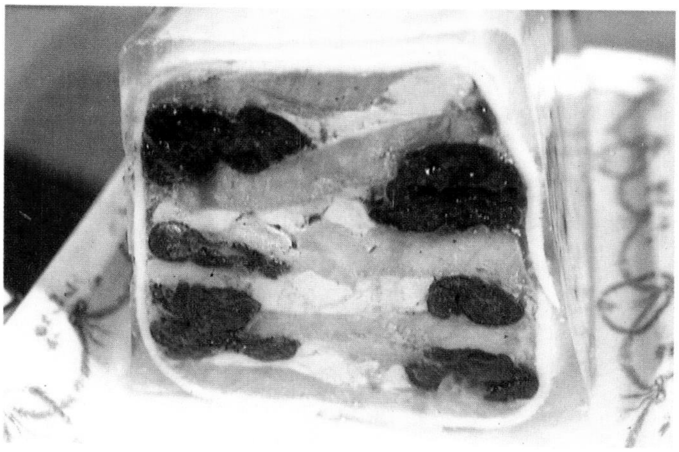

**Cooking**

Place the terrine in a water bath and start the cooking at 150 °C (275 F). Lower the heat to 95-100 °C (200 F).

Since foie gras makes up a substantial portion of this terrine it is recommended to use a steamer if available. This method usually lowers the amount of juices that are rendered from the foie gras.

It is also possible to place the terrine in a vacuum pouch and cook in the same manner as the foie gras terrines in chapter 5.

The terrine is cooked when the probe thermometer inserted into the center registers 74-75 °C (165 F).

The juices on the surface of the cooked terrine will absorb into the terrine as it cools and make it easier to slice.

Cool the cooked terrine quickly.

**Storage**

This terrine will keep for 1 week in the refrigerator.

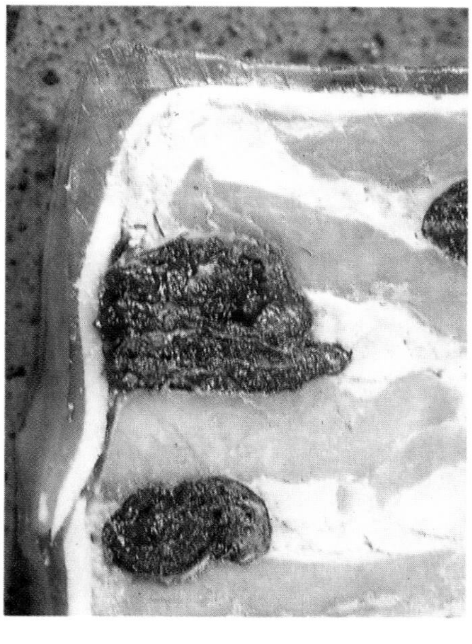

When the terrine is completely cooled, it can be placed in a vacuum pouch to prolong the storage time and make it easier to handle and transport.

If the terrine is cooked in a vacuum pouch it is recommended to enclose it in a second vacuum pouch to ensure freshness for up to 20 days.

**Presentation**

As with all terrines, there are two ways to present this preparation:

- Glazed with aspic and sliced directly from the terrine.

- Unmolded and coated with aspic.

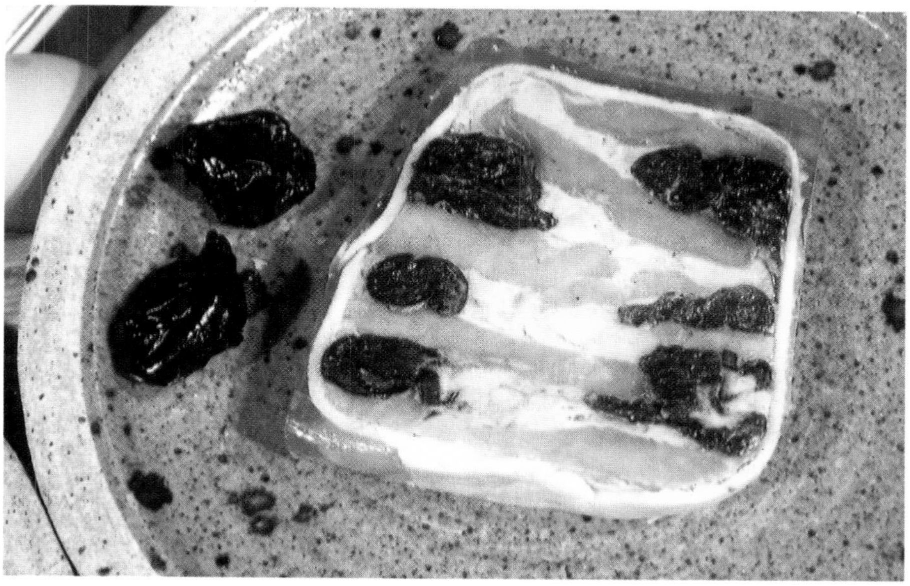

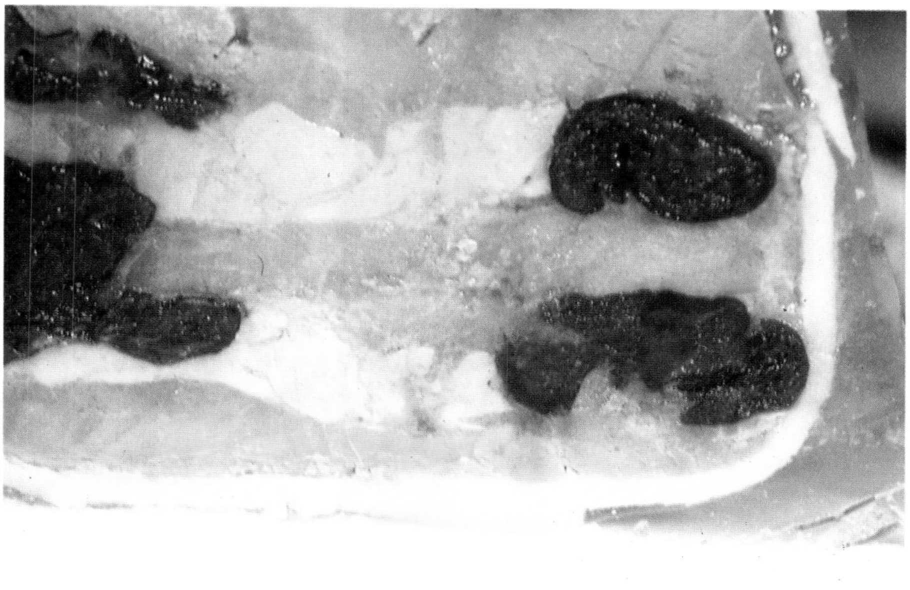

# Ballotine of Bresse Chicken with Crayfish

## Introduction

The marriage of poultry and shellfish is not an invention of "nouvelle cuisine". In the 17th century chicken was served with fresh water crayfish. This version with saltwater crayfish is a logical variation.

## Equipment

Knives, horizontal chopper, stainless steel bowls, sauté pan, conical sieve, parchment paper, kitchen towel, galantine band

## Ingredients

1 top-quality chicken (from Bresse if available)
1 kg (2.2 lbs) pork (belly and jowl)
800 g (1 lb 10 oz) lean pork
1 kg (2.2 lbs) saltwater crayfish
300 g (10 oz) peeled pistachios
200 g (7 oz) mushrooms
100 g (3 1/2 oz) chopped parsley
2 garlic cloves – 4 eggs
200 ml (scant 1 cup) heavy cream
Aromatic vegetables – Madeira

Cognac – Tomato paste
200 g (7 oz) shallots
Dry white wine
250 ml (1 cup) fish stock
3 tomatoes
Butter and oil
*Seasonings (per kilo (2.2 lbs))*
18 g (generous 1/2 oz) curing salt (sodium nitrite with fine salt)
2 g (1/16 oz) white pepper
2 g (1/16 oz) sugar or dextrose
Cayenne pepper

**Preparing the Ingredients**

***The Bresse Chicken***

Choose a top quality hen that weighs about 2 kilos (about 4 1/2 lbs) which will yield about 1 kg (about 2 lbs) of meat.

Pass the bird over a flame to burn off any small feathers that remain and remove the innards. Bone the chicken by first making a slit down the back. It is important to not pierce the skin during this procedure.

Leave the breast meat whole.

Trim the meat from the legs and cut the largest pieces into strips. Reserve all bits of meat trimmed from the bones to make the forcemeat. With the carcass and bones make a stock following the classic recipe. When the stock is cooked, cool it quickly. Reduce 1 liter (about 1 quart) of the stock to a glaze, set aside.

***The Pork and Marinade***

Choose lean pale pork from a top-quality cut. Cut the trimmed pork into strips (lèches).

Trim the belly and jowl and cut into pieces (classic forcemeat).

With the liver of the Bresse chicken (add more chicken livers for a total of 200 g (7 oz)) make a “gratin” (see pages 259-260).

In two stainless recipients, place the “lèches” of pork and chicken in one and the belly and jowl with the gratin in the other. Coat evenly with the corresponding amounts of seasonings. Sprinkle the strips with armagnac and the forcemeat/gratin with madeira. Cover and marinate in the refrigerator for 12 hours.

***The Saltwater Crayfish***

Choose perfectly fresh shellfish.

By hand twist the heads off and set aside. Cook the tails for 6-8 minutes (depending on the size) in boiling salted water.

The heads are used to make a classic “américaine” sauce:

Break up the crayfish heads by pounding with a pestle.

Heat a little butter and olive oil and sauté the crayfish shells.

Chop the shallots and garlic and add to the pot with the shells and cook until browned.

Pour off the fat then flame with armagnac and deglaze the pot with dry white wine, reduce by half.

Cover with fish stock and add the reduced chicken glaze.

Add the fresh tomatoes (peeled, seeded and chopped) and a little tomato paste. Add chopped parsley and a pinch of cayenne pepper.

Cover and cook for 15 minutes.

Pass the liquid through a conical sieve and press on the shells to extract maximum flavor. Season to taste. Cool then remove the layer of fat that forms on the top.

Reduce the cooled liquid to 150 ml (generous 1/2 cup).

***The Forcemeat***

In the horizontal chopper, place the marinated belly and jowl (“farce”) and the gratin. Process until finely ground and blend in the eggs. Add the cooled, reduced americaine sauce and lastly the cream. Stir in the crayfish by hand.

The mixture should be cold (below 15 °C (60 F)) during processing. Chill the bowl of the chopper if necessary.

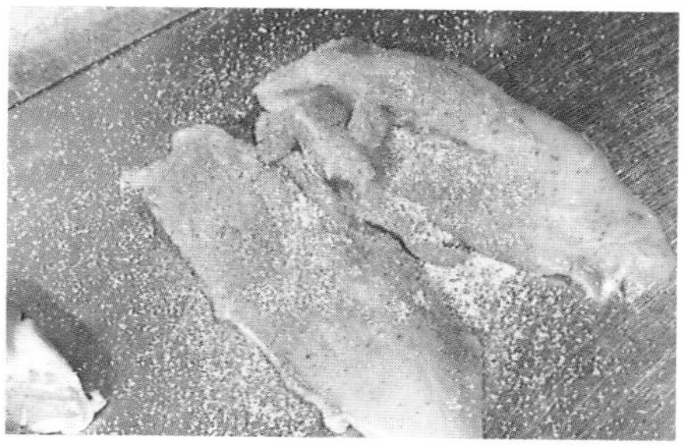

***The “Rosace”***

Make a “rosace” or rosette shaped cylinder for the center of the ballotine as described in the recipe

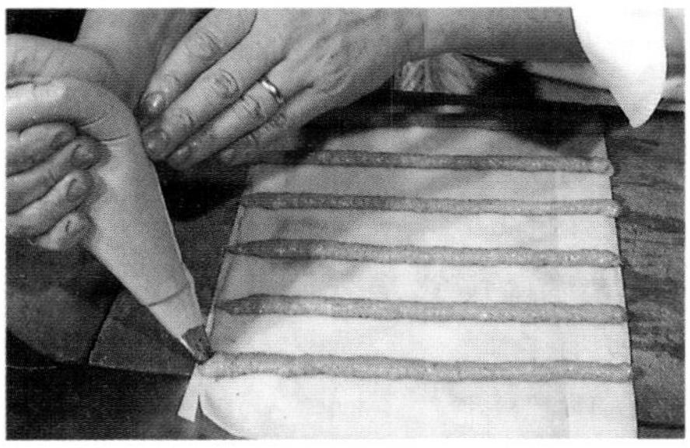

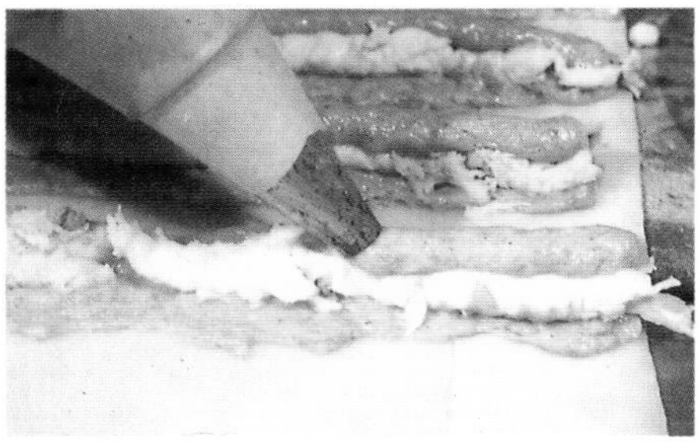

for " young pig with rosace " (page 224).

After the petals have been formed and frozen briefly to stiffen, stick them together with the forcemeat.

Arrange rows of peeled pistachios between the petals, pressing them into the forcemeat to hold.

Place the rosace in the freezer until the ballotine is assembled.

**Assembling the Ballotine**

Spread a sheet of moistened parchment paper on the work surface. Spread out a sheet of barding fat the size of the ballotine (that is the size of the rosace).

Spread a thin layer of forcemeat

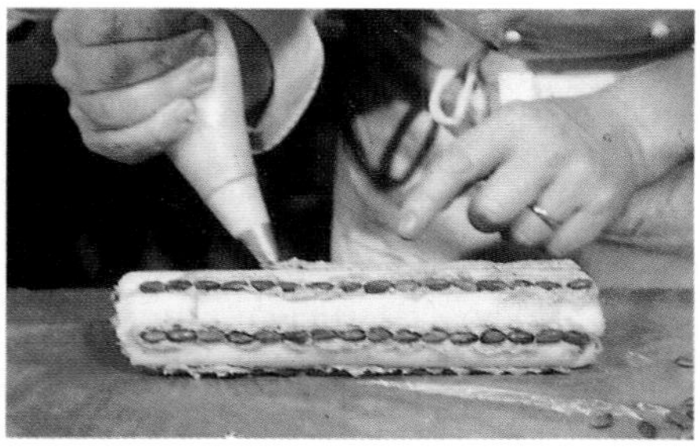

on the barding fat. Place the two chicken breasts in the center.

Blend the remaining forcemeat with the strips of chicken and pork and spread to make a layer about 3 cm (about 1 in) thick.

Place the rosace in the center.

Roll the paper, barding fat and forcemeat around the rosace to form a ballotine making sure that the rosace stays in the center (and that the paper does not get rolled inside.) Tie the paper at the two ends, pulling a little to give the cylinder an even shape.

Roll in a handtowel then secure the wrapping with a long linen strip

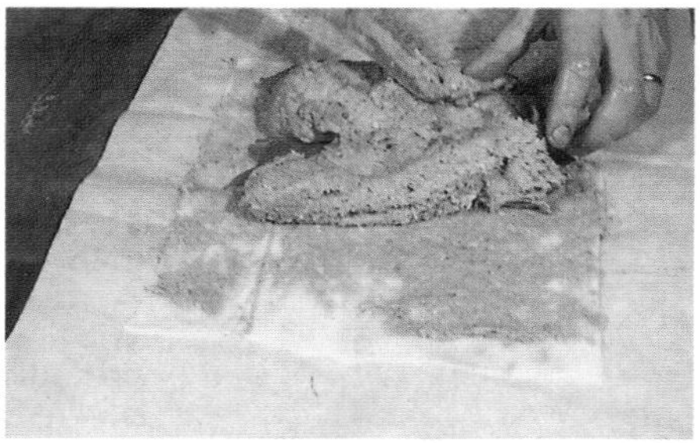

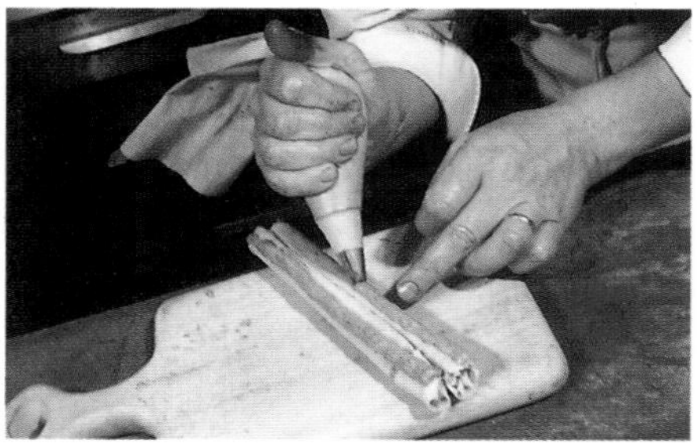

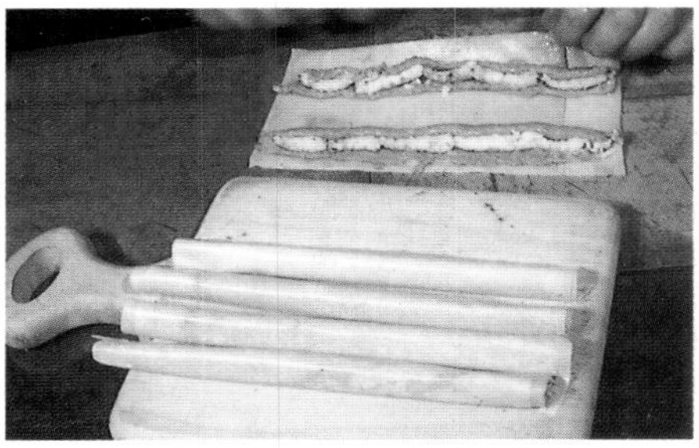

(used to tie pigs' fet) or other sturdy strip of cloth.

**Cooking**

The ballotine is poached in chicken stock. (Pork stock can be added if necessary.)

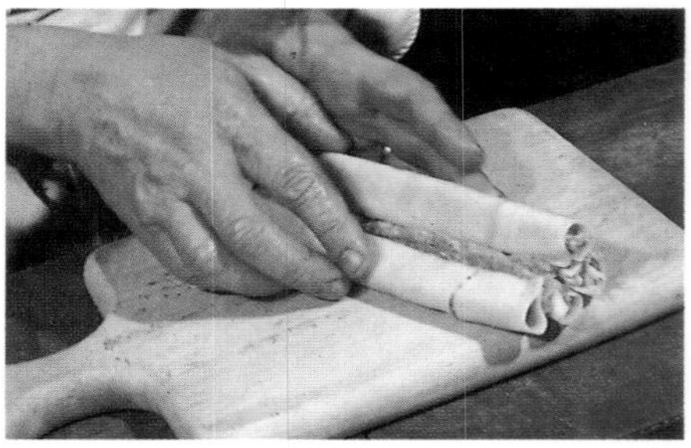

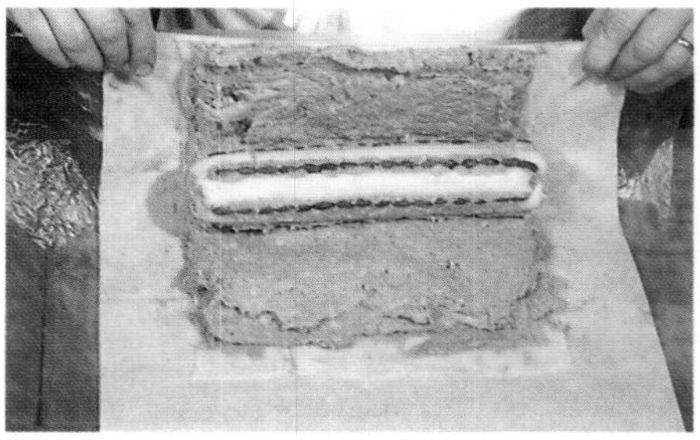

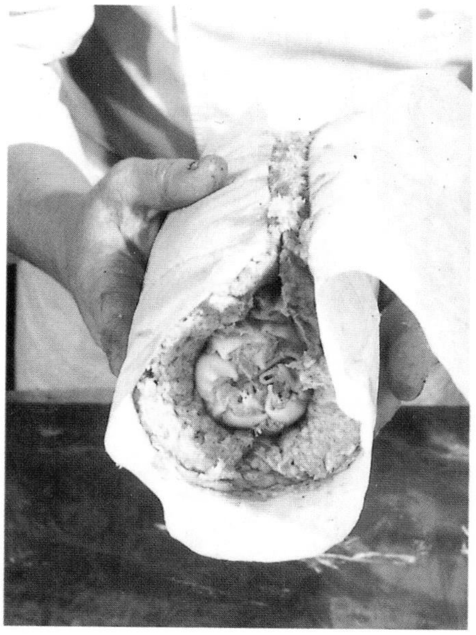

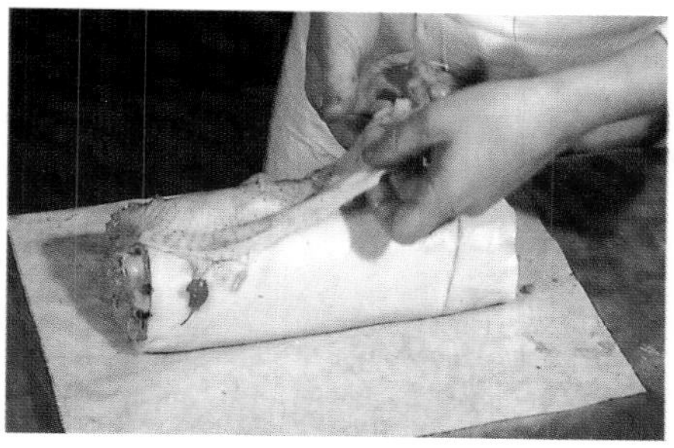

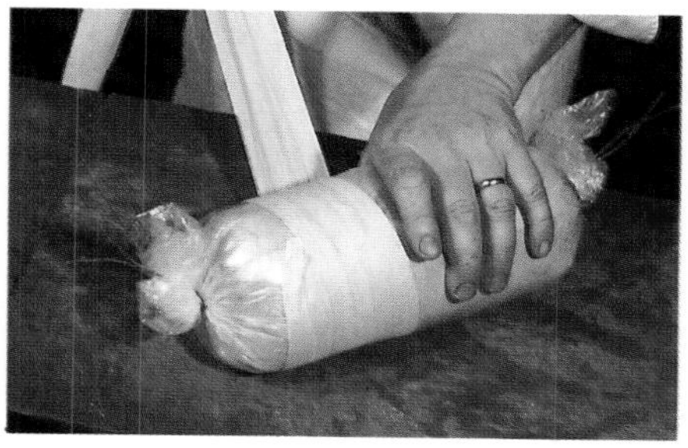

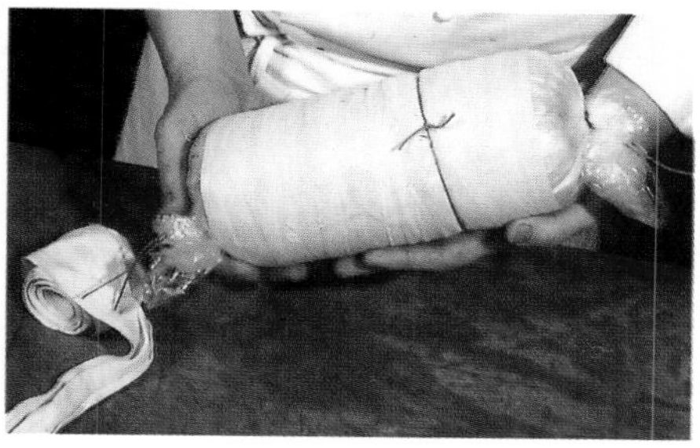

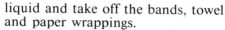

Place the ballotine in the cold stock and bring the liquid to 80-85 °C (175-185 F) and skim all fat and impurities that rise to the surface. Maintain the temperature of the cooking liquid at 80 °C (175 F) and cook until the internal temperature of the ballotine is 76-78 °C (170 F) (checked with a probe thermometer.)

The cooking time depends on the diameter of the ballotine.

Remove the cooked ballotine from the liquid and tighten the ends and tie another piece of string to secure. Bring the cooking liquid to a boil and skim all fat and impurities that rise to the surface.

Place the ballotine in a deep recipient and cover with the strained cooking liquid.

Cool quickly in the liquid.

**Storage**

This preparation will keep in the liquid for 10-12 days.

**Presentation**

Remove the ballotine from the liquid and take off the bands, towel and paper wrappings.

Rinse the surface to remove the stock that adheres to it. Place in the refrigerator to completely dry for 1 hour.

Decorate with fruits and/or vegetables cut in attractive shapes.

Glaze with aspic; either brush on several coats of slightly thickened aspic or use a ladle to pour over a thin smooth layer of aspic.

# Terrine of Duck Confit with Parsley

**Introduction**

This original preparation is inspired by the classic molded ham and parsley of Burgundy. The rich confit (duck cooled and preserved in fat), a product of southwest France marries well with the filling made with parsely.

" La terrine de confit de canard à la bourguignonne " is a delicious dish that is quite easy to prepare.

**Equipment**

Knives, horizontal chopper, ladle, stainless steel bowl, mold

**Ingredients**

24 duck legs " confits "
300 g (10 oz) carrots
200 g (7 oz) shallots
200 g (7 oz) parsley
4 calves' feet, cooked
Barding fat

*Seasonings (to taste)*

Fine salt
Freshly ground pepper
Nutmeg

**Preparing the Ingredients**

***The Carrots***

The carrots are added primarily for their color. The small pieces of bright orange look very attractive with the dark green filling that holds the meat in place.

The carrots are peeled and cut into " brunoise "; tiny dice (about 5 mm × 5 mm (1/4 in)). The dice are simply blanched in boiling water or steamed.

They should remain " al dente "; slightly firm. When the carrots are just barely cooked, they retain their neat shape, the bright color as well as the taste.

Cool the cooked dice of carrots in cold water, drain and set aside in the refrigerator.

### *The Duck Legs*

Our recipe for making " confit de canard " is included in volume 1 of this series. It is preferable to use duck that has been prepared yourself.

Take 24 duck legs that have been cooked in fat and heat gently to melt all the fat that adheres to them.

Remove the skin then pull the meat from the bone and set the meat aside in the refrigerator.

### *The Calves' Feet*

Cook four calves' feet in the classic manner (see instructions for cooking pigs' feet).

While the cooked feet are still warm, remove all the meat from the bones and drain.

Keep the meat from the feet warm.

## Making the Filling

Place the shallots (peeled) and parsley (washed and stemmed) in the horizontal chopper and process until finely chopped.

Add the warm, drained meat from the calves' feet.

Process until finely ground and season to taste with salt, freshly ground pepper and nutmeg.

## Assembly

Line the terrine mold with a sheet of barding fat.

Layer the various preparations into the mold:

First spread a smooth layer about 2 cm (3/4 in) on the bottom.

Sprinkle the diced, cooked carrots over this layer.

Next place a layer of meat removed from the leg of duck (confit). Piece together the shapes of the boned meat so that there are no gaps.

The duck meat should form a neat, even layer in each slice of the terrine.

Repeat the layers to fill the mold with a layer of the filling on the top.

(Each layer should be even so that each slice is symmetrical.)

Fold the barding fat over the top.

Cover with a sheet of aluminum foil and place a baking sheet on top.

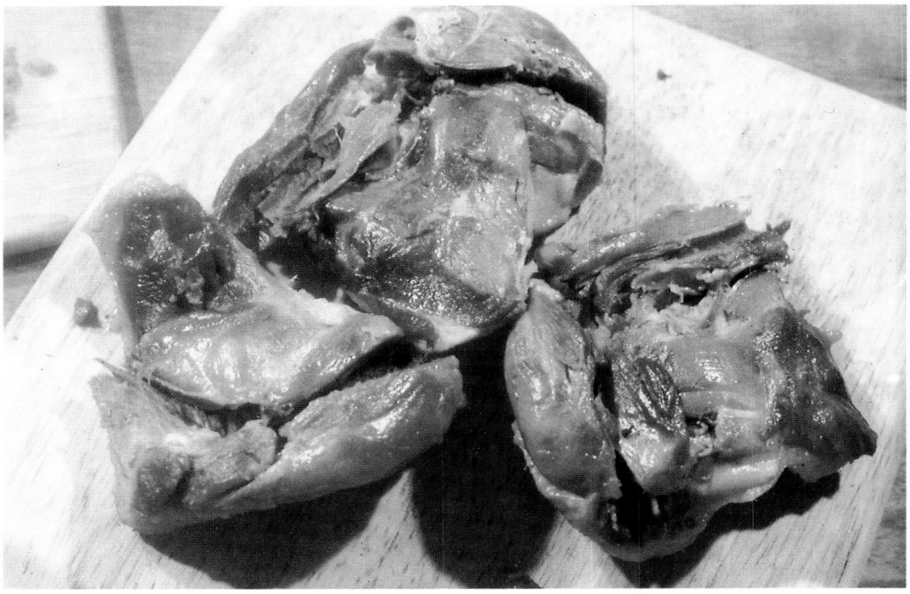

**Cooking**

All of the elements are cooked in advance except the parsley and the shallots.

The cooking stage serves the same purpose as for the headcheese; to sterilize the combination of ingredients by heating in a 170 °C (350 F) oven for about 1 hour.

Place the molds in a water bath (in a deep recipient with 2-3 cm (about 1 in)) hot water.

The internal temperature does not need to be checked because the ingredients are already cooked; this is simply a security measure.

Place a light weight (500 g (1 lb)) on top of the heated terrines and cool quickly.

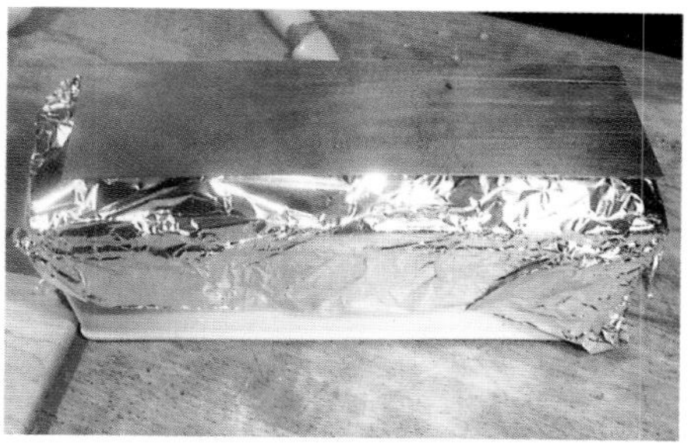

**Storage**

This terrine will keep for 8-10 days.

This product is so easy to prepare that it is advised to make small batches more often rather than storing large quantities in vacuum pouches.

**Presentation**

As with all terrines, this preparation can be presented two ways:

• Left in the mold; top decorated and brushed with aspic then slice directly from the mold.

• Unmolded; the bottom of the cleaned mold is layered with aspic and the decoration is placed in the mold. After pouring in a little thickened aspic the terrine is placed back into the mold and refrigerated to set the aspic.

The terrine is then unmolded after 4-6 hours and presented on a platter.

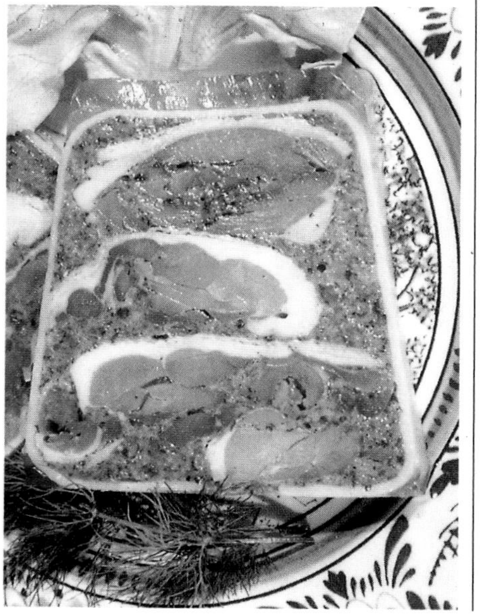

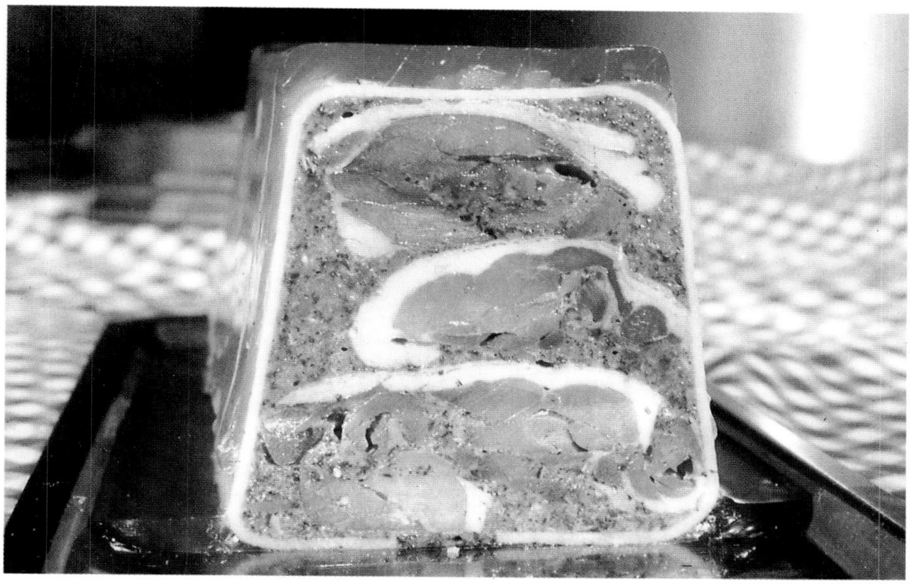

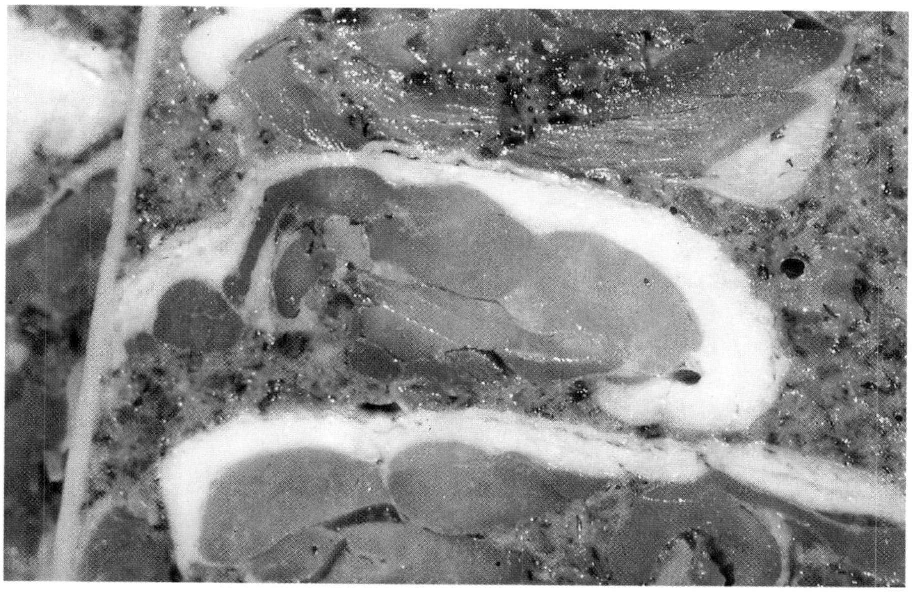

# Terrine of Guinea Hen with Sweetbreads and Morels

## Introduction

Sweetbreads contribute their special blend of rich taste and texture to several unique terrines in this series.

The flavor of this unctuous ingredient marries wonderfully with many other foods.

This combination of guinea hen and morels makes " la terrine de pintadeau aux ris de veau et morilles " an outstanding dish.

## Equipment

Knives, horizontal chopper, braising pans, stainless steel bowl, conical sieve, platter, terrine mold

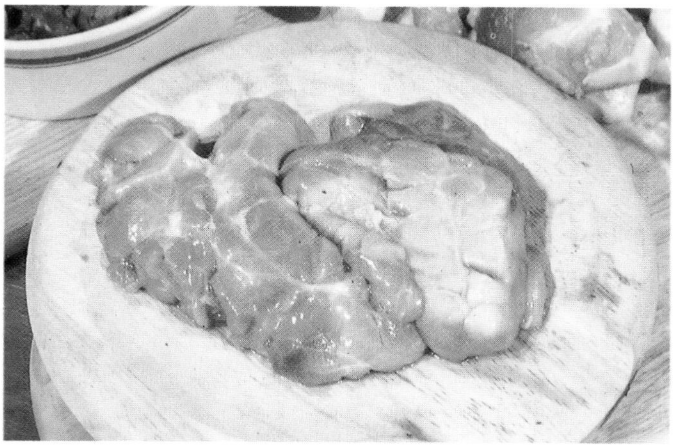

**Ingredients**

1 guinea hen
800 g (1 lb 10 oz) sweetbreads (untrimmed)
1 kg (2.2 lbs) jowl and belly (forcemeat)
300 g (10 oz) dried morels
200 g (7 oz) peeled pistachios
3 eggs
Aromatic vegetables
200 g (7 oz) chicken livers (for " gratin " see p. 259-260 for ingredients)
Madeira
Cognac
Chicken or duck stock
Pork stock

***Seasonings (per kg (2.2 lbs) of meat)***

18 g (generous 1/2 oz) curing salt (sodium nitrite with fine salt)
2 g (1/16 oz) sugar or dextrose
2 g (1/16 oz) ground pepper
1 g (1/32 oz) four spice powder

**Preparing the Ingredients**

***The Guinea Hen***

Choose a young guinea hen that weighs 1.5-1.6 kg (about 3.5 lbs).

Flame the bird to remove remaining feathers, remove the innards in the classic manner.

Remove the meat from the bone. There should be about 750-800 g (1 lb 10 oz) of meat.

Leave the breast meat whole and cut the large pieces from the leg into strips (lèches). Reserve the trimmings for the forcemeat and set aside the bones to make a stock.

Coat evenly with the corresponding amount of seasonings, sprinkle with cognac and marinate in the refrigerator for at least 12 hours.

***The Sweetbreads***

Cover the sweetbreads with cold water and degorge for 6-8 hours (change the water when it becomes pink from the blood).

Blanch for a few minutes in boiling salted water and cool immediately.

Trim any excess fat.

Prepare the aromatic vegetables to form a flavorful bed for the sweetbreads to braise on (onions, carrots, celery, parsly stems, thyme and bay leaf with a little goose fat).

Place the sweetbreads on the vegetables and season with salt and pepper and place a few nuggets of butter on top.

Cook in a hot oven (180-200 °C (375-400 F)) to brown the top.

Turn the meat over and add poultry stock to the pan to cover the vegetables (2-3 cm (1 in)).

Brown the second side then cool the sweetbreads quickly. The center should remain very pink (the sweetbreads will cook again when the terrine is cooked). Strain the braising liquid, skim the fat off the top and reduce to a glaze.

***Stock made with Guinea Hen Carcass***

Chop the bones and carcass of the guinea hen. Brown the bones in a little goose fat.

Add aromatic vegetables (peeled and cut in small pieces).

Brown the vegetables, pour off the fat and flame with cognac.

Cover the bones with pork stock.

Simmer the stock for 2 1/2 hours, skimming all fat and impurities that rise to the surface. Strain the stock through a conical sieve, pressing on the bones and vegetables to extract as much flavor as possible.

Cool the stock quickly.

Take 1 liter (about 1 qt) of the stock and reduce to a glaze.

***The Morels***

Soak the morels in water for four hours.

Wash the mushrooms in several basins of water until no sand or grit is left on the bottom.

Poach the morels for 4-5 minutes in a little poultry stock.

Drain the morels and reduce the cooking liquid to a glaze.

***The Forcemeat***

Trim the skin from the belly and jowl and cut in large dice (2.5 cm (1 in)). With the chicken livers (plus the guinea hen liver) make a " gratin " (see pages 259-260).

Place the meats and the cooled gratin in a stainless steel recipient and add the corresponding amount of seasonings, and marinate in the refrigerator for at least 12 hours.

The cooked morels can be added to the marinade to contribute a robust flavor then removed before the forcemeat is ground.

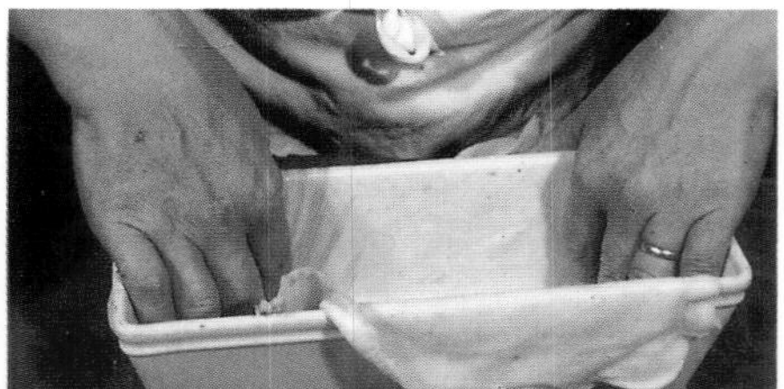

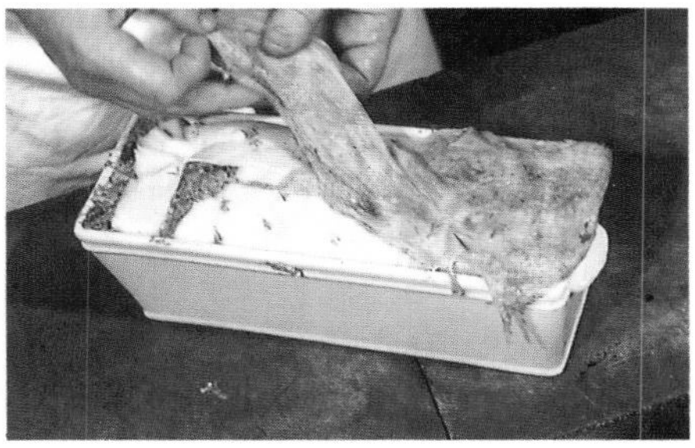

### Making the Filling

The filling (also called a " farce " or forcemeat) is made by first chopping the marinated gratin and pieces of belly and jowl (morels removed and set aside). Add the eggs and the three reductions (guinea hen, sweetbreads and morels).

Process until smooth. Note that the temperature of the mixture should not exceed 14-15 °C (60 F); chill the bowl of the chopper if necessary. Transfer the forcemeat to a large stainless steel bowl.

Cut the cooked, cooled sweetbreads into large dice (2.5 cm (1 in)). If the morels are large, cut in half or thirds.

Gently fold in the sweetbreads, morels, pistachios, and the strips of meat. This can be done in a mixer at low speed.

### Assembly

Line the mold with a sheet of barding fat. Fill the mold halfway with the forcemeat.

Lay the marinated breast of the guinea hen in the center.

Fill the mold to the top with forcemeat and fold the edges of the barding fat over the top to cover.

### Cooking

Place the mold in a water bath and start the cooking at 190-200 °C (400 F). When the top has browned a little, turn the heat down to 110 °C (225 F).

Cook until the internal temperature registers 76-78 °C (170 F) on a probe thermometer.

Drain off the fatty juices rendered by the terrine during cooking. Replace these juices with the guinea hen stock (which has been brought to a boil, skimmed then strained).

Place a light weight on top and cool quickly.

### Storage

This terrine will keep in the refrigerator for 8-10 days. After the terrine cools completely, it can be placed in a vacuum pouch to prolong storage.

### Presentation

Like the other terrines in this series, this preparation can be decorated and sliced directly from the mold or unmolded, decorated, glazed and presented on a platter.

# Chicken Terrine " à l'Ancienne "

## Introduction

This interesting terrine made with ordinary ingredients is a creation of Jean-Pierre Odeau.

The procedure is simple enough for an amateur cook in a home kitchen and does not call for any fancy equipment.

All the ingredients are foods that are easily procured except for the truffles which is an optional ingredient.

Despite the common ingredients and straight forward procedure, this is a delicious product that takes its place among top-quality " nouvelle " charcuterie preparations.

## Equipment

Paring knife, chef's knife, terrine mold, stainless steel bowl, hotel pan, mixer

**Ingredients**

*For a terrine of 2 kg (4.4 lbs)*

900 g (scant lb) chicken filets
1 kg (2.2 lbs) sowbelly
4 eggs
6 g (1/6 oz) potato starch or cornstarch
40 cl (1 3/4 cup) port
20 g (2/3 oz) truffles (optional)
Barding fat

***Seasonings***

36 g (about 1 oz) curing or " plain " salt
4 g (scant 1/6 oz) saltpeter with red food color
4 g (scant 1/6 oz) ground white pepper
1 g (1/32 oz) ground nutmeg

**Preparing the Ingredients**

Chicken filets are available in bulk from wholesalers. They are often thawed for sale after having been stored at – 18 °C (0 F). This is usually not indicated on the label so the charcutier does not always know just how fresh the product is.

It is best to use fresh, unfrozen filets to ensure the quality of the final product. It is our firm belief that fresh ingredients are essential for good results.

The sowbelly is trimmed of skin, bones and cartilage then sliced about 7-8 mm (about 1/4 in) thick (about the thickness of a chicken filet).

An electric slicer will ensure more even slices.

The chicken and pork is seasoned with salt and port.

Cover and marinate in the refrigerator for 12 hours.

Add a little food color if using. (The French use " sel rose " which is a blend of salt peter with food color).

Check manufacturers instructions.

However, plain salt can be used, resulting in a white appearance preferred by many clients.

Chef Odeau sometimes assembles the terrine immediately without marinating the meats. In this case it is necessary to use curing salt.

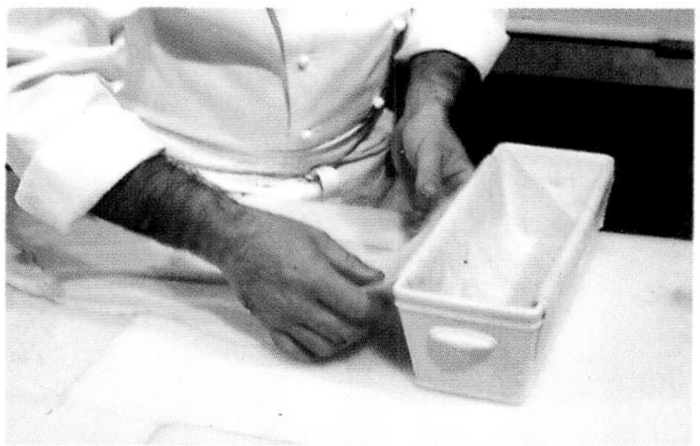

**Procedure**

Place the marinated meats in a large bowl.

In a stainless steel bowl, whisk together the eggs, starch, pepper and nutmeg.

Pour this mixture through a strainer over the meats, add the chopped truffles if using and stir to coat the meat evenly. This procedure could also be done in a mixer at low speed.

The eggs are the " ciment " in this recipe. They serve as a binder to hold all the ingredients together.

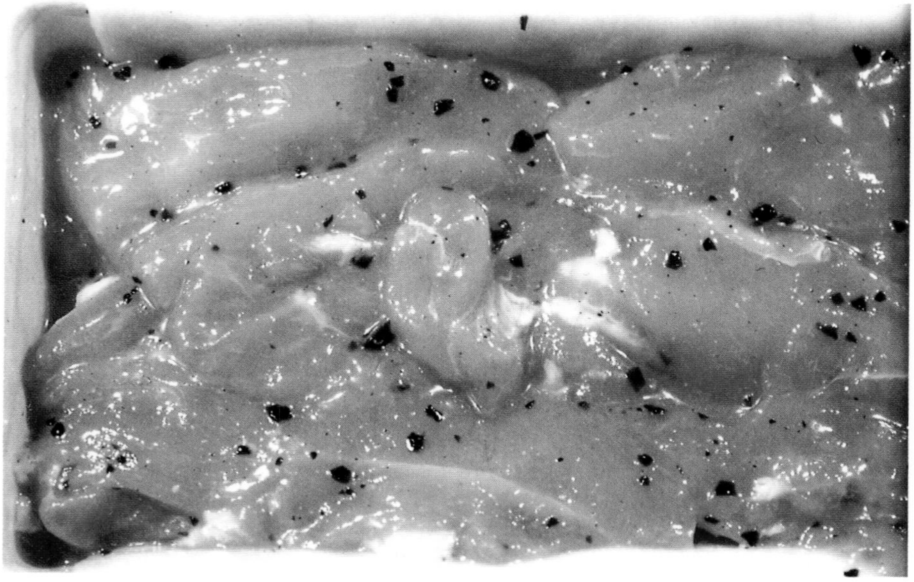

**Assembling**

Line the mold with a thin sheet of barding fat large enough to cover the top.

Alternate layers of chicken filets and sowbelly.

Repeat the layers to fill the mold. It is important to scoop up some of the egg mixture that settles to the bottom of the bowl and spoon it over every other layer.

Pour all remaining egg mixture over the top and fold the barding fat over to cover.

Cover with aluminum foil or set a baking sheet on top.

This terrine does not need to be browned on top.

### Cooking

The terrine is cooked immediately in a water bath. Set the oven to 170 °C (350 F), place the terrine in the oven then turn down the temperature to 100-110 °C (210 F) and cook until the internal temperature is 74-75 °C (165 F).

Pour off the cooking juices and replace them with full-flavored stock that has been previously brought to a boil and skimmed of all impurities.

Place a light weight on top of the terrine to eliminate air pockets then cool rapidly.

### Storage

This terrine will keep for 6-8 days.

It is so easy to prepare that it is recommended to make it often rather than making large batches and storing in vacuum pouches.

### Presentation

Remove the barding fat from the top of the terrine and cover with a thin layer of aspic.

The chicken terrine "à l'ancienne" should be sliced rather thickly as the eggs do not bind as well as a forcemeat.

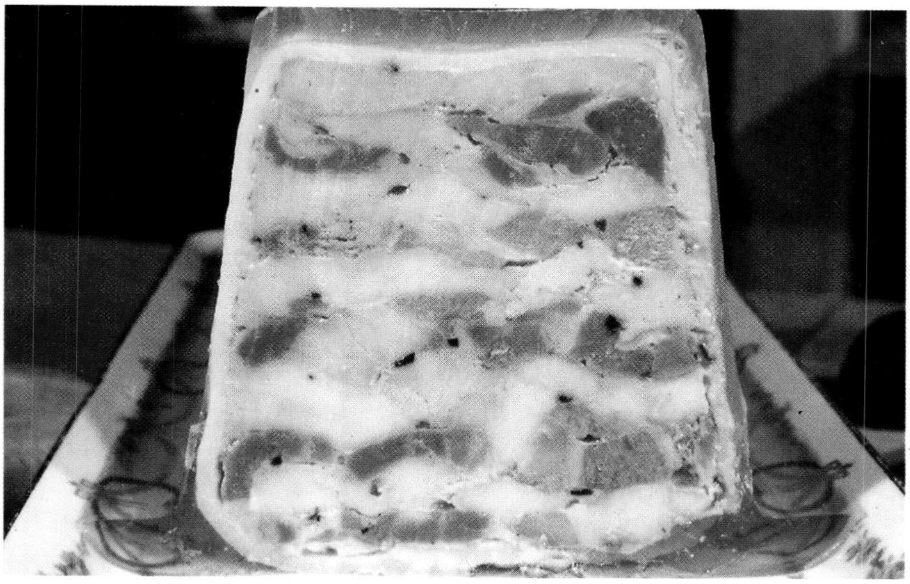

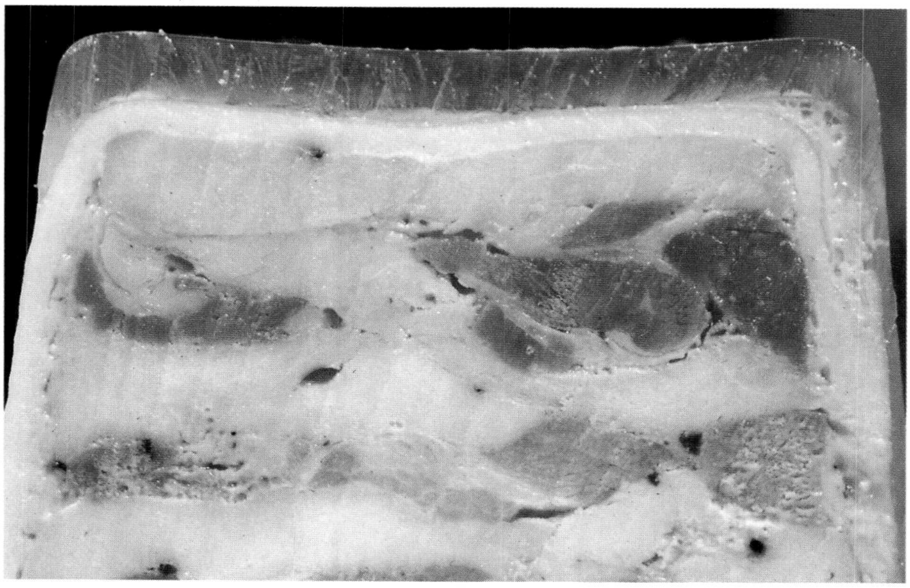

# Terrine of Duck "à l'Orange"

## Introduction

The marriage of sweet and sour flavors in this terrine is fairly new in charcuterie. The combination is inspired by the well known " canard à l'orange " of classic cuisine. This hot dish is made with a " bigarrade " which is a sweet and sour sauce base made with caramelized sugar and vinegar.

Many delicious terrines have been developed using fruits. The most successful combinations respect the character of all the ingredients and are a well balanced blend.

**Equipment**

Grinder of chopper, large bowl, plastic scraper, terrine molds, strainer, drum sieve, saucepan, paring knife, large pot, mixer

**Ingredients**

*For 10 kg (22 lbs) of mixture*

1 kg (2.2 lbs) duck meat
3.5 kg (7.7 lbs) lean pork
3 kg (6.6 lbs) pork jowl and belly
360 g (12 oz) eggs 8-10 oranges (untreated)
1 tablespoon currant jelly
1 dl (scant 1/2 cup) wine vinegar
100 g (3 1/2 oz) sugar
50 cl (2 cups)
Cointreau
Reduced duck stock

***Seasonings***

160 g (1/3 lb) curing salt (sodium nitrite blended with salt
20 g (2/3 oz) freshly ground pepper
10 g (1/3 oz) ground nutmeg

**Preparing the Ingredients**

***The Meats***

Bone the ducks and cut the meat into strips about the size of the filet found on the underside of the breast. (These strips are called " lèches " in French.) Save the trimmings, pieces of fat, bones and skin.

Choose top grade lean pork and cut into " lèches " as well.

Remove the skin from the jowl and belly, cut in large even cubes and combine with the fat and trimmings from the duck.

With the bones of the duck make a full-flavored stock using pork stock instead of water.

Marinate the strips of duck and pork with curing salt, Cointreau, and orange zests.

Marinate the jowl and belly meat (forcemeat) with curing salt and Cointreau.

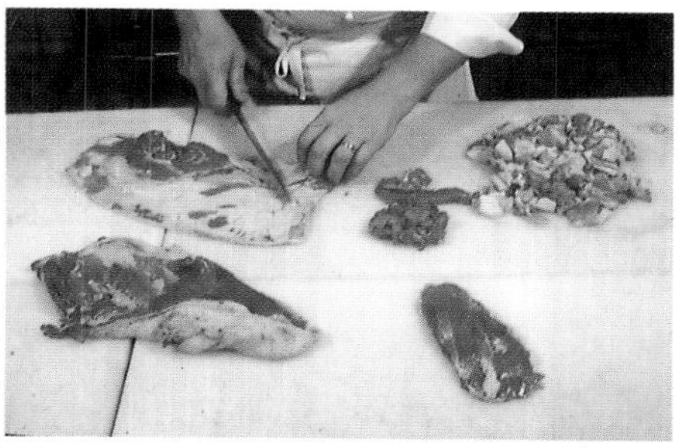

Cover the two recipients with plastic wrap and refrigerate 12 hours.

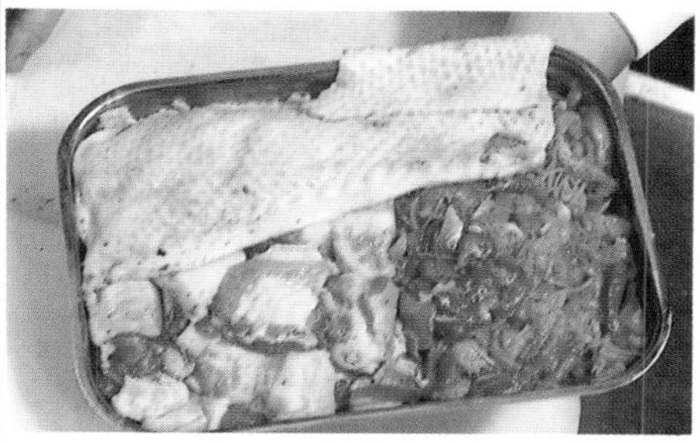

**The Oranges**

Choose untreated oranges if possible. Wash them thoroughly then remove the zest which is the orange rind without the bitter white pith. Cut the zest into thin strips (julienne).

Cook the zest in boiling water for 1-2 minutes, drain and refresh with cold water.

Drain well and add to the marinade for the strips of duck and pork meat.

**The " Bigarrade "**

Put the sugar and a little vinegar in a saucepan. (Use " vinaigre de vin vieux " (vinegar made with aged wine) if available.)

Heat the mixture, stirring often, until it turns into a light caramel.

Add the juice of two oranges (or use the reserved ends of several oranges as shown--the center portion is set aside for the decoration).

Bring to a boil and add the currant jelly. Stir to blend the ingredients.

Reduce by 1/4.

Pour the sauce through a strainer and set aside.

**The Forcemeat**

Reduce 1/2 L (2 cups) of duck stock to a glaze.

Place the jowl and belly meats with the eggs into the chopper along with the duck glaze and spices.

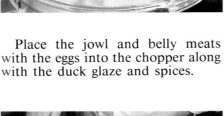

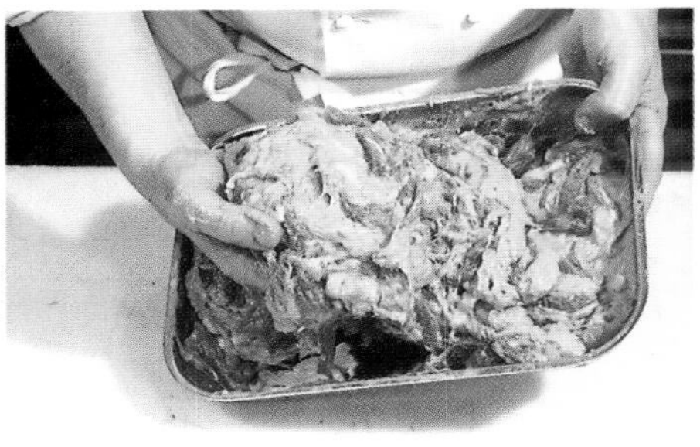

Process these ingredients until smooth being careful to keep the temperature of the mixture at around 12-14 °C (55 F).

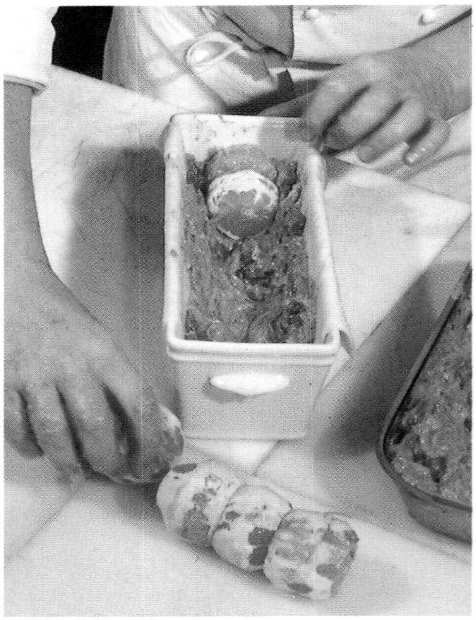

**Assembling the Terrine**

Cut slices of oranges to arrange in the center of the terrine.

Line the mold with a thin sheet of barding fat (with enough hanging over the edge to fold over the top).

Fill with alternating layers of forcemeat and strips of duck and pork with one row of orange slices arranged in the middle.

Fill the mold to the top with layers of forcemeat and meat strips.

It is also possible to remove all the peel from the oranges, lift out the sections with a paring knife and cut into pieces. These pieces are then delicately folded into the forcemeat .

Fold the barding fat over the top and lay the skin of the duck on top.

**Cooking**

This terrine is cooked in a water bath in the oven.

Start the cooking at 200 °C (375 F) until lightly browned then turn the temperature down to 100-110 °C (210 F) and cook until the internal temperature is 78 °C (170 F) (measured with an electronic probe).

Pour off the fat and juices of the cooked terrine and replace them with a full-flavored duck stock that has been boiled and skimmed and flavored with Cointreau.

Refrigerate at least 24 hours before slicing.

**Storage**

This terrine will keep covered in the refrigerator for 6-7 days.
To store the terrine up to 12-15 days, place in a vacuum pouch.

**Presentation**

Remove the barding fat, decorate with slices of oranges and brush with aspic. It is served cold in medium slices.

# Terrine of Duck with Rosemary

### Introduction

All of the fragrant herbs from the southern region of Provence marry very well with duck.

Rosemary goes particularly well with duck making " la terrine de canard au romarin " a star in the line-up of new terrines.

### Equipment

Grinder or chopper, plastic scraper, large bowl, hotel pans, terrine mold, drum sieve, conical strainer, knives, large pot, saucepan, mixer

## Ingredients

*For 10 kg (22 lbs) of mixture*

3 kg (6.6 lbs) duck meat
3 kg (6.6 lbs) lean pork
3 kg (6.6 lbs) jowl and belly
400 g (14 oz) eggs
500 g (1 lb) " gratin " of chicken livers
Cognac or Armagnac
100 g (3 1/2 oz) rosemary

### *Seasonings*

160 g (1/3 lb) curing salt (sodium nitrite with fine salt)
18 g (1/2 oz) freshly ground pepper
10 g (1/3 oz) ground nutmeg

## Preparing the Ingredients

### *The Meats*

Choose a meaty duck and remove the meat from the bones. Cut the meat into strips (" lèches ") about the size of the filet found on the underside of the breast. Reserve the trimmings, skin, fat and bones.

Choose top grade lean pork and cut it into strips the same size as the duck.

Remove the skin and cartilage from the jowl and belly and cut into large even pieces.

Marinate the lean meats and the forcemeat ingredients (jowl and belly) separately with curing salt and cognac. Add the gratin (see below) to the forcemeat.

Make a full-flavored stock with the duck bones. First brown aromatic vegetables (onion, carrot, celery) in duck or goose fat. Break up the bones and add them to the vegetables and brown together. Add pork stock to cover, add a bouquet garni and bring to a boil.

Skim the impurities that rise to the surface then lower the heat and cook gently for 3 hours, skimming occasionally.

### The " Gratin "

This preparation that is often used in game forcemeats is added here to intensify the flavors of the base ingredients.

The gratin however contributes a deep color as well which is appropriate for game terrines but not always desirable for forcemeats made with more delicate meats.

The amount of gratin added to a forcemeat ranges from 50-250 g (2 oz-1/2 lb) per kilo (about 2 pounds). In this recipe, 500 g (1 lb) represents about 150 g (5 oz) per kilo (2 lbs).

### Gratin Ingredients

1 kg (2.2 lbs) lightly salted slab bacon
250 g (1/2 lb) carrots
250 g (1/2 lb) shallots
1 kg (2 lbs) white mushrooms
1.5 kg (3 lbs) chicken livers
150 g (5 oz) chopped parsley
Madeira
Salt and pepper
Goose fat

### Procedure

Trim the slab bacon of skin and cartilage and cut into small strips (" lardons "). Blanch the lardons in boiling water, drain and squeeze dry in a clean handtowel.

Cut the carrots and onions into tiny dice (" brunoise ").

Wash the mushrooms, peel then slice thinly.

Trim the chicken livers of nerves and traces of bile (green stains).

In a large saucepan, heat a little goose fat. Add the lardons then the diced carrot and onion.

Cover and cook over medium heat for a few minutes. When soft but not browned, add the mushrooms.

Cook over medium high heat to evaporate the liquid without browning.

Lastly add the chicken livers and cook just a little--they should remain rare.

Season with salt and pepper (remember that the bacon is salty).

Add madeira to almost cover the ingredients. Cook to reduce a little.

Remove from the heat and stir in the chopped parsley. The livers should still be moist and pink on the inside.

Cool quickly and store in a stainless steel recipient covered with plastic wrap.

Refrigerated (2-4 °C (35 F)) the gratin will keep 10 days.

### Making the Mixture

Place 1 L (1 qt) of strained and degreased duck stock in a casserole.

Add the branches of rosemary.

Bring to a boil then simmer for 10 minutes to infuse the rosemary into the stock. Taste and reduce if necessary to achieve a rosemary flavor. The amount of flavor will depend on the freshness and quality of the rosemary. This herb has a very strong character--the chef is striving for a well-balanced taste where no one ingredient dominates.

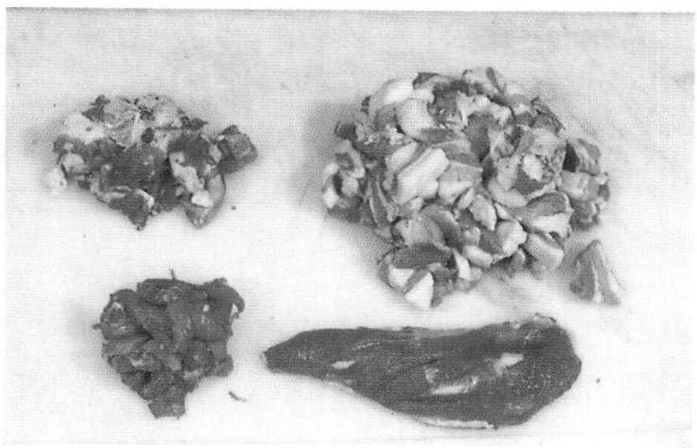

The leaves of rosemary are not used " as is " in the terrine. The pointed leaves are hard and are unpleasant to bite into.

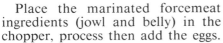

Place the marinated forcemeat ingredients (jowl and belly) in the chopper, process then add the eggs.

Process until finely chopped and smooth then add the rosemary infused stock.

Process until smooth then incorporate half of the pepper and nutmeg.

The temperature of the mixture should not go above 14-15 °C (60 F) during the mixing procedure.

**The Decoration**

Cut 8 strips of barding fat the same length as the terrine mold and 4 cm (1 1/2 in) wide.

Pipe out a line of forcemeat on each strip and fold over and press the seam to form a petal or teardrop shape.

It is recommended to weigh each " petal " to make sure they are the same size so that the motif is balanced.

Place the petals on a baking sheet and harden in the freezer for about 20 minutes.

Take the hardened petals from the freezer and cover with forcemeat and assemble them in a " rosace " or flower pattern.

Put the assembled rosace in the freezer to harden.

This pattern is a classic decoration for the interior of fancy terrines and can be made for a variety of preparations using the method outlined here (see Blood Sausages, volume 1).

The charcutier may choose to use other shapes to enhance the slice of his terrines. In France there are forms available for forming triangles, teardrops and other shapes. The metallic forms are filled with forcemeat and frozen like the rosace.

**Assembling the Terrine**

In a large bowl, mix the strips of lean meat with about 10 % of the forcemeat and the remaining pepper and nutmeg.

This will help hold the strips to the other ingredients so that the terrine will slice more neatly.

In a mold lined with thin sheets of barding fat, place even, alternating layers of forcemeant and strips of meat to fill the mold halfway.

Place the frozen rosace in the center then fill the mold with the remaining forcemeat and meat strips.

Fold over the sheet of barding fat and cover with the duck skin.

**Cooking**

The terrine is cooked in a water bath in the oven.

Set the oven at 180-200 °C (375 F) and cook briefly to brown the surface. Lower the temperature to 100-110 °C (225 F) and cook until the internal temperature is 76-78 °C (170 F).

Pour off the fat and cooking juices and replace them with full-flavored duck stock that has been infused with rosemary and brought to a boil and skimmed.

Place a light weight on top to compress the terrine slightly.

Cool quickly and refrigerate 24 hours before serving.

**Storage**

After the terrine is completely cooled, place in a vacuum pouch to store for up to two weeks.

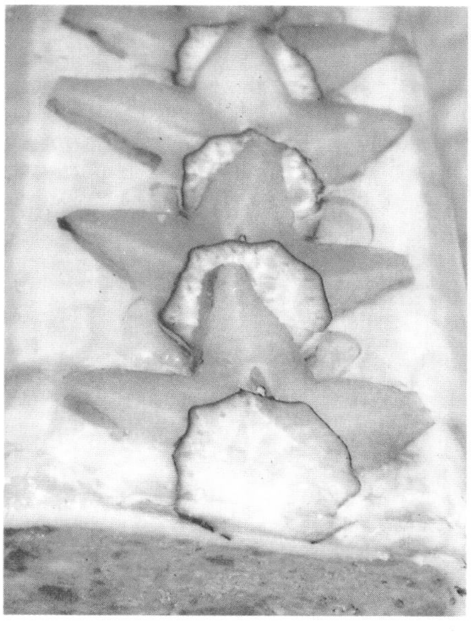

**Presentation**

To serve, remove the barding fat and glaze with amber colored aspic. The top can first be decorated with branches of rosemary that have been blanched to guarantee cleanliness.

# Chicken Terrine with Lemon

**Introduction**

This terrine fills the new demand for " lighter " charcuterie products. A portion of the meat is chicken which is very low in fat. The tart taste of the lemon marries well with the chicken and the pork which contributes moisture to the forcemeat.

**Equipment**

Knives, horizontal chopper with fixed or removable bowl, plastic scraper, stainless steel bowls and hotel pans, casserole, drum sieve, conical sieve, earthenware mold

**Ingredients**

*For 10 kg (22 lbs) of mixture*

2.5 kg (5.5 lbs) chicken meat
4 kg (8.8 lbs) lean pork
3 kg (6.6 lbs) pork jowl and belly
6 eggs
250 ml (1 cup) heavy cream
6 lemons

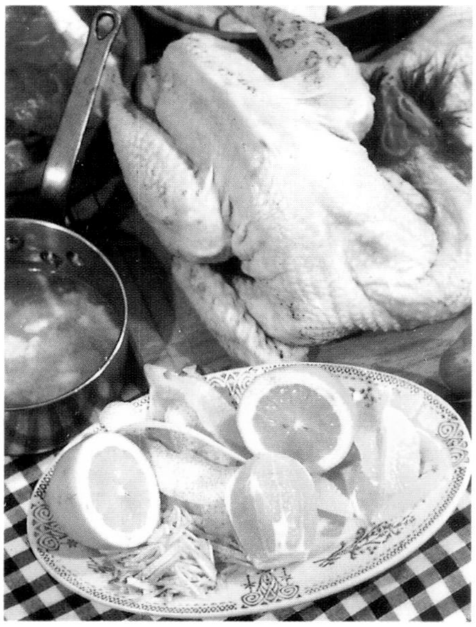

*Seasonings*

170 g (scant 6 oz) curing salt (sodium nitrite with fine salt)
18 g (generous 1/2 oz) white pepper
10 g (1/3 oz) nutmeg
500 ml (2 cups) cognac

**Preparing the Ingredients**

***The Meats***

Choose top-quality chickens with firm flesh. Bone and trim all nerves and fat. Cut the meat into strips (" lèches ") about the size of the filet which is on the underside of the breast.

Small trimmings from the bones can be used in the forcemeat. Set aside the bones to make a stock.

Choose pale-colored pork from a lean, tender cut. (Terrines made with poultry should be light in color so the pork must be very pale.) Cut the lean pork in strips the same size as the chicken strips.

Trim the jowl and belly (half and half) which are used to make the forcemeat. The lean portion of the jowl can be cut into strips and added to the lean pork. Cut the jowl and belly into large even cubes. Refrigerate the meats until ready to marinate.

***The Lemons***

The peel of the lemon is used in this recipe so the lemons should be untreated if possible.

In any case, wash the lemons well. Remove the zest from four lemons and trim any white pith that remains on the zest. Cut the zest into very thin strips (julienne). Blanch the zest in boiling water for one minute. Drain, rinse with cold water and dry on paper towels. Set aside. Cut the remaining peel off the four lemons and remove the sections of fruit by slicing between the membranes. Cut the sections into small cubes.

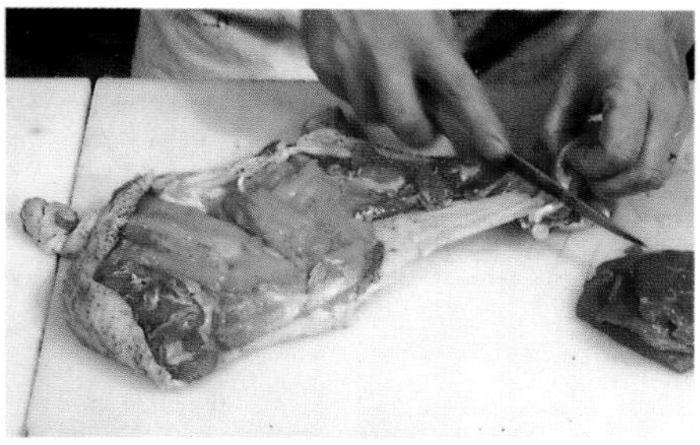

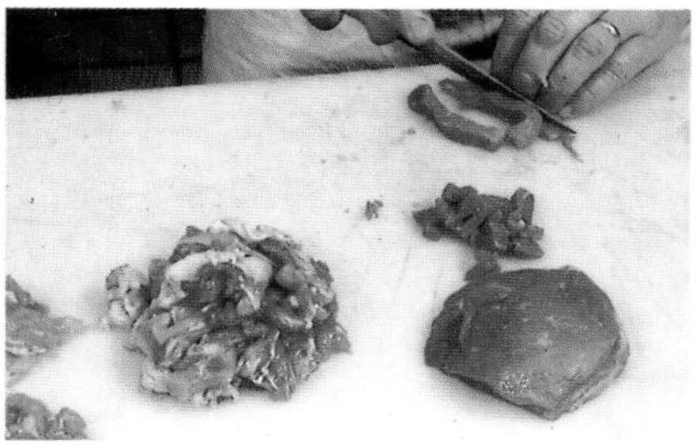

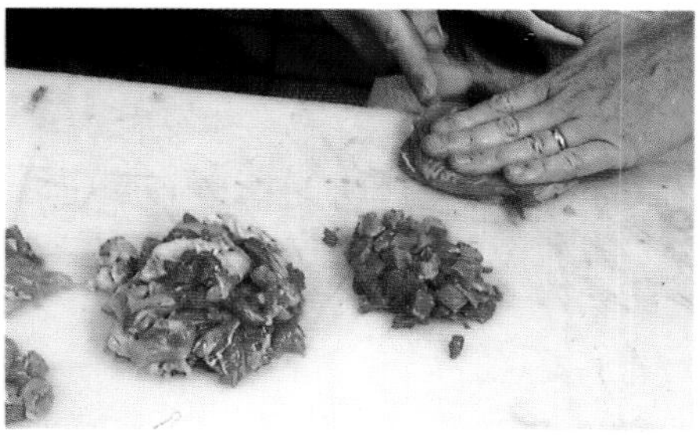

***The Marinade***

Marinate the strips of chicken and lean pork with the corresponding amount of seasonings, the julienned zest and the juice of the two remaining lemons.

Season the jowl and belly separately and add cognac.

Cover and marinate in the refrigerator for 12 hours.

***The Chicken Stock***

Make a chicken stock with the carcass and bones of the chicken following the classic method. After skimming and straining the stock, reduce 1 liter (1 qt) to a glaze and refrigerate the rest.

**Procedure**

Chill the bowl of the chopper. Chop the marinated jowl and belly (forcemeat) and add the eggs, cream and the meat glaze. Process until the mixture is smooth and unctuous. The temperature should not exceed 15 °C (60 F). Transfer the forcemeat to a mixer and incorporate the strips of pork and chicken and blend until evenly distributed.

Lastly add the cubes of lemon and blend just enough to incorporate.

**Assembly**

***Decoration***

Prepare a decoration for the interior of the terrine. Spread a sheet of barding fat, the same length as the mold, on the work surface. Spread with meat strips mixed with forcemeat. Roll the fat around the forcemeat to make a cylinder about 3 cm (1 in) across. Place in the freezer for 15 minutes to harden.

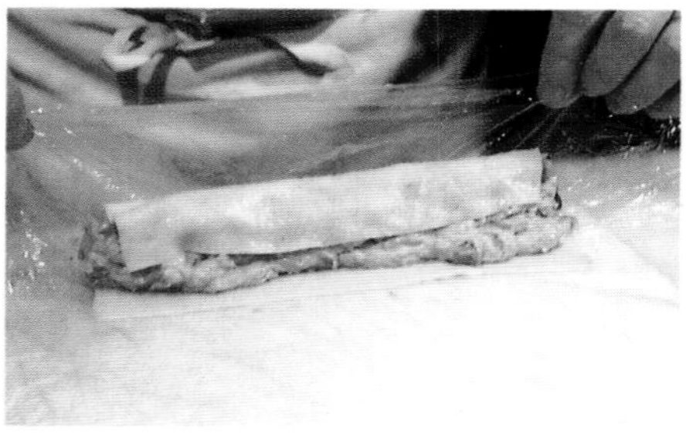

***Filling the Mold***

Line the mold with barding fat and fill halfway with forcemeat, lining up the meat strips lengthwise as much as possible.

Place the cylinder in the center and fill the mold to the top with forcemeat (lining up the meat strips).

Fold over the barding fat to cover the top. The skin from the chicken can be placed on top for extra flavor.

**Storage and Presentation**

This terrine will keep for 8-10 days in the refrigerator. To store for up to 3 weeks, place the chilled terrine (24 hours in the refrigerator) in a vacuum pouch.

The chicken terrine with lemon can be presented in the mold or unmolded and glazed with light-colored aspic. Lemon in various forms (zest, sections etc.) would be an appropriate decoration.

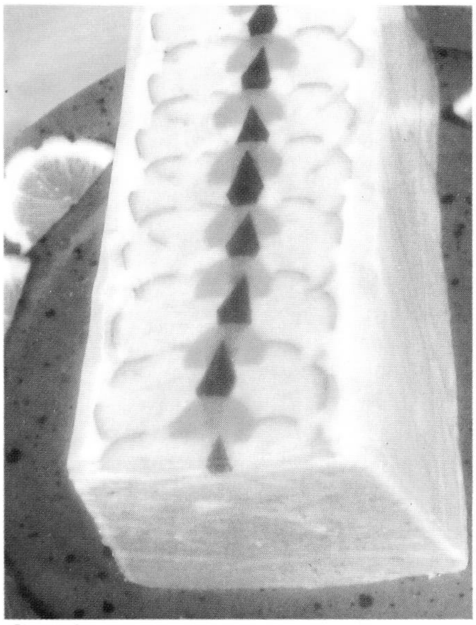

**Cooking**

The terrine can be cooked immediately or covered and refrigerated for several hours to allow the flavors to develop.

Cook in a water bath. Place in a hot oven (180-200 °C (375-400 F)) and brown the top. Turn the heat down to 100-110 (225 F) and cook until the internal temperature is 76-78 °C (170 F).

Pour off the fatty juices rendered during cooking and replace these juices with full-flavored chicken stock that has been boiled, skimmed and strained.

Place a light weight (300 g (10 oz)) on top and cool quickly.

# Terrine of Quail with Sweetbreads

**Introduction**

Without question this is one of the best terrines featuring luxurious ingredients. Even though the quail are farm-raised and therefore not quite as flavorful as wild birds, they are still a delicious match for the subtle flavor of the sweetbreads.

Molding the mixture in a terrine mold is an easier procedure than reforming the birds as in the recipe for " stuffed quail with raisins ".

**Equipment**

Knives, chopper, braising pan, bowls and hotel pans, plastic scraper, conical sieve, sauté pan, casserole

**Ingredients**

8 Quail (180-200 g) (6-7 oz)
1 kg (2.2 lbs) sweetbreads
500 g (1 lb) pork jowl
500 g (1 lb) lean veal
100 g (3 1/2 oz) chicken livers
100 g (3 1/2 oz) goose fat
1 calves' brain
100 ml (scant 1/2 cup) heavy cream
100 g (3 1/2 oz) fresh bread crumbs
100 g (3 1/2 oz) shallots
100 g (3 1/2 oz) mushrooms
100 g (3 1/2 oz) carrots
3 eggs
Aromatic vegetables
Port
Armagnac

*Seasonings (per kg (2.2 lbs))*

18 g (generous 1/2 oz) curing salt (sodium nitrite with fine salt)
2 g (1/16 oz) sugar or dextrose
2 g (1/16 oz) white pepper
5 g (1/64 oz) nutmeg

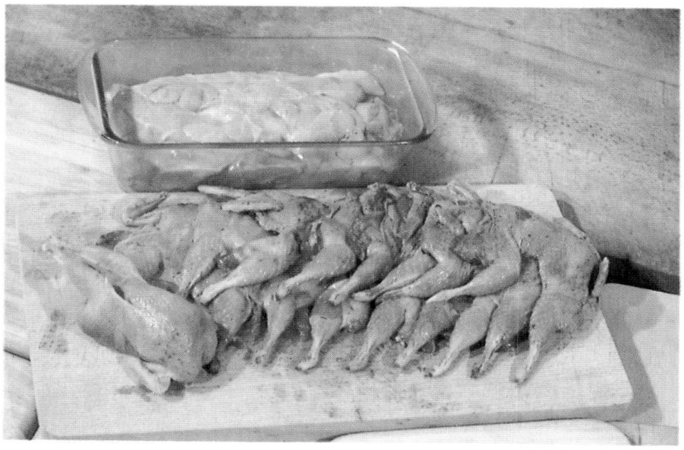

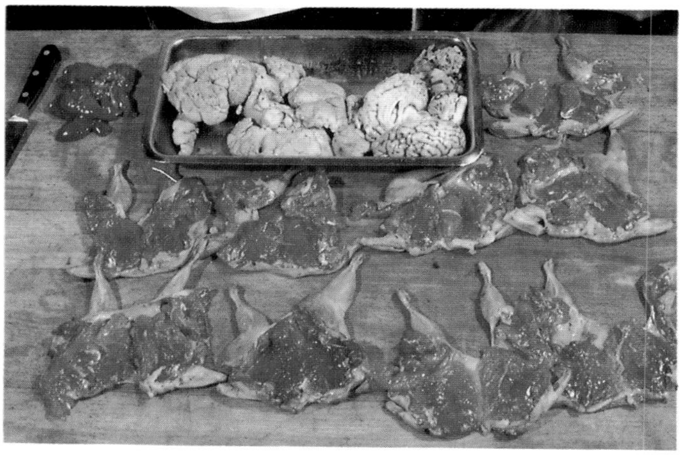

**Preparing the Ingredients**

***The Quail***

Pass the bird over a flame to remove all remaining feathers and carefully remove the innards.
Bone the quail from the back. Remove all the bones (wings and legs). Leave the breast meat whole (with skin attached).
Coat the quail with the corresponding amount of seasonings, sprinkle with armagnac and marinate for 12 hours.
Make a stock with the bones and carcasses of the quail:
Chop the bones (including the feet and heads) and brown in a little goose fat.
Add aromatic vegetables (carrots, white part of leek, onions) and brown.
Pour off the fat and deglaze with armagnac.
Cover the bones with pork stock and bring to a boil, skimming all fat and impurities that rise to the surface.
Add a bouquet garni and lower the heat to a simmer.
Cook for 2 1/2-3 hours, skimming occasionally.
Strain the stock through a conical sieve, pressing on the bones and vegetables to extract maximum flavor.
Reduce 1 liter to a glaze and refrigerate the remaining stock.

***The Sweetbreads***

Degorge the sweetbreads in cold water for 6 hours. (Change the water occasionally.)
Trim fat then blanch in boiling, salted water for 4-5 minutes.
Refresh in cold water, drain and pat dry.

Braise the sweetbreads:
Brush a coat of goose fat on the braising pan.
Prepare the aromatic vegetables: onions, carrots, white of leek, celery, parsley, thyme and bay leaf and place them in the braising pan.
Set the sweetbreads on the bed of vegetables, season with salt and pepper and place a few nuggets of butter on top.
Brown in a hot oven (180-200 °C (375-400 F)).

Pour veal or chicken stock over the sweetbreads (enough to cover the vegetables). Turn the sweetbreads and brown the other side. They should remain pink; they will be cooked again in the terrine.
Refrigerate the sweetbreads and strain the braising liquid.
Reduce half of the liquid to a glaze and add to the reduced quail stock (to be later added to the forcemeat). The remaining juice is added to the quail stock which will be poured over the cooked terrine.

***The Forcemeat***

Trim the skin and glands from the pork jowl and cut into cubes (2.5 cm (1 in).

Cut the veal into strips (the veal can be trimmings from another preparation). Coat the meats with the corresponding seasonings, sprinkle with port and marinate in the refrigerator for 12 hours.

***The Calves' Brain***

Wash and trim the thin outer covering from the brain.

Poach in salted water with a bouquet garni (or chicken stock).

Cool the cooked brain quickly and completely.

***The " Gratin "***

Cook the shallots and carrots in goose fat. Add the trimmed livers and brown quickly on all sides (the livers should remain very pink).

Add chopped parsley and a little madeira, cook a little.

Cool quickly, set aside.

**Making the Forcemeat**

In the chopper, process the jowl and veal along with the " gratin " of liver.

Add the eggs, the stock reductions, cream and bread crumbs.

Process until the mixture is smooth and unctuous. The temperature of the mixture should not exceed 15 °C (60 F) during processing. Chill the bowl of the chopper if necessary.

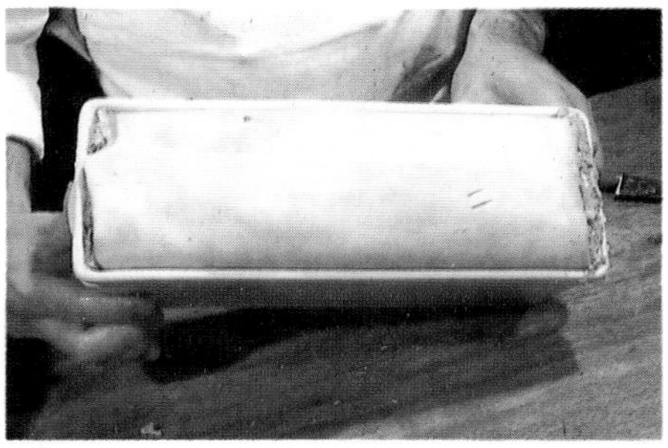

## Assembly

Line the mold with barding fat.
Cut the cooked brain into cubes (1.5 cm (about 1/2 in)).
Set aside 300 g (10 oz) of forcemeat and blend the rest with the strips of meat (lèches).
Cut a sheet of barding fat the same length as the mold and spread it with an even layer of forcemeat.
Arrange the sweetbreads in the center and roll the barding fat and forcemeat around the sweetbreads to form a cylinder that will be placed in the center of the terrine.
Roll the cylinder in a sheet of plastic wrap and tie the two ends, pulling tight to give the " roulade " a smooth and even shape. Place in the freezer for 20 minutes to harden.
Gently fold the cubes of brain into the forcemeat and fill 1/3 of the mold.
Blend the 300 g (10 oz) of reserved forcemeat with the breast meat and arrange an even layer of this mixture in the mold (any " extra " breast meat can be placed on the top).
Remove the plastic wrap from the sweetbreads and place the cylinder in the center of the terrine.
Fill the mold with the remaining forcemeat.
Fold the barding fat over the top to cover.

## Cooking

Place the mold in a water bath and place in a hot oven (180-200 °C (375-400 F)). Turn the heat down to 100-110 °C (225 F).
Cook until the internal temperature is 76-78 °C (170 F).
Drain the fatty juices rendered during cooking.
Replace these juices with the quail stock and braising juices (from the sweetbreads) which have been brought to a boil, skimmed and strained.
Place a light weight on top and cool quickly.

## Storage

This terrine will keep for 8 days in the refrigerator.
As with all terrines, the storage time can be prolonged by placing the cooled terrine in a vacuum pouch.

## Presentation

The terrine can be served directly from the mold. Clean around the edges, decorate the top and glaze with aspic. Note that the terrine will stay fresher if left in the mold.
To present the terrine unmolded, pour clarified aspic into the bottom of the cleaned mold.
Arrange a decoration on this layer of aspic. Pour in a little more aspic and slide the terrine back into the mold. Chill for 6 hours to set the aspic and unmold onto a platter.

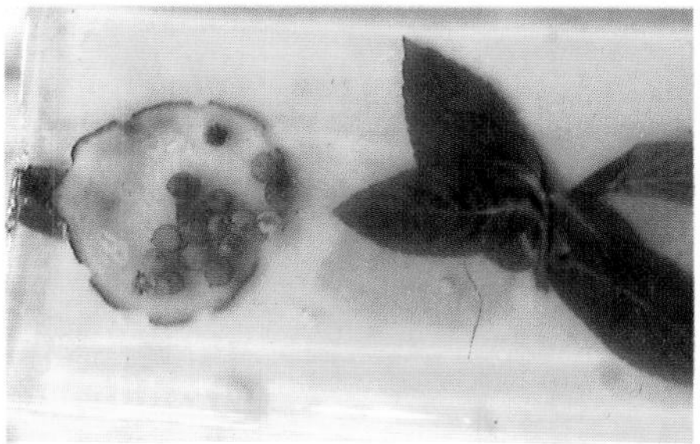

# Turkey Mousse with Vegetables

## Introduction

There is a growing demand for charcuterie products with a lower fat content. This mousse featuring turkey with an addition of vegetables marries ingredients with little or no fat in a flavorful blend of tastes.

Turkey is the leanest of all meats and the vegetables have practically no fat at all.

Here is a charcuterie product suitable for the strictest of diets.

## Equipment

Knives, horizontal chopper, casserole, sauté pan, spoon, mold, platter

## Ingredients

***The Forcemeat***
2.5 kg (5.5 lbs) turkey breast
5 eggs
500 ml (2 cups) heavy cream

***The Vegetables***
750 g (1.5 lbs) broccoli
2 red bell peppers
2 medium zucchini
500 g (1 lb) carrots
500 g (1 lb) green beans

*Seasonings (per kilo (2.2 lbs)*
*(for the forcemeat)*

18 g (generous 1/2 oz) curing salt sodium nitrite with fine salt)
2 g (1/16 oz) sugar or dextrose
2 g (1/16 oz) white pepper

**Preparing the Ingredients**

*The Turkey*

Trim the large nerve that runs the length of each turkey breast, cut in cubes, then season with curing salt and sugar.

A little port or madeira can be sprinkled over the meat. The recipe does not list any alcohol to make the dish more dietetic.

***The Vegetables***

*The Broccoli*

The broccoli is rinsed then cooked " al dente " by steaming or poaching in salted water. Refresh immediately in cold water, drain and set aside.

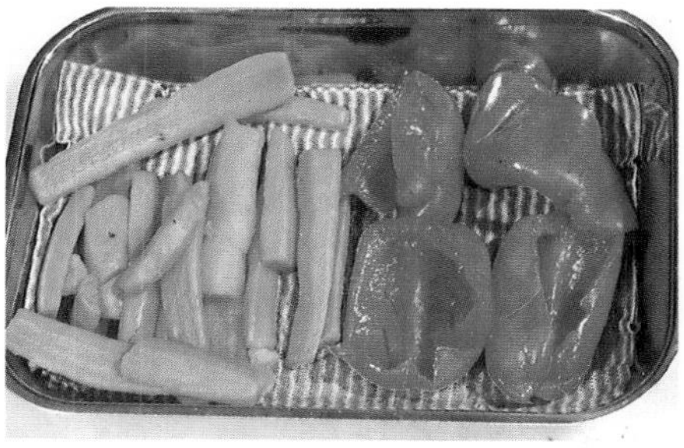

*The Peppers*

Place the peppers in a hot oven to loosen the skin. Peel then cut in half and remove the seeds.

The peppers need no further cooking. Cut into strips.

*The Zucchini*

Wash the zucchini and cut them lengthwise.
Cook in boiling salted water for just a few minutes until cooked but firm.

*The Carrots*

Choose carrots that are all the same size. Peel and rinse the carrots.
Cut in half lengthwise and steam or cook in boiling salted water until " al dente ".

*The Green Beans*

Wash the beans and remove the ends and strings. Cook in boiling salted water just long enough to make them tender but still firm.
Refresh in cold water to stop the cooking and set the color.

It is important that all the vegetables be just barely cooked. They will cook again when the terrine is cooked in the oven. If the vegetables are too soft, they will become mushy in the final product.
The appearance of each slice as well as the taste would be adversely affected by overcooked vegetables.

**Making the Mousse**

Chop the marinated turkey in the chopper, add the eggs then the cream and process until smooth. The temperature should not exceed 14-15 °C (60 F); chill the bowl of the chopper if necessary.

Season with pepper and nutmeg, taking into account that the vegetables will absorb some of the seasoning.

The vegetables should not need any extra salt because they were cooked in salted water. However if the vegetables were steamed (which retains more of the vegetables' flavor) the forcemeat may need a little more salt to compensate for the unsalted vegetables.

**Assembly**

Butter the mold.
Spread a thin layer of the mousse on the bottom.
Arrange the carrots then cover with mousse.
Line up the green beans neatly, pressing them gently into the mousse. Cover with a thin layer of mousse.
Arrange the broccoli and press on it gently. Cover with a thin layer of mousse.
Continue with the remaining vegetables, layering each with a little turkey mousse in between.
The order of the layers or the pattern of the vegetables can vary and be an expression of the chef's creativity.

**Cooking**

Cook the assembled terrine immediately.

Place the terrine (in a water bath) in a 180-190 °C (350-375 F) oven then lower the heat to 100-120 °C (225 F).

Cook until the internal temperature reaches 75-76 °C (170 F).

Place a weight on the cooked terrine (500 g (1 lb)) and cool quickly.

**Storage**

The turkey mousse will keep for 1 week covered in the refrigerator. The storage time can be prolonged by placing the cooled terrine in a vacuum pouch.

**Presentation**

The mousse can be unmolded and can be also decorated, glazed with aspic and sliced directly from the mold.

# Saddle of Rabbit with Mild Garlic

## Introduction

Garlic has long been an ingredient in charcuterie preparations as well as medical " cures ".

In modern times, it is no longer acceptable to smell of garlic like in the days of King Henry IV.

Therefore modern recipes include much less garlic than their ancient counterparts.

There are techniques of preparing garlic to diminish the undesirable side effects. The garlic is this recipe is prepared so that it contributes a delicate flavor without the inconveniences.

**Equipment**

Knives, cleaver, food processor, sauté pan, plastic scraper, conical sieve, casserole, mold

**Ingredients**

1 rabbit (2.5 kg (5.5 lbs))
2.5 kg (5.5 lbs) lean pork
2 kg (4.4 lbs) belly and jowl
4 eggs
100 g (3 1/2 oz) shallots
250 g (1/2 lb) rabbit liver
100 g (3 1/2 oz) carrots
250 g (1/2 lb) mushrooms
300 g (10 oz) garlic
Chopped parsley
" Marc de Bourgogne " or cognac
Barding fat
Pork stock

*Seasonings (per kg (2.2 lbs))*

18 g (generous 1/2 oz) curing salt (sodium nitrite with fine salt)
2 g (1/16 oz) white pepper
1 g (1/32 oz) four spice powder
0.5 g (1/64 oz) nutmeg
Thyme
Sage
Tarragon

**Preparing the Ingredients**

***The Rabbit***

A rabbit weighing 2.5 kg (5.5 lbs) will yield about 1.5 kg (3.3 lbs) of meat. (This recipe is based on the boned weight.)

Bone the rabbit completely, keeping the filets whole (boned from the saddle).

Cut the large pieces from the thighs and shoulder into strips (lèches) and set aside all the meat trimmings for the forcemeat.

Make a stock with the bones and carcass of the rabbit:

Chop the bones with a cleaver and brown in a little goose fat.

Add sliced onions and carrots and lightly brown.

Pour off the fat and deglaze with white wine.

Cover with pork stock and bring to a boil, skimming all fat and impurities that rise to the surface.

Cook for 2 1/2-3 hours then strain through a conical sieve, pressing on the bones and vegetables to extract maximum flavor.

Reduce 1 liter (about 1 qt) to a glaze and cool the remaining stock.

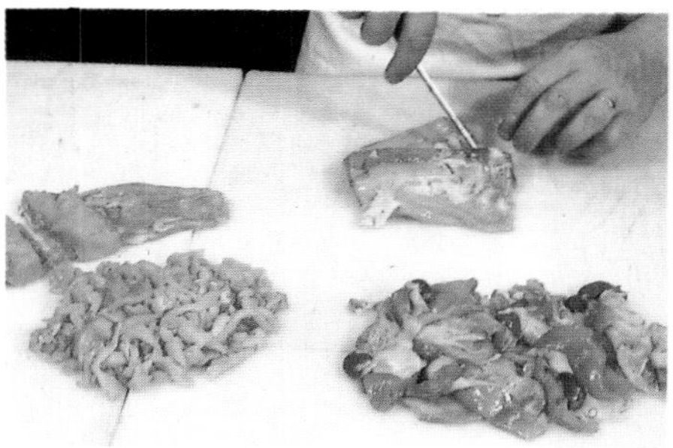

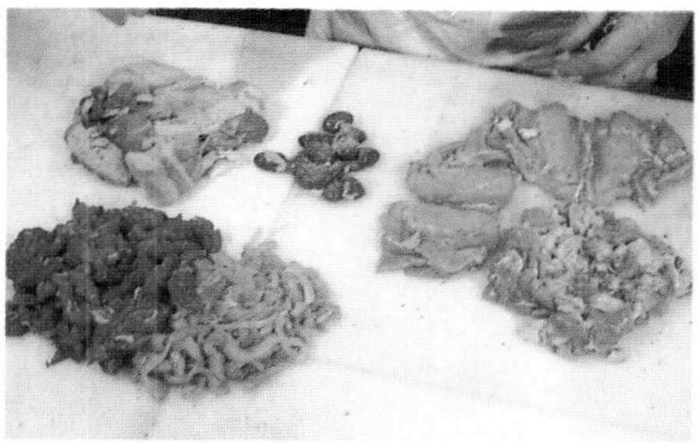

***The Pork***

Choose lean pork from a top quality cut, trim and cut in strips (lèches).

Trim the pork belly and jowl and cut in cubes (2.5 cm (1 in)).

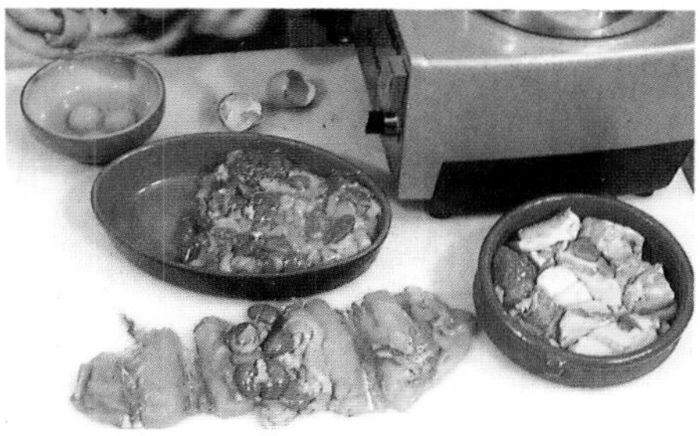

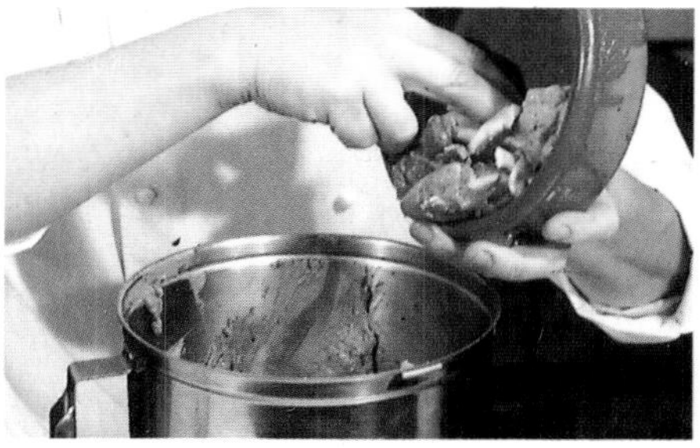

***The Marinade***

In one stainless steel recipient place the meats (rabbit (filets and pieces) and strips of pork) and in another place the forcemeat (jowl and belly) with the gratin. Season with the corresponding amounts of curing salt and spices, cover and marinate in the refrigerator for 12-24 hours.

***The " Gratin "***

With the rabbit liver (combined with chicken livers to make 250 g (1/2 lb)), make a gratin:

Cook the sliced shallots and carrots in goose fat.

Add the sliced mushrooms then the pieces of liver and brown quickly on all sides. The liver should remain very pink.

Add chopped parsley and madeira and cook a few minutes.

Cool the mixture quickly. Marinate the cooled gratin with the forcemeat (belly and jowl).

***The Garlic***

Choose plump heads of white or purple garlic and peel the cloves.

Cut each clove in half and remove the green sprout or " germ " which can be very bitter.

Chop the garlic in the food processor; it should be finely chopped (1 mm (very tiny dice--not puréed)).

Bring 2 liters (about 2 qts) of salted (10 g (1/3 oz salt)) water to a boil.

Poach the chopped garlic for four minutes.

Drain and set aside in the refrigerator.

The poaching process transforms the overwhelming odor of the garlic and gives it a mild, delicate flavor.

**Making the Forcemeat**

Process the marinated belly and jowl with gratin. Add the eggs, stock reduction and the garlic.

Process until smooth making sure that the temperature of the mixture does not exceed 14-15 °C (60 F).

**Assembly**

Cut a sheet of barding fat the same length as the mold and spread it with a thin layer of forcemeat.

Place the filets in the center of the barding fat. Mix the meat strips with the remaining forcemeat and add

enough of this mixture to make a cylinder about 5-6 cm (about 2 in) across.

Roll to make an even cylinder, wrap in plastic wrap and tie the ends tightly to maintain the shape.

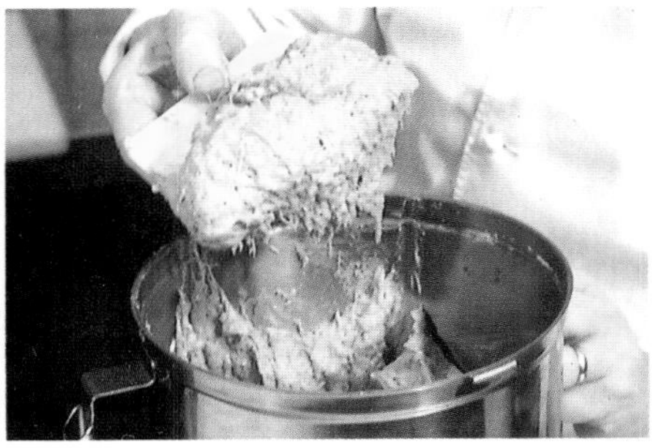

Place in the freezer for 30 minutes to harden.

Line the mold with barding fat.

Spoon a layer of forcemeat with meat strips in the bottom of the mold (about 2 cm (3/4 in)).

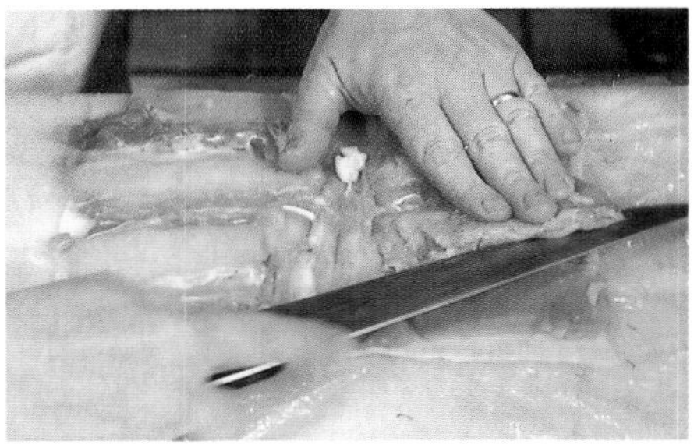

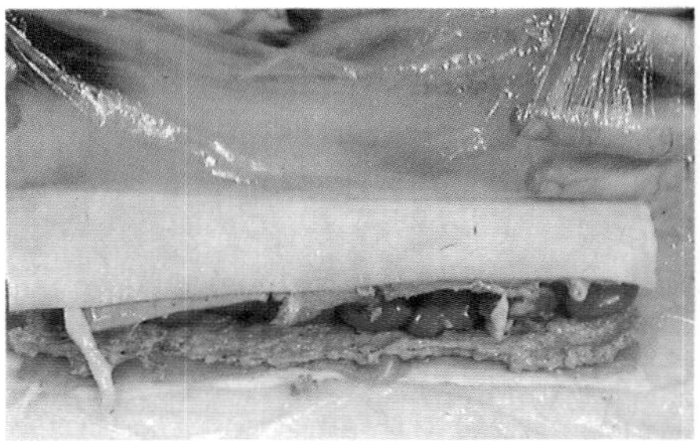

Remove the plastic wrapping from the cylinder and place it in the center of the terrine.

Fill the mold with the remaining forcemeat and fold the barding fat over the top to cover.

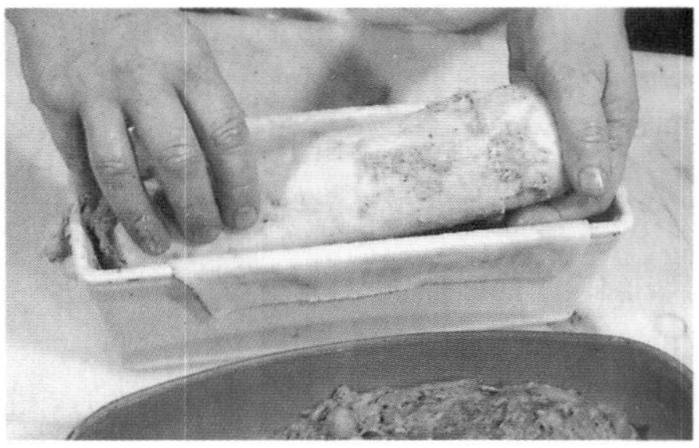

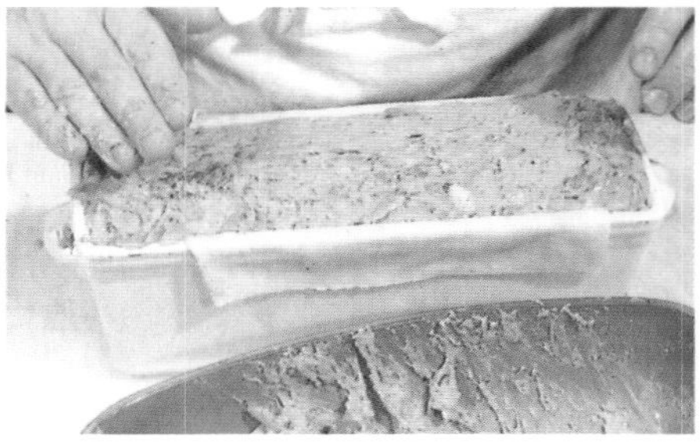

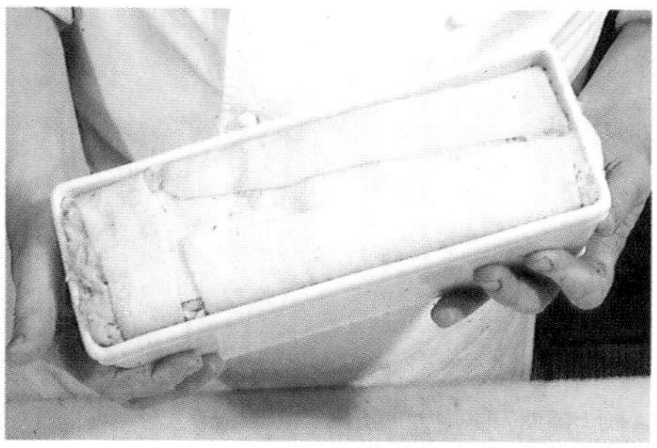

## Cooking

The terrine can be cooked immediately following assembly or placed in the refrigerator to " mellow " and allow the flavor to develop.

Cook the terrine in a water bath. Place in a hot oven (180-200 °C (375-400 F)). After the top browns a little, turn the heat down to 100-110 °C (225 F) and cook until the internal temperature is 76-78 °C (170 F).

Pour off the fatty juices rendered during cooking.

Replace these juices with rabbit stock that has been brought to a boil, skimmed and strained.

Place a light weight on top and cool quickly.

## Storage

This terrine will keep 6-8 days in the refrigerator.

The storage time can be prolonged to 15-18 days if the cooled terrine is placed in a vacuum pouch.

## Presentation

The terrine can be sliced directly from the mold. Decorate the top with poached garlic sliced thinly and other pieces of blanched vegetables then glaze with carified aspic.

To present the terrine unmolded, pour aspic into the bottom of the cleaned mold.

Arrange a decoration on this layer of aspic. Pour in a little more aspic and slide the terrine back into the mold. Chill for 6 hours to set the aspic and unmold onto a platter.

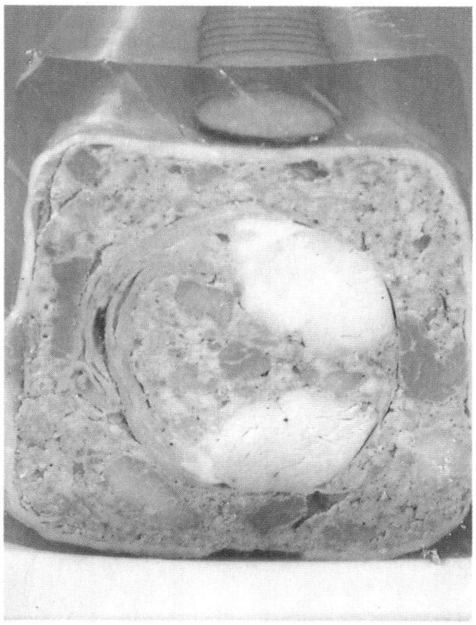

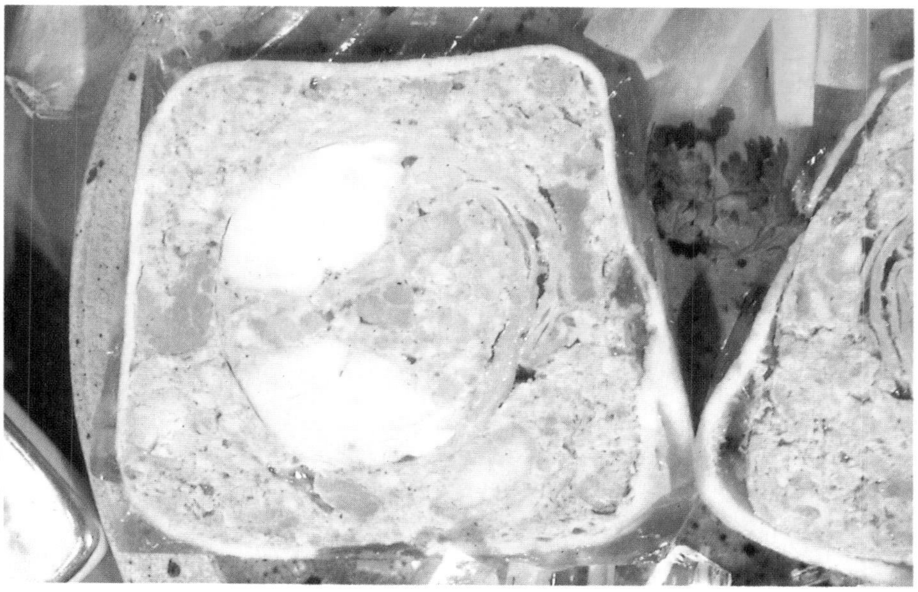

# Rabbit Terrine with Mushrooms

## Introduction

Rabbit and mushrooms is a classic combination that is used in cooked dishes as well as charcuterie.

In cooked dishes the mushrooms are usually a garnish, in charcuterie mushrooms are used to flavor the "gratin" that is often added to forcemeat or are folded into the mixture separately.

To attain the full flavor from the mushrooms, they must be very fresh.

## Equipment

Knives, vertical chopper (food processor), stainless steel bowls and hotel pans, kettle or large stockpot, platter

## Ingredients

1 rabbit with liver
2.5 kg (5.5 lbs)
2.5 kg (5.5 lbs) pork belly and jowl
3 eggs
800 g (1 lb 10 oz) white mushrooms
500 g (1 lb) "gratin" (p. 15)
Aromatic vegetables
Pork stock
Dry white wine
Butter and oil

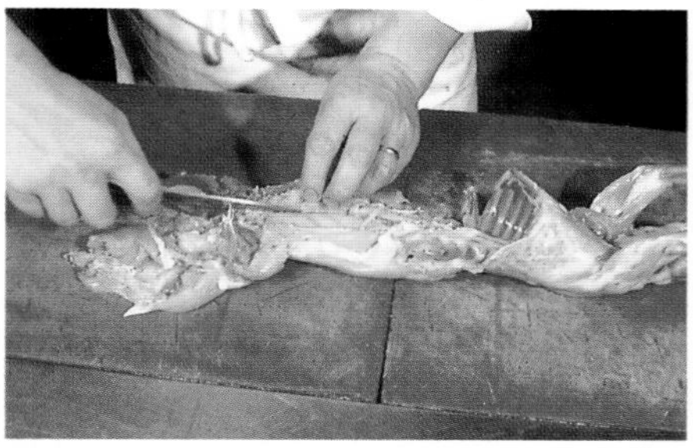

*Seasonings (per kg (2.2 lbs))*

18 g (generous 1/2 oz) curing salt (sodium nitrite with fine salt)
2 g (1/16 oz) sugar or dextrose
2 g (1/16 oz) ground pepper
1 g (1/32 oz) four spice powder

**Preparing the Ingredients**

Choose a rabbit that is 2 1/2-3 months old weighing about 2.5 kg (about 5.5 lbs). This size rabbit will provide about 1.5 kg (3 1/4 lbs) of meat (with liver). This is the weight used in this recipe.

Note that rabbit meat is low in fat, it can be used to make many delicious low fat dishes.

To make a forcemeat for this terrine the lean rabbit must be blended with pork belly and jowl to add moisture.

Bone the rabbit and keep the filets whole to be used as a garnish in the terrine. Cut the remaining meat into small even pieces. Refrigerate until marinated.

***The Stock***

Make a stock with the bones and carcass of the rabbit :

Chop the bones and brown in a little lard.

Prepare aromatic vegetables (2 carrots, 2 onions, 2 stalks of celery, large bouquet garni, 2 cloves). Add to the bones and brown.

Pour off the fat and deglaze with dry white wine.

Reduce the wine to a glaze then add 4 liters (about 4 quarts) pork stock to cover the bones.

Bring to a boil and skim all fat and impurities that rise to the surface.

Lower the heat and simmer for 2 1/2 hours, skimming occasionally.

Strain the stock through a conical sieve, pressing on the bones and vegetables to extract maximum flavor.

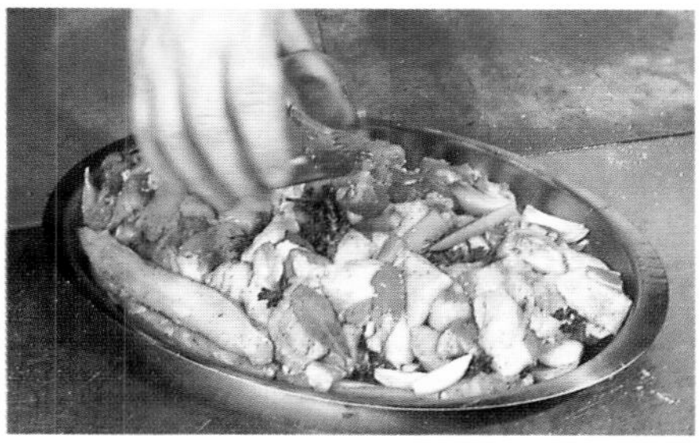

***The Pork***

Trim the belly and jowl and sort the meat so that the ratio is about 1/3 fat and 2/3 lean.

Cut in even dice (about 2.5 cm (1 in)).

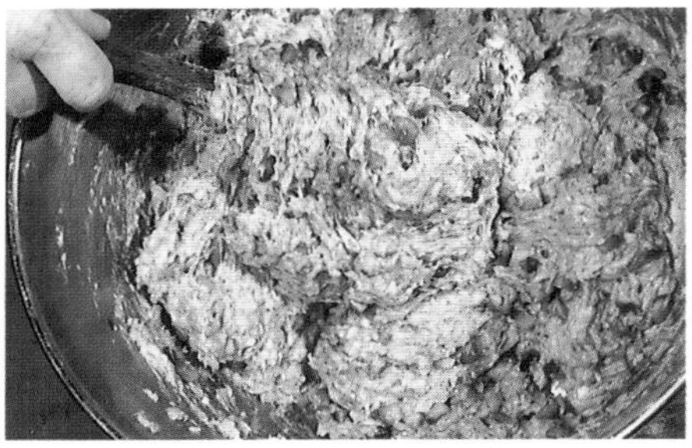

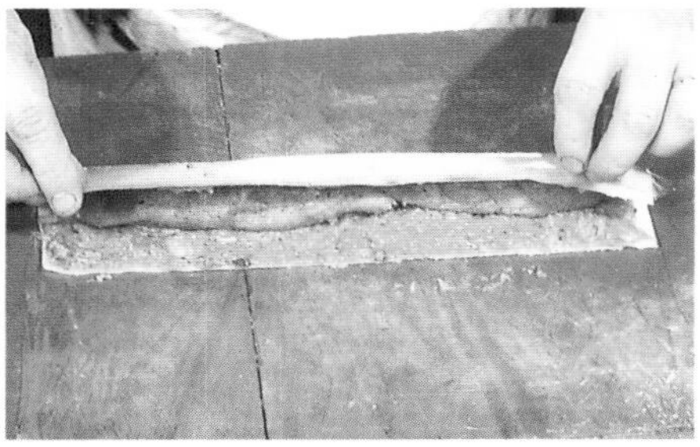

### *The Marinade*

Prepare aromatic vegetables (carrots, onions, shallots, celery, thyme, parsley and bay leaf). Cut the vegetables in thick slices so that they can be retrieved easily from the marinade.

Add the rabbit meat and pork to the vegetables, toss with the curing salt and sugar and sprinkle with dry white wine.

Marinate in the refrigerator for at least 12 hours.

### *The Mushrooms*

Remove the sandy stem of the mushrooms.

Wash in a large basin of cold water, let the sand and dirt settle to the bottom. Lift the mushrooms out and repeat the process to ensure that the mushrooms are clean.

Slice or cut in large dice.

Brown the mushrooms lightly in oil and butter (half and half). Continue to cook to evaporate the liquid rendered by the mushrooms.

Drain the mushrooms and reserve the liquid.

## Procedure

### *The Forcemeat*

Add the mushroom liquid to 1 liter (about 1 qt) of the rabbit stock.

Reduce by 3/4; almost to a glaze.

Cool but do not let the gelatinous liquid solidify.

Purée the gratin and the rabbit liver in the food processor.

Add the marinated pork and small pieces of rabbit (not the filets). (Save the vegetables from the marinade.)

Process the meats until coarsely ground, add the eggs and the stock reduction.

Process again to blend and chop the meats to a medium " grain ". Stir in the mushrooms (by hand or in a mixer at low speed).

The mushrooms should be evenly distributed and the mixture should be homogeneous.

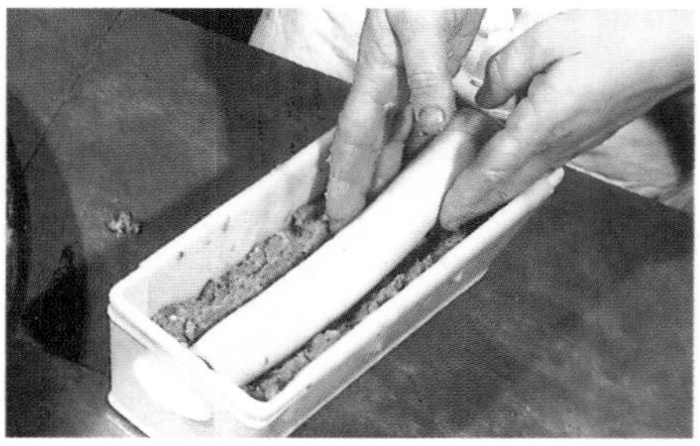

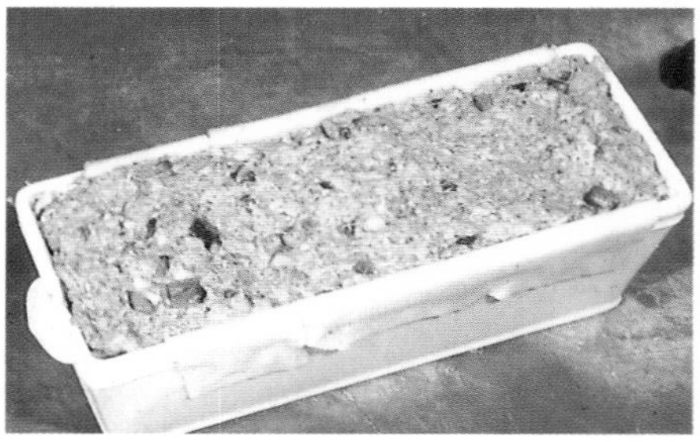

### *The Garnish*

The filets are wrapped in barding fat to make an attractive garnish for the middle of the terrine.

Spread out a sheet of barding fat the same length as the mold.

Spread a little of the forcemeat on the barding fat and place the rabbit filets in the center.

To form a perfect cylinder, wrap in parchment paper or plastic wrap and tie the ends.

Place in the freezer for 15-20 minutes to stiffen.

### Assembly

Line the mold with a sheet of barding fat and fill halfway with the forcemeat.

Place the cylinder of rabbit filets in the center then fill the mold with the remaining forcemeat.

Fold over the barding fat to cover the top.

### Cooking

Place the terrine in a water bath and start the cooking in a hot oven (180-200 $^0$C (375-400 F)).

When the top has browned a little, lower the heat to 120 $^0$C (250 F).

The terrine is cooked when the probe thermometer inserted in the center registers 75-76 $^0$C (170 F).

Drain the fatty juices from the cooked terrine and replace with rabbit stock that has been brought to a boil, skimmed and strained.

Place a light weight on top and cool quickly.

### Storage

The rabbit terrine with mushrooms will keep in the refrigerator for 10 days.

When the terrine is completely chilled it can be placed in a vacuum pouch to store the product for 2-3 weeks.

As with all the terrines, the taste is best after about 2-3 days. However only the experts can tell if a terrine has been stored longer than that.

### Presentation

The terrine can be sliced directly from the mold. Decorate the top and glaze with aspic.

To serve unmolded, clean the mold and pour a little aspic in the bottom. Arrange the decoration on this layer of aspic, pour in a little slightly thickened aspic and replace the terrine.

Refrigerate for a few hours to set the aspic, unmold and serve on a platter.

# Terrine of Hare with Olives

**Introduction**

Olives are often served with a slice of terrine as an accompaniment. Here olives are incorporated in the terrine and the taste marries well with the rabbit. Other meats are delicious when cooked with olives--pork, duck and chicken for example. In this recipe olives are used for their flavor as well as for the lovely color and design they add to each slice. The green of the olives is especially pretty with the rosy color of the meat.

**Equipment**

Paring knife, chopper, casserole, conical sieve, large bowl, terrine mold.

**Ingredients**

1 rabbit with liver
Pork (2/3 lean-1/3 fat)
250 g (1/2 lb) green olives
Aromatic vegetables
Pork stock
Dry white wine
Eggs
80 g (2 1/2 oz) shallots
Barding fat.

*Seasonings (per kilo (2.2 lbs))*

18 g (1/2 oz) curing salt
2 g (1/16 g oz) sugar or dextrose
2 g (1/16 g oz) ground pepper
1 g (1/32 g oz) four spice poweder

The weight of the rabbit will determine the quantities of the other ingredients. The ratio for these are given on the following pages.

**Preparing the Ingredients**

***The Marinade***

Remove all the meat from the carcass of the rabbit keeping the tenderloins whole.

Weigh the rabbit meat and use twice that weight in pork (trimmings from the belly, pork jowl).

Set aside the tenderloins and liver and cut the remaining rabbit meat and the pork into 2 cm (3/4 in) cubes.

Place the meats (and liver) in separate stainless steel recipients and season with curing salt, sugar and a little dry white wine. Cover and refrigerate for 12 hours.

***The Rabbit Stock***

Chop up the rabbit bones and carcass with a cleaver.

Heat some lard in a large heavy casserole and add the bones.

Brown the bones over medium high heat and add two sliced onions and three sliced carrots and continue cooking to brown the vegetables.

Deglaze the pot with dry white wine and reduce to cook off the alcohol. Add 4 L (about 4 qts) pork stock.

Add a bouquet garni and slowly bring to a boil, skimming all impurities and fat that rise to the surface.

Lower the heat so that the stock is

at a low boil and cook for 2 1/2 hours, skimming from time to time.

Strain the stock through a conical sieve, pressing on the bones to extract the maximum flavor. Reduce one liter (1 qt) of the stock to about 100 ml (scant 1/2 cup).

Set aside the glaze and the remaining stock in the refrigerator.

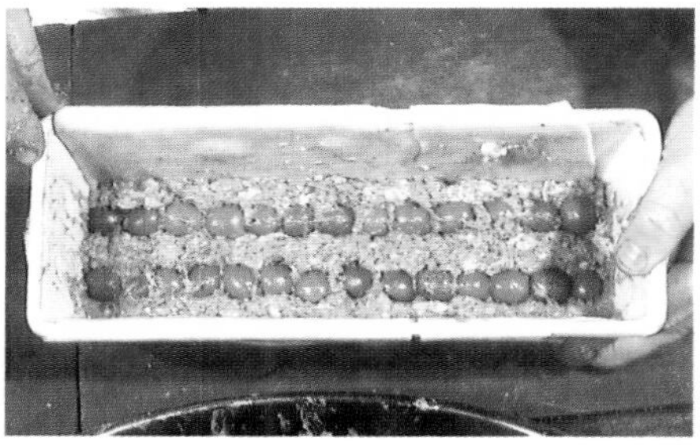

***The Olives***

It is necessary to soak the olives in cold water for 12 hours to remove excess brine.

It is recommended to not substitute black olives in this recipe because they have a tendency to discolor the meat.

Remove the pits after they have soaked.

**Procedure**

***The Forcemeat***

Remove the rabbit liver from the marinade. Peel and slice the shallots and cook them in lard until soft but not browned.

Add the liver and brown it quickly on all sides. It should remain very pink inside. Set aside in the refrigerator.

Process the cooled liver with the cubes of marinated rabbit until smooth.

Add the marinated pork and the eggs (2 per kg (2.2 lbs) of forcemeat) and lastly the meat glaze and spices.

Process until the forcemeat is the desired texture.

It may be necessary to blend the ingredients in a mixer to avoid chopping the meats too finely.

***The Olives***

Use a pastry bag with a small tip (6 mm 1/4 in)) to fill each olive with forcemeat.

Set aside in the refrigerator.

***The Rabbit Tenderloins***

Cut a rectangle of barding fat the length of the mold. Spread a thin layer of forcemeat on the barding fat and place tenderloins in the center.

Roll the barding fat neatly around the meat to make a cylinder with the tenderloin in the middle.

**Assembly**

Line the mold with sheets of

barding fat. Spread a layer about 2 cm (3/4 in) thick on the bottom of the mold.

Arrange two rows of stuffed olives down the length of the mold then fill the mold halfway with another layer of forcemeat.

Place the cylinder of tenderloins in the center (pressing on it so that it is in the middle of the finished terrine). Cover with forcemeat then arrange two more rows of olives (in the same position as the first rows of olives). Fill the mold to the top with forcemeat and fold over the edges of barding fat. So that each slice is symmetrical (and identical) it is important to place the garnishes at even intervals and in neat rows.

If time allows, cover the assembled terrine with plastic wrap and refrigerate for 12 hours so that the flavors have a chance to " mellow " and develop.

**Cooking**

The terrine is cooked in the classic way – in a water bath in the oven.

Place in an oven preheated to 180-200 °C (375-400 F) and cook until the fat on the top browns.

Place a baking sheet on top and lower the heat to 110-120 °C (200 F).

The terrine is cooked when a probe thermometer inserted into the center registers 76-78 °C (170-175 F).

It is important to remember that the terrine will continue to cook after it is removed from the oven. Since the temperature will rise another 1-2 degrees before it starts to actually cool, it is important to closely monitor the cooking. This is a general guideline for all charcuterie products.

Pour off the fatty juices rendered during cooking. Replace them with the reserved rabbit stock. Bring this stock to a boil, skim the impurities, strain then pour it over the terrine until it comes to the top.

Place a light weight on top to compact the terrine slightly.

Cool as quickly as possible. Remove the weight, cover with plastic wrap and store in the refrigerator (2-4 °C (35 F)).

This terrine will keep for about 8 days. The storage can be prolonged by placing the cooled terrine in a vacuum pouch.

**Presentation**

***In the mold:*** It is possible to keep the terrine in the mold and cut slices to order. The barding fat is removed and the top is decorated (geometric patterns featuring green olives for example). It is then coated with a thin layer of aspic.

***Unmolded:*** The terrine is unmolded and the barding fat is removed and the surface is wiped off. The mold is cleaned and a thin layer of aspic is added. Before the aspic sets, arrange a decoration of cut-out vegetables and green olives.

Slide the terrine back into the mold and refrigerate for several hours to set the aspic around the terrine. Dip the mold in a basin of warm water to loosen the aspic and unmold onto a serving platter.

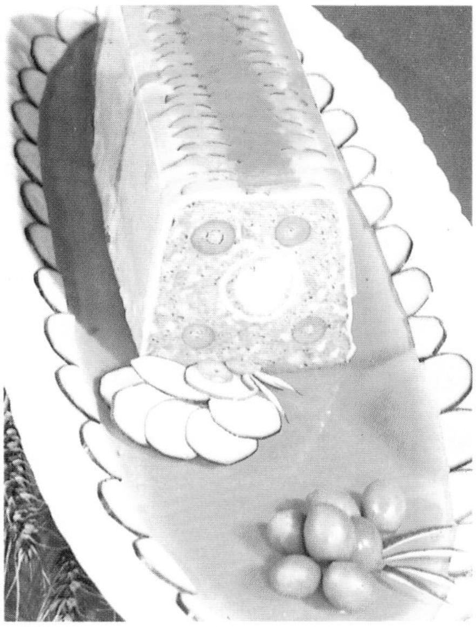

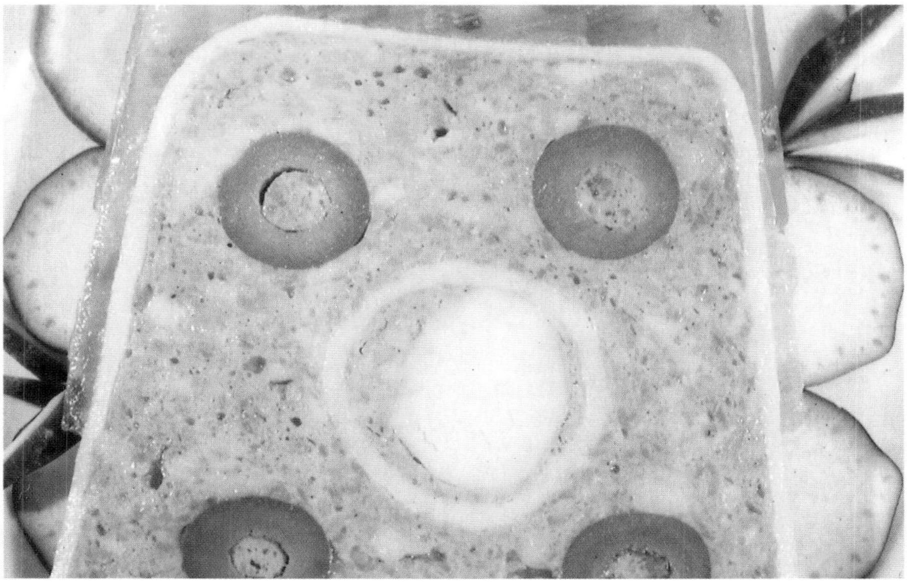

# Squab with Foie Gras

### Introduction

This is a very luxurious preparation. The reformed bird is lovely and the substantial amount of foie gras used for each serving makes it delicious.

The rich taste of the squab marries well with the foie gras; a favorite combination of many connoisseurs.

### Equipment

Knives, hotel pan, horizontal chopper, cleaver, aluminum foil

### Ingredients

4 squab
800 g (1 lb 10 oz) foie gras
800 g (1 lb 10 oz) forcemeat (pork belly and jowl)
200 g (7 oz) chicken livers
100 g (3 1/2 oz) shallots
100 g (3 1/2 oz) carrots
100 g (3 1/2 oz) fatback (lightly salted)
150 g (5 oz) mushrooms
150 ml (generous 1/2 cup) cream
1 egg
Cognac
Madeira
Truffles
(30 g (1 oz) per kg (2.2 lbs))

*Seasonings*

18 g (generous 1/2 oz) curing salt (sodium nitrite with fine salt)
1 g (1/32 oz) white pepper
1 g (1/32 oz) four spice powder

**Preparing the Ingredients**

***The Squab***

The squab used here is farm-raised. In France wild squab (pigeon) is hunted (controversial practice) and could be used for this dish.
The taste of the wild bird is very delicate but it is almost impossible to find them on the market.

The farm-raised bird is usually 5 weeks old. Without feathers and innards, the bird weighs about 300-400 g (10-14 oz).
Even the farm-raised squab are expensive and when combined with foie gras make a dish that can only be offered for special occasions.

The squab is prepared like other poultry; feathers are burned off over a flame, and the innards are carefully removed. The skin must remain intact for this presentation so this operation is delicate.

The boning process is also similar; the bird is slit down the backbone and boned carefully (using the tip of a paring knife) without piercing the skin.
The wing bones and the lower leg bone are left in so that the bird can be reformed.
The feet and the head (and neck) are cut off. The head can be plucked and poached and used as a decoration.

Make a stock with the bones and carcasses of the squab:

- Chop the bones with a cleaver.
- Prepare the aromatic vegetables.

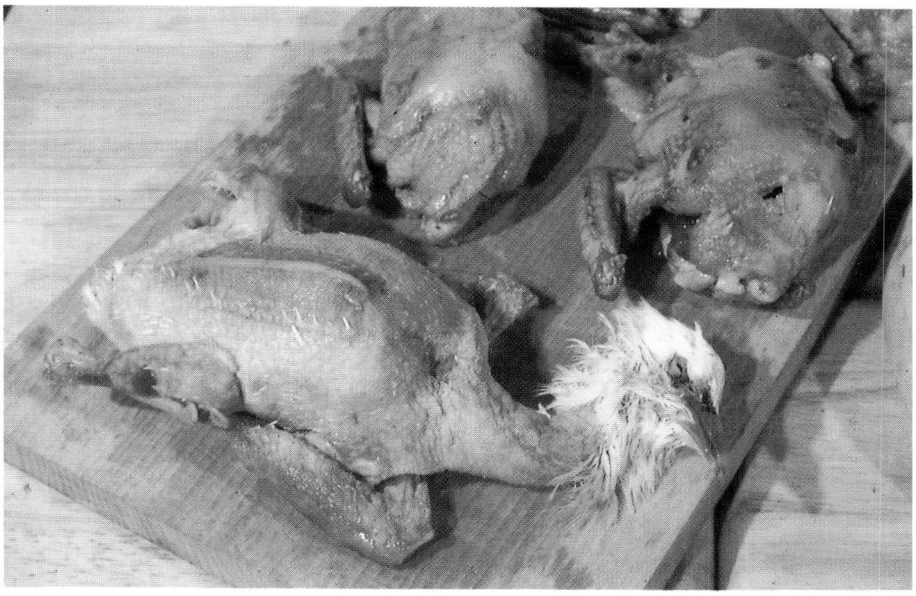

- Brown the bones in a little goose fat.
- Add the vegetables and brown.
- Pour off the fat and deglaze with cognac.
- Cover the bones generously with pork stock.
- Simmer for 2 1/2-3 hours.
- Skim often.

# Squab with Foie Gras *(continued)*

- Strain the stock through a conical sieve, pressing on the bones and vegetables to extract maximum flavor.
- Cool then reduce 1 liter (about 1 qt) to a glaze.

The boned squab are seasoned and sprinkled with cognac and marinated in the refrigerator for 12-24 hours.

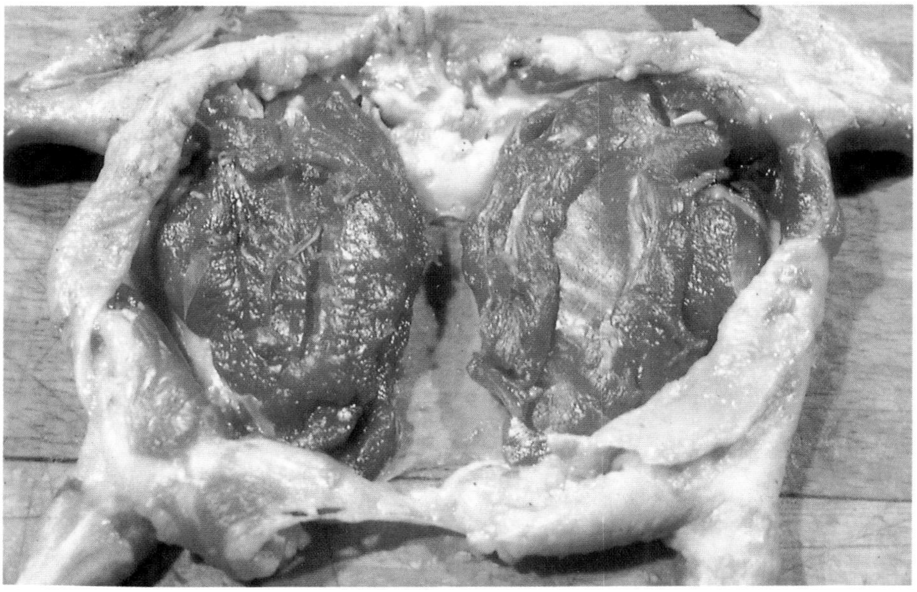

### *The Forcemeat*

The forcemeat is made with a " farce " of trimmed belly and jowl (2/3 lean, 1/3 fat) and " gratin ".

Cut the pork into large cubes (2 cm (3/4 in)) and marinate with seasonings and cognac.

The gratin is made with the squab livers and chicken livers:

- Cook the shallots in a little fat.
- Add carrots and dice of blanched backfat.
- Add the mushrooms.
- Add the trimmed livers and brown on all sides without overcooking; they should remain very pink.
- Add chopped parsley.
  Cover the mixture with madeira. Simmer for 1-2 minutes.
- Cool the mixture quickly.
  Check page 15 for more information on " gratins ".

The cooled gratin can be mixed with the belly and jowl meat and marinated together (12-24 hours in the refrigerator).

For the best flavor the seasoned squab can be layed flat (skin side up) on top of the marinated forcemeat so that there is an exchange of flavors during the marinating process.

### *The Foie Gras and Truffles*

We have chosen top-quality goose foie gras to lower the risk of melting during cooking.

The foie gras is prepared and seasoned like the foie gras in chapter 5 (marinated for 12 hours).

The marinated foie gras is then formed into a cylinder about 3.5-4 cm (1.5 in) across.

The " roulade " of foie gras is split and a row of truffles is added to the center. The cylinder is then rolled in a sheet of barding fat and refrigerated.

The final dish should include 3% truffles. If the foie gras does not contain enough truffles, additional chopped truffles can be added to the forcemeat.

**Procedure**

***The Forcemeat***

Place the pork and gratin in the chopper and process with the egg. Add the cream and the meat glaze and process until the forcemeat is smooth.

The temperature should be kept under 14-15 $^0$C (60 F) during processing. Chill the bowl of the processor if necessary.

The meat glazes used in this type of forcemeat often sodify due to the high gelatin content. To blend them evenly into the forcemeat they should be warmed slightly to melt. If they are too hot when added they might cause the mixture to ferment.

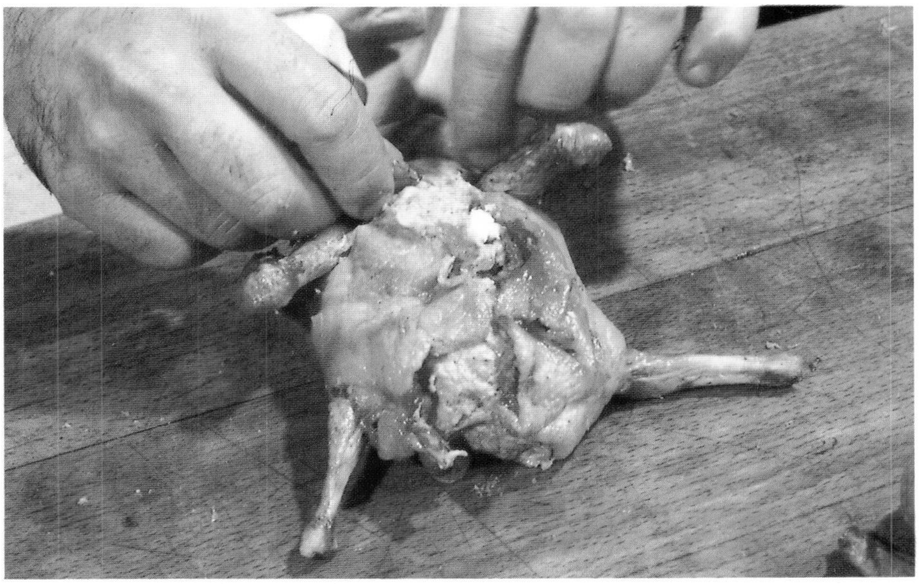

**Assembly**

Spread the seasoned squab on the work surface.

Divide the forcemeat into four equal parts.

Spread each squab with an even layer of forcemeat.

Press on the forcemeat so that it fills the crevasses and sticks to the meat.

Cut the cylinder of foie gras into four even portions that will fit inside the squab.

Close each bird around the filling, keeping the foie gras in the center.

Prepare four doubled sheets of aluminum foil large enough to wrap around each squab.

The squab will be cooked in a sense " en papillotte ".

It is recommended to refrigerate the assembled squab for 6 hours before cooking (for better flavor and form).

# Squab with Foie Gras *(continued)*

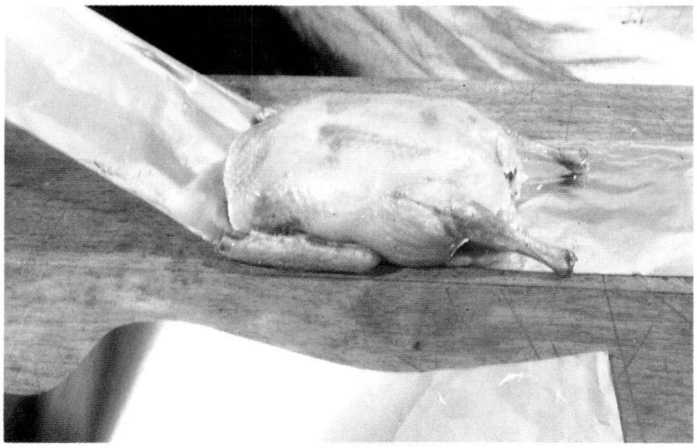

### Cooking

Poach the squab in a full flavored cooking liquid made with:

- the remaining squab stock,
- pork stock,
- and aromatic vegetables.

Bring the liquid to 85 $^{0}$C (185 F) and skim all fat and impurities that rise to the surface. Lower the heat to 80 $^{0}$C (175 F) and cook the squab until the internal temperature is 65-67 $^{0}$C (about 150 F).

The thermometer is actually testing the doneness of the foie gras. That is why we have chosen goose foie gras which can be cooked to 65 $^{0}$C (150 F).

Cool the cooked birds immediately and quickly.

### Storage

Covered with the strained cooking liquid the stuffed squab will keep in the refrigerator for 1 week.

### Presentation

Remove the cold squab from the liquid.

Remove the foil wrapping.

Clean all the stock that adheres to the birds and dry in the refrigerator for 1 hour.

Decorate with fruits or vegeatables or truffle slices.

Glaze with aspic that has been chilled to thicken it slightly. Dip the birds into the aspic or brush it on with a pastry brush.

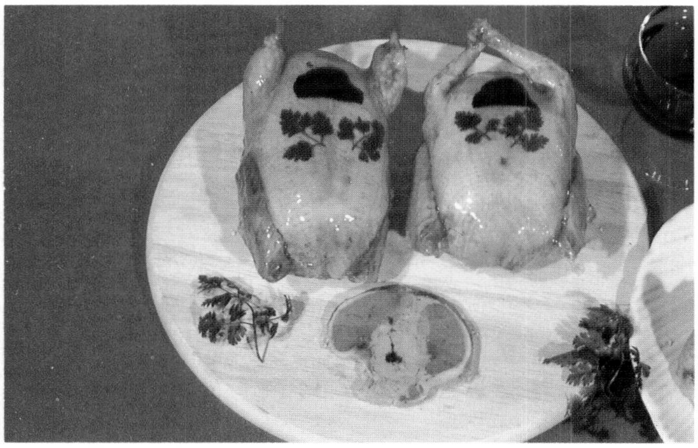

# Stuffed Quail with Raisins

**Introduction**

Quail has become a big industry in France as well as the United States. The abundance of the product means that quail can now be purchased at reasonable prices.

Although wild quail are no longer marketed, perfectly delicious dishes can be made using the farm-raised quail which will be enjoyed by even the most discriminating gourmets.

The quail can be presented two ways; reformed or molded. Here we use a special mold called a " terrine à mauviette ". " Mauviette " is an old culinary term for meadowlark.

**Equipment**

Knives, bowls and hotel pans, conical sieve, horizontal chopper, sauté pan, aluminum foil, terrine mold

**Ingredients**

8 quail
800 g (1 lb 10 oz) belly and jowl (forcemeat-1/3 fat, 2/3 lean)
200 g (7 oz) " gratin " (p. 15)
250 g (1/2 lb) raisins (currants or " smyrne ")
2 eggs
100 ml (scant 1/2 cup) cream

*Seasonings (per kg (2.2 lbs))*

For the forcemeat:
18 g (generous 1/2 oz curing salt (saltpeter with red color)

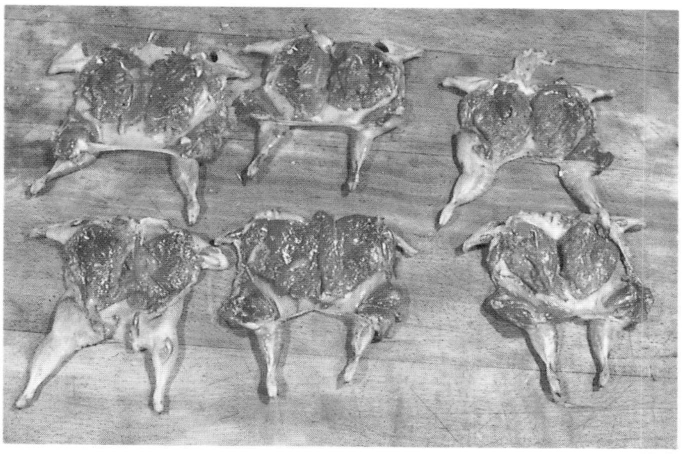

2 g (1/16 oz) sugar or dextrose
2 g (1/16 oz) pepper
1 g (1/32 oz) four spice powder

*For the quail*
18 g (generous 1/2 oz) curing salt (sodium nitrite with fine salt)
2 g (1/16 oz) pepper
1 g (1/32 oz) four spice powder
Cognac
Pork stock

**Preparing the Ingredients**

***The Quail***

As with all poultry, pass the birds over a flame to burn off all remaining feathers and carefully remove the innards.

Cut off the heads and reserve for the presentation. Cut off the feet then slit the back open.

Carefully bone the birds from the back without piercing the skin.

Bone the wings and the thigh but leave the lower leg bone in so that the bird can be reformed .

***The Raisins***

Choose raisins from " Corinthe " (currants) or " Smyrne " (or other good tasting raisin). Soak them for a few hours in water with an addition of 10% cognac.

***The Forcemeat***

Trim the belly and jowl and sort out 1/3 fat and 2/3 lean. Cut in cubes (2 cm (3/4 in)).

***The " Gratin "***

Make a " gratin " using the livers from the quail with chicken livers. Refer to page 15 for more information.

***The Marinade***

Season the quail and the pork. (The gratin can be marinated along with the pork belly and jowl (forcemeat.)) Cover and refrigerate for about 12 hours.

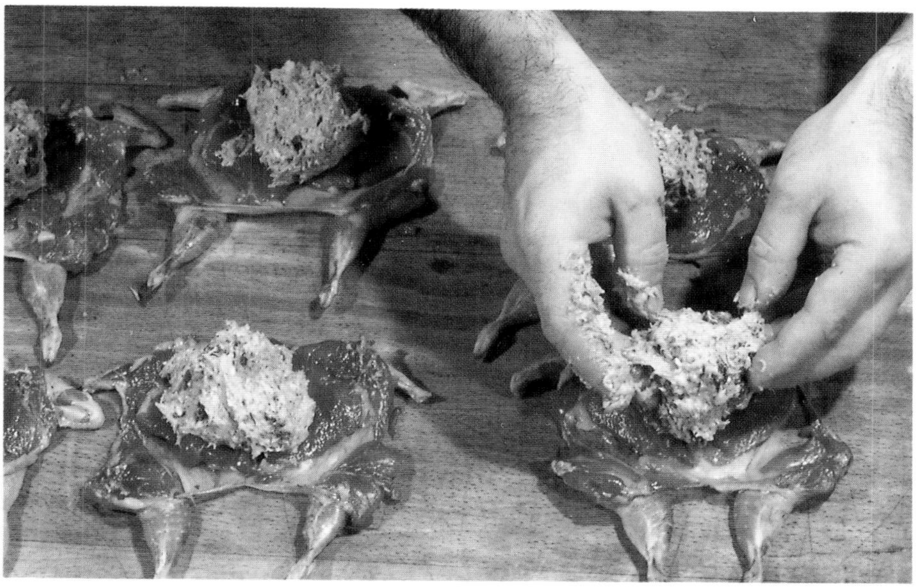

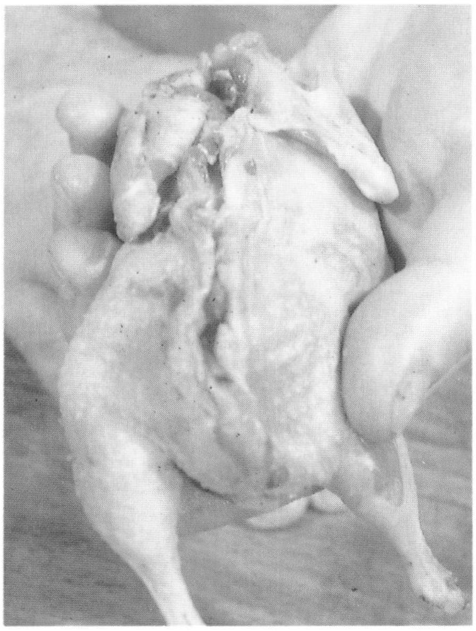

*The Quail Stock*

Make a stock with the bones and carcasses of the quail and aromatic vegetables.

Brown the bones in a little goose fat or lard.

Add the bones and brown them. Add the vegetables and brown.

Pour off the fat and deglaze with a little cognac then add pork stock to cover.

Simmer for 2 1/2-3 hours, skimming often.

Strain the stock through a conical sieve, pressing on the bones and vegetables to extract maximum flavor.

Reduce one liter (about 1 quart) of the stock to a glaze. Refrigerate the remaining stock.

**Making the Forcemeat**

Place the marinated forcemeat ingredients (gratin, belly, jowl) in the chopper.

Chop coarsely then add the eggs and the reduction. Lastly incorporate the cream and process until the mixture is smooth and homogeneous.

The temperature should never exceed 15 °C (60 F); chill the bowl of the chopper if necessary.

Transfer the mixture to a bowl. Drain the raisins and gently fold them into the forcemeat.

Set aside in the refrigerator.

**Assembly**

Spread the boned quail on the work surface.

Divide the forcemeat evenly and fill each bird with enough so that it can be reformed as a " plump bird " without bursting.

***In a Mold***

Brush fat on the molds (butter, goose fat or lard). Use the form of the mold to guide the placement of

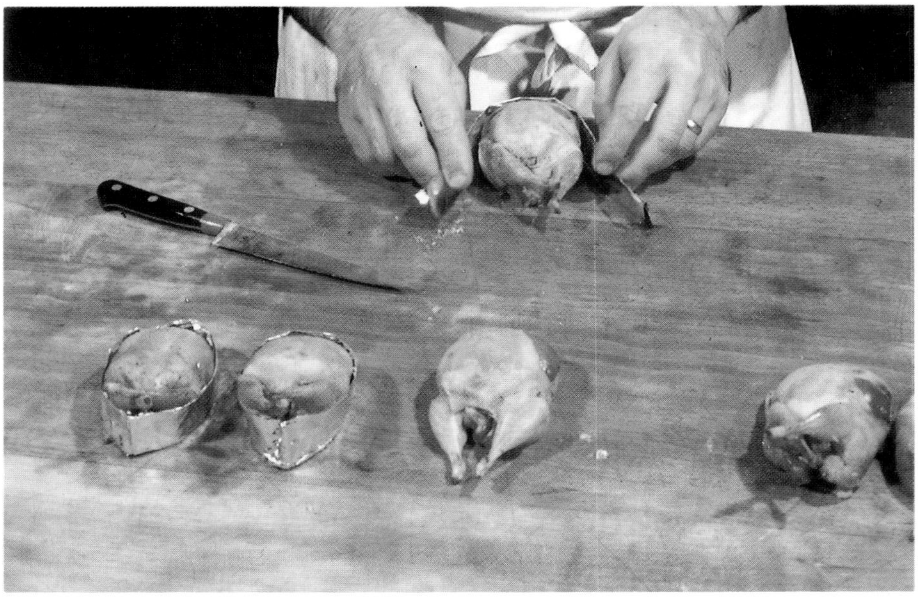

the bird, placing the breast and legs of the bird in the natural position.

***Without a Mold***

Make bands of aluminum foil (four for each bird) which are wrapped around the quail to keep the shape. The principle is just like the mold but there is no base.

The quail can be tied with kitchen string to hold the shape.

**Cooking**

The molded quail are cooked in a water bath.

Place the quail in a hot oven (180-200 °C (375-400 F)) and immediately turn the heat down to 110-120 °C (225 F). The quails are cooked when the internal temperature is 75-78 °C (170 F).

The quail in the foil wrappers are placed in a " water bath " but the water is replaced by quail stock. The internal temperature of the cooked quail is the same. Cool quickly, in a " cooling chamber " if available.

**Presentation**

The molded quail can be kept in the molds which are cleaned and the top of the quail is decorated before glazing with aspic.

The quail in the foil wrapping are rinsed to remove the stock that adheres to them, decorated then glazed with aspic. They can be dipped in thickened aspic or the aspic can be brushed on.

This preparation will keep for several days. The version in the molds will keep a little longer.

To use the heads for decoration, pluck the feathers and flame. Poach for a few minutes then cool. Secure the head in place with a sturdy toothpick.

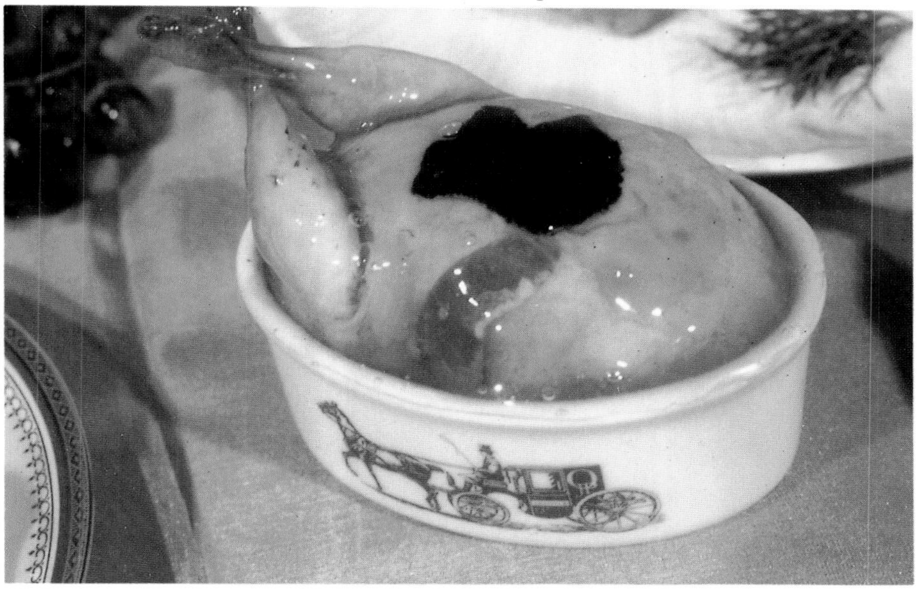

# Stuffed Rabbit " à la Bordelaise "

## Introduction

This delicious dish is a standard offering in many French charcuteries. " Le lapin farci à la Bordelaise " gets its name from an addition of white wine from Bordeaux.

Rabbit is a very lean meat which is also extremely flavorful. This preparation is a good example of a simple and rustic dish that has an elegant taste.

## Equipment

Knives, grinder, conical sieve, cleaver, horizontal chopper, mixer, sauté pan, stainless steel bowls and hotel pans, casserole

## Ingredients

1 rabbit (2.5 kg (5.5 lbs) untrimmed)
1 kg (2.2 lbs) sausage meat
400 g (14 oz) pork jowl (trimmed)
150 g (5 oz) rabbit liver
300 g (10 oz) mushrooms
100 g (3 1/2 oz) chopped parsley
2 eggs
Caul fat
Pork stock
30 g (1 oz) tomato paste
Dry white wine (Bordeaux)
Cognac

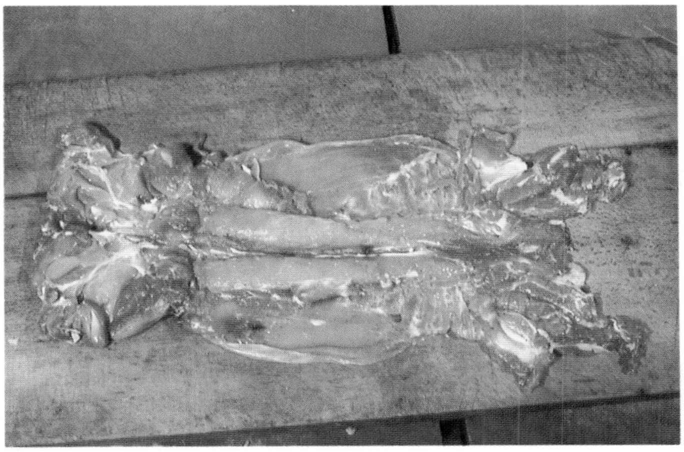

*Seasonings (per kg (2.2 lbs))*

18 g (generous 1/2 oz) curing salt
(sodium nitrite with fine salt)
2 g (1/16 oz) pepper
Tarragon
Thyme
Savory

**Preparing the Ingredients**

***The Rabbit***

A rabbit weighing about 2.5 kg (5.5 lbs) untrimmed will yield approximately 1.5 kg (3.3 lbs) of meat.

Slit the rabbit down the back and remove all the bones without piercing the skin.

This is a delicate and time consuming operation. There are a lot of tiny bones, especially in the rib section and shoulder.

Check that all the small bones are removed; any bones left could ruin the slice or worse yet end up on a consumer's plate.

The head is not used in the recipe but it can be cleaned and poached in stock and used as a decoration for the finished dish.

With the bones and carcass of the rabbit make a stock following the classic method:

Chop the bones with a cleaver.

Brown the bones with a little lard.

Add aromatic vegetables and brown them.

Pour off the fat and deglaze with dry white wine.

Cover the bones with pork stock, bring to a simmer and skim all fat and impurities that rise to the surface.

Cook the stock or 2 1/2-3 hours, skimming occasionally.

Strain the stock through a conical sieve, pressing on the bones and vegetables to extract maximum flavor.

Reduce 1 liter (about 1 qt) to a glaze and refrigerate the remaining stock.

***The Pork Jowl***

Trim the skin and glands from the jowl and cut into even cubes (2 cm (3/4 in)).

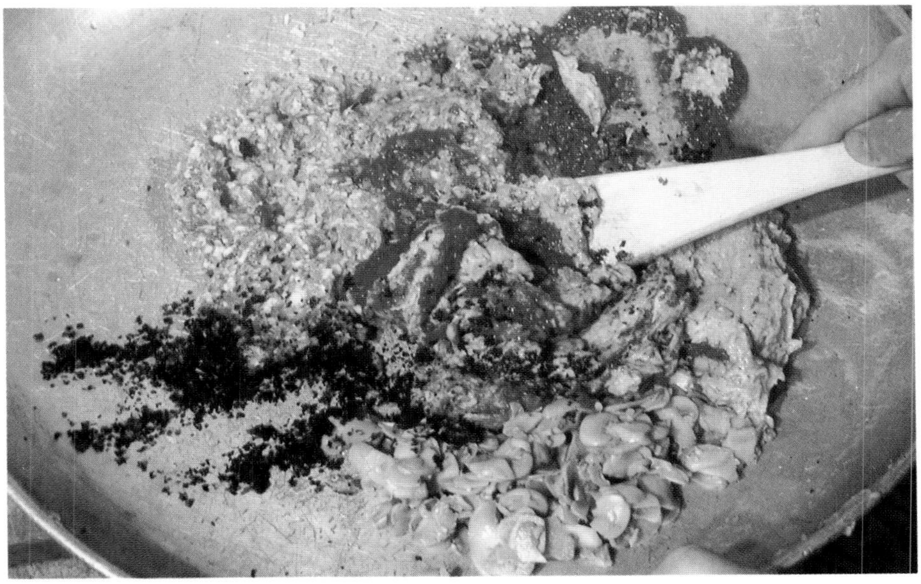

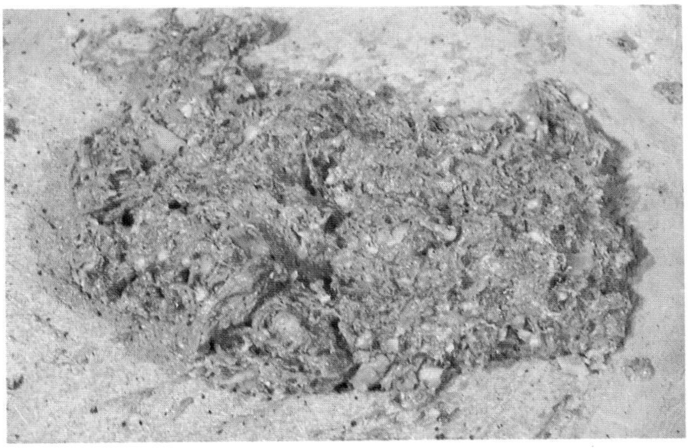

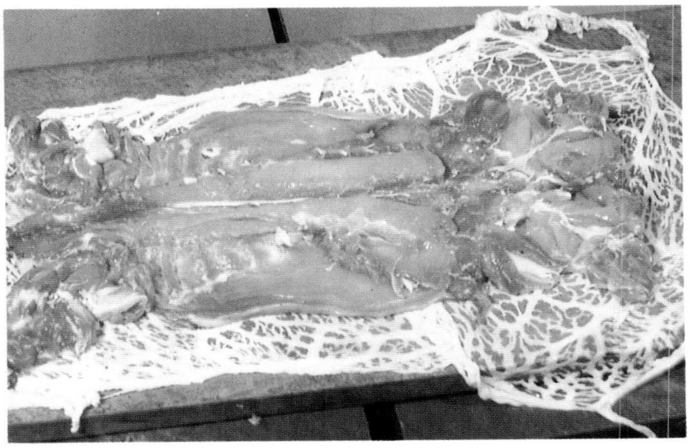

***The Marinade***

In a stainless steel recipient, season the rabbit and sprinkle with dry white wine.

In another recipient season the jowl and sprinkle with cognac.

Cover and marinate in the refrigerator for 12-24 hours.

***The " Gratin "***

Make a gratin (recipe on pp. 259-260) with rabbit livers. Chicken livers can be used to obtain 150 g (5 oz).

Set aside in the refrigerator.

**Making the Forcemeat**

Grind the marinated jowl and the gratin through a 2 mm (about 1/8 in) disk.

Place the ground meats in a mixer and at low speed incorporate the eggs and the meat glaze.

Fold in the mushrooms (which have been sliced, sautéed in goose fat, seasoned with salt and pepper and cooled).

Add the chopped parsley and sausage meat (volume 1).

Turn the mixer at low speed to blend all the ingredients until homogeneous.

**Assembly**

Wash, rinse and dry the caul fat. Spread it out on the work surface.

Spread the rabbit on the caul fat with the filets in the center.

Cut a little meat from the thighs and place it around the shoulders to even out the distribution of meat.

Spread the forcemeat evenly on the rabbit.

Roll the boned rabbit around the filling and wrap in the caul fat.

Tie the rabbit like a roast to give an even shape. Do not tie the cylinder too tightly because the meat expands slightly when cooked and flavorful juices would be lost.

**Cooking**

Place on a greased baking sheet and brown in a hot oven (180-190 (375 F)).

When the rabbit is browned, transfer to a container with the rabbit stock (a fish poacher is ideal). Deglaze the baking sheet with white wine and add the juices to the rabbit stock.

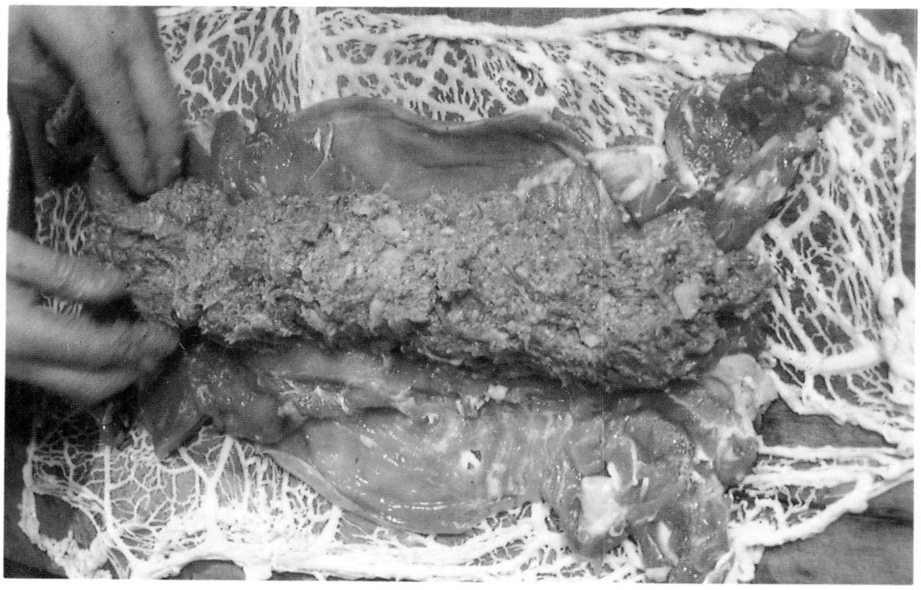

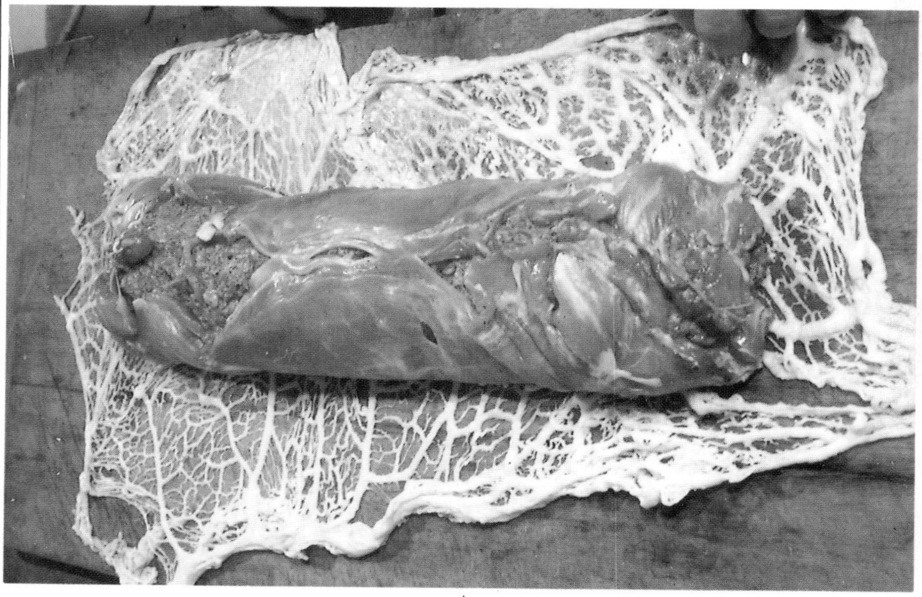

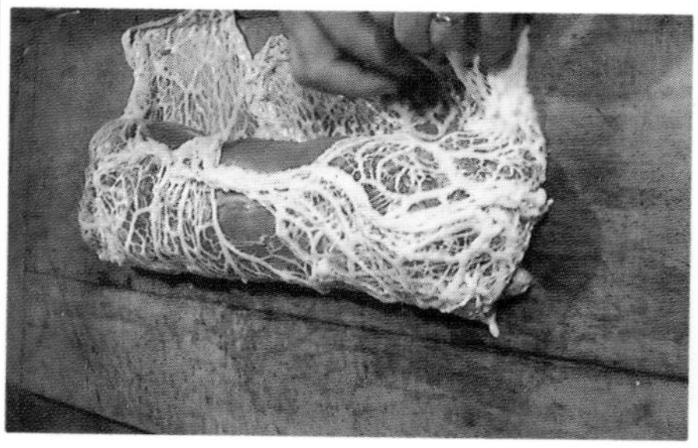

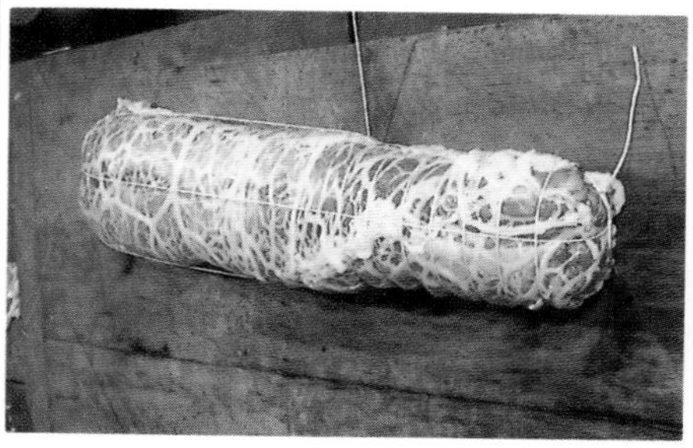

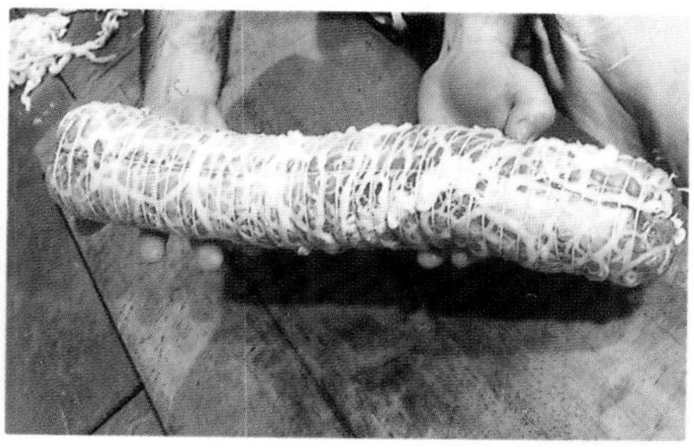

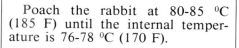

Poach the rabbit at 80-85 $^{0}$C (185 F) until the internal temperature is 76-78 $^{0}$C (170 F).

Skim all fat and impurities that rise to the surface during cooking.

Cool the rabbit quickly in the cooking liquid.

**Presentation**

When the rabbit has completely cooled, remove it from the stock, take off the strings and caul fat, rinse off the stock that adheres to the skin. Dry the skin and decorate with fuits and/or vegetables cut in attractive shapes. Brush on a coat of aspic that has been chilled to thicken it slightly.

The stuffed rabbit can be stored in the cooking liquid for 6-8 days.

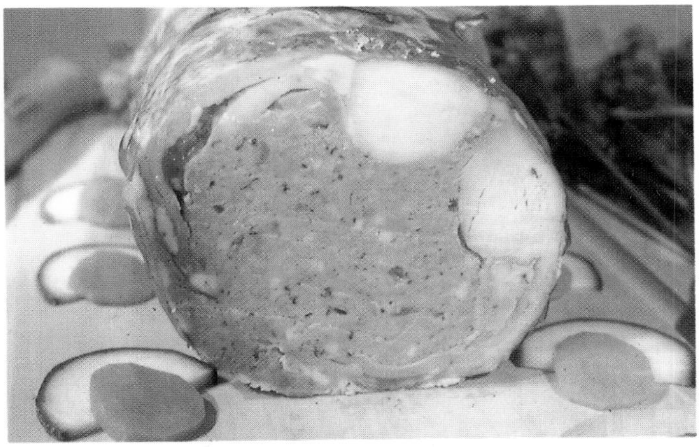

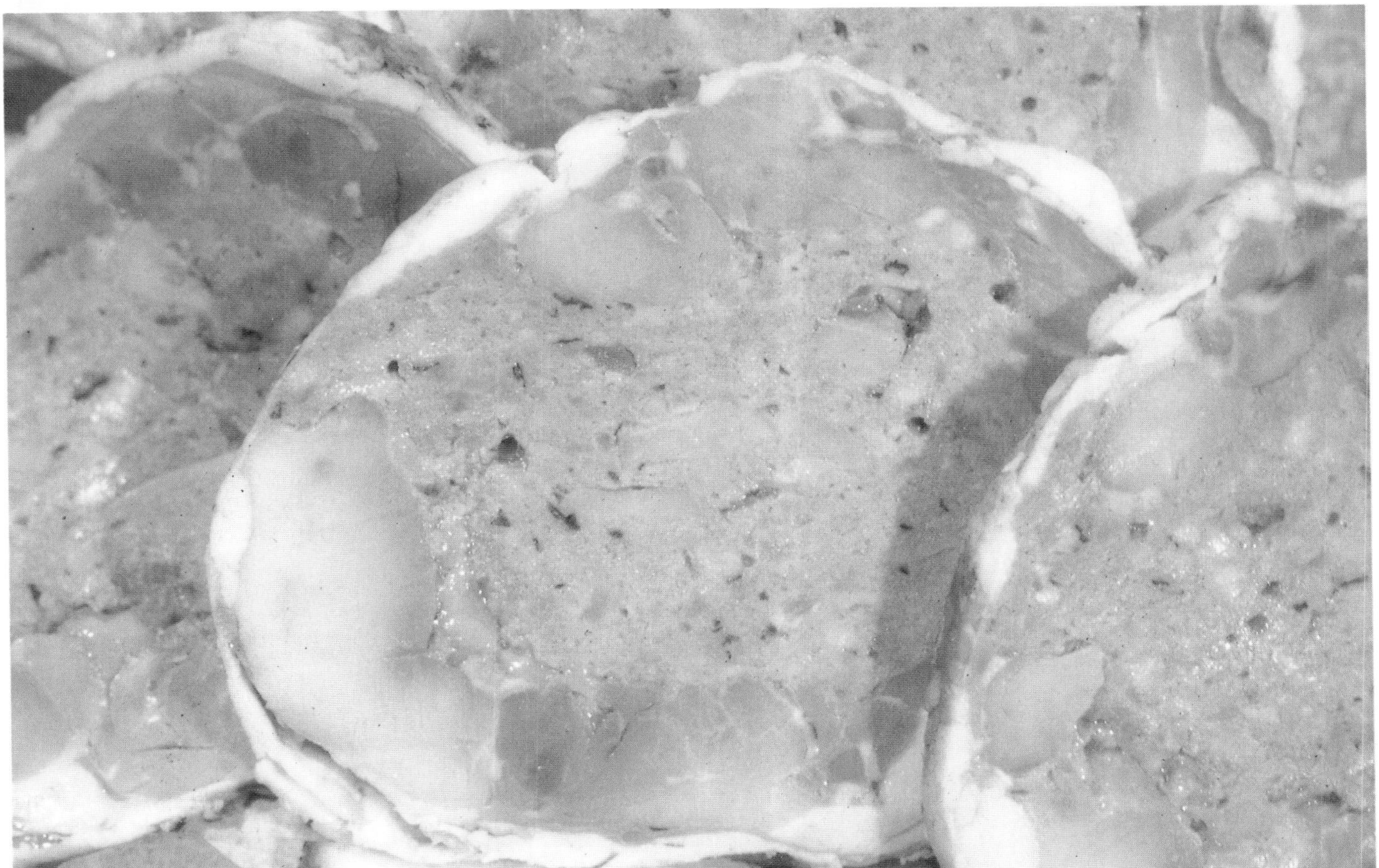

# Terrine of Guinea Hen with Wild Mushrooms

**Introduction**

Guinea hen, like quail has been domesticated for the mass market. Related to partridge, the farm-raised guinea hen has retained some its wild, musk-like flavor.

The wild mushrooms add a woodsy taste that marries perfectly with the dark flesh of the guinea hen.

**Equipment**

Knives, chopper, sauté pan, stainless steel bowls and hotel pans, conical sieve, cleaver, platter

**Ingredients**

1 guinea hen
(about 1.8 kg (4 lbs))
1.5 kg (3.3 lbs) pork belly
and jowl (forcemeat)
3 eggs
300 ml (generous 1 cup) heavy cream
250 g (1/2 lb) chicken livers
800 g (1 lb 10 oz) wild mushrooms
(cèpes, chanterelles for example)
Madeira
Cognac
Aromatic vegetables
Barding fat
Chicken stock
Pork stock
Goose fat
150 g (5 oz) chopped parsley

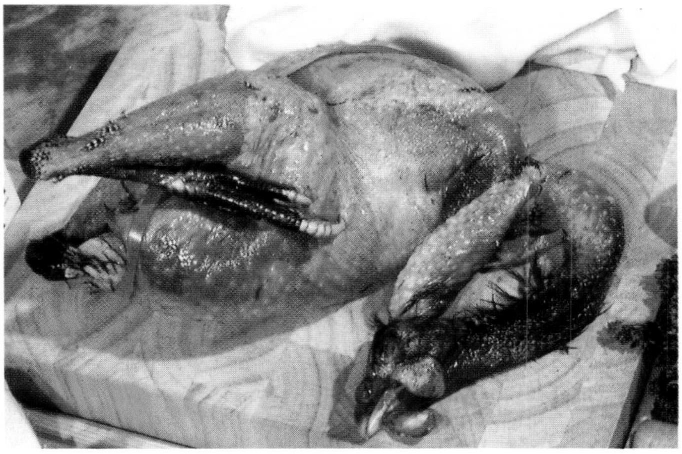

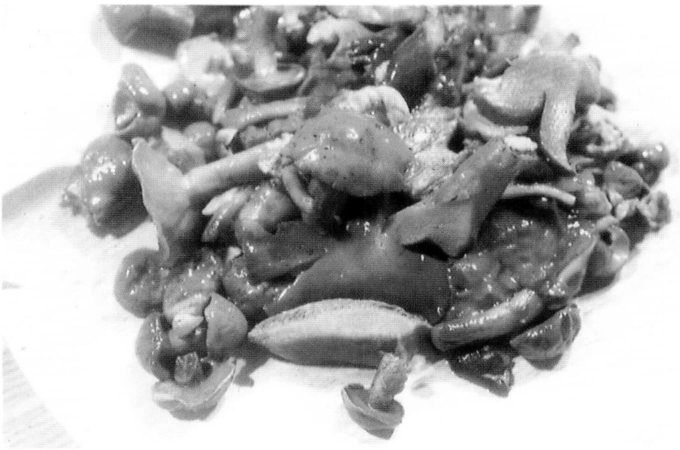

*Seasonings (per kg (2.2 lbs))*

18 g (generous 1/2 oz) curing salt (sodium nitrite with fine salt)
2 g (1/16 oz) sugar or dextrose
2 g (1/16 oz) white pepper
1 g (1/32 oz) four spice powder
0.5 g (1/64 oz) nutmeg

**Preparing the Ingredients**

***The Guinea Hen***

Choose a female bird that weighs about 1.8 kg (about 4 lbs). The female is meatier and more tender than the male.

Prepare in the classic manner: burn off the remaining feathers, remove the innards and bone from the back.

Keep the breast meat whole, cut the large pieces of meat into strips and add the trimmings to the forcemeat (pork belly and jowl).

***The Guniea Hen Stock***

Chop the bones and carcass of the guinea hen and brown in a little goose fat.

Prepare the aromatic vegetables (1 onion, 2 carrots, 3 celery stalks, parsley, thyme and bay leaf). Add the onions and carrots and brown.

Pour off the fat and deglaze with cognac.

Add the parsley, thyme and bay leaf and cover with pork stock.

Bring to a boil, skimming all fat and impurities that rise to the surface.

Lower to a simmer and cook for 2 1/2-3 hours, skimming occasinally.

Strain the stock through a conical sieve, pressing on the bones and vegetables to extract maximum flavor.

Reduce 1 liter (about 1 qt) to a glaze and refrigerate the remaining stock.

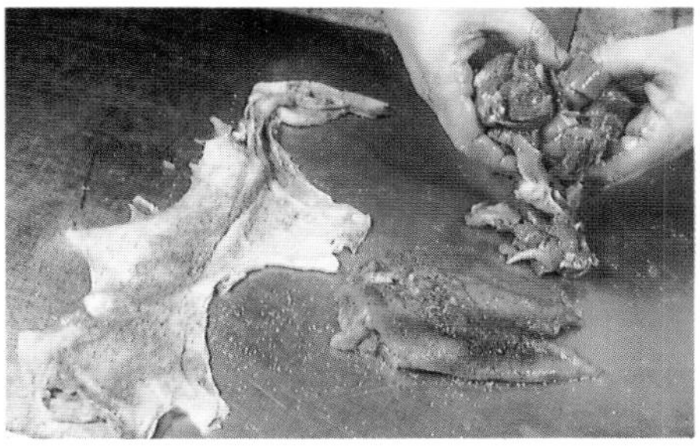

***The Forcemeat***

Remove the skin from the pork belly and jowl and trim glands and nerves.

Cut into large cubes (2.5 cm (1 in)) and set aside with the trimmings of guinea hen.

*The " Gratin "*

With the chicken livers (including the liver from the guinea hen), make a " gratin " (page 259) and cool completely.

*The Marinade*

Season the prepared ingredients:

- Guinea hen meat (breast, strips)
- Forcemeat (belly, jowl, trimmings)
- " Gratin "

Place them separately in a hotel pan, cover with the skin from the guinea hen and marinate in the refrigerator for at least 12 hours.

***The Mushrooms***

Wash the mushrooms thoroughly to remove all traces of dirt and sand. Dry on paper towels.

Heat some goose fat (or butter and oil) in a sauté pan.

Add the mushrooms to the hot fat and sauté a few minutes.

Season with salt and pepper, add chopped parsley and drain (reserve the juices.) Set aside in the refrigerator.

Deglaze the pan and reserve all the mushroom juices.

**Making the Forcemeat**

Purée the gratin in the chopper.

Add the " forcemeat " ingredients (marinated pork belly, jowl and trimmings).

Process a little then incorporate the eggs, the meat glaze and the mushroom juices then the cream.

Process until homogeneous. Note that the temperature of the mixture should never exceed 15 °C (60 F). Chill the bowl of the chopper if necessary.

Cut the larger mushrooms in half or thirds so that all the pieces are about the same size as the smallest mushrooms.

In a mixer at low speed or by hand, blend the forcemeat, the marinated meat strips and the mushrooms.

Stir until the ingredients are evenly distributed.

**Assembly**

Line the molds with barding fat and fill halfway with forcemeat.

Cut the breast meat in thin slices (on the diagonal (" scallops ")) to cover the surface evenly with meat.

Fill the mold to the top with the remaining forcemeat.

Fold the barding fat over the top to cover and prick with the point of a knife to keep it from curling during cooking.

**Cooking**

Cook the terrine in a water bath. Place in a hot oven (180-200 °C (375-400 F)). After the top browns a little, turn the heat down to 100-110 °C (225 F) and cook until the internal temperature is 76-78 °C (170 F).

**Presentation**

The terrine can be sliced directly from the mold. Decorate the top then glaze with aspic.

To present the terrine unmolded, pour aspic into the bottom of the cleaned mold. Arrange a decoration on this layer of aspic. Pour in a little more aspic and slide the terrine back into the mold. Chill for 6 hours to set the aspic and unmold onto a platter.

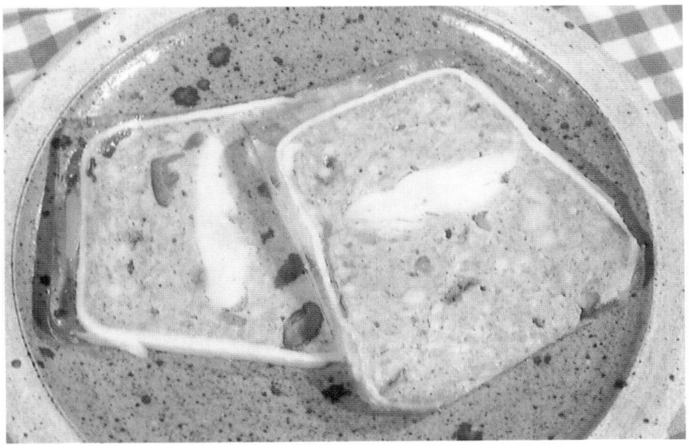

Pour off the fatty juices rendered during cooking.

Replace these juices with guinea hen stock that has been brought to a boil, skimmed and strained.

Place a light weight (300 g (10 oz)) on top and cool quickly.

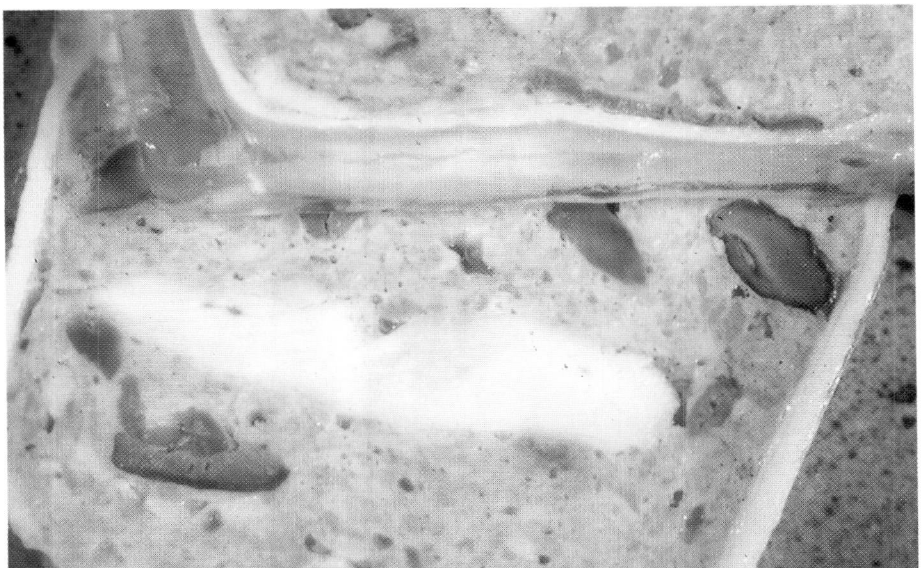

**Storage**

This terrine will keep 10-12 days in the refrigerator. The storage time can be doubled if the cooled terrine is placed in a vacuum pouch.

First published as *Traité de Charcuterie Artisanale* by Editions St-Honoré, Paris, France: copyright © 1991.
English translation copyright © 1991 by Van Nostrand Reinhold for the United States of America and Canada; by CICEM (Compagnie Internationale de Consultation *Education* et *Media*) for the rest of the world.

Van Nostrand Reinhold
115 Fifth Avenue
New York, New York 10003
Nelson Canada
1120 Birchmount Road
Scarborough, Ontario MIK 5G4, Canada
ISBN 0-442-30443-9 (Vol. 2)

All rights reserved. No part of this work covered by copyright hereon may be reproduced or used in any form or by any means –graphic, electronic, or mechanical, including photocopying, recording, taping, or information storage and retrieval systems– without written permission of the publisher.

CICEM, 36, rue St-Louis-en-l'Ile
75004 PARIS (France)

© CICEM ISBN 2-868715-019-0
Dépôt légal janvier 1991
Photographies Pierre Michalet – Réalisation graphique CICEM
Composition : Imprimerie Alençonnaise - Photogravure : Studio Maguyva
Imprimé en France par l'Imprimerie Alençonnaise

Library of Congress Catalog Card Number 90-47382

**Marcel Cottenceau, Jean-François Deport, Jean-Pierre Odeau**

Collective title: Charcuterie Series

**Contents:**
Vol. 1. Hams, Sausages and Sausage Meats – Blood Sausages and White Sausages
Rillettes, Rillons, Confits and Smoked Pork
Vol. 2. Pâtés, Terrines and Ballotines made with Poultry, Veal, Pork and Liver –
Andouilles and Andouillettes – Foie gras
Title : Charcuterie Series
ISBN 0-442-30433-9 (Vol. 2)